ADMIRALS

ADMIRALS

The Naval Commanders who Made Britain Great

ANDREW LAMBERT

faber and faber

First published in 2008
by Faber and Faber Limited
3 Queen Square London WC1N 3AU

Typeset by Faber and Faber Ltd
Printed in Great Britain by MPG Books Ltd, Bodmin, Cornwall

A CIP record for this book is available from the British Library

ISBN 978–0–571–23156–0

—

2 4 6 8 10 9 7 5 3 1

For Zohra and Tama

Contents

List of Plates

Preface

On 21 October 2005 it was my privilege to deliver the bicentenary address at Burnham Thorpe, birthplace of the greatest admiral. I spoke in the church where his reverend father had officiated for over forty years, alongside the memorials to his parents and two long-forgotten brothers. That day the triumph and tragedy of Trafalgar stretched across the globe: few could have been unaware of the hero, his life and deeds.

Yet while Britain restored Nelson to his rightful place as national hero and defining genius, the celebration of his unique talents seemed to diminish the achievements of every other admiral, consigning them to the dusty footnotes of history, as if Nelson was enough. That would be a gross injustice: Nelson knew that he stood on the shoulders of giants, and he inspired others to carry on the art of the admiral in the centuries that followed. This book places Nelson in context by tracing the development of naval command across four centuries, thus revealing what it was that made him unique.

The eleven British admirals whose careers are examined here all exercised the highest command, in war and peace, at sea and ashore. They directed the most consistently successful fighting force in world history, one whose triumphs were achieved through sustained excellence rather than individual genius. The Royal Navy was never perfect, even at Trafalgar, and has had its fair share of fools and knaves; but it has always been able to recover from setbacks to emerge victorious, even against such recent foes as the Treasury and the Royal Air Force.

This study charts how the art of naval command has evolved within a single organisation over a period of four hundred years.

The figures discussed are not necessarily the best admirals in history, even supposing such a thing could be measured, but each undoubtedly contributed to the evolution of the art; studied together, their careers form a coherent pattern. Each should be seen in the context of his own period: to compare Lord Howard and Lord Cunningham, for example, would be an injustice to both, and wholly unhistorical.

It is noteworthy that while the newly cleaned Nelson stands in majesty in Trafalgar Square, the other great admirals are conspicuous by their absence. If one judged purely by the statues on display in central London, one might imagine that Britain's history was made solely by soldiers, politicians and airmen! We fail to recognise the importance of the sea to our national history: Britain's development as a modern democratic state, the global dominance of the English language and the nation's continuing prosperity are the legacy of the admirals represented here, and yet their names are mostly forgotten. History is not a mere record of the past, but a constant reminder of the way in which we reached the present. As Britain grapples with some of the biggest questions it has ever faced, returning the sea to the centre of public debate will help us better understand how it became the multicultural nation we know today.

In the course of writing this book I have once again trespassed on the good will of family and friends, colleagues and students. Teaching naval history remains the single most important influence on my work: students and their questions are the key to keeping an open mind. The striking renaissance of the discipline of naval history in the past two decades has created an impressive body of literature, one that makes a crucial contribution to broader discussions of national identity, state policy and scientific endeavour.

I have profited greatly from the advice of many readers. I taxed John Beeler, John Brooks, David Davies, Richard Harding and Alan James with individual chapters, while Michael Tapper read the entire draft. Their generosity and insight have saved me from errors of fact, balance and judgement and much improved the final result, but I alone must be responsible for what remains. This is my second book with Julian Loose at Faber, and I can only repeat what I said in 2004: it has been a pleasure from start to finish.

Having had the opportunity to write this book while continuing in a full-time teaching post is a reflection of the support given by my colleagues in the Department of War Studies at King's College, London. It is my privilege to work in the ideal environment for naval history, where the study of war, strategy and the armed forces is the basis of the curriculum, with students of the highest quality at all levels. King's has been the academic home of naval history for well over a century, and continues to lead the field. I am indebted to many colleagues, but the Principal, Professor Rick Trainor, and Vice-Principal, Professor Sir Lawrence Freedman, deserve special mentions for their support. My colleague in the Laughton Naval History Unit, Dr Alan James, has not only doubled the number of naval historians in the department, but has done so to remarkable effect. Likewise the community of research students: an unrivalled gathering of talent and application, they hold out the brightest prospects for the future of the discipline. Much of this has been made possible by the support of the Tubney Charitable Trust, and others. If the development of naval history in the twenty-first century is to be sustained, we must hope that such generosity will be replicated.

My family continues to suffer the burden of having a historian in the house without protest, arriving at some unusual destinations in the process. Zohra and Tama have tolerated these admirals, and I can only hope they will appreciate the results. The support of my parents has been a source of strength and sustained my connection with things that really matter.

Andrew Lambert
Kew

INTRODUCTION

Searching for the Sublime

For four hundred and fifty years a group of small islands off the north-west coast of Europe, moderately populated and not especially favoured by their climate, exerted a disproportionate influence on world affairs. First they defied the superpowers of the age – Spain and then France – then in the process they themselves became a superpower. By the middle of the nineteenth century they had become the base of a unique world empire of trade and profit, the first global power – and in the twentieth century they cashed in those assets to play a vital role in winning three titanic conflicts.

This astonishing run of success was based on one critical advantage: naval power. The admirals who shaped and secured the unique instrument of British global pre-eminence possessed rare talents, consistently turning ships, seamen and money into a war-winning tool of state power, unrivalled in efficiency, economy and energy. Over the centuries the art of the admiral developed to meet new challenges and fresh foes – but it never failed.

This book concerns eleven men whose careers created, refined and reconfigured the role of the admiral. Their work was of the utmost public importance because it was on the Navy, 'under the good providence of God, [that] the Wealth, Safety and Strength of this Kingdom chiefly depend'.[1] While other nations looked to armies for their security, England – and after 1704 Great Britain – looked to the sea, and for over three hundred years the Royal Navy dominated the ocean. The end of empire and the relative decline of Britain should not obscure the critical role that its admirals played in creating the modern British state, and much else besides.

The art of the admiral is a curious compound of seamanship,

tactics, diplomacy and judgement. It calls for leaders of courage and authority, able to inspire their followers and overcome all odds. Like most arts, that of the admiral has a presiding genius, who with a unique combination of experience, education, insight and dedication elevated the art of war at sea to the sublime, creating a command style that was startlingly simple and stunningly complete. Horatio Nelson's battles were special – they changed the course of history.

The log book of HMS *Victory* recorded the moment of Nelson's death amidst the details of a battle that was then drawing to a close.

Observed one of the Enemy's Ships blow up and 14 sail of the Enemy's ships standing to the Southward – Partial Firing continued until 3.40 when a Victory having been reported to the Rt. Hon.ble Viscount Lord Nelson KB and Commander in Chief he died of his wounds.[2]

There was something curiously complete about that juxtaposition of explosion, conclusion and transfiguration. It was truly sublime. As a self-conscious hero Nelson was well aware of the new artistic sensibilities that echoed contemporary political passions. Joseph Addison, one of his favourite authors, used the sublime as a suitable discourse to describe the deeds of heroes: noble, heaven-born figures who could elevate mere mortals to a higher plane. The defining texts of Addison's sublime were the apocalyptic passages of the Bible, Nelson's constant guide.[3]

The year before Nelson was born, Edmund Burke defined the sublime as anything that, when contemplated, inspired terror – the strongest of human emotions. Immanuel Kant took the idea a stage further, describing it as 'the extreme tension experienced by the mind in apprehending the immensity or boundlessness of the grandest conceptions'.[4] Kant's conception offers a compelling explanation of what happened to Pierre de Villeneuve on the morning of 21 October 1805. Transfixed by the steely glare of Nelson's remaining eye, paralysed by the grandeur, the simplicity and the power of his design, Villeneuve froze – immobilised by the awful majesty of British naval power for the second time in his career.

The sublime of Burke and Kant is not the preserve of art critics, teasing out meaning from vast landscapes: the notion is equally applicable to the art of war, nowhere more than to the titanic explosion that destroyed *L'Orient*, the dramatic highlight of the battle of the Nile. This unprecedented pyrotechnic display briefly turned night into day, while the detonation silenced the men of both fleets – and left Villeneuve stunned. There was a similar cataclysm, rich in metaphorical resonance, in each of Nelson's great battles: first the *Dannebrog* at Copenhagen and then *L'Achille* at Trafalgar gave a cultural meaning to Nelson's obsession with annihilation. When Philippe Jacques de Loutherbourg[5] painted the 'Battle of the Nile', he employed the artistic imagery of the apocalyptic sublime, setting a catastrophe of biblical proportions in the land of the Pharaohs.

While any competent British admiral would have won a victory off Cape Trafalgar, only Nelson could have done so in a manner that achieved a decisive strategic effect. It was his unique ability to transcend the rules and restrictions of the art that made him, by any calculation, a genius. While there are many definitions of 'genius', Kant's version – 'Genius is the natural ability which gives the rule to art . . . a talent for producing that for which no definite rule can be given'[6] – is both nearly contemporary with Nelson and of great significance to students of warfare. Unlike the prosaic British, with their focus on character and courage, continental Europeans sought a more cerebral understanding of military genius. In his seminal work, *On War*, Carl von Clausewitz, Prussian general, educator and theorist, developed Kant's concept in his attempt to comprehend the nature of genius. While Clausewitz selected Napoleon as his case study, his results offer important insights for students of Nelson. Clausewitz believed that genius, 'a very highly developed mental aptitude for a particular occupation',[7] was found in those of superior intellect, whose careers had been shaped by a sophisticated and systematic appreciation of their profession. It was 'a harmonious combination of elements' that allowed those who had mastered all the principles of their profession through study and experience to develop the ability to transcend the rules. In addition, military genius involves taking quick decisions in complex situations, achieving an instinctive understanding of situation, the *coup d'œil* that marked out the great commander.

Napoleon argued that the calculations required on the battlefield would tax a Newton; but as decisions had to be made immediately, only highly educated instinct could hope to succeed.[8] Nelson undoubtedly had this quality, as Cuthbert Collingwood observed with characteristic insight: 'an enemy that commits a false step in his view is ruined'.[9] For Clausewitz, genius was ultimately an intangible quality that could not be taught; but superior intelligence also needed to be focused, as Nelson's was, through a lifelong dedication to professional education. Clausewitz concluded his discussion of genius with the pointed observation that a commander-in-chief must also be a statesman, without ceasing to be a warrior: 'on the one hand he is aware of the entire political situation: on the other, he knows exactly how much he can achieve with the means at his disposal'.[10]

This is precisely how Nelson saw his role. His political acumen – displayed in his role as strategic adviser to two prime ministers, Henry Addington in 1802–3 and William Pitt in 1805 – is often overlooked, due to the lack of written records and the British tendency to favour tales of heroic action. But while Clausewitz tells us that 'Everything in war is simple, but the simplest thing is difficult,' Nelson reversed that truth, raising the art of war at sea to the sublime by the simplicity and grandeur of his ideas.[11] After Trafalgar, Cuthbert Collingwood, his oldest friend, noted:

He possessed the zeal of an enthusiast, directed by talents which nature had very bountifully bestowed upon him, and everything seemed, as if by enchantment, to prosper under his direction. But it was the effect of system, and nice combination, not of chance. We must endeavour to follow his example, but it is the lot of very few to attain his perfection.[12]

Indeed it is.

But while no other naval commander has attained Nelson's perfection, he did not invent the art of the admiral. He inherited a rich tradition stretching back two hundred years: his mentors feature in this book, as do his protégés. To understand this tradition, we need to look beyond the unique genius of one man and see how mere mortals exercised leadership and command in the most complex and demanding of environments.

The demands of trade and security ensured that the English state would acquire a maritime character, and Britain remains the most 'maritime' of the major economies, undertaking more trade by sea than any other G8 nation. The admirals in this book opened the world to British trade, and they kept it open against all comers; and while the political empire has receded into history, Britain remains a global trading nation. The Royal Navy may no longer be the world's largest, but it remains second to none in quality, and above all in its people. While two generations of miserable post-1945 historians competed to write off Britain and its navy, history is not circular, and decline is not inevitable. The Falklands conflict of 1982 marked a watershed; the Nelson celebrations of 2005 reminded the world of Britain's matchless naval heritage; while the decision in June 2008 to order two 65,000-ton aircraft carriers, HMS *Queen Elizabeth* and HMS *Prince of Wales*, demonstrates just how far the pendulum has swung since 1966, when the last carrier programme was cancelled. Britain has recovered her maritime perspective and recognised that in an age of global opportunities and threats naval forces remain essential. The business of naval leadership will inevitably change, but the underlying demands are constant. Admirals have a future.

But just what is an admiral? The very word is full of mystery, originating in Muslim North Africa rather than the classical European languages.[13] The fact that it was quickly adopted by medieval Europeans suggests a yawning gap in their own languages, similar to that filled by the Arabic zero in mathematics. Mediterranean navies used specialist warships – oared galleys – which required sophisticated systems of command and control. This was a very different environment to that facing their northern European contemporaries.

By the late thirteenth century the term 'admiral' had reached England, and it would be there that the art of the admiral – the business of commanding fleets, leading men in battle, administering the naval service – would be developed and defined. The early admirals were heavily involved in questions of law and revenue, becoming wealthy men, but their role in war was limited by the inability of medieval ships to stay at sea for very long or to intercept hostile forces. In northern Europe medieval naval warfare was largely a matter of assembling sailing ships, getting alongside the enemy and letting the infantry fight it out. Admirals were men of high social rank, often with military experience, but never mariners: seamanship was not the business of a gentleman. In essence, the King's Navy was a collection of ships assembled for the purposes of military transport, hastily equipped to fight, and used to land the troops overseas. Edward III fought a naval battle at Sluys to ensure that he invaded France, rather than the King of France invading England:

the battle occurred so far inland that the site is now dry land. After Agincourt, Henry V built a powerful fleet to secure communications with his French possessions, but the navy was so expensive that his successors abandoned the idea, and his mighty flagship, *Grace Dieu*, was left to rot in the River Hamble.

Throughout the medieval era navies were optional, and largely created in wartime. They could not stop invasions, lacking both the seaworthiness to keep station for any period and the firepower to sink other ships. Admirals were part-timers, usually aristocrats temporarily placed in charge of armed ships. That situation began to change, however, at the end of the fifteenth century. After his own successful invasion, Henry Tudor declared himself King Henry VII, and moved to prevent others from following in his footsteps. He built a fort at Milford Haven, where he had landed, and constructed two big warships, the *Regent* and the *Sovereign*, armed with guns capable of crippling a ship and many more intended to kill the crew. These were the first English battleships: ships capable of fighting other ships entirely with projectile weapons. They were relatively manoeuvrable and capable of operating at sea for weeks at a time. However, with only two large ships and a handful of forts, Henry proved unable to prevent invasions. In this strange era, uneasily balanced between the medieval and the modern, the art of the admiral first emerged from the chaos of hand-to-hand combat afloat.

Unlike his father, King Henry VIII saw a world full of opportunity, not danger. He wanted to emulate the heroic deeds of earlier kings, Henry V and Edward III, invading France to recover the lands that were once English. His fleet would command the narrow seas and secure the supply lines for his army. But first he needed an admiral to command his ships.

I

THE COURTIER

Charles, Lord Howard
of Effingham

1536–1624

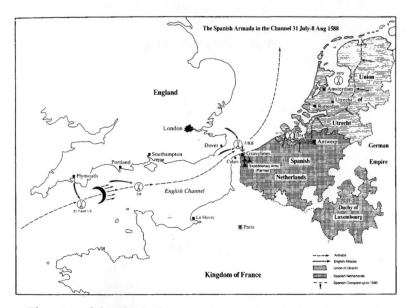

The crisis of the Elizabethan state began when the Spanish Armada entered the Channel: Lord Howard's victory off Gravelines proved decisive

IN 1513 HENRY VIII WAS AT WAR with France. The English fleet, led by the Lord Admiral, Sir Edward Howard, chased the French fleet into Brest harbour. Before Howard could turn his success to account, raiding the coast and attacking merchant ships, French reinforcements arrived: six Mediterranean war galleys armed with heavy cannon. The tables were well and truly turned when the galleys sank one of the English ships, damaged another and took up position in a shallow bay: Blanc-Sablons, where they were both safe from the cumbersome English sailing ships and handily placed to attack isolated vessels. The sudden arrival of these terrifying warships unsettled the English sailors and threatened to drive the fleet off the coast. The occasion demanded leadership. The admiral had to act. Short of food and stores, Howard decided to attack, hoping speed and enthusiasm would solve his problems. Late in the afternoon of 25 April, Howard launched an impetuous frontal assault with two small galleys, two row barges and two boats. The French ships were moored with their sterns on the beach, every gun facing the English. Despite heavy fire, Howard and a few men boarded the French admiral's galley, trying to tow it out to sea, but his cable was cut and his boat drifted away. Isolated on the Frenchman's deck, Howard and his companions were quickly driven overboard by French pikes. The other English boats saw nothing of the Lord Admiral's attack, too busy fighting their own battles. The last anyone saw, Sir Edward was struggling in the water, vainly calling for assistance. Realising he could not be saved, Howard calmly rolled up the gold whistle and chain of his office and hurled them into the sea.[1] He had paid a heavy price for relying on personal courage and energy.[2]

This was no way to lead a navy: courage and audacity were admirable qualities, but they offered no solution to the problems that faced Sir Edward Howard. It would take the English a long time to learn how to deal with the galley, and to decide how an admiral should command the fleet. Seventy-five years later Sir Edward's nephew, Charles Howard, was Lord Admiral. He commanded the largest fleet that England had ever assembled in the first great sea battle of the modern age. In the process he defined the art of the admiral and launched England's enduring love affair with the Royal Navy.

The introduction of heavy cannon in the early sixteenth century enabled warships to inflict serious damage on each other, as an alternative to capture by boarding. Improved sailing rigs and construction methods allowed ships to grow so that they could carry enough guns to be effective. These developments were timely, for the usurpation of 1485 left the Tudor dynasty vulnerable to European-backed claimants to the throne. A navy was needed to assist shore defences. Henry VII built two great ships, and expected rather more of his admirals. His son built a big fleet, and used it for war and diplomacy. They were the founders of the modern naval mission – and of a permanent navy. Henry VIII used stone, timber, cash and bells sequestered from the dissolved monasteries to build forts at the major invasion anchorages, and more ships. He also created a potent gun-founding industry to arm his wooden walls with bronze guns and his stone walls with iron pieces.

Although Henry VIII's military ambitions were thwarted and the last remnant of England's European empire did not long survive him, his wars created the modern Royal Navy. He built many warships, and used them to defend his realm against a French invasion. The need to account for and administer these ships created the first permanent naval bureaucracy, which in turn prompted the development of a modern state. The cost of maintaining a navy capable of defending the British Isles forced England, and later Britain, to become a modern tax-raising bureaucratic state long before other European powers. Naval might came to define the character, politics and identity of the nation. The development of English politics was largely directed by Parliament's ability to control the funds needed for the navy. The link between naval power and commercial opportunity was obvious, building a political consensus that favoured the navy, the 'senior service', over the army.

Charles Howard

For much of the Tudor era, the office of Lord Admiral, which combined a great and profitable office of state with command of the fleet, was held by the Howard family. Closely connected to the royal family by blood and marriage, the newly ennobled Howards rode the Tudor roller-coaster with varying degrees of success. Several fell foul of their monarchs: Charles's great-grandfather, the first Duke of Norfolk, died fighting for Richard III at Bosworth Field, while his cousin and contemporary Thomas, fourth Duke of Norfolk, was beheaded for high treason in 1572. Charles Howard was born in 1536. His father William, later the first Lord Effingham, was too poor for treason – invariably a rich man's sport – and stuck close to the throne, occupying several prominent offices, including Lord Admiral, and later Lord Chamberlain. After a medieval education, living in the noble house of his uncle Norfolk and then with a leading Huguenot family in France, Charles Howard entered a court that was full of his relatives. He first went to sea when his father became Queen Mary's Lord Admiral in 1554, and did so at intervals over the next thirty years. However, there was no intention that he should become a seaman. His role was command, lending honour and rank to the work of the professionals, men of humble origin who had mastered their art through long experience. Howard himself had not been educated for any profession, but noble birth and connections ensured that his lack of sophisticated learning proved little handicap, while excellent French made him a useful ambassador.

In an age of religious strife, when otherwise sane men burned other human beings because they differed over the details of a church service, Howard's lack of education saved him from those crises of conscience that afflicted so many of his contemporaries. He was a Christian and shared his faith with his queen, be she Catholic Mary or Protestant Elizabeth. Consequently he viewed the Spanish as civilised and humane enemies, if they were of his class and breeding. Nor did he reach middle age worn out by years of responsible and demanding service. Though he became the royal emissary to the French court at twenty-three, where he conducted himself with dignity and effect, otherwise he was just one of the young peacocks strutting about the early Elizabethan court, hoping the latest fashions would secure royal favour or profitable employment. In such company he had advantages: his father held a crucial royal office, and he himself was tall, handsome and well-made in an age when conspicuous display required a fine physique. He looked the part – and he acquired an additional connection in 1562 when he married Catherine Carey, Queen Elizabeth's cousin and intimate companion. Howard evidently knew how to play the court game.

In 1570 Howard commanded an English squadron sent to escort a Spanish fleet carrying Anne of Austria from Flanders to marry King Philip II. While his fellow commander William Winter was the seaman, Howard's presence demonstrated that England took the charge seriously. Aware that Spanish and papal agents believed that the Spanish fleet could be used to invade England, overthrowing Queen Elizabeth in favour of Mary, Queen of Scots, Howard's squadron combined polite gestures with significant force.

Nor was Howard restricted to military functions: in 1574 and 1575 he acted as Lord Chamberlain while the Earl of Sussex was indisposed. His father had held this office until his death in 1573 and Howard knew the routine, delighting in the public display, parade and pomp of courtly life. But while he remained a peacock for the rest of his days, there was more to Charles Howard than vain display. In January 1584 Elizabeth appointed him Lord Chamberlain in his own right, a truly magnificent office; but in May 1585 he was promoted to Lord Admiral.

Howard took up this office at the age of forty-nine, but unlike many of his contemporaries, notably the reclusive office-bound spider Philip II, only seven years his senior, he was in fine health. Raised in a noble household, Howard enjoyed the great medieval outdoor pursuits. A champion of the tiltyard and tournament, the ultimate noble sports, he pursued deer with a passion that matched his zeal in dealing with the Queen's enemies. Among the most prized rewards of his fame were the charge of several royal forests and guardianship over the deer they contained. He was the kingdom's most prominent breeder of hunting dogs, and when he went to war he took the language of the chase with him. He also enjoyed his falcons.[3] These royal sports had trained the eye and judgement of princes and warriors for generations. They developed energy and endurance, qualities that saw Charles Howard through a ten-day campaign of unrelenting tension and drama. Not once did he complain about his health or energy levels. He took great pride in the lithe athletic body he retained to the end of his long life.[4] His one great portrait, by Daniel Mytens in 1620, shows a very old man, posing in front of his two great triumphs, at the time he ceased to be Lord Admiral. The finely formed leg that dominates the foreground emphasises the enduring vanity of an aristocratic Elizabethan peacock. The Hilliard miniature of 1605, meanwhile, gives us a jaunty, self-confident sixty-nine-year-old, bejewelled hat set at a rakish angle, a gaze full of power and confidence.[5]

Two years before becoming Lord Admiral, Howard had chaired a commission investigating corruption charges that had been levied against the Treasurer of the Navy, John Hawkins. Fortunately for the navy, Hawkins was exonerated: his contribution to building and maintaining the fleet was unequalled. The investigation introduced Howard to the navy's administrative routine, and he continued to take real pleasure in the ships and stores under his control. But rank and quality were his recommendation, not administrative expertise. Royal powers could only be assumed at sea by a great nobleman, a critical qualification when much of his work would involve dealing with foreign powers. Nor were his officers amenable to modern concepts of discipline. Howard's authority to command stemmed from his social status and royal office; there were no Articles of War. Tudor naval leadership required more carrot than stick, and the most useful asset the Queen gave him was the authority to knight men who distinguished themselves in her name. It was a power he would use to great effect.

The relationship between the Lord Admiral and his queen was an important demonstration of his abilities and her expectations. Although a Privy Counsellor, holding one of the great offices of state, Howard was not one of her inner circle of advisers on state policy. He lacked the application and intellectual penetration to be useful, and furthermore had a reputation for revealing rather more than he ought, as if unable to hold his tongue when trusted with political confidences. But unlike some of his more cerebral and discreet contemporaries, he was trusted to employ the navy within the political framework of Elizabethan government. Such was his standing that he could contradict the royal pleasure and challenge the

Queen's judgement without sanction. Acting as the link between a cautious queen and her daring mariners, he knew enough of the sea to base his arguments on practical issues.

Howard enjoyed his status, which he used to great effect, representing England abroad and settling the bitter squabbles of the seamen. In the spring of 1588 two key sea officers, John Hawkins and William Winter, were quite literally at daggers drawn: Howard reconciled them. He was equally successful in handling the mercurial and prickly Francis Drake. Nor were such quarrels a question of hard words and handbags. In an age noted for outrageous public displays of pride and pomp, the potential for slights and disagreements to end in violence was clear. Drake had hung one colleague, and very nearly did the same to William Borough in 1587. Fortunate to escape with his life, Borough could not be employed with the fleet the following year. The danger increased whenever Howard was not with the fleet: personal issues erupted into violence with sickening frequency, invariably compromising operations.

The post of Lord Admiral was a powerful and profitable one, combining command of the fleet at sea with oversight of the Navy Board, which Henry VIII had established to direct the navy's day-to-day administration, and the Admiralty Courts, which controlled maritime disputes, international trade and piracy. While the war with Spain lasted, court fees and other perquisites arising from the legal side of his brief would make Howard a very rich man. This had been part of the Queen's purpose in appointing him. He had been an obvious choice: loyal, almost of royal blood, well-known to the Queen, and with ample experience at sea. He received the opportunity for wealth as a reward for his services and his loyalty. Not that he had absolute control over the only English standing military force – the Queen was far too astute for that. Instead, Howard shared his authority over the navy with the Privy Council and the Lord Treasurer, who had to find the necessary money. Ultimately Elizabeth settled the big issues and left Howard to control the fleet. She was expecting trouble, and chose a man she trusted to command her ships.

No sooner had Howard entered office than the crisis of the sixteenth-century English state broke. He was one of the commissioners who condemned Mary, Queen of Scots to death, and he urged Elizabeth to approve the sentence. Mary's death removed the last reason that had persuaded Philip II to stay his mighty hand. He saw no good reason to overthrow the heretic bastard Elizabeth simply to put French Mary on the throne. With Mary dead he had a good claim to the English throne, and the power to uphold it. He had seized the throne of Portugal on the same grounds only a few years before. Moreover, Philip had a noble aim: he was going to kill thousands to restore the benighted English to the bosom of the true church.

Spain, the superpower of the sixteenth century, had just absorbed Portugal and her immense trade empire in Asia, adding jewels and spices to the silver of the New World. But not everyone in the Spanish Empire was content. The Protestant Dutch had rebelled; Elizabeth provided money and manpower to support their efforts, as she did to those of the Huguenots who opposed Spanish influence in France. Her subjects were also conducting a predatory campaign against Spanish trade and colonies in the Caribbean. Most were opportunistic plunderers picking up what they could in rich but almost defenceless regions. But some, especially Devonian pirate raider Francis Drake, brought a burning Calvinist zeal to their work.[6] For Drake this was personal: he hated the Catholic Church, the King of Spain and all their works with an intense but controlled fury, delighting in sacking Catholic churches and royal treasuries. He had sailed the seven seas, the first Englishman to circumnavigate the globe, but never lost the instincts of a pirate and an outsider. By 1585 his name was known around the world, terrifying superstitious Spaniards and spoiling the supply of silver from the New World that funded King Philip's empire. The voyages of Drake and other privateers were supported by the investments of merchant corporations, traders and aristocrats such as Howard (who put money into the 1585 raid[7]), and such investors expected a healthy return. The construction of large, militarily useful ships had been encouraged by tonnage bounties on big ships. Most were well-armed, especially those trading into the Mediterranean, where Muslim corsairs cruised against Christian shipping for prizes and slaves. If the nation was to be defended, it would need every man of ability and every ship of force. Drake and his like were the best fighting seamen in the world.

Drake dominated the first two years of the undeclared war. A raid on the West Indies and an outrageous attack on the Spanish fleet in

Cadiz harbour in 1587 reinforced his celebrity status, ensuring him a prominent role in 1588. It was already common knowledge that Philip was assembling an invasion force, and while a Spanish victory seemed inevitable to many, wiser and better informed men disagreed. The Pope was in no hurry to send Philip any money; instead he provided a Holy Banner and a high-value IOU to be redeemed after the conflict was over. His Holiness was taking an each-way bet on the event, and fancied Elizabeth to win: Sixtus V feared a Spanish monopoly on power and had a sneaking admiration for the feisty heretic Queen.

In December 1587 the Queen ordered Howard to collect and take command of the royal, private and armed commercial ships that made up the English navy. While war had not been declared, it was already being waged with some enthusiasm, and the invasion threat could not be ignored. Initially the English hoped the mobilisation of the fleet would persuade Philip to abandon his efforts – though even if it did, the Duke of Parma's powerful army, based in modern Belgium, would have to be watched.[8] Howard had little interest in the nuances of the international position: like any good admiral he acted on the instructions of the political leadership. His political views were simple: the Kings of Spain, France and Scotland formed an unholy, treacherous trinity. He was equally forthright about ongoing negotiations with the Duke of Parma, governor of the Spanish Netherlands, which he was convinced were treasonous.[9] In truth the negotiations were skilfully exploited by the Queen's ministers to uncover the Spanish design. While they lasted, Parma could not seize the Channel port he needed for his invasion flotilla. Nor, despite Howard's complaints, did the talks hamper defence preparations.[10]

England's Finest

The test for Lord Howard would be to collect and control an unruly crew of self-interested prima donnas, aristocrats, villains and rogues in ships belonging to the Queen, the great merchant companies and private individuals and transform them into a national fleet. If he achieved that, he might do some damage to the Queen's enemies. However, the warships Howard commanded were designed to fight in an entirely new way. Here social rank proved to be a major advantage. Despite his seafaring experience, Howard was not such a fool as to think he knew how to fight a sea battle. He assembled an expert council, containing Drake, Hawkins, the pirate Martin Frobisher and the royal captain Thomas Fenner, as well as his cousin Lord Thomas Howard and his nephew Lord Sheffield. The experts wanted to head for Spain to destroy the Armada before it could set sail. Initially Howard was dubious, but he was prepared to reconsider, and came round to their way of thinking: 'I did ever and will ever yield ever unto them of greater experience.'[11] The Queen disagreed: she ordered the fleet to remain at home, fearing that if it missed the enemy on the coast of Spain there would be nothing to stop an invasion. Even so, Howard continued to press for the offensive strategy. Once rumour had the Spanish at sea, the Queen relented enough to allow the fleet to head south three times in May, but foul weather and the lack of intelligence saw them return to Plymouth.

Having accepted the advice of his staff, Howard was frustrated by the Queen's reluctance to see things in the same light, a frustration evident in the letter he wrote her on 23 June: 'For the love of Jesus Christ, Madam, awake thoroughly, and see the villainous treasons round about you.'[12] He also bombarded her key advisers, Lord Burghley and Sir Francis Walsingham, with the same opinions. At the same time, he had to restrain independent spirits in the fleet, not least Drake, and try to find the money and food to keep his men happy.

The fleet Howard commanded was strikingly different from the one his uncle had directed back in 1513. In place of the great lumbering fortresses and rowing barges designed for close-range action and boarding, the new Elizabethan galleons were low, fast and armed with heavy cannon. Their fine-lined hulls made them significantly quicker and handier than anything in the Armada. They were designed to fight beyond the range of muskets and small arms, relying on heavy iron shot to cripple rival ships. The design had evolved over the past fifty years, largely in response to another brush with French galleys at Spithead in 1545, when the *Mary Rose* sank. Henry VIII had already developed low-lying sail and oar warships to support his heavy ships, and later that year they defeated the French galleys. The new ships were handy: they could turn quickly, and by mounting many guns bearing forward they could engage galleys with every chance of success. The key to the new design was the steady increase in the quantity of heavy-cast bronze artillery pieces. While guns were scarce, it made sense to use only one or two on each ship, but once there were enough guns it made sense to build more powerful ships. Despite the limited utility of galleys and galleasses in rough English waters, they retained a terrifying grip on the imagination of English sailors until the end of the century.

The combination of skilled master shipwrights like Matthew Baker, who designed and built many of the galleons, and advice from Treasurer John Hawkins, a vastly experienced seaman and warrior, produced a unique English warship. It was ideal for the defence of the realm, and for relatively limited cruising in the eastern Atlantic. By 1588 these ships carried an armament that accounted for 8 per cent of their displacement, more than double the weight of armament in the best ship in King Philip's fleet. The twenty or so large galleons that had been built since the early 1570s were the backbone of the English fleet: they would be supported by private armed vessels, armed merchant ships and minor warships. To use this new type of warship, designed for speed and firepower, the English relied on seamen, with trained gunners to help the sailors fight. Any soldiers on board were part of the ship's company and answerable to the ship's captain. The English ships had another critical advantage: their heavy guns were mounted on compact gun carriages, with four small solid wooden wheels, or trucks. This allowed the guns to recoil inboard for reloading and to be shifted on the deck to permit angled fire. The same basic design would outlast the wooden warship. However, rates of fire were still very low. One round an hour was normal for the English in 1588, rather more by 1596. This does not sound very impressive, but Spanish ammunition returns make it clear they only fired their heavy guns once a day. The Spanish had less than half the number of heavy cannon mounted by the English, and they were generally of smaller calibre. At the end of the Armada campaign the Spanish had run out of small shot for their anti-personnel weapons. While they took almost all their heavy-calibre shot home, where it was very properly counted back into the storehouse, the English exhausted their supplies.[13]

Warships armed with heavy cannon could inflict serious damage on other vessels, without the need to board and fight hand to hand. This was critical, for whatever advantages the English possessed in seamanship, ships and artillery, the Spanish were the acknowledged masters of infantry combat. Close-quarters fighting with Spanish soldiers would only end one way, and the English made no attempt to prepare for it. Instead, the new warships were designed with a combination of heavy forward fire, high speed and quick turning. They would engage the enemy with the bow-chasers, then fire a broadside, the stern-chasers and then the other broadside in a turning movement before retiring to reload. These tactics mirrored those employed by contemporary pistol-armed cavalrymen. In both cases the object was to use firepower to inflict damage and casualties until the enemy formation broke. At that point the demoralised, scattered enemy would be run down, boarded and taken. For as long as heavy artillery remained the primary weapon, battle tactics remained essentially unchanged: break the enemy's formation through superior firepower and exploit the ensuing chaos. The only problem in 1588 was that no one had ever used these tactics against competent opponents. Going to war with Spain was a massive gamble: could a navy defend England, did the new ships and tactics work, and was Charles Howard a battle-winning admiral? Could he keep control of his fleet, impose the correct tactics and subordinate personal glory to national needs?

Fortunately for the English, the pace of war remained slow, allowing Howard to operate his council as a prototype staff. He summoned his advisers, firing a gun and hoisting a flag, almost every day of the Armada campaign. The council met for discussion, decision and the distribution of fresh orders. They were fighting for the highest stakes, with little or no experience to guide them. In the event, the early days of the Armada battle did more to develop fleet tactics for sailing ships armed with heavy guns than everything that had gone before. This was a brave new world, and it required an admiral who would consult, reflect and adjust. Any fool could be brave, but an impetuous dash at the enemy in 1588 would have cost far more than the life of a hot-headed Lord Admiral. Could Howard keep his cool under pressure and under fire? Was he the man for a crisis?

Spanish Armada

The threat he faced was substantial, for Philip II was not a man to do things by halves. He had been offered two invasion plans for the

'Enterprise of England'. The Marquis de Santa Cruz, his senior admiral, advised sending a fully equipped invasion force direct from Spain, but that was financially impossible. His general in Flanders, the Duke of Parma, favoured a sudden descent from the Low Countries, relying on stealth. Philip combined the two plans, placed Parma in charge, to satisfy papal concerns, and left key details unresolved. Santa Cruz would sail to the English Channel, link up with Parma and land a combined army in Kent. No one worked out where the two forces would meet. Parma did not control a single deep-water harbour on the Channel or North Sea coast; his army was hemmed in by shallow-draught Dutch warships. Without control of the narrow seas and the Flemish shallows the Spanish forces could not combine. Nor, given the communications technology of the age, could the naval and military commanders act in harmony. The key, as Howard knew, was the presence in the Armada of galleys and galleasses. Only heavily armed shallow-draught oar-driven warships could secure the anchorages Parma needed to embark his troops.[14]

However, such problems were put to one side while Philip grappled with the greatest administrative task his kingdom had yet essayed. To assemble 141 ships, 7,600 sailors and 20,500 troops, Philip stripped his empire of ships, guns, food and manpower. By early 1588, just keeping the Armada in being was eating up four fifths of Spain's enormous revenue. By then the mission was in crisis, and nothing was ready. When Philip demanded answers, Santa Cruz died. He was replaced by the thirty-eight-year-old Duke of Medina Sidonia, a grandee with considerable experience of maritime administration and war.[15] The Duke tried to escape his fate, but Philip was adamant. In the event Medina Sidonia performed miracles, the Armada sailing almost as planned and with most of the inventories filled. However, mere numbers disguised the sad reality of Spanish power. Every corner had been cut, some cannon were so badly cast they could not be used, much of the food was imperfectly preserved and barrels had been made of unseasoned wood. But above all, no one had considered how the Armada would link up with Parma: it seemed getting the Armada to sea was the only test that mattered. Well aware that English ships were faster and handier than Iberian models, and armed with 'ship-killing' heavy guns, Philip did not seek answers in this world. One Spanish admiral advised a papal diplomat: 'We are sailing against England in the confident hope of a miracle.'[16]

In truth, the sailing of the Armada *was* something of a miracle. It left Lisbon on 18 May, only to find much of the food and water unfit for consumption. Medina put into Corunna on 9 June, where he performed a second miracle, reassembling his storm-scattered force, finding the necessary provisions and getting back to sea on 11 July.

The English were waiting, and they appeared remarkably calm. England possessed a mature naval administrative system, and as Elizabeth was chronically short of money she did not assemble the fleet until intelligence confirmed the Spanish were about to sail. In December 1587 rumours that Santa Cruz had been ordered to sea prompted Elizabeth to mobilise, which in turn led Philip to delay. Consequently the alarm in England subsided, and half the men were paid off, which left the fleet perfectly capable of sailing while reducing dangerous overcrowding. In March the fleet was once again brought up to full strength and Howard was sent to join Drake's small squadron at Plymouth to guard the Western Approaches and the south coast of Ireland. Lord Henry Seymour's small squadron occupied the Straits of Dover to ensure Parma could not act alone. With powerful threats at either end of the English Channel the easy option was to prepare against both, but Howard resisted this.

From February 1588 Howard flew the Royal Standard in the *Ark Royal*, a brand new eight-hundred-ton galleon, originally built as *Ark Raleigh*, a private warship for the famous Elizabethan adventurer. The *Ark* possessed remarkably good sailing qualities, which helped Howard observe and direct the battle and to be in the right place at the right time.[17] He had no more than thirty serious fighting ships with him; two more galleons were under Seymour's command. The other vessels in his force, from large armed merchant ships to small coasters, lacked the firepower and structural strength for heavy fighting.

While he attempted to prepare the fleet for war, Howard faced a serious problem: Lord Treasurer Burghley was anxious for peace.[18] His reasons were economic: the country could not afford to mobilise its full strength for any length of time. Credit was short, treasure and cash shorter still. Ministers lacked the resources with which to meet Howard's demands and consequently seemed to him mean-spirited and devious. In desperation, Burghley shifted the cost of mobilising the navy onto coastal towns and counties, and delayed mobilising the troops until the Armada arrived.[19] Howard considered such methods too risky, urging Secretary of State Sir Francis Walsingham to lever open the coffers:

I am sorry her Majesty is so careless of this most dangerous time. I fear me much, and with grief I think it, that her Majesty relieth upon a hope that will deceive her and greatly endanger her; and then will it not be her money nor her jewels that will help; for as they will do good in time, so will they help nothing for the redeeming of time being lost.[20]

Howard was increasingly frustrated by Burghley's penny-pinching and the continuation of negotiations with Parma, both of which might ruin the kingdom. By the end of May the fleet was short of food, which posed real problems for the maintenance of morale. As Howard declared, 'My good Lord, there is here the gallantest company of captains, soldiers and mariners that I think was ever seen in England. It were a pity they should lack meat when they are so desirous to spend their lives in her Majesty's service.' The fleet was the only safety for the nation: the amateur soldiers ashore would be frightened by the arrival of the Armada.[21] While anxiously begging his political masters for more men, money and munitions, Howard managed to preserve a calm and confident demeanour for his followers.[22]

If the Spanish did send their fleet, Howard needed to know where it was going. To defeat the Armada he would need every warship in one place, but the Spanish could land in Ireland or Scotland as easily as in England. Anxious for hard intelligence, he deployed several pinnaces at sea and off the coasts of Spain and France, intercepted neutral ships for news and consulted his seamen on the effect of the weather. They were convinced that the best option was to attack the Spanish in their own harbours, where they could be found more easily than at sea. With the wind from the west the fleet at Plymouth could do nothing about a landing in Ireland or Scotland. A lack of intelligence paralysed the council in London, leaving Howard to wish the Queen had spent some money to obtain the Spanish plans.[23] Instead of being able to launch a preemptive strike, he was held back by uncertainties and fears in London. The candour of Howard's language at this time reflected the strains of exercising high command with inadequate intelligence and failing logistics. His anxiety to attack the Armada as soon as it could be located stemmed from a growing awareness that when the food ran out, the men would desert. He feared that the campaign was shaping up to be a repeat of 1513, while maintaining that if the men were 'kindly handled', they would 'run through fire and water' for the Queen.[24] But he feared the Spanish would keep the Armada in being until the English fleet ran out of food, and then strike.[25]

Gradually intelligence and diplomacy began to reduce the uncertainty. By early July Walsingham knew the French would neither join nor assist the Spanish by opening their harbours. Howard acknowledged the report but did not place great faith in French honesty.[26] By this stage the pinnaces and flyboats sent out to the Spanish coast and the western approaches of the Channel were bringing in news that the Armada had been forced into Ferrol by a storm, and that it was once more at sea. His forces reduced by disease, Howard needed to recruit again: 'God of his mercy keep us from sickness, for we fear that more than any hurt the Spaniards will do if the advertisements be true.'[27]

By July the main fleet was at Plymouth. With Seymour's squadron ready to prevent Parma crossing the Channel, the bulk of the fighting ships were in position to meet the Armada. Howard knew that if the Armada could not drop anchor, it could neither stage an invasion nor link up with Parma; he described his plan in sporting terms as 'coursing the enemy as that they shall have no leisure to land'.[28] Now he had to translate the ideas and experiments of the past seventy-five years into a tactical system that would enable his fleet to defeat the Armada without coming to close quarters. Reckless, foolhardy bravery would be worse than useless. Only disciplined, controlled professional methods would suffice. It was his job to impose them on the fleet. Furthermore, his options were constrained by the limited endurance of any fleet at sea, particularly one such as this where the men were crowded on board ship. Not only were contemporary food and drink supplies highly perishable, but shipboard standards of hygiene were low. Hunger, thirst, scurvy, dysentery and typhus were common problems. Howard could not afford to go to sea a moment too soon, or a moment too late.

The sighting report arrived on Friday 19 July: the enemy were off the Lizard. Howard hurried his fleet to sea. He made no mention of

Drake stopping to finish a game of bowls – they were in too great a danger for play-acting. If the Spanish pushed into Plymouth Sound, they could trap the fleet in an ideal place for a close-range battle. Only when the tide turned after dark that evening could the ships be towed out by their boats. Some of the Spanish admirals had advised Medina Sidonia to attack Plymouth, but his orders were explicit. He was not to land; his job was to rendezvous with Parma. By contrast, Howard had been given a wide discretion, always the key to success at sea. No one in London or Madrid could anticipate the wind and weather or the play of events at Plymouth. The very different approaches the two monarchs adopted to exercising command at a distance would play a critical part in the forthcoming campaign: while Medina Sidonia had to do as he was told, Howard was left to use his judgement.

By the time he reached the Channel, Medina Sidonia had lost a key asset: the four galleys that could have cleared the Flemish shallows of light sailing ships failed to make it through the Bay of Biscay.[29] However, he still possessed four Neapolitan galleasses, massive hybrid sail- and oar-powered warships that combined the firepower of fifty guns with mobility in a flat calm. These were the craft that most concerned the English: Howard was quick to count them when he saw the Armada.

As the ships of the two fleets spread their sails, the campaign of 1588 opened with all the pomp and splendour of a royal function. Every ship was brightly painted about the upper works with patterns, designs and heraldic crests, executed in gold, green, red and black. The sails carried crosses, and were topped off with gaudy banners and pennants. Nor were the ships alone in making a vainglorious display: officers appeared in their best clothes, dressed to kill, thus ensuring that if captured they would not suffer the fate of the lower orders. It was still customary to throw captured seamen and soldiers overboard, 'making water-spaniels of them', while reserving men of quality for ransom or exchange. Amidst this proud display Howard stood out: his height, greying hair and golden badge of office could not be mistaken. A great deal of time and money had been devoted to ensuring that ships and officers looked fit to represent the religious and royal interests of their respective nations. It remained to be seen if their actions would live up to the boasts their appearance conveyed.

On the 20th the Spanish pressed on into the Channel, and when Howard spotted them at around 15.00, he used the south-westerly wind to work across the front of the Armada and out to sea. The speed and sailing qualities of the English ships impressed the Spanish sailors as they saw how easily Howard had secured the weather gauge. Once upwind of the enemy, Howard could control the battle, while Drake's smaller squadron remained inshore. On Sunday 21 June the weather was wet, with low visibility. Howard and Drake were astern of the Spanish, who had deployed in a thick line abreast, with trailing wings. By placing his fighting ships at the stern and on the flanks, Medina would protect his troop transports. This was the formation used by the treasure fleets that he administered and his admirals escorted. Their mission was to rendezvous with the Duke of Parma on the Flemish coast, not to win a sea battle or to launch an invasion. The Armada was an amphibious transport convoy, not a battle fleet, and Medina knew better than anyone that the safe and timely arrival of the convoy was the only measure of success. He would ensure the formation was held at any cost, eventually hanging a captain who broke ranks. He was not looking for a fight, but he would go to Flanders whatever the English did. Philip knew the English were superior in seamanship and gunnery, but he still had faith that they would be vulnerable at close quarters, where their ships could be boarded. His admirals did not share that faith.

With the chivalry of a grandee, Howard issued a formal challenge, sending in a pinnace to fire a single shot, before the two English formations attacked the wings of the Spanish crescent. These tactics must have been settled before the fleet left Plymouth. If the English galleons could break the Spanish formation, the transports and troop ships would be easy prey for the smaller armed vessels. The Spaniards reported that the English came into the attack in line astern, one ship after another sailing up to fire their heavy bow-chasers, broadsides and stern-chasers in a figure-of-eight turning movement before retreating to reload. An afternoon of almost continuous English attacks failed to break the Spanish formation or to do any serious injury to their ships. Occasionally a Spanish ship would heave to, so her carpenters could plug shot holes, but nothing more. The Spanish were unable to reply effectively – their small guns were outranged, their heavy weapons were almost impossible to reload – but they held their formation and pressed on. Howard was quick to praise his captains, and to beg for more ammunition: 'Sir, for the love of God and our country, let us have with some speed some great shot sent us of all bigness; for this service will continue long; and some powder with it.'[30] The English had begun the battle with no more than thirty rounds of heavy ammunition for each gun; that would not last two days. The first lesson of 1588 was the need for ample firepower.

As night fell the Armada appeared uninjured, but appearances were deceptive: two Spanish warships had been crippled. In manoeuvring to repel the English the powerful galleon *Nuestra Señora del Rosario* collided with another ship, leaving her without a bowsprit or foremast and quite unmanageable. The *San Salvador*, meanwhile, had been shattered by a gunpowder explosion. Spanish attempts to tow the *Rosario* failed and Medina abandoned her with an admiral and a pay chest containing fifty thousand ducats. That night Howard detailed Drake to follow the enemy fleet, keeping the *Revenge*'s stern lantern lit to guide the English fleet. Instead, Drake extinguished his lantern and slipped away to take the valuable *Rosario*. He claimed to have seen sails and gone to check, but the fact that he was close alongside the crippled Spanish flagship the next morning suggests that his piratical instinct simply got the better of naval discipline. The Spanish admiral surrendered without a fight, leaving Drake a rich prize and a better idea of what English gunnery had achieved. It was not an impressive result in either political or strategic terms. The other professional plunderers, especially Frobisher, were furious, while Howard was none too pleased. At first light the fleet was widely dispersed, and the *Ark Royal* was alone, uncomfortably close to the Armada. Later that day the fleet picked up the abandoned *San Salvador*, but Drake's actions ensured there was no fighting on 22 July.[31]

On Tuesday 23 July the fleets were off Portland Bill, when the wind veered round to the south-east, giving the Spanish the weather gauge. The English tried to work round them along the shore in order to regain their advantage. Medina Sidonia squeezed the English against the coast, but Howard was quick to change course, heading out to sea. However, Frobisher's squadron, led by the large and, by English standards, rather slow *Triumph*, was hard pressed by the four galleasses. But Frobisher knew what he was doing, relying on local knowledge to counter Neapolitan mobility: once they reached the Portland Race the galleasses were left floundering in a powerful tidal rip, an easy target for English gunners. Howard was quick to support Frobisher, and exchanged fire with Medina Sidonia as their ships passed. Medina Sidonia hauled his wind, offering Howard the chance for a heroic close battle, but Howard knew better. He led his squadron past, just beyond musket shot, subjecting the Spanish flagship to a furious cannonade. The action that day cost the English far more ammunition than they could afford, but at least Howard had kept his fleet together and the Spanish showed no sign of trying to anchor.

The next morning the wind failed. The English fleet, once more astern, surrounded a Spanish straggler. This time the galleasses rowed back to recover the ship. In the afternoon Howard called a council. Despite several days of fighting, English gunnery had not stopped the Armada. The fleet was reorganised into four squadrons: Howard, Drake, Hawkins and Frobisher would direct the attacks. The change proved timely. The following day, Medina Sidonia tried to anchor in the Solent, where he could wait until he had located Parma, but that afternoon a heavy attack by Drake's squadron drove his seaward flank too close to Selsey Bill and the Owers Shoal for comfort, and the Spaniards had to haul back out to sea.[32] Drake achieved this by engaging at close range – fifty to a hundred yards, where every shot told. To celebrate the achievements of the campaign to date, and to encourage the rest to emulate his best officers, Howard used his royal authority to knight the leading figures: Hawkins, Frobisher and George Beeston of the *Dreadnought* were joined by Roger Townsend, Thomas Howard and Lord Sheffield.

Howard's overriding concern was to prevent the Spanish seizing an anchorage and landing their troops. Waiting in the Downs to watch Parma's forces, the veteran sea officer William Winter was delighted by Howard's 'wise and honourable carriage' in preventing the enemy anchoring at Spithead, the only useful anchorage in the Channel for the big Spanish ships. Once past the Isle of Wight they would 'have but a bad place to rest in'.[33] To add to his problems, Medina Sidonia did not know if any of his messages had got through to Parma. They had, but Parma had no idea where Medina was, and had no intention of embarking his army until he did.

Having won a major strategic victory and learnt how to damage the enemy, the English fell back to conserve their powder and shot.

They could simply follow the Spanish up the Channel until they reached Dover because the only suitable anchorage at the Downs had been heavily fortified by Henry VIII. Howard took every opportunity to demand additional ammunition from national and local supplies, but the captured Spanish vessels were his best sources. With impeccable logic Howard elected to save the last reserves of ammunition for the decisive battle when the Armada reached the coast of Flanders. Either stunned or stupefied, Walsingham responded to his urgent request for more powder and shot by demanding an itemised inventory!

Medina Sidonia would have to link up with Parma on an open coast, without a deep-water harbour. Without galleys he could not control the local shallows and open the passage for Parma's invasion barges in the face of Dutch and English light warships. On the night of Saturday 27 July the Armada anchored off Calais, in a dangerous open roadstead. While the ships were reasonably close to Parma, they were also hard against a sandbank and exposed to westerly gales. Nor was Parma ready: he had not moved his men, and it was becoming clear that he had never possessed much enthusiasm for the mission.

Howard anchored to windward of the Armada, and was joined by Lord Henry Seymour's squadron. Seymour, who had been relieved on the coast by a Dutch force, had full magazines, but his food was running low. Something had to be done, and quickly, for the English had no way of knowing just how long it would take Parma to embark. It was Parma's army, rather than the Armada, that really frightened the sea officers. Though confident they could handle any fleet in the world, they knew no one could match Parma's veteran Spanish infantry – certainly not the shambolic feudal levy that the Earl of Leicester had summoned to Tilbury. Time was of the essence when Howard summoned his council on the morning of Sunday 28 July.

The English had to get the Armada off the Flemish coast in order to prevent the link-up with Parma. They decided to employ eight small or medium-sized vessels, hastily fitted as fireships. Several of them belonged to Drake, who claimed every possible penny of compensation. Even at the inflated estimate of five thousand pounds, however, they proved excellent value. For maximum effect the fireships were sent down with the late tide, after dark. Medina was ready – he had ordered a guard of rowboats and given detailed instructions to meet the threat – but this was a tight corner, one he had only entered to satisfy the imperious orders of his king. With the English fleet to the west, lethal shoals to the east, and the coast to the south he had few options. His standing orders were to cut anchor cables, make sail, avoid the fireships and then re-anchor. The entire fleet managed the first three steps, but the fourth was beyond them. Many of the transport and smaller vessels lost contact with the Duke's well-handled rearguard. The fireships were unsettling weapons, particularly when the Italian engineer Giambelli, whose exploding 'hell-burners' had been used to devastating effect at Antwerp only three years earlier, was reported to be in the pay of the English. The blazing ships, their guns firing at random, were sufficiently diabolical to terrify exhausted and nervous Iberian seafarers, far from home and desperately short of local knowledge.

Although not one of the fireships took effect, they forced the Spanish to cut their cables and stand out to sea. In the process they lost the cohesion that had been their strongest suit. The next morning Medina found himself with only five fighting ships. The English responded by closing the range to fifty yards. The battle off Gravelines was the main event of the campaign, and the English committed their last reserves of powder and shot. Short of ammunition for the small guns, and unable to reload the big ones, the Spanish were heavily pounded.

Howard left Drake to lead the attack while he engaged the flagship galleass *San Lorenzo*, which was beached off Calais harbour. Some have argued that he would have been better employed directing the rest of the fleet rather than chasing glory.[34] In reality Howard knew that the oar- and sail-equipped galleass was vital if the two Spanish forces were to be linked, while the move inshore might herald the arrival of Parma at Calais. None of the smaller warships of the English and their Dutch allies stood a prayer against an oared vessel with twenty heavy cannon, sixteen light cannon and numerous small-calibre breech loaders. Her destruction would be a major blow to Spanish amphibious plans. Although the galleass was already under attack from Seymour's pinnaces, Howard took to his boats to finish the job. While the *San Lorenzo* was unable to fire her cannon at the English, she still had three hundred soldiers on board, but after half an hour of musketry the Spanish captain was killed, and his men lost heart. Cheered on by the Lord Admiral, the English boarded, drove the crew ashore and ransacked their prize. When the governor of Calais proved that the town was still under French control, and not Parma's, Howard abandoned the galleass. Afterwards Drake would imply that he, not the Lord Admiral, had won the battle off Gravelines. Howard was sufficiently concerned to produce a quasi-official rebuttal. He need not have worried: the destruction of the galleass was the highlight of the 29th.

Having devoted little more than an hour to the vessel's destruction, Howard hastened to take command of the fleet for the afternoon. Despite furious English attacks, Medina Sidonia steadily reassembled the Armada. The Spanish ships suffered severely – one sank, two more were driven ashore to be captured by the Dutch, the rest were badly battered – but still they managed to reform as night fell. As Drake put it, 'I hope in God the Prince of Parma and the Duke of Sidonia shall not shake hands this few days; and whensoever they shall meet, I believe neither of them will greatly rejoice of this day's service.'[35] As the *Vanguard* alone fired five hundred shot, the Spanish had ample cause to lament.[36]

That night it seemed that the heroic efforts of the Spanish sailors would be in vain: wind and wave were driving the entire Armada to certain destruction on the Zealand Bank. A fortuitous shift in the wind early the next day allowed them to head north. Howard continued the pursuit but did not attack: he had run out of ammunition.

After that fight, notwithstanding that our powder and shot was well near all spent, we set on a brag countenance, and gave them chase, as though we had wanted nothing, until we had cleared our own coast, and some part of Scotland of them.[37]

While the English fleet had shepherded the Armada north, there was still a danger that Parma might attempt an invasion in his small craft, so on the 30th the Council agreed that Lord Henry Seymour would have to go back to the narrow seas with six warships and four pinnaces to join the Dutch. Drake and Howard were concerned that Parma, whom they feared far more than Medina Sidonia, might stage a surprise invasion. This was no idle alarm: Parma had embarked eighteen thousand men by 12 August and stood ready to act until the 31st. Howard's decision reflected a clear strategic vision, while Seymour's limited grasp of the big picture was evident from the fact that he protested.

On 1 August Howard assembled the council, which agreed to pursue the Armada as far as the Firth of Forth, in case it tried to land in Scotland. Then they would return south to defend their own coast, in case the Spanish force doubled back. The English fleet was compelled to break off the pursuit when lack of victuals compounded the absence of ammunition.[38] Winter explained that Howard's stratagem was based on the knowledge that the Spanish had no anchorages available to them, other than the Forth or the Naze of Norway, where they would be safe from another fireship attack. By following closely he could maintain this threat and keep them moving. Without spare anchors and cables the Spaniards simply could not risk another fireship attack.[39]

The English lost sight of the Armada when they hauled to the west at midday on 2 August, following a final council. There were still approximately a hundred Spanish ships in company. Drake and Howard thought they might go to Denmark or Norway for masts, anchors and stores, before returning to the Channel. On the morning of the 3rd the fleet headed south to anchor at Margate, where they would revictual and prepare for further service. Without certain knowledge of the Armada's movements, Howard saw no reason to stand down the fleet or the army. He believed the Spanish would go home, but would not risk the kingdom on gut feeling. He favoured attacking Parma's shipping at Dunkirk.[40]

Howard's anxiety reflected the simple fact that no one knew where the Armada had gone. Nor did anyone seem to know where the provisions for the English fleet had been sent. Howard arrived off Margate on 8 August, but had to move on to Dover for supplies before the fleet starved. Hawkins found the victualling ships at Harwich the same day.

Typhus and the Treasury

When Howard arrived off Margate, his overriding concerns had been to keep the fleet ready and to take care of the seamen who had won the battle. Howard cared about his men and shared their dangerous world. Unfortunately the Queen's fear of invasion was very quickly replaced by a return to the strictest fiscal probity. Burghley and Walsingham were anxious to disarm and save money, but Howard's correspondence left them uncertain. When Walsingham lamented, 'I am sorry the Lord Admiral was forced to leave the prosecution of the enemy through the wants he sustained. Our half-doings doth breed dishonour and leaveth the disease uncured,' it was not entirely clear whether the disease he feared was the Spanish threat or a massive increase in defence spending.[41] Nor was he in any hurry to expend funds: 'For the sending of some money to the fleet for the relief of the decayed men, I think the same may be deferred until her Majesty's return.' He wanted to know how many ships would be kept in service before paying off those no longer required. However, he did agree with Howard on the key question: 'It were not wisdom, until we see what will become of the Spanish fleet, to disarm too fast, seeing her Majesty is to fight for a kingdom.'[42] The Lord Treasurer was prepared to send some money to the fleet, but only when the Treasurer of the Navy, John Hawkins, sent him the details.[43] That Hawkins was commanding a squadron of the fleet made this little more than a convenient device for delay. Burghley knew there were 119 ships at sea, including royal vessels and those of merchant venturers. They were manned by 11,120 men.[44]

While Burghley hoarded his cash and waited for an invoice, Howard faced a crisis:

There is a number of poor men of the coast towns – I mean the mariners – that cry out for money, and they know not where to be paid. I have given them my word and honour that either the towns shall pay them or I will see them paid if I had not done so, they had run way from Plymouth by thousands. I hope there will be care had of it.[45]

That the men placed so much faith in Howard's word was significant. The Lord Admiral was a man of rank and honour. Unlike the merchants and adventurers they normally served, he would not lie to them or cheat them of their pay. While he was genuinely concerned for the men, Howard also had to protect his reputation. If he ever deceived the mariners of England, he would never regain their trust – a commodity that would be vital in years to come.

On the 10th sickness – probably typhus, a common complaint when large numbers of unwashed bodies were left in confined spaces – broke out on the galleon *Elizabeth Jonas*. The undernourished and ill-clothed men of the fleet died in droves. 'It would grieve any man's heart to see them that have served so valiantly to die so miserably,' he told Burghley, but he may have misjudged the extent to which the treasurer's heart was capable of human feelings.[46] The need for clean clothes and money to discharge the men was glaring, but little was done. Instead, the officers began to argue: predictably, Frobisher attacked Drake over the *Rosario* and called him a coward.[47] Drake did not lower himself to Frobisher's level by replying in kind; instead, he employed courtly writers to create the legend of Sir Francis defeating the Armada single-handed. In the process he would expunge from the commonly accepted version of the story not just the belligerent Frobisher, but also the real commander.

On the 13th the English suspended the mobilisation of the militia for service in the south-east, but left the seventeen thousand men under the Earl of Leicester at Tilbury. The Queen sailed down to inspect them on the 17th, and launched the post-battle propaganda campaign with a famous speech stressing that she, with the heart and stomach of a king of England, was willing to die among them. Whoever wrote the speech, and it may well have been Elizabeth, was expert both in the English language and the politics of the image. It was grand theatre, beautifully contrived, and delivered with a wider audience in mind. In fact, the Queen only arrived at Tilbury after the danger of invasion had passed. Two days later the army began to demobilise, and by the end of the month only fifteen hundred men remained.

Still the fleet was denied funds: by 22 August Howard was reduced to pressing the Queen to urge measures on her Privy Council, sending his letter in the hands of Thomas Fenner, captain of the *Nonpareil*, to ensure he was not misunderstood. Fresh reports that day claimed the Armada was returning, and the fleet was in no condition to meet it. Decimated by disease, it needed fresh men, clean ships and money. Without money to pay the men, their discontent would only increase.[48]

On the 23rd Drake provided the voice of reason. Although he acknowledged the intelligence picture remained uncertain, despite Howard sending out scouting pinnaces, he did not think the Spanish would return via the North Sea unless compelled by stress of weather – and the wind had not been in the right quarter.[49] Later that day news from Flanders revealed that Parma had disbanded his fleet and marched inland, while the vessels detailed to watch the Armada reported it to the west of the Orkneys.[50]

Now the fleet could be disbanded, but Burghley's economical hopes were frustrated by the need to pay wages to dependants of the deceased, as well as those men discharged.[51] The Queen fancied recovering the cost of defeating the Armada by capturing the annual Spanish bullion convoy, but her fleet was in no shape for such an operation. Howard sent Drake to explain such seamanlike facts to Walsingham.[52] Paying off the fleet had begun on the 21st, was suspended on the 22nd, and resumed two days later. The merchant vessels and the smaller warships were steadily reduced, but Burghley was far from satisfied, sending Hawkins a 'sharp' letter about the need to economise. Grappling with the first full-scale fleet pay-off in English history, Hawkins protested that he and his staff were doing all they could.[53]

The typhus epidemic saved the state: dead men drew no pay. Some £400,000 had been spent on the campaign, of which a mere £180 went as sick and disabled benefits. Howard thought this was disgraceful, and was quick to upbraid his monarch. He used his own money to buy food and wine, sold his silver dinner service to buy clothes, and seized some of the *Rosario* treasure to pay the men their just deserts. Money was the problem: 'If I had not some to have bestowed upon some poor and miserable men, I should have wished myself out of the world,' he declared. His aim was not charity, but naval service. He would need these men again, and made sure Secretary of State Walsingham recognised the fact.

It were too pitiful to have men starve after such a service. I know Her Majesty would not, for any good. Therefore I had rather open the Queen's Majesty's purse something to relieve them, than they should be in that extremity; for we are to look to have more of these services; and if men should not be cared for better than to let them starve and die miserably, we should very hardly get any men to serve. Sir, I desire that they may be but double allowance of but as much as I [give] out of my own purse, and yet I am not the ablest man in [the realm]; but before God, I had rather have never penny in the world than they should lack.[54]

Two days later he arrived at Court to reinforce the point.[55] Only a man of Howard's rank and prestige, royal connections and personal status dared to challenge the Queen; and no one else ever did so on behalf of commoners.

By 4 September half the fleet had been paid off, retaining only royal ships. Confident the Spanish had gone, Hawkins was anxious to refit the fleet.[56] By early October reports began to come of the disastrous passage of the Armada along the west coast of Ireland, of ships wrecked with massive loss of life – and of survivors being massacred. But there were still items to account for. The eight Calais fireships cost £5,111 and ten shillings, while Burghley was still quibbling over £623, ten shillings and eleven pence worth of special victuals Howard had issued to the sick at Plymouth. Howard, with a gesture typical of the man, made his point, and then declined to press for a refund on the large quantity of wine and beer he had supplied from his own purse.[57] Fortunately he could afford to be generous; it is unlikely that Burghley was embarrassed.

English guns and fireships had prevented the Spanish linking their forces – the critical move of the campaign – and wrecked it as a fighting force, but they had not destroyed the Armada. That role would be filled by the elements, the coast of Ireland and the inevitable collapse of Spanish logistics on a prolonged voyage. Driven north, and then north-east by the wind, the Spanish struggled to keep together. Medina Sidonia knew he had to get out into the Atlantic and avoid the Irish coast, but his battered ships and starving men were caught in the tail end of a south-westerly hurricane, and many sought shelter. Some ships, mostly Mediterranean-built transports, were simply unequal to the weather; others were badly damaged by gunfire and, short of anchors and cables, could not hold the ground. Few escaped the treacherous coast, while any men who reached the shore received a murderous welcome. Even despite all these perils, however, half the fleet made it back to Spain – a testament to Medina Sidonia's professional leadership.

Although Charles Howard held the post of Lord Admiral for another four decades, he could not hope to surpass the achievement of 1588. He commanded the fleet that defeated the Spanish design, preventing it from linking up with the Duke of Parma's army in Flanders. He led the fleet as a great officer of state, but he was no mere knight on the ocean: like other gentlemen officers of the day, he had learnt the business of seafaring. If he did not possess the knowledge and skill of Drake or Frobisher, the practical seamanship of the boatswain, he knew enough to command ships and fleets at sea. His social rank, moreover, gave him the authority to command:

he spoke for the Queen. He was a leader who consulted and accepted the advice of the experts. His council played a crucial role in deciding his plans, and he had the greatness to accept their superior knowledge. He settled old enmities, and maintained harmony afloat; he restrained the impetuous, of whom there were many, chided lethargic, penny-pinching administrators ashore about ammunition and food, and forcefully reminded his queen of what should be done. Only Charles Howard could have held together the diverse collection of royal warships, armed merchant vessels and private enterprise craft that made up the English fleet. In the first naval campaign settled by heavy guns, Howard's caution avoided defeat: he made fewer mistakes than his Spanish opponent, and if he did not hang any of his captains, as Medina Sidonia did, he achieved his aim. He won.

In 1588, in northern waters, Howard created the art of the admiral: the system and ideas that would govern the management of sailing-ship fleets for the next two hundred years. His Spanish opponent was a titled bureaucrat: brave, resolute, but ultimately unable to deal with the changing demands of war at sea under sail. His juniors were fine seamen, and brave souls, but their grasp of the wider context was minimal. Only Howard combined first-hand knowledge of the sea with the rank, authority and military experience necessary to produce an effective meld of sailing and fighting.

Howard had learnt what all great admirals know: that navies are about people. The English had better ships in 1588, but they also had better men. The Lord Admiral cared enough about the English sailor to spend his own money on their food and to risk the wrath of his queen on their behalf. This was the first truly national force to fight in defence of England, built on the qualities of Howard's seamen and ships. English warships were manned by a well-organised crew which employed the differing specialist skills of seamen, soldiers and officers to great effect. The Spanish, by comparison, did not embrace the concept of a dedicated naval service: their leaders were not much enamoured of the sea and did not value their men.

In 1590 Howard took action to ensure the seamen would never again face poverty and sickness without funds. Together with Drake and Hawkins, he set up the Chatham Chest, an early form of insurance, whereby small deductions from the seamen's pay were used to pay for burials, pensions and disability compensation.[58] This was an important development: the Chatham Chest established a deeper sense of connection between ordinary seamen and the service for which they worked.

Propaganda

By modern standards the campaign had been 'indecisive', but the results were clear. To the contemporary mind, the role of God in a religious war could not be overestimated. The English, their Dutch allies and other Protestant groups were quick to launch a full-scale propaganda offensive, which was so effective that one historian observed: 'It is hard to resist the conclusion that the victory was of the pen rather than of the sword.' History is written by the winners, and here the key battle was about to begin. Within days of the victory the state moved against its internal enemies: suspected Catholic agents were rounded up, tried and hung. On 8 September several captured Spanish banners featured in a second service of thanksgiving at St Paul's Cathedral, with some of the naval commanders present. A third and more magnificent event on 24 November was attended by the Queen, who arrived in a chariot 'imitating the ancient Romans'. But while this was the capstone of the official pageantry, the propaganda offensive was only beginning. The Queen was the focal point for the national effort, but it would be Howard who would create the more enduring monument to naval glory. He did so in his own interest, but the scale and style of the work ensured it was soon appropriated for national purposes.

For all the triumphant celebration that followed the dispersal of the Armada, Howard was well aware that many did not understand how the battle had been fought, or what it had achieved. He quickly commissioned an 'official' account of the campaign from the Florentine scholar Petruccio Ubaldino, who worked at court. Howard's notes were worked up into a narrative in October 1588. This prompted Drake to provide Ubaldino with information, and a second narrative was produced in April 1589 to justify Drake's actions. Here the key audience was the court, and especially the Queen, for whom an Italian account would be doubly useful: it lent a stamp of impartial authority to the story, and it was easily accessible to key foreign observers. Drake's version was overtaken by events. His disastrous 1589 expedition to Lisbon saw him fall out of favour, and his manuscript was given to Lord Chancellor Hatton.[59] It was subsequently lost to view for three hundred years. Ubaldino's first version, translated into English in 1590 and printed and circulated by Howard, thus became the basis for Armada history. Like any good historian, Ubaldino served his patrons and his public. He attributed the victory to divine inspiration, although as a Catholic he may have had some difficulty reconciling such views with his conscience. He also drew attention to the skill and courage of his two patrons, Howard and Drake.

Ubaldino's account was accompanied by eleven charts, based on information supplied by Howard and drawn by Robert Adams, Surveyor of the Queen's Buildings.[60] These drawings provide a step-by-step overview of the campaign. Although the immediate purpose of Ubaldino's work was to establish Howard as the dominant figure, so that he could reap the political and financial rewards, these sources dominated the literature and art of the campaign for centuries and quickly became part of national mythology.

For his personal pleasure, meanwhile, Howard ordered a series of tapestries to celebrate the defeat of the Spanish Armada from Dutch master weaver Francis Spiernicx. The ten cartoons were designed by the pioneer Dutch sea painter Hendrick Vroom (1566–1640), who transformed the Adams drawings into images with remarkable skill. The ten designs were in the tradition of Bayeux and other great celebratory wall hangings: they were composed to be seen from below, picking out the key moments of the story and providing a full cast of characters in the broad borders, with sea monsters, charts and other conventional adornments for good measure. The truly novel aspect of the designs was that their perspective was taken from a ship, not land. Howard, who had seen an earlier set by Spiernicx commemorating the Spanish conquest of Tunis in 1554, was so pleased with them on their delivery in 1596 that he gave Vroom an extra hundred guilders. It is not the least of the ironies of this oeuvre that Vroom (a name that means 'godly' in Dutch) was almost certainly a Catholic.[61]

After hanging in Howard's Chelsea manor, the Armada tapestries were moved to his London residence, Arundel House on the Strand, in 1602. Although many thought he would give them to Queen Elizabeth, they were actually bought by James I in 1612 for the royal quarters at the Tower of London – by then Howard was desperate for money. In 1650 Cromwell transferred them to the House of Lords, where they dominated the chamber. Within a few years he would be engaged in his own naval war with Spain, and he well understood the symbolic importance of the tapestries: by placing images of suitably Protestant character at the heart of the legislature, Cromwell effectively exploited the continuing resonance of the Armada story for the emerging national identity.

Engravings of the tapestries were produced in 1739, ready for another war with Spain, this time propelled by the ambitions of the commercial elite, who sought to profit from the conflict. Once again, current events had sparked a renewal of interest in the images. Tragically the original tapestries were destroyed by fire in 1834, and were replaced in the new Parliament building by frescoes of Trafalgar and Waterloo. It is to Vroom, however, that we owe the most commonly repeated images of the Armada, and it is fortunate that he also produced a painting of the fireship attack off Gravelines, again drawing on Adams' chart.[62] Among the first sea-battle pictures to deal with a specific historical incident, it profits from Vroom's nautical experience.

In 1590 a new portrait of Elizabeth, painted by George Gower, presented her between two scenes of the campaign: one showing the fleets, the other the wreck of the Spanish ships on the coast of Ireland. Overhead is the canopy used in the St Paul's procession; the crown to the right symbolises royal power, while the globe under her hand denotes the worldwide extent of that power. The picture is reputed to have been owned by Drake. Like the ballad attributed to the Queen, it conveys the divine power that 'made the winds and waters rise, to scatter all mine enemies'. In the aftermath of the victory, Elizabeth was regenerated as a national icon.

Alarms and Panics: 1589–95

After the Armada, the English looked to hit back, but the efforts of Drake, Hawkins and others miscarried. In 1591 a small fleet was intercepted by a powerful Spanish force while searching for the treasure fleet, and Drake's Armada flagship, the *Revenge*, was lost in a heroic but utterly foolish battle with a Spanish fleet. Sir Richard Grenville, for all his courage, had no idea how a race-built galleon should be used in battle: after firing his heavy guns to great effect he carried on the engagement with small arms. While there were many brave and bold English captains, there seemed to be no admiral other than Howard. Without his strategic view and presence, command and control broke down. A more disciplined, coherent national strategy was required. The age of freebooters ended when Drake and Hawkins died in the West Indies in 1595, on a futile piratical cruise.

Howard himself had no wish to see an end to licensed predation: his income as Lord Admiral was heavily dependent on the fees and spoils of the war against Spanish commerce. He fitted out his own privateers, invested with his friends, and then had the Admiralty court bend the rules to condemn dubious prizes. In this he found an amenable ally, Admiralty judge Sir Julius Caesar, who combined the ambition of his namesake with a fair legal mind. War with Spain made Howard wealthy. The grandee of the ocean lived like a prince, using his income to keep up the image rather than acquiring land and capital investments. He may have believed that the war would last for ever.

Howard had shown how to lead a national fleet whose central core of powerful royal warships, commanded by men of unquestioned loyalty and unequalled skill, was supported by various vessels whose private financiers mixed patriotism and religious zeal with pardonable avarice. Improvements were steady, if not spectacular. After the defeat of the Armada, however, he remained at home for seven years: there were no missions that called for a Lord Admiral, no operations on a scale appropriate to his office and reputation.[63] It was not until 1596 that the time came for another national effort requiring a fleet large enough to warrant the Lord Admiral going afloat. The target was Cadiz; the purpose, as it would be so many times in the history of the Royal Navy, was to pre-empt the enemy in his own harbour, to prevent an invasion by laying waste to the very base of the Armadas. Howard shared command of the army and navy with the headstrong young Earl of Essex – a most unsettling colleague, not only because of his habit of changing his mind with the suddenness of a summer shower, but also because the old Queen personally begged Howard to make sure her favourite returned unharmed. The English were joined by a Dutch squadron, bringing the total force to more than a hundred warships and transports, carrying ten thousand soldiers and sailors. Sailing from

Plymouth on 1 June, their destination remained secret. Few in the fleet knew, and the Spanish were in ignorance until Howard passed Cape St Vincent on the 19th, by which time it was far too late. The fleet anchored off Cadiz on the 20th and sailed into the bay at high water the next morning, capturing or destroying thirteen Spanish warships. The fighting in Cadiz harbour pitted the latest English galleons against Spanish galleys. It was no contest: accurate and rapid English gunnery easily sank or drove off the galleys. Unfortunately Howard, as joint commander, lacked the authority to control Essex, and the operation was marred by amateurish glory-hunting, with a consequent loss of focus and discipline. Anxious to make his name, Essex stormed and sacked the city, before destroying the fortifications and public buildings. Howard, concerned to bring the earl home in one piece, had little choice but to reinforce the land attack, rather than move against the Spanish ships that had retreated to the head of the bay. The outward-bound West India convoy would have paid for the expedition twice over, but they were burnt by the Spanish the day after Essex's headlong rush to seize the town.[64]

The Spanish defences were inadequate, and for once the English soldiers were well-behaved. Once again Medina Sidonia, the local grandee, found himself commanding a hopeless endeavour against the rampant English. Howard took the greatest delight in reminding the Duke, in elegant Latin, of 1588. With Drake dead, it was all the more important that the Spanish saw 1588 as Howard's victory. Predictably, Essex was no sooner ashore than he wanted to hold the city, despite the Queen's orders. Howard insisted they must return, demonstrating why he had been sent.[65] He had no wish to explain to an incandescent queen why her earl was not coming home.

Cadiz was a triumph, striking the enemy's fleet in harbour with trifling losses, presaging the Royal Navy's methods in the years that followed. Although combined operations are notoriously the most difficult form of war to command, especially when admirals and generals hold joint and equal authority, Howard ensured the project was carried to a successful conclusion despite the distractions of Essex. The meaning of Cadiz and the Armada was clear: England amounted to something in the world, for the first time in two hundred years. As Sir Francis Bacon put it in 1597:

But thus much is certain; that he that commands the sea is at great liberty, and may take as much and as little of the war as he will; whereas those that be strongest by land are many times nevertheless in great straits. Surely at this day with us of Europe the vantage of strength at sea (which is one of the principal dowries of this kingdom of Great Britain) is great; both because most of the kingdoms of Europe are not merely inland, but girt with the sea part of their compass; and because the wealth of both Indies seems in great part by an accessory to the command of the seas.[66]

However, the Queen had more immediate concerns than enduring strategic concepts. The divided command structure had compromised the efficient execution of the plan. She was infuriated to find it had cost her a treasure fleet, but had only herself to blame.[67] To make matters worse, the loot from the expedition trickled through the fingers of the royal servants: only a tithe was ever collected, although many men got rich at Cadiz. Spain, meanwhile, had been humiliated: her silver fleets were disrupted for the second year in a row, and she was forced into bankruptcy. Philip quickly sent another Armada, but it was caught in a gale on the coast of Galicia in mid-October and a quarter of the ships were sunk. When the English sent a force to attack the remnants at Ferrol the following year, Essex had sole command. Without Howard, Essex quickly ran out of control, wasting the entire season. At the age of sixty, Lord Howard might no longer be the prettiest boy at court, nor the most brilliant mind, but he was remarkably sure in his judgement of men and affairs, a loyal servant of his queen, and the bedrock of national security. Philip tried again while Essex was off on his pointless cruise. This time the Spaniards were within thirty miles of the Lizard when the gale struck: twenty-eight ships were sunk, while others limped into English ports to surrender.

News of Essex's folly arrived in London shortly after Howard was ennobled as Earl of Nottingham. The title was an old one, making him at a stroke the second peer in the realm. It was the culmination of a career pursuing power, place and precedence. A contemporary engraved equestrian image of Howard, complete with the Armada and the sack of Cadiz in the background, emphasised the religious character of his triumphs. This was not how Howard saw his work: for him, his faith was incidental to the fact that he had saved his country. Now King Philip was dying, and Spain was unable to find any more ships, men or money. It seemed that England was safe at last.

Securing the Kingdom

As it turned out, however, the last years of Elizabeth's reign had yet more surprises in store, as Philip III took up his father's Armada habit. To meet the threat, Howard was created Lord Lieutenant General of England in 1599, offering unprecedented powers that reflected the Queen's reliance on him. In 1601 he took a key role in the trial and condemnation of his headstrong colleague Essex. In this, as in much else, Howard allied his loyalty, military prestige and sound judgement to the brilliant talents of Burghley's son, Robert Cecil.[68] By the end of Elizabeth's reign Howard was her most trusted minister. When Lady Nottingham, the Queen's closest confidante throughout her reign, died suddenly, the despairing monarch followed within the week. Howard was left to bury them both and ensure the smooth transition of power to James VI of Scotland.

Howard remarried, remaining highly visible in the life of the Jacobean court, but the end of the war with Spain severely reduced his income. His last great public duty was an embassy to Spain at the signing of the peace in 1604, which he carried off in style. However, peace and royal ignorance left the navy budget vulnerable. Soon corrupt officials and small budgets had whittled away the once-dominant Tudor fleet. Howard's age and rank meant that his stewardship of the navy was distant, and his subordinates found opportunities for corruption hard to resist. In 1619 he sold the office of Lord Admiral to the Duke of Buckingham for a much needed three thousand pounds and an annuity of a thousand pounds. He had never seen the office as anything other than a personal possession, although it was one that he embellished and upheld in ways that made the nation more powerful. Though by modern standards this action would mark him as corrupt, by those of his own day he was a successful operator in a complex world where offices were never salaried and office holders lived on perquisites. The office of Lord Admiral was a medieval sinecure, long overdue for the reform that was already in the air: Howard proved to be the last man to use the Admiralty of England as a private financial resource.

By this time, his once-handsome body enfeebled by age, his bright prospects and seemingly endless wealth drained away, Howard was little more than a living shadow of former glory, acutely conscious that he had failed to establish his dynasty. He died on 14 December

1624, with little more wealth than he had begun with, and his title died with his youngest son. Soon there was little left to remind the world what he had been in his pomp, save a majestic tapestry. Nonetheless, Howard's contribution to the navy had been huge, laying the foundations of the nation's future naval glory.

Lord Howard of Effingham was no seaman: he was a great leader who held together a disparate collection of self-interested and self-willed men, ensuring they worked together in harmony. He used rank and authority to control and conciliate ill-assorted captains and make them an effective fighting force. The mark of his greatness was the failure of every other Elizabethan officer to match his achievement. In battle he provided the voice of sense and reason, avoiding unnecessary risk and ensuring orders were executed with a nicely judged combination of obedience and initiative.

Howard created the role of admiral in the late sixteenth century, when heavy cannon and effective sailing ships provided new options for war at sea. The combination of high rank, a close relationship with the Queen, early experience and solid common sense made Howard effective. He resisted the temptation to chase glory, ignoring Medina Sidonia's challenge to close-quarter battle, either ship to ship or fleet to fleet. He was safe, reliable and perfectly capable of acting the grandee. In addition he knew that great navies are made by men, not ships. While Francis Drake remains the 'star' of Elizabethan seafaring enterprise, it was the safe, secure figure of Charles Howard who defeated the Armada. In battle and in the propaganda round that followed, Howard did more to make England a naval nation than anyone else: within a year the navy was the Englishman's proudest boast. In the centuries to come, navy and nation would look back on 1588 as their finest hour, and revive the memory whenever they felt alarmed.

In an age when English monarchs sat nervously on their thrones, fearing assassination, usurpation and treason, Howard earned his rank and privilege by absolute loyalty. As a consequence, his monarchs were content to ignore his enthusiastic exploitation of his office. Howard used the Admiralty Court, privateer licences and pirate forfeits to maintain a princely lifestyle. Perhaps he lived too long: eighty-eight years was more than his monarch, his naval and political contemporaries, and his wife. He died less than two decades before civil war brought down the Stuart kingdom he had done so much to create and alienated the navy from the monarchy. Yet he left a glorious legacy. In his two seagoing commands he won great victories: the first defined a nation, the second blasted the last hopes of a crumbling superpower. He was also a man of cultured taste, supporting a troupe of actors in London, though sadly the admiral who gave Drake his orders never had the chance to command Shakespeare.

2

GOD'S REPUBLICAN WARRIOR

Robert Blake

1599–1657

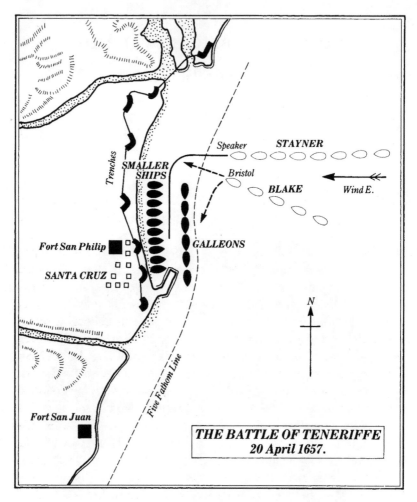

Speaker

STAYNER

Trenches

SMALLER
SHIPS

Bristol

BLAKE

Wind E.

Fort San Philip

GALLEONS

SANTA CRUZ

N

Five Fathom Line

Fort San Juan

**THE BATTLE OF TENERIFFE
20 April 1657.**

A triumph of will power: Robert Blake's last and greatest victory at Santa
Cruz de Tenerife exemplified heroic leadership

UNLIKE CHARLES HOWARD, Robert Blake had no hereditary claim to a position of command at sea. Nothing in his lineage, nor in the first forty years of his life, hinted that he might become an admiral.[1] Only the social and political turmoil of the English Civil War opened the path to a naval career. His early biographers invented a boyhood enthusiasm for ships and fabricated early sea voyages, as if the fact that Robert Blake took command of the English fleet at the age of fifty-one without prior seafaring or naval experience were a reflection on the profession's integrity. The first significant study, however, could only claim that he 'probably' learnt of ships and the sea from his father.[2] All these early writers missed the real key to his success: it was because Robert Blake was neither a seaman nor a professional warrior that he would transform the art of the admiral.

The eldest son of a large middle-class family of landowners, merchants and mayors in the Somerset port town of Bridgewater, Blake was baptised on 27 September 1598 and educated at the local grammar school. Rather than entering the family business, he was propelled by his academic ability and family resources to Oxford University. He studied first at St Alban's Hall and then Wadham College – the latter only recently founded, by a Somerset man – and graduated in February 1618. Although he remained at Wadham for the next six years, any hopes he might have had of an academic career foundered on the rock of his beliefs. Blake was by this time a committed Puritan: he viewed bishops and kings as a barrier to the building of a New Jerusalem on earth.[3] But beyond his all-consuming faith, his personal life remains shrouded in mystery. A shy, introspective man, he never expressed any interest in women, never married, and seems to have found what little companionship he needed among preachers, soldiers and sailors. He had little regard for money, and rarely pursued outstanding back pay, though he died relatively wealthy because he never spent his income. His activities in the two decades after leaving university remain obscure. After his father died in 1625, he bought the property adjoining the family home, which had been left to him and his brother Humphrey, who ran the family business. It is likely that he lived on the proceeds of the family lands at Crandon-cum-Puriton: if he engaged in overseas commerce, as some biographers believe, he did not do so to any great effect.

He did, however, establish a significant local standing, serving briefly as a Member of Parliament in 1640. As the nation became increasingly divided on questions of religion and governance, his support for Parliament against the Crown remained steadfast. Nor was he slow to take up arms in the Civil War, joining his friend and fellow Puritan Colonel Edward Popham in raising and commanding local troops. While he began his military career in the cavalry, Blake spent most of the first civil war defending towns. In July 1643 he commanded an important fort at Bristol, the last to surrender; the following year he led the successful defence of Lyme Regis, and then held Taunton against three Royalist sieges between October 1644 and June 1645. Though Blake was not a professional soldier, he nonetheless displayed many of the essentials of leadership: he drew from deep reservoirs of faith and conviction to produce stirring rhetoric that inspired troops and townspeople alike, while showing a paternalistic concern for their well-being and morale. He was also quick to learn the military techniques that the situation demanded: charged with the defence of indefensible towns, he soon mastered the art of the timely counter-attack, and on numerous occasions he would catch the besieging army off guard or off balance, deflecting them from their own operations.

Although he began the Civil War without any military experience, and remained essentially an amateur warrior, Blake was an educated man with a receptive mind – at least where earthly matters were concerned. He realised that the key to success did not come from the superior tactics and skills of career soldiers like his contemporary George Monck, but from the hearts of his men. His leadership was energetic and conveyed a sense of drama: like a preacher, he found inspiration both in words and deeds. He shared Cromwell's belief that the foundations of success were faith and discipline: both men were severe on traitors and cowards. The absolute conviction of his faith gave Blake's leadership a zeal and authority that left no one in any doubt as to his purpose or resolve. His disregard for precedent, and disdain for the time-honoured military traditions of plunder and personal profit, meant that he could hold apparently indefensible towns such as Lyme Regis which a professional would have surrendered.[4] Reduced to the point of starvation in Taunton, he told his men he would eat three of his four pairs of boots before surrendering the town. His strengths were not confined to the day of a battle: attention to detail and effective precautions were critical to his defensive endeavours. He placed a high value on loyalty to his men, and to his political leaders, even if he disagreed with their policy.

Elegant appearances played no part in Blake's leadership: every part of him, square-built, graceless and only five foot six, shouted his status as a bourgeois merchant. Yet the face that looms out from the only surviving portrait also conveys reflection and determination, suggesting a man as strong in his faith as in his armoured body.[5] It would be interesting to know how and when the image was created, for Blake was not the sort of man to commission a portrait, and he had no wife who might want one. Someone evidently wanted a personal memento of this mighty warrior: perhaps Cromwell, who valued the heroic image as a tool of statecraft, needed a suitable icon to help him in his dealings with foreign ambassadors.[6] By the time the first civil war ended Blake had acquired a national reputation, while his enhanced standing in Somerset saw him return to Parliament in September 1645. His overriding agenda was the establishment of a national church on Presbyterian lines, with lay elders and ministers. He did not look kindly upon the increasingly factionalised sects that had emerged within the army, and used his civic authority to close an independent meeting house in Taunton. Although Blake pledged not to negotiate with Charles I, he took no part in the creation of the Commonwealth government or the trial and execution of the King. In the face of royal duplicity, he accepted a republic as the best option.

General at Sea

The execution of the King and the establishment of the Commonwealth made the army the real power in the land. Threats to its authority remained, however: the Stuart cause was alive and well, much of Europe looked on the regicide republic with horror, and both Ireland and Scotland offered opportunities to potential invaders. The critical issue facing England was whether the new regime could be established in perpetuity without bankrupting the country. The army was a costly instrument, and it was not the only institution required to ensure national security.

In March 1649 Blake was appointed one of three 'generals at sea', army officers detailed to command the navy. These 'generals' were sent to impose the government's authority on an unreliable, mutinous and dangerous force. Though the navy had largely sided with Parliament in the Civil War, playing a critical role in the outcome of the conflict, it was an independent-minded force, and both its officers and its men took a narrow, personal view of their duties. They expected to be indulged and had no intention of submitting to the sort of 'New Model' discipline that the army had accepted. There was a clash of cultures that reached an inevitable crisis point when the government sacked a popular admiral and appointed an obnoxious replacement: the resulting mutiny saw half the fleet sail off to join Prince Charles in Holland. Though the widely respected Earl of Warwick, reinstated as Lord High Admiral to deal with the emergency, had performed well, he was closely linked to the old navy, and the Army Council had no faith in him. Indeed, the soldiers did not trust any seaman: instead, they detailed Richard Deane, Robert Blake and Edward Popham to take control of the rebellious navy. Cromwell was about to sail to Ireland and wanted to ensure that the committee headed by his brother-in-law appointed a man whom he trusted: Deane, a Plymouth merchant, had traded in Baltic naval stores before the war and earned Cromwell's admiration as the artillery commander of the New Model Army. Deane clearly knew and respected Blake, whom he suggested, and Blake in his turn suggested Popham, who at least had some naval experience. As a regicide, Deane's commitment to the Commonwealth was beyond doubt, but both Blake and Popham had to sign a declaration of loyalty to the new regime before they could take office. Political reliability was the overriding requirement for the job: there were many officers with similar experience of war, and rather more knowledge of the sea and naval warfare. The naval role of the three new appointees was not considered permanent or exclusive, however: all would be offered land commands over the course of the following decade.

The first task of the 'generals at sea' was to restore the fleet to order and impose discipline, as the Commonwealth needed warships to support the Irish campaign and to deal with Prince Rupert's Stuart fleet. The business of practical seamanship, meanwhile, had to be left to experienced navigators and mariners. If they were to achieve the necessary discipline, it was essential that the generals did not alienate the fleet, and this may in part explain Blake's appointment: his views were far closer to those of the majority of seamen than the hard-line republican convictions of Deane.[7]

Whatever the motives behind their appointment, the new men quickly realised that the fleet would only be effective if they avoided politically motivated witch-hunts. Once in office, they turned against the committee that had appointed them, insisting that promotion be based on merit. They secured the loyalty of the seamen with improved rations, while all ranks appreciated a new Prize Code and regulations. Finally, the Lord Admiral's share of prize was set aside to fund pensions for the wounded and widows. It appears that Blake was the author of these developments: he drafted a written engagement for the seamen, which they signed with enthusiasm. He had done the same at the siege of Taunton.

The new men had little time to enforce their authority before the navy's services were required. Rupert led the Royalist fleet to sea from his base in Holland, attacking English merchant shipping with impunity. The generals quickly chased Rupert off his cruising ground in the Western Approaches and into the Irish port of Kinsale. His colleagues went ashore, leaving Blake to blockade Rupert's ships from late May 1649. It was tedious work, but Blake, who had no reason to be anywhere else, found inner strength in his own company and felt a growing identification with the navy. Consequently he refused Cromwell's lucrative offer of a major-general's post ashore in Ireland, although only after consulting Popham.[8] Remaining at sea strengthened his commitment to the fleet, but Cromwell cannot have been unaware that Blake did not share his political views, and could not be bought or flattered. This perhaps gave Cromwell two good reasons to leave Blake where he was: he was obviously well suited to the task, and keeping him 'at sea' neutralised the potential threat he represented. In late October a gale drove Blake off-station, allowing Rupert to escape just before Cromwell's army reached Kinsale. Once released from their watch, Blake's ships supported the pacification of southern Ireland.

Blake must have been encouraged by the speed with which the fleet had accepted the new leadership, and by their determined performance throughout the year; only the escape of Rupert's fleet marred his first season afloat. He had spent far more of the year afloat than his colleagues, becoming the most experienced 'general at sea' and by far the most popular. The Council of State was quick to send him to Lisbon, where Rupert was looking to set up a new base in order to continue harassing English trade. The new mission would take Blake into the world of international diplomacy, Catholic courts and Muslim corsairs. Would his simple faith clash with the complex commercial and political interests of the English state?

Portugal had achieved a fragile independence from Spain only in 1640, and was still at war with Madrid. As Spain was also at war with France, Portugal had the support of Paris and the commercially motivated backing of the Dutch. Anxious not to add the powerful English fleet to his enemies, the Portuguese King tried to be even-handed. However, Blake's opening move was anything but subtle: he attempted to sail into Lisbon harbour and sink Rupert's 'pirate' ships at anchor. This was more than the Portuguese would tolerate.[9] The forts opened fire, forcing the English ships to back off. Months of tedious blockade and devious diplomacy followed. King John was anxious to get rid of Rupert as quickly as possible, though without handing him over to Blake; as long as the stand-off lasted, the Portuguese military efforts were diverted from the Spanish frontier and their vital Brazil treasure fleet was left vulnerable.

On 3 September Rupert attempted to escape from the Tagus, aided by a thick sea mist. While he had thirty-six ships, Blake was left with only three: some were lost in the fog, and the others had been sent home. Blake reported the ensuing action with his usual modesty:

By God's good providence, the enemies [sic] fleet was all to the leeward of us, so we keeping the wind made toward them being resolved to encounter Prince Rupert, who was the headmost of the fleet. Coming within reach we gave him a broadside, so did the two frigates, which the Lord was pleased so to direct that his foretopmast was shot off by the cap. Whereupon he bore up in the midst of the fleet and the thick mist taking them again out of our sight, we stood off to seek the rest of our squadron.[10]

Another account had Blake holding a collision course with Rupert's flagship until the Prince gave way. No one ever doubted Blake's resolve. Two weeks later he seized half the incoming Brazil convoy, a move that threatened Portugal with bankruptcy, before sailing for Cadiz to refit and deal with four French frigates that had attacked English shipping in the Straits of Gibraltar. He captured the French flagship and put into Cadiz, only to learn that Rupert had left Lisbon. Blake wasted no time on regrets: he put to sea in haste, encountered six Royalist ships off Alicante and chased them into Cartagena, capturing one and driving another ashore to be burnt by her crew. The rest were wrecked when they tried to escape: 'it pleased God to determine the business by a storm of wind, by force whereof and their own wilfulness all four were driven ashore the next day and spoiled'. Blake discovered that there were limits to the efficacy of such divine intervention. Rupert was not with his squadron – 'the will of God being otherwise I must acquiesce in it'.[11] Nonetheless, his mission was complete: the Royalist fleet would do no more harm. Parliament awarded Blake a thousand pounds and voted a Day of Thanksgiving.

No sooner had Blake returned to Somerset for a rest than his services were required again. His original orders to capture the Isle of Man from the Royalists were overtaken by events, and he was now detailed to the Scilly Islands, where the Royalist garrison was funding itself by extensive privateering, to the annoyance of Dutch traders. When the Dutch sent Admiral Tromp to demand satisfaction, the Commonwealth hastened Blake to the scene to ensure they did not seize the islands. The first attempt to land proved abortive, but Blake adjusted his method, using seamen to spearhead the assault landing. This time he succeeded, securing control of the key anchorage at the cost of only four dead. Now he could blockade and bombard the Royalist positions. He was fortunate to escape unharmed on 4 May when a cannon firing on Royalist ships exploded: the gunner and an ensign were less fortunate.[12] The islands surrendered in June and were quickly turned into a propaganda triumph.[13] When the Scots army invaded England to restore the monarchy, Cromwell called Blake ashore, but his plans were changed by Popham's sudden death from a fever. With Deane already employed in Scotland, Blake was the only general still at sea.

There he remained. He spent the autumn capturing Jersey from the Royalists, using the experience he had gained in the Scillies to plan a skilful landing that minimised casualties. The Isle of Man, meanwhile, surrendered without his involvement. Having recovered its lost islands, the English Commonwealth was complete, and Blake might have expected to be released from service. In fact, he would find no peace this side of the grave: his services to date would turn out to be little more than a belated apprenticeship in naval command. Thus far his biggest problem had been getting at the enemy, since once engaged Rupert's ships had shown little fight and not much skill. It was perhaps fortunate that Blake had faced no sterner test while learning his new profession.

The First Dutch War

Having created a powerful navy in order to protect commercial shipping and recover isolated fragments of the state from the defeated Royalists, the Commonwealth now found itself in possession of a major instrument of national policy, one ideally suited to promoting the power, prestige and prosperity of the English state. In 1652 England was already engaged in an undeclared, low-level maritime war against France, but it would be the Dutch Republic that felt the first impact of the Commonwealth's power.

At first glance the English Commonwealth and the Dutch Republic had a great deal in common on questions of politics and religion, and might have seemed obvious allies, but the reality was very different. The cost and economic dislocation of a civil war and its aftermath, together with a series of poor harvests, left English finances in a ruinous condition. The end of the Thirty Years War, which had offered a market for English merchant ships, proved equally catastrophic. The Dutch dominated European shipping: the combination of powerful banking houses and cheap ships with small crews allowed them to secure the bulk of the continent's carrying trade, and treaties with Denmark and Spain in 1649 and 1650 only enhanced those advantages. When the Commonwealth created a new naval administration, it naturally tapped into the expertise of English ship-owners and merchants, men who found Dutch competition particularly galling. These men sponsored legislation in 1650 that banned foreign ships from trading with English colonies, and the 1651 Navigation Act that required goods bound for England to be conveyed either in English ships or those of the producing country, thus cutting Dutch carriers out of the import business. The aim was clear and deliberate, although the policy would take years to reach fruition. The Dutch were not overly concerned: the English market was not particularly important to them. They did object, though, to the rough, occasionally lethal activity of English privateers looking for Royalist or French cargoes.

Religion soon overrode such rivalries. Confident that they were acting in God's name, the English leaders offered the Dutch a federation, hoping for a Protestant league to overthrow their Catholic rivals – the Pope, Spain and France. The Dutch rejected the offer of an alliance, to the surprise of religious hard-liners in England, who could only account for their decision by declaring they must be bad Protestants who required chastising to make them see the error of their ways. To compound the problem, Dutch diplomatic attempts to settle a series of commercial questions were backed up by a mobilisation of the fleet. Far from being deterred, the Commonwealth, convinced the Dutch meant war, acted accordingly. As the English would later learn themselves, deterrence only works against political entities that are rational and calculating. The Commonwealth government was neither of these things; it simply fitted out eighty ships for war.

Having annihilated the last Spanish fleet to enter the English Channel in 1639, the Dutch had good reason to be confident: they had large merchant fleets, excellent seamen, and in Maerten Tromp an admiral of outstanding ability, greatly admired by his men. The Dutch tactics exploited their seamanship and numbers, using well-handled ships in an aggressive mêlée style of close-range fighting. Their object was to capture enemy ships by boarding, while difficult opponents could be dealt with by fireships. However, two of the three critical Dutch trade routes, their economic lifelines, passed close to the English coast. To secure this trade the Dutch would have to defeat the English fleet – and therein lay the core of their problem. While the English had been using a fleet of armed merchantmen and small warships to deal with Stuart privateers and isolated islands, they also possessed a powerful battle fleet of great warships, some built by the very 'ship money' programme that had sparked the Civil War. These big ships mounted heavier cannon than the small Dutch vessels, and in this war it would be guns, not ships, that made the difference.[14]

Although James I had taken little interest in the fleet, Charles I had appreciated that the strength of his personal position was intimately linked with the nation's naval power. With this in mind, he built several powerful warships, a process that reached a fitting climax with his prestige flagship, the *Sovereign of the Seas*, the largest warship in the world. This massive gilded propaganda statement broadcast Charles's claim to English rule of the ocean, so that he could tax those who used the seas and enforce a salute to his flag from every ship passing through the English Channel. The Dutch had nothing like the hundred-gun three-decked *Sovereign*: indeed, Tromp complained that the English had fifty ships more powerful than his own flagship. Despite these salutary facts, the Dutch government ordered Tromp to salute the English flag in the Channel only if the English ships were superior.

Bloodshed was the inevitable consequence of such impolitic orders in a period of heightened tension. On 19 May 1652 squadrons led by Tromp and Blake met off Dover. Blake took in sail and waited for the Dutch, determined to enforce the salute. Outnumbered forty-two to thirteen, Blake could have avoided the confrontation, but that was neither in his character nor, in the event, necessary. With Tromp's flagship less than a hundred yards away Blake fired two guns to signal his demand that Tromp strike his flag. Rather than conform, Tromp hung out the red battle flag, and after Blake had fired three shots at his ensign, the Dutchman loosed off a full broadside. Blake was anxious to keep the Dutch to seaward, and his fleet fought without forming a line. Although heavily outnumbered, Blake held his own, the Dutch charge and mêlée tactics making it easy for his ships to use their firepower. Blake's flagship, the *James*, was frequently surrounded:

We have received above seventy great shots in our hull and masts, in our sails without number, being engaged with the whole body of the fleet for the space of four hours, and the mark at which they aimed.[15]

Despite that bombardment, casualties were light: six killed, nine badly and twenty-five slightly wounded, although the mizzen mast was shot off. Blake owed a good deal to his stout old ship, built many years before, in King James's reign. When nine more English ships arrived under Admiral Nehemiah Bourne, the Dutch were driven off, leaving a prize in English hands. There was very little skill involved in the action off Dover, just resolute fighting. Blake led by example, with words and deeds calculated to rouse the spirits of his men: in return, he expected absolute commitment.[16] This approach to discipline proved to be the key asset for the English: their Dutch opponents were a fractious collection of ships and men from several distinct regional admiralty authorities, divided by political faction and personal loyalties. Under pressure, the fragile discipline of the Dutch invariably broke, and they were quick to blame each other. After Dover, Blake recognised that the more heavily built and armed English ships would win if they stood their ground, supported one another and trusted in God. It was not a war he wanted to fight, but a man who demanded loyalty from those he commanded must do as he was bid by those who held supreme authority.

The lessons of the battle were equally clear to Tromp: the wily old admiral knew his fleet had little chance against such ships and such men as the English could deploy. Anxious to avoid a war, he wrote to Blake to ask if he could have his ship back, hoping to calm the situation. Filled with righteous indignation by the sight of dead and wounded men, Blake, reminding his opponent that he was the commander of 'the fleet of the Parliament of the English Republic', rebuffed the approach.[17] As Tromp had anticipated, his government was anxious to avoid conflict, but the English declared war on 8 July. The English war aims were clear enough: as the Dutch envoy Pauw lamented, 'We are attacking a mountain of iron, they are attacking a mountain of gold.'[18] This golden mountain was to be found at sea, and Blake was ordered to the Orkney Islands to locate it, in the form of a Dutch East India convoy. Tromp followed. Such was the lure of the convoy that both main fleets, between eighty and a hundred ships strong, were soon heading due north, directly away from the main theatre of operations. The English captured some small Dutch warships guarding their fishing fleet and managed to avoid the storm that scattered Tromp's force, sinking some of his ships and some of the long-lost convoy. When the storm abated, Tromp found his convoy and brought them home safely. He was promptly dismissed by a republican regime that did not share his

Orangist politics. Many of his warships did not reach Holland for weeks to come and missed the fighting that autumn. Perhaps God really was an Englishman.

Thus far, battle tactics were little different from those used in 1588: fleets charged into one another bow-on, manoeuvred for advantage, and tried to board crippled opponents. However, the heavy English ships were not very agile. They carried their main armament on the broadside rather than at the bow, and were better suited to linear combat. By fighting in a closely ordered line, they could use their heavy guns to negate the superior speed and manoeuvrability of the Dutch, crippling their ships and killing their men before they could get to grips with the English fleet. These tactics could be used because Dutch strategy required their fleet to escort vital convoys up and down the English Channel. With the immense strategic advantage of a commanding position across a vital choke point, the English only had to watch and wait. While the Dutch ships were faster and more agile, they had to fight on English terms to keep their economy running. Consequently all the major battles were fought to secure the passage of Dutch convoys.

Returning to the Channel in mid-August, Blake hastened to repair the storm-damaged ships of the fleet. In early September he was ordered to seize a French convoy heading for the privateer port of Dunkirk. The day after he executed his orders, Dunkirk surrendered to the Spanish. This was the final straw for Paris, which was quick to recognise the republic and send an ambassador to London. Naval power was a mighty instrument of Commonwealth state policy.

On 28 September the English and Dutch fleets met off the Kentish Knock shoal. Admiral de With's Dutch fleet was slightly outnumbered but heavily outgunned. Although de With proved the more adept tactician, his advantage was negated once the heavy English ships entered the fray, especially Blake's flagship the *Resolution* and the awe-inspiring *Sovereign*.[19] These were the prestige vessels of James I and Charles I, the largest, strongest and most heavily armed warships on the planet. At one stage the gilded *Sovereign* ran aground, but once in action she brushed aside the attentions of twenty Dutch vessels, leaving a trail of shattered, blood-stained hulks in her wake. Although decorated like a fairground ride, a hundred bronze cannon made her irresistible: awe-struck Dutchmen called her the 'Golden Devil'. Once again, Blake led the fleet by example, and he insisted they hold their fire until the enemy came in close. He won a significant victory, taking three ships and a Dutch admiral. English casualties were light: bigger, stronger ships with superior firepower quickly subdued their opponents. That night both fleets remained close, repairing their ships. The following morning the Dutch fled, and a partial chase action ensued, but they could not be brought to battle. On the third morning the fleets were still in sight, but the Dutch fled as soon as the English bent on sail.

Blake's official report of the battle is spare and undemonstrative, as befits a modest God-fearing man. It also reveals his absolute dependence on professional advice. His course during the second night, he reports, 'was advised by the captain, master and mates, the pilot and others'. For tactical decisions he assembled 'the Vice and Rear Admirals, and also a great part of the captains, being then come onboard for the supply of some necessaries, we advised together what was fittest to be done'.[20] In essence Blake led the discussion of strategy and tactics, but he deferred entirely to the mariners when it came to ship-handling and navigation, especially after both his flagship and the *Sovereign* touched the Kentish Knock shoal.

Much more could have been achieved if the English had held better discipline and acted as a unit. The partial success produced differing reactions on either side of the North Sea: the Dutch were energised, recalling Tromp to command, while the English became rather complacent, paying off ships for the winter. When Tromp emerged with a massive outbound convoy in late November, Blake was still waiting in the Downs, but the balance of force had been completely reversed: Blake had only forty-two ships to pit against the eighty-eight commanded by Tromp. Despite a council of war recommending that he avoid action, it seems that Blake simply could not resist the challenge. Rather than let Tromp pass unmolested, he shadowed the Dutch as they pushed south-west down the Channel, using the shoals to keep the fleets apart.

When the fleets reached Dungeness Point on 30 November, the English were pinned against the shore; Tromp hung out the red battle-flag and steered for Blake's new flagship, the *Triumph*. Although he missed his mark, his intentions were made clear as he took two English ships in desperate hand-to-hand fighting. The *Triumph* was heavily engaged, suffering six killed, ten wounded and significant damage to her rigging. Blake was unable to support the two ships that Tromp boarded after his foretopmast was shot away and the mainstay cut through. Having cleared the Channel, Tromp took his convoy out into the Atlantic.

For Blake the defeat was peculiarly bitter. He knew that some twenty ships, half the fleet, had not done their utmost to engage the enemy:

There was much baseness of spirit, not among the merchantmen only, but many of the State's ships, and therefore I make it my humble request that your Honours would be pleased to send down some gentlemen to take an impartial and strict examination of the deportment of several commanders, that you may know who are to be confided in and who are not.

In essence he wanted a court martial; he declared the command was a burden 'far too great for me', and begged to be released now that two new generals had been appointed.[21] He might be forgiven a little melodrama, given that this was his first defeat, but the government had no intention of removing its most popular and successful naval commander after a defeat that reflected more on the inadequacy of their own preparations than his errors. The Council of State rejected Blake's offer to resign: as he intended, this forced them to take action to address the weaknesses highlighted off Dungeness, to meet his request for an enquiry, and to tighten up discipline and subordination. Blake had carried the day with typical determination: as Samuel Gardiner observed, he was 'the incarnation of the war spirit', and his 'fierce patriotism was widely shared'.[22]

With the enemy 'far too strong for us', meanwhile, Blake retreated to the mouth of the Thames, where the shoals gave him added security.[23] Tromp took his merchant convoy down the Channel – and gathered some tasty prizes. In London, the defeat was a salutary reminder that the navy faced a major opponent and, with the Thames virtually blockaded, commodity prices began to rise.[24]

While the fleet waited on the defensive, a court of enquiry considered the conduct of certain captains, among whom four (including his younger brother Benjamin) had failed to support Blake and another was dismissed for incompetence. At the council of war these men had argued that fighting was not the best option when facing overwhelming odds, and had been ignored. When they did not follow their leader into battle with the necessary enthusiasm, the meaning of their action was obvious: they were registering their dissent. Blake used the Council of State to establish his authority. He required absolute obedience to his will, and used the Court of Enquiry to set an example. It was no coincidence that three of the suspects were considered politically unreliable.[25] In the event four of the five victims of this purge were quietly reinstated; though two of them were killed at the Texel the following year, the lesson remained clear. The admiral needed absolute authority: while Howard had exercised an authority drawn from the Queen's personal mandate, Blake imposed a discipline founded on the will of Parliament.

Blake also advised that his two fellow generals at sea, the experienced Deane and the newly appointed George Monck, be sent to sea to lighten his own burden of command. He recommended that in future armed merchant ships should be commanded by state officers, not their owner's nominees, as the latter tended to think about the value of the ship they were hazarding, rather than the service they might do the state. Furthermore, several leading merchant-ship owners were politically suspect.[26] At Blake's insistence, too, seamen's pay was increased. He also secured a new disciplinary code giving the commander-in-chief authority to court-martial and punish officers who failed to do their duty. To make sure no one misunderstood the import, there were twenty-five offences for which death was the punishment, among which treason featured prominently – although the charge was never laid in the Common-wealth period.[27] Having discovered the limits of leadership by example and zeal, Blake pushed the government to apply the pro-fessional military standards that were in force ashore to the fleet. A new Admiralty Committee was set up to oversee the fleet, and Blake occasionally attended their meetings. The largest tax increase of the Commonwealth period was voted through to fund these improvements. With more money and more authority, the navy prepared for the new season.[28]

On 18 February Tromp returned up the Channel with the home-bound shipping, encountering Blake off Portland. Once again, the English had failed to scout effectively and were caught with the bat-tle fleet stretched across the Channel between Portland and Alderney to ensure they did not miss their prey. With the eye of an experienced seaman, Tromp saw in an instant the opportunity to overwhelm an isolated fragment of the English fleet. He sent his merchant ships to windward and attacked the most northerly English ships, led by Blake and Deane, sailing together on the *Triumph*.

With the enemy fast approaching, Blake was in his element. This was how he liked to fight: nothing complex, no manoeuvres, just downright hard fighting. The result would be decided by God's judgement. While they waited for the Dutch charge, the English ships were ordered to close ranks and take in sail. They greeted Tromp with an effective cannonade. Blake and Deane were in a dangerous position until the superior skill and seamanship of Vice Admiral John Lawson brought timely reinforcements to break the Dutch concentration and release the generals. When Monck's frigates threatened his convoy, Tromp was obliged to break off. Although he left nine Dutch warships and twenty-four merchant ships in English hands, Tromp would get the rest home. The English lost only one ship, but many fine officers fell. Blake's captain and secretary were killed at his side, and he himself was hit on the thigh by an iron bar that had already sliced through Deane's coat and breeches. It was his first serious injury in ten years at war. Even so, he retained command throughout the day, lest his departure might discourage the men, and the official report made no mention of the injury.[29] The capture and recapture of at least three English warships, and heavy casualties on the flagship, demonstrated that the small number of English ships with Blake had not been able to stop the Dutch charge. Moreover, most of the fighting had been at close range, where the Dutch could still do serious damage. A better system would be required to exploit superior English firepower to the full.

That night the English repaired their rigging and sails, and reinforced their heavy ships with manpower from the less powerful units. The following day battle resumed, if only briefly, before the Dutch fled for home.[30] The Dutch ships were badly damaged and short of ammunition, having received no fresh stocks since before Dungeness. Yet most of their ships survived. That night Tromp used the shoal waters around Cape Gris Nez to evade the deep-draught English ships. While this has often been praised as an outstanding example of seamanship, it was in truth a desperate measure, forced on Tromp by the prospect of absolute disaster if battle was rejoined. For the English, meanwhile, victory off Portland restored the energy and enthusiasm that had been severely dented by the defeat off Dungeness.[31]

For all the glory and grandstanding, the English had failed to crush an inferior, beaten enemy at Portland. This was perhaps more obvious to the new general, Devon-born George Monck, for whom this was his first naval battle. As a professional soldier and artillery specialist, Monck provided vital expertise when the generals refined their tactical system to reflect the overwhelming importance of gunnery and firepower.[32] The generals' 'Instructions for the better ordering of the Fleet in Fighting' of March 1653 stressed the importance of maintaining a linear formation, astern of the flagship. These were the first tactical and doctrinal instructions issued to the fleet. If the Dutch ships could be prevented from coming to close quarters by heavy gunfire, their seamanship and mobility would be negated. Blake's part in this process was limited by his wound and the fever he picked up shortly afterwards. He spent the spring in London driving the naval administration to produce the ships, men, food and money required for victory at sea.

Although far from well, Blake went to sea on 1 June with a squadron of new ships, promising he would 'with God's grace do such service as the infirmities of my body will bear, which I find increase upon me'.[33] It did not take him long to find the fleet. After a quiet summer, the two fleets had met again off the Gabbard Shoal in the mouth of the Thames on 2 June. Blake missed the first day, when Deane and Monck formed the line and battered the lightly armed Dutch into submission. Deane was killed at the outset of the fighting, his head knocked off by a cannonball, leaving Monck to cover his body with his cloak in order not to dishearten the men. When Blake's fresh ships appeared late the next day, the Dutch broke and fled. Little wonder. After the English had used six thousand barrels of gunpowder to drive heavy iron shot through their flimsy ships, the Dutch had neither the ammunition nor the stomach for any more. That they only lost twenty ships reflected another heroic effort by Tromp, who used the Wieling shoal to escape from the English and prevent a complete catastrophe. As de With confessed to the Dutch government, 'The English are now our masters and command the sea.'[34] He was not exaggerating: the English fleet blockaded the Dutch coast 'the better to improve upon the victory God hath given us', quickly bringing economic life to a standstill.[35] Grass grew in the once busy streets of Amsterdam. After a month the English withdrew, short of food and water, their crews falling sick.[36]

After the battle, Blake joined Monck on the *Resolution*, despite complaining of pains in his head and his left side, the latter partly due to gravel in his kidneys. The exact nature of his illness is uncertain, but in his weakened condition the fevers that swept through the fleet that summer may have affected him. There were eighty sick on the *Resolution* alone. He was ashore when Monck won the last battle of the war off the Texel on 31 July. In contrast to Blake's passionate, impulsive and slightly chaotic 'follow my leader' approach, Monck's fleet formed a tight line of battle, and used it to smash the shambolic Dutch formation. In a battle between well-ordered lines of broadside-firing capital ships and a swarm of agile boarding platforms, the English would win as long as they maintained their discipline, and discipline was Blake's greatest contribution to the cause.

In the event, Tromp was killed early in the battle, and as the news spread through his fleet Dutch resistance collapsed. On 1 October Blake went ashore at Portsmouth, travelling to Bath to take the waters for his gravel. Within a fortnight he was back at the Admiralty in London. He remained in harness ashore until late January 1654, when he went back to sea on board the *Swiftsure* with Admiral William Penn,[37] but saw no further combat in this war.

Although some historians have argued that the First Anglo-Dutch War witnessed the beginning of line-of-battle tactics, the development was by no means clear-cut. On the evidence of the instructions of 29 March 1653 and the subsequent battles, any judgement must remain uncertain. The instructions call for a line to be formed astern of the general, 'upon pain of the severest punishment'. This reads like Blake's response to the failure of his squadron to follow his lead at Dungeness, rather than the dawn of a tactical revolution.[38] Blake also insisted on keeping good order while sailing, and threatened to cashier defaulters.[39] It is significant that the instructions for summoning captains aboard the flagship were far more detailed than the provisions for the order of battle or of sailing.[40] Blake was not the man for formulaic tactical systems: for him discipline was the basis of all naval action, and without it the systematic linear tactics employed by Monck would have been unthinkable.

There was another reason why Blake did not introduce the linear system: it was regarded as essentially defensive, a method of preventing the Dutch from closing to board, or worse, loosing their deadly fireships. Mêlée battle provided ample opportunity for distracted or damaged ships to be grappled by incendiaries, and all right-minded seamen feared fire on board their wooden walls. None could swim. The new instructions stressed the use of English flotilla craft to deal with the threat.[41] Robert Blake was not a man to let fear override his aggressive instincts: he was happy enough with the existing system in which the admiral led the fleet and all conformed to his movements. However, it would require stronger doctrine, and more firmly entrenched standard procedures, to make it work in the way Blake wished. Such doctrines and procedures were well established in military service. To the zeal and commitment upon which Blake relied, Monck added a requirement for professional judgement from his sea officers, to avoid the sort of pointless bloodshed that Blake had indulged off Dungeness. It was fortunate for Blake he would never again face fellow republican Protestants: against Tunisians and Spaniards, he could enthuse his followers with religious fervour and indignation, while relying on their seamanship being superior to that of their foes.

Dealing with the Lord Protector

The political climate had changed significantly during the war. Cromwell staged a *coup d'état* on 23 April 1653, expelled the Rump Parliament and set up a government dominated by extremist independent preachers who supported the war. While Richard Deane had approved, Blake held his silence: this was not what he had been fighting for. Nor was it very popular across the nation. Recognising the need for a more acceptable political system, Cromwell took office in December as Lord Protector and settled terms with the Dutch. This time Blake made his loyalty clear.[42] When the Treaty of Westminster was signed the following March, Cromwell ensured that princes of the House of Orange, hereditary holders of the supreme command and other quasi-royal figures were excluded from the Dutch government. As the infant Orange prince was a grandson of Charles I, the possibility of Orange support for the Stuart cause was significant, and Cromwell took care to prevent them controlling the only fleet that could successfully invade England.[43] He also took care to retain the loyalty of his own fleet, putting his faith in Robert Blake to help him do so.

This was a potentially risky course for Cromwell to take: Blake's religious and political views were different from his own, and his popular fame, nurtured by the English identification with the sea, threatened to outstrip that of the Lord Protector. Blake had lost his seat when Cromwell dissolved Parliament, though he did not regret the passing of a factious, divisive House that had done little to advance the causes he held dear. His faith was the key to his return to the hundred-seat 'Barebones' Parliament, where he represented the Somerset congregations. When Cromwell finally dismissed Parliament in December 1653, Blake was relieved, though hardly pleased, since this act made Cromwell king in all but name. Blake could have pursued his own political career, drawing on the overwhelming support he enjoyed among the Puritan congregations of Somerset, who elected him to every parliamentary assembly summoned between 1645 and his death, often without him even standing. It has been argued that Blake abandoned his political career for a naval one because he was disillusioned with the whole political process.[44] If this was so, one suspects that Cromwell was only too pleased to keep him thus employed. By 1654 Robert Blake had become a compelling leader: absolutely incorruptible, deeply concerned for the welfare of his men, both in this world and the next, and utterly resolute in the face of all adversity.

Having built a mighty fleet and humbled the acknowledged masters of the sea, England possessed both a potent reputation and the tools to back it up. It was tempting for Cromwell to deploy this asset before it wasted away into underfunded lassitude. He had been forced to change his foreign policy, as his plans for a Protestant league foundered on the mutual hostility of the four leading powers. Instead, he decided to support France against Spain because he believed Spain to be the more powerful of the two Catholic belligerents. He would use his naval power to seize Spanish territory in the New World, relying on her treasure fleets to provide the war chest. Despite the Elizabethan emphasis on plunder, Cromwell's plan would have established the nucleus of a great empire had he possessed the funds to bring it to fruition. His emphasis on strategic bases was sound: Dunkirk would give England command of the North Sea, while Gibraltar or Minorca would enable the fleet to control the entrance to the Mediterranean, securing English commerce against Flemish privateers and barbary corsairs.[45] In fact, it would not be for another century that an English strategist had the means to execute such designs. However, Cromwell's naval power did succeed in securing the seas for English commerce, and here Blake proved to be as mighty an instrument as the wooden walls he commanded.[46] On 16 May he was invited to dine with the Lord Protector, the Lord Mayor of London and members of the London Common Council,[47] in a symbolic demonstration of the faith Cromwell placed in naval power as a means of achieving both political aims and commercial profit.

A New Enemy

The war Cromwell ultimately chose was motivated not by religion but by national interest and commercial gain. When one of his officers asked why they were fighting Spain, who had done England no harm, Blake's legendary response was: 'It is not for us to mind State Affairs, but to stop the foreigner from fooling us.'[48] While the words may be apocryphal, it is clear that Blake saw the navy's task as executing state policy, not debating it. He insisted his officers must obey without question, and he in turn had no option but to obey his government.

Cromwell himself had no intention of revealing his hand before he was ready. Dispatched to the Mediterranean with twenty ships, Blake had orders to block a French attack on Naples and force them to accept an alliance on English terms, before chastising the Barbary corsairs. The French expedition reached Naples, but retreated in disorder before Blake arrived. As the latest and most powerful political instrument to enter the complex world of Mediterranean politics, the English fleet was assiduously courted by the great and not so great states of the littoral, but Blake remained on his ship and steadfastly refused to meet any envoys or potentates. There were a number of reasons for this – including ill-health, distaste for Catholic courts and their rituals, a sense of increasing isolation – but whatever the truth, the general's invisibility and inscrutability lent a degree of mystery to the fleet that made it seem all the more powerful.

Within weeks, Blake could see that the French were in disarray, and he hastened to fulfil the second part of his instructions: to chastise the Barbary corsairs. The Tunisians affected to be unimpressed. While the fleet revictualled for another sortie along the Barbary

Coast, Blake learnt that an Ottoman Turkish fleet was assembling in North African ports for an attack on Venetian-held Crete. Inspired by the heroic actions of the Venetian admiral Mocenigo, and reminded of the generous behaviour of the Serene Republic during the Dutch War, Blake was prepared to stretch his orders.

A second visit to the Tunisians found them 'more wilful and untractable than before, adding to their obstinacy much insolence and contumely, denying us all commerce of civility, and hindering all others as much as they could from the same. These barbarous provocations did so far work upon our spirits, that we judged it necessary for the honour of the fleet, our nation, and religion, seeing they would not deal with us as friends, to make them feel us as enemies.'[49] The Dey was confident the English could do him no harm. However, Blake located a squadron of eight Ottoman warships in nearby Porto Farina, along with a recently captured English merchant ship, and waited for the weather to favour an attack.

At first light on 3 April 1655 his fleet used the sea breeze to stand into the bay, every ship laying out an anchor on a long cable as it went. The attack unfolded exactly as planned: the smaller ships closed on the anchored Ottoman vessels; the heavy ships were deployed to deal with the forts that surrounded the bay. Blake knew that success depended on getting as close as possible to the Tunisian forts – and he anchored within musket shot, less than a hundred yards away. The effect was immediate: the troops were driven out of the forts by overwhelming fire, and the ships were abandoned. By 08.00 boarding parties had set every ship ablaze. When Blake was content, he signalled for the fleet to withdraw. His crews then abandoned their guns and simply hauled on the cables, dragging their ships back out to sea. It was all over by 11.00. A mere twenty-five of the fleet had been killed and eighty wounded, mostly in the boarding parties. Porto Farina was, as one officer observed, 'a piece of service that has not been paralleled in these parts of the world'.[50]

There was something terrifying in the calm, deliberate nature of Blake's attack. He had turned the rules of war upside down: ships were not meant to defeat forts with trifling losses. The attack succeeded despite the risks of running aground or of catastrophic damage from enemy guns because Blake had an iron grip on his fleet. To remove any personal pecuniary temptation that might conflict with the prompt execution of duty, he insisted that no prizes be taken: all enemy vessels were to be destroyed. Monck had used this method to maintain cohesion at the Texel. For all the tactical success of the battle, judgements on its political consequences tend to be negative. The Dey was not impressed; after all, they were not his ships, and their destruction did not greatly delay Ottoman success in Crete. However, the unspoken assumptions of the Mediterranean world were reshaped to take account of the English fleet as a decisive force. Algiers was quick to sign a treaty, release all English and Irish slaves, and open the port for the fleet to be supplied.[51]

After the event, Blake, a trifle nervous he might have exceeded his orders, blamed his decision on 'the barbarous carriage of those pirates'.[52] He need not have worried. Cromwell was delighted: 'We have good cause to acknowledge the good hand of God towards us in this action . . . so I think myself obliged to take notice of your courage and good conduct therein, and do esteem that you have done therein a very considerable service to this Commonwealth.' Now the corsairs had been chastised, it was time for the main event – war with Spain.[53]

The Spanish Threat

In the weeks that followed his success at Porto Farina, Blake's mission shifted from opposing France and the corsairs to preparing for war with Spain. An alliance with France was about to be sealed, and Cromwell had sent a fleet to the West Indies to begin his war with an attempt on the Spanish treasure fleet. He needed Blake to blockade Cadiz, and was already negotiating a treaty with Portugal that would open Lisbon to the English fleet. However, instructions from London were vague, and Cromwell kept updating his programme, leaving Blake in a very difficult position. When he located the Spanish fleet on 15 August, boisterous weather prevented him from engaging for two days – which 'checks of Providence did put us upon second thoughts' – and he decided that his instructions did not permit him to take hostile action, as the Spaniards were not heading for the West Indies nor escorting treasure ships.[54]

Blake's decision was contrary to Cromwell's wishes, but the Lord Protector only had himself to blame, having provided his general with rather opaque instructions. The problem was compounded by the failure of his naval administration to keep Blake's ships supplied:

the victualling ships sailed late, only to be driven back to England by storms. By September Cromwell, recognising the failure of his West Indies plan, was anxious to prevent the Spanish reinforcing their fleet in the Caribbean. Yet however much he might have desired to keep the fleet on station, seize the treasure ships and blockade Cadiz, he accepted that with no 'certain knowledge of the Spanish and English fleets' he could give 'no positive orders to engage' and would have to leave Blake 'to handle the rein'.[55]

That autumn the fleet began to show the effects of a long cruise: sickly men, shortage of provisions and increasingly unseaworthy ships. Recognising the need to return to England, Blake requested permission, but set off before the Lord Protector had a chance to reply. With his battered and sickly body in steady decline and his mental reserves exhausted, a depressed Blake spent more and more time alone in his cabin. On 6 October the fleet anchored in the Downs.

Blake's campaign had struck a chord with the people of England, distracting them from domestic turmoil and an unpopular regime.[56] While this public-relations triumph was a useful by-product, Cromwell was astute enough to see that Blake's twelve-month cruise had been the key to the French alliance. His actions had forced the French to concede Cromwell's terms – critically, his demand that the allies begin the war on Spain by capturing Dunkirk for the English. Nor was Spain ignorant of the effect that an English war would have. As 1655 closed, Blake and the English navy were the most potent force in European diplomacy.

Domestically, however, there was chaos, to which Cromwell reacted by taking dictatorial powers and imposing his iron will on army, navy and nation. He bolstered his regime by altering the composition of the army, disbanding Presbyterian regiments and retaining those with radical independent religious views.[57] He could not control Robert Blake in this way, however: the republican general had the loyalty of the fleet in his pocket and rebuffed every attempt Cromwell made to secure his personal loyalty. Against a man of iron faith and unshakeable conviction, bribes and flattery were no more effective than coercion and threat.

Blake requested a new general at sea to accompany him back to the coast of Spain. Cromwell responded by appointing the courtier and soldier Edward Mountagu, a well-connected young man of

Royalist sympathies who proved an adept student of command at sea and of seamanship. Though appointed by Cromwell to ensure the political loyalties of the fleet, mainly by purging it of those opposed to the Protectorate, Mountagu earned Blake's friendship by his attention to duty and collegial conduct.[58] This potent reassertion of authority and discipline was exactly what Blake wanted – loyalty above faction. Blake would direct the fleet, leaving Mountagu to handle the political decisions and negotiations with foreign powers. As Blake was too ill for shore operations, Mountagu's presence also guaranteed reliable military command.[59] While it must have stuck in his throat to address Cromwell as 'Your Highness',[60] the republican religious ideologue was fast becoming a thoroughly modern professional admiral. His only political concern was the funding of his fleet.

Although Blake was well aware that he had little chance of returning from the cruise, there was no point giving up his mission because he had no home in which to spend his final days. He enjoyed the company of his officers, and it seems the challenge of command helped to keep him alive.[61] Instead, he took the time to settle his earthly affairs: he left a hundred pounds each for the poor of Bridgewater and Taunton, divided his property and possessions amongst his relatives, and set aside fifty pounds to ensure that his black servant Domingo was educated 'in the knowledge and fear of Jesus Christ'.[62]

The fleet that Blake and Mountagu took to sea from Plymouth on 18 March included over forty heavy ships, led by the brand-new hundred-gun first-rate *Naseby*, the prestige ship of the Commonwealth. Diarist John Evelyn, no fan of the 'Usurper Oliver', had seen the ship launched with great ceremony at Woolwich in 1655, but he was not impressed:

In the prow was Oliver on horseback trampling 6 nations under foot, a Scot, Irishman, Dutch, French, Spaniards & English as was easily made out by their several habits: A fame held a laurel over his insulting head, & the word God be with us.[63]

With such a figurehead no one could mistake the purpose of the Commonwealth, or the prestige of the Lord Protector. Cromwell's English state had no hesitation in throwing its weight about – or reminding the rest of the world why it could.

[67]

Unfortunately for Cromwell's designs, Blake sailed too late to catch the small spring treasure fleet, which reached Cadiz before the English arrived. Nor could the fleet execute his other short-term objectives: to destroy Cadiz and the Spanish fleet, or capture Gibraltar to give England a naval base in the Straits.[64] The first was too strong and too well prepared; the second would require too many troops.[65] The Spaniards had learnt the lessons of 1587 and 1596: their preparations were impressive, their troops numerous. At least the appearance of the fleet in the Tagus persuaded the King of Portugal to ratify the 1654 Treaty with England.[66] Blake was happy to let the diplomats settle the terms: he had no desire to attack the formidable defences of Lisbon. It was far better to use the river as a base to attack the less heavily defended Spanish Atlantic ports and destroy Spanish commerce – a task Blake conducted with his cruisers. When the novice General Mountagu wanted to seize the Brazil fleet and use force to secure Portuguese ratification, Blake had to restrain his enthusiasm.[67]

Once the generals had dashed his hopes for amphibious operations, Cromwell recalled ten ships to blockade Dunkirk.[68] Cadiz was also blockaded, but Blake knew it would be fruitless as long as it was kept up with great force. Consequently he split the fleet into three: Mountagu went to negotiate a treaty at Sallee, the main corsair port on the Moroccan Atlantic coast; Blake took the main body to cruise off Cape St Vincent; while a small squadron under Captain Richard Stayner observed Cadiz from over the horizon. Lulled into a false sense of security by the disappearance of the English, the incoming treasure fleet made a dash for Cadiz, only to run into Stayner's ships. On 8 September all six galleons were captured, burnt or run aground. Much of the treasure was lost, but two hundred thousand pounds went home, which Cromwell immediately turned into coin. Stayner's success renewed enthusiasm for the war and persuaded the House of Commons to fund the conflict. No doubt it was these very practical considerations that persuaded Cromwell to order a National Day of Thanksgiving on 5 November.

Cromwell had already decided that part of the fleet must remain on the coast of Spain through the winter before Stayner struck. If the blockade was going to defeat Spain, the fleet needed to capture the treasure fleet, cut Spanish links with Flanders and protect English trade with Lisbon and the Mediterranean. For this unprecedented mission he put his faith in his best commander: 'We would have General Blake to stay with the fleet.'[69] Mountagu went home with the big ships, carrying Blake's urgent appeal to have the fleet revictualled: 'My hopes do very much depend upon your noble self, who I doubt not will use your utmost endeavour to set all wheels at work to quicken an expedition of so great consequence.'[70] After a season in harness, he knew his colleague and trusted him. He did not mention the state of Blake's health to Cromwell, finding comfort in the strength of his faith and the mercies of his God through 'the Great Tempests of Wind that we have encountered without the Straits and within' through the winter.[71]

Blake continued the blockade, anxiously looking for the next supply of beer while dispatching 'bitter complaints' to the Admiralty. In the absence of beer, the fleet used watered wine as a substitute, but there was not enough wine in Lisbon to satisfy the English thirst. Fortunately Mountagu proved as good as his word, and victuallers began to arrive with fresh frigates. Cromwell had heard that the treasure fleet was waiting at Havana: this time there should be no mistake. However, time was of the essence: the whole operation depended on Blake, and he was fading. The leg wound from Portland had never healed properly, the gravel in his kidneys proved a constant source of pain, and now he was afflicted with dropsy. With his digestive system in ruins he ate nothing but soups and jellies. The prognosis was grim: Blake was slowly dying. He admitted as much to Mountagu:

The Lord hath been pleased in great mercy to provide for our safety and in particular for my self in supporting me against the many indispositions of my body so that by his blessing I doubt not to be enabled to continue out in the service the ensuing summer.

Even in adversity Blake's faith remained strong: though his ships were short of men, God was with them.[72] Shortly afterwards, however, a furious gale drove the fleet south to Tetuan, and while Blake's heart was as resolute as ever, he knew the flesh was fast fading, declaring that 'I hope the Lord will support me till the appointed time.' His fleet was in little better state, with sickly seamen and ships too foul to chase the enemy.[73]

To add to Blake's woes, a Dutch fleet arrived in the Mediterranean. Many feared it had come to help the Spanish escort their treasure fleet and challenge the English blockade. Such rumours proved incorrect, as the small Dutch force dealt with French and Barbary commerce raiding. Blake had quite enough on his plate without vengeful Dutchmen: the blockade of Cadiz was maintained, and he kept a watchful eye on Morocco and Algiers. The weather was no help, as a gale blew the fleet into the Mediterranean and left many ships badly damaged. But the blockade of Cadiz was sustained through the winter, breaking the flow of American silver into Spain. This demonstration of power sent a frisson of fear across Europe: the English navy was proving to be a mighty force.[74] Although English finances were in a parlous condition, Cromwell did not think of giving up the war, instead borrowing money from the City of London to pay Blake's fleet. That he was prepared to play for such high stakes – he needed to hit the treasure-fleet jackpot to balance his budget[75] – was testament to his faith in Robert Blake.

Finally an English merchant ship brought Blake news of the 1657 treasure fleet: the galleons were anchored in the harbour of Santa Cruz on the island of Tenerife. Unable to get their vital treasure home, the Spanish had elected to wait until the English departed, but they had reckoned without Blake. He acted decisively, taking almost the entire fleet to the Canary Islands. Arriving on the evening of Saturday 18 April, Blake elected not to fight on the Sabbath, using the day to check his location and call a council of war.

The purpose of the council was to give orders to his officers: Blake had no intention of allowing them to dictate the course of action. He had decided to repeat the method employed at Porto Farina, and when Rear Admiral Stayner had the temerity to propose a quick attack by the smaller ships, Blake lost his temper, giving the captains such a tongue-lashing that none dared to respond. This was perhaps forgivable: he was terminally ill and about to risk his fleet in a desperate attack on well-prepared positions. To secure a sea breeze the fleet would attack early the next day, 20 April. That morning he called another council, inviting his officers to seek God's blessing before they went into battle.[76] Then he settled the tactical details: twelve frigates would open the attack; the heavy ships would follow. The frigate captains chose Stayner to lead the attack. Blake knew the galleons contained no treasure, since the Spanish had taken it all ashore. His object was the destruction of the Spanish fleet, and his purpose to deny the treasure to Madrid. He had no interest in prizes or profit. He had never cared for money, and despite the more worldly concerns of his captains resolutely refused to countenance any diversion from the Porto Farina model. Sink or burn was his motto.

This would be no easy operation. Santa Cruz was heavily defended, with powerful shore fortifications, while the harbour contained seven great galleons and nine smaller ships, all of which were armed, and was supported by newly completed trenches and batteries. The galleons were anchored in four fathoms, with their broadsides facing out to sea; the smaller ships were moored inboard, with their sterns to the beach. Furthermore, the Spanish had ample time to prepare and a large supply of men and guns. But before they could get to grips with the enemy, the English would have to sail into a harbour noted for the fickle winds and gusts created by the mountains and valleys behind the town. Little wonder the Spanish were confident.[77]

Stayner led the frigate squadron into position from the forecastle of his flagship, the *Speaker*, to make sure he took up the proper berth close alongside the galleons. Blake had ordered the frigates to hold their fire until they had moored, both to preserve the all-important first broadside and to allow them to see where they were going. Although a thirteenth ship joined Stayner's formation without orders, the English ships had moored as required by 08.00, opening with a furious bombardment of the Spanish ships. Blake followed in with the heavy ships to engage the Spanish forts. Most of the guns on shore were simply overwhelmed by an iron tornado of heavy English shot, their gunners killed or driven from their posts. A few shore batteries escaped this treatment, but only because their guns were masked by the Spanish ships and the gunners were unable to see the target. By 12.00 the line of anchored Spanish ships was effectively beaten: only the admiral and vice admiral's ships were still in action, the rest having either surrendered or caught fire. The inevitable took a little longer this time, but at 13.00 the admiral's ship exploded; the vice admiral's was already blazing furiously and detonated soon afterwards. Blake's men quickly completed their work, boarding and setting ablaze the huddle of smaller ships tied up inshore, covered by heavy fire directed at the remaining shore positions.

As the Spanish ships sank or burnt to the waterline, they uncovered additional shore batteries and entrenched musketeers whose fire made withdrawal the hardest and costliest part of the battle. Despite express orders to the contrary, two admirals, including Stayner, and three captains tried to tow out prizes. Blake had to repeat his orders three times before they were obeyed. He knew that the ships would need all their men to warp out of the bay under fire. After a day of hard fighting, the men had to turn to the capstan and haul themselves to safety. This was no easy affair, nor was it soon completed. The withdrawal began at 15.00 and lasted until 19.00, all the while under fire from the main castle and other shore positions. One of the frigates took the ground, but eventually all worked their way out against the wind. Stayner, who had led the attack with skill, only to fall prey to the Drake syndrome, was the last out. The *Speaker* had been hit hard, and was barely afloat by the time she had been warped out of artillery range. With almost nine feet of water in the hold, the carpenters nailed hides over the shot holes and held them in place with barrel staves. Only the bowsprit could carry sail, and hardly a rope in the rigging was undamaged. Blake had ordered the *Swiftsure* to tow her clear, but she unaccountably cast off the tow while the *Speaker* was still in range, exposing her to further punishment. Only when the sun went down did the shore breeze finally carry her out of range. Almost immediately her foremast went over the side, followed by the main and mizzen, before the *Plymouth* could take her in tow. The rest of the fleet sent carpenters and crew to help with repairs and pump out the hold. The *Speaker* had fifteen killed and thirty wounded, about a quarter of the losses for the entire fleet.[78] The following day the ship was repaired and her masts replaced.

By any standards Santa Cruz was a remarkable achievement. The completeness of Blake's victory bore testament to his skill and forethought at the planning stage, his iron discipline ensured all followed his orders, while the astonishing firepower of the English fleet reflected a decade of hard fighting. This battle marked the birth of the modern naval service, and it stunned all Europe. When he heard the news, Royalist exile Edward Hyde, later Earl of Clarendon, felt proud to be an Englishman:

The whole action was so miraculous that all men who knew the place concluded that no sober men with what courage soever endued, would ever undertake it; and they could hardly persuade themselves to believe what they had done.[79]

Unfortunately there was no great artist present to render Blake's greatest moment, or its intense, close-quarters combat, at once shrouded in smoke and sparkling with gilt-work. Only art could capture the intensity and terrible beauty of the struggle. A painting of Santa Cruz would have been a potent propaganda tool for the Protectorate, a warning to any that doubted the power of England at sea.

Because the English captured no treasure, some have argued then and since that the triumph was barren.[80] Nothing could be further from the truth: the whole of Europe quickly understood that it was 'the most important naval engagement since the Armada'.[81] Every country with ports and seagoing trade had good cause to be alarmed. Santa Cruz was a well-defended harbour, and yet the English had destroyed everything that floated and smashed the shore defences at the cost of fewer than a hundred casualties. Spain was ruined by the battle, the treasure of two seasons either sunk or left bottled up and useless in Tenerife. The figures are clear: between 1650 and 1655 Spain received 8.7 million pesos in bullion. Between 1656 and 1660 this figure dropped to 4 million, while the all-important royal share of bullion imports collapsed from 2.6 to 0.7 million.[82] Without bullion Spain could not wage war: unpaid soldiers do not fight. Though the Spanish army captured the border fortress of Olivença, the key to Portugal, in May 1657, after that the money ran out and the army disappeared. Nor could Philip IV honour his promise to fund an army for Charles II to recover his kingdom.[83] Little wonder Spain had to make peace with France in 1659, having lost Dunkirk to an Anglo-French army. Soon after this, Philip had to admit that his crusade to recover Portugal had failed.[84] The freedom of Portugal was ultimately the greatest prize of England's war with Spain. While Lisbon was in Portuguese hands, English trade could travel to the Mediterranean and cross the Atlantic in safety. Together with the neutrality of Flanders, the independence of Portugal was a vital prerequisite of Britain's later rise to global power. Blake's destruction of the Spanish bullion fleets had secured this independence.

Death of a Hero

After Santa Cruz, Cromwell ordered the fleet on the coast of Spain to be reduced, and finally recalled Blake. A day of thanksgiving was voted by Parliament, and Secretary Thurloe declared, 'It is the Lord's doing, and the glory be His.'[85] Cromwell recognised the skill that had ensured the total destruction of the enemy, while preserving the English ships and men: 'We cannot but take notice how eminently it has pleased God to make use of you in this service, assisting you with wisdom in the conduct and courage in the execution.' The jewel worth five hundred pounds that Parliament voted as a mark of favour was a portrait of Cromwell set with four diamonds.[86] What Blake made of such a kingly gesture is unknown – and it is unlikely he lived to receive it.

Uninterested in praise or frippery, Blake carried on with the business at hand. The fleet spent five days repairing the worst of their injuries off Tenerife, and then returned to blockade Cadiz. Not that a blockade was necessary: news of the victory was quite enough to keep the Spaniards in harbour. When he crossed the Straits to Sallee, Blake found the Sultan of Morocco, well aware of what had happened just off his coast, suddenly most anxious to conclude the long-delayed treaty. Having settled the diplomacy, Blake returned briefly to Cadiz, and then headed for home with ten ships on 9 July. During a brief stop to revictual at Lisbon, the English agent realised that the general was dying. Having completed his life's work, Blake relaxed, his indomitable spirit finally giving in to the very human infirmities of dropsy and scurvy. Anxious to step on English soil one last time, he headed for Plymouth, perhaps hoping his God might spare him to return to Somerset, but he was fated only to glimpse his homeland. Blake died at 10.00 on 7 August, just as the *George* entered Plymouth Sound. His last thoughts were for the fleet he had left behind on the coast of Spain, begging that their supplies might not be forgotten.

Blake's death was widely lamented: the simplicity and selflessness that made him a great admiral were irreplaceable. At Cromwell's direction, Blake was given the same public funerary honours as his friend and fellow general Richard Deane. His body was embalmed and taken to lie in state at Greenwich Palace. The body was buried on 4 September in Henry VII's chapel at Westminster Abbey, a most unusual place for a man of his simple faith and republican principles. The hero's funeral, which Cromwell himself was too ill to attend, was motivated more by the need to sustain his war than by a desire to honour the late general's wishes.[87] Bridgewater would have been a more appropriate burial place and would have avoided the need for the restored Stuart government to remove Blake's remains from the vault, along with those of the rest of the Interregnum elite. They were reburied in an unmarked grave in the churchyard of St Margaret's, Westminster, on 12 September 1661.[88]

But while the Stuart regime cast out Blake's body, it was more cautious in distancing itself from his legacy. As the Earl of Clarendon observed:

He was the first man that declined the old track, and made it manifest, that the science might be attained in less time than was imagined; and despised those rules which had been long in practice, to keep his ships and men out of danger, which had been held in former times a point of great ability and circumspection; as if the principal art requisite in the captain of a ship had been to be sure to come home safe again. He was the first man who brought ships to contemn castles on shore, which had been thought ever very formidable, and were discovered by him to make a noise only, and to fright those who could be rarely hurt by them. He was the first that infused that proportion of courage into the seamen, by making them see by experience what mighty things they could do if they were resolved, and taught them to fight in fire as well as upon water; and though he hath been very well imitated and followed he was the first that drew the copy of naval courage and bold and resolute achievement.[89]

In six years Robert Blake turned the ramshackle, free-spirited English fleet into the most formidable political instrument on earth. He banished swearing, profanity and ungodliness from his ships and fleets, turning his seamen into Christian warriors.[90] He imposed an iron discipline on his officers, demanding absolute obedience – and in his turn he paid the same tribute to a state that increasingly disappointed his religious and political hopes. In return for their loyalty, Blake gave his all for his officers and men: he was careful not to risk their lives, he improved their pay and conditions, and secured pensions to compensate them for their wounds and to support their dependants if they were killed.[91] He made the navy the pre-eminent instrument of national policy, and he did so at a time when Cromwell's New Model Army was reckoned the best in Europe.

The state used this 'new model' navy to increase England's share of oceanic trade and colonial territory: it succeeded because Blake and his fellows could batter and blockade the Dutch into submission, bankrupt Spain and chastise the Barbary corsairs to stop them preying on English shipping.

Although he began his seagoing career as a brave, resolute soldier, Blake grasped the complex art of the admiral and elevated it to a higher plane. He was never a great seaman, unlike his brilliant Dutch contemporaries, Tromp and de Ruyter. He did not seek tactical finesse; he understood that discipline and simplicity were the key to success. He learnt quickly and built his own style of leadership on faith and the force of his will. He, and he alone, had the authority to break the link between war and predation, state violence and personal gain that had disfigured naval warfare in the past. He imposed this doctrine by sheer force of will. No one disobeyed Blake, no one argued with him twice. His orders were obeyed, and at Santa Cruz he provided the English navy with a truly sublime moment.

When Horatio Nelson planned his own attack on a Spanish treasure shipment at Santa Cruz in 1797, he turned to the history books for inspiration and an example of resolute leadership in battle. Sharing the precedent with his commander-in-chief, Admiral the Earl St Vincent, he observed:

I do not reckon myself equal to Blake; but if I recollect right, he was more obliged to the wind coming off the land, than to any exertions of his own: fortune favoured the gallant attempt, and may do so again.[92]

Nelson was misinformed: the wind did not shift until long after the English ships had left the scene of the action. Success was down to Blake's skilful planning and forethought.[93] In the event, Nelson's attack failed where Blake's had succeeded because Nelson was still learning his craft. He placed undue faith in suspect intelligence and made a second, frontal assault on well-prepared defences. In 1797 he was not Blake's equal, but in the eight years that followed he would profit from the bitter and painful experience of defeat, just as Blake had done.

Despite Nelson's endorsement, Blake proved a troublesome figure for the service that he did so much to create.[94] He served in the navy of the Parliament of England, the Republic and the Lord Protector, rather than the King. Although he was not a regicide, he was a loyal servant of the regime that killed Charles I, yet his defeat of the Dutch and annihilation of the Spanish were the basis of the restored regime's international standing. Although Charles II had Blake's mortal remains removed from Westminster Abbey, he rewarded Mountagu for bringing Cromwell's navy over to his cause and knighted Richard Stayner for the triumph at Santa Cruz. Blake was only allowed into the Royal Navy's pantheon of immortals in 1808, when a battleship was named in his honour, but the gesture was potent and it was frequently repeated. It is an indictment of the Ship Names Committee that HMS *Blake*, paid off in 1982, was the last major Royal Navy warship named after an admiral.

3

THE KING

James II, Duke of York

1633–1701

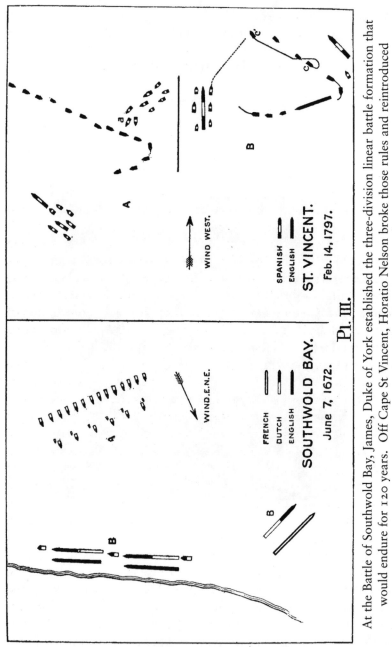

Pl. III.

WIND WEST.

SPANISH
ENGLISH

ST. VINCENT.
Feb. 14, 1797.

WIND.E.N.E.

FRENCH
DUTCH
ENGLISH

SOUTHWOLD BAY.
June 7, 1672.

At the Battle of Southwold Bay, James, Duke of York established the three-division linear battle formation that would endure for 120 years. Off Cape St Vincent, Horatio Nelson broke those rules and reintroduced initiative into naval warfare

In DECEMBER 1659 THE ENGLISH navy blockaded the Thames, forcing the army to recall Parliament. Admiral John Lawson insisted that the country should be governed by constitutionally elected civilians, and not 'a puppet of the soldiers'.[1] The navy had tolerated Cromwell but had no intention of seeing power pass to other generals. Lawson's blockade defeated the New Model Army in ten days, without firing a shot. Arriving at the head of an army from Scotland, George Monck maintained the momentum towards a restoration of the monarchy, placing Edward Mountagu in command of the fleet.

The lesson for the restored monarchy was clear: the navy – a mighty instrument of internal as well as external power – must be secured for the dynasty. Under Blake, the navy had acquired an unrivalled reputation for discipline, but since the removal of his iron hand it had begun to intervene in domestic politics, with chaotic results. The newly restored Royal Navy needed a period of peace and sound administration in order to restore internal order. Continuity, represented by Mountagu – now ennobled as the Earl of Sandwich for his role in bringing the monarch back to the country – and his cousin Samuel Pepys, would lay the foundations for the modern professional service. This process took place under the close personal supervision of two Stuart princes.

By combining the military zeal of the Commonwealth fleet with professional standards and personal loyalty to the monarch, these men created a recognisably modern Royal Navy. However, while the Stuart princes Charles and James brought expertise and commitment to the project, their aims were dynastic and personal. This fleet belonged to the royal house, and it would bear the stamp of James

II long after his death. When he fled the country in 1688, James reluctantly handed control of his beloved fleet to the House of Commons. This process would be at once the cause of many of the navy's problems and a sure guarantee of its long-term success.

James II has had a bad press, but his highly successful naval career must be disentangled from his failures as a monarch and a man. For two hundred and fifty years it was simply not politic to bring this up: a navy that retained a deep-rooted aversion to the Catholics it abusively termed 'left-footers', long after the passions of the seventeenth and eighteenth centuries had cooled, had no wish to be reminded that it owed so much to James, or that it had betrayed him in his hour of need. In 1846 Edward Law, Second Earl of Ellenborough, the new First Lord of the Admiralty, was so impressed by the part James had played in creating the office[2] that he proposed erecting an old bronze statue of the King by Grinling Gibbons in the Admiralty forecourt; this would be passed by every officer and statesman who entered the old building and would be visible to everyone who walked along Whitehall. The more finely tuned political instincts of the prime minister, Sir Robert Peel, rejected the idea as impolitic: anti-Catholic legislation imposed after James's flight from England in 1688 had been revoked fewer than twenty years ago, and with Ireland in turmoil Peel had no desire to remind the world of England's last Catholic king.

It was a wise decision. Two years later Thomas Babington Macaulay would inaugurate the notion of 'Whig' history with an account that firmly cast James as a villain. Macaulay viewed history from the perspective of the Whigs, an aristocratic clique that prided itself on replacing royal absolutism with a constitutional monarchy – ancestors of the modern Liberal Party. Macaulay had been a Whig/Liberal MP when his party attained their ultimate goal, the 1832 Reform Act, which they believed would enfranchise their supporters, exclude the working classes and restrain the monarch. Every chapter of Macaulay's English history aimed to explain how the country had reached its present state of perfection. The upward trajectory of the nation had been achieved, according to Macaulay, by constraining the monarchy, giving powers to Parliament and securing civil liberties and religious tolerance, as enshrined in the Revolution Settlement of 1689. Those who had opposed this inevitable progress were pilloried and traduced. In

Whig history James II was more caricature than character: an absolutist tyrant who used a foreign army to impose an alien religion on
his people, trampling on their liberties in the process. In this version there was no room for light and shade: history was a simple
tale, and James was simply a very bad man.[3] After all, had he not
been a villain, the events of 1688 would have looked like an act of
naked usurpation.

While few histories even mention James's naval career, or give him
credit for anything positive, there is ample evidence to suggest he
deserves a fresh look. While he was a flawed human being and a disastrous king, Ellenborough may well have been right that James,
Duke of York was a brilliant naval administrator. He might also
have been a fine sea officer. Perhaps personal failings and political
ineptitude do not disqualify an officer from achieving greatness in
his profession.

James's claim to a successful naval career was developed in the
twentieth century, largely by Catholic historians following the lead
of the pioneering Catholic scholar of the nineteenth century, John
Lingard.[4] However, where Lingard had been a professional before
his time, Hilaire Belloc and those who followed his line proved partisan and doctrinaire, and were linked to the anti-democratic movements of the 1930s. Nonetheless, their articulation of the revisionist
case generated a useful debate, and James was given a measure of
credit for his earlier career in naval administration and empire building – though praise was always offset by an acknowledgement of his
failure as a king.[5] He remains a controversial figure to this day,
although lacking the romantic allure of his grandson, 'Bonnie Prince
Charlie', leader of the last Jacobite rising.

Royal Admiral

James Stuart was born at St James's Palace on 14 October 1633, the
second surviving son of King Charles I and Queen Henrietta Maria.[6]
He was only five when Charles appointed him Lord High Admiral.
The office had been vacant since the murder of the Duke of
Buckingham, who had bought it from Charles Howard in 1619.
James would be the titular head and – something of vital importance
in an age of limited royal funds – the recipient of the revenues, leav-
ing the Earl of Northumberland to command the fleet as Lord

Admiral. James would inherit the seagoing office when he came of age: the funds it offered would help to support the 'spare' prince. However, Charles's 'ship money' tax provoked widespread opposition, the collapse of relations between King and Parliament, and ultimately civil war. James's quiet, cloistered childhood came to an abrupt end when he witnessed the opening battle at Edgehill. Although the war took him to Oxford, his education was interrupted, to be replaced by hunting and campfire tales of military glory. Nor did he occupy a significant place in his father's thoughts, left behind when the King fled the city to become a prisoner of Parliament. Not for the last time, Parliament misjudged their prince: they saw him as a malleable alternative to King Charles and the Prince of Wales who could be raised to the throne on their terms. They soon discovered, however, that the King's stubbornness and pride were not the result of a flawed education but a genetic attribute of the Stuart family. James had all the arrogance of his father and the military zeal of his cousin Rupert, but none of his elder brother's political insight. He refused to play the game. Where a more reflective captive might have humoured his gaolers, if only for better treatment, James made himself thoroughly objectionable, a skill he would exercise at every stage of his career. Parliament soon tired of him, and the turbulent prince was probably allowed to escape to the continent.

When a squadron of English warships rebelled against Parliament in 1648 and sailed to Holland, James rushed down to Helvoetsluys to exercise his authority as Lord High Admiral. His elder brother Charles, Prince of Wales, was not impressed by the resulting chaos, removing James from command and replacing him with Rupert. Prince or not, James was still a boy of only fifteen. He was fortunate that he had not been sent out to fight Robert Blake.

The execution of King Charles I early in 1649 bound the brothers in adversity. For the rest of his life James remained convinced that the blame for this catastrophe, and all his woes, could be laid squarely on the shoulders of the republicans. He did not indulge in the more extreme forms of mourning that many Royalists affected, treating the death of his father as a deeply personal matter. He also concluded that it was his father's willingness to compromise with the republicans that had led to his death, a fundamental misjudgement that would lead to his own downfall three decades later. His response to the travails of his youth was to create a strong, author-itarian government, based on military power and always informed by his own profound fear of imprisonment.[7]

By the time the exiled Stuart court moved to Paris in 1651 James had reached the age when he could begin a career. After Cromwell's victory at Worcester and Blake's island campaign, the royal cause was in ruins. There were no more Stuart territories for him to administer: foreign military service was the only honourable option remaining for a prince of royal blood. The French army was then at the peak of its prestige, size and professionalism, the envy of all Europe. James spent the Commonwealth years learning the soldier's trade, initially in the army of his cousin Louis XIV, under the tute-lage of the greatest soldier of the age.

When James joined the staff of Marshall Turenne in April 1652, France was at war with Spain, providing a fine field for the young prince to display his courage, horsemanship and keen eye – not to mention his royal blood. He earned Turenne's praise and was rap-idly promoted to lieutenant general at the age of just twenty-one. For much of the 1650s James was the poster boy of the exiled dynasty, a brave English soldier earning his laurels at the head of English troops. The same courage and composure under fire would excite the admiration of his own subjects when he led them into battle. In four years he made a real impact on the French, and always reckoned his time as a general in King Louis's service the happiest of his life. He had found his calling, and men he could fol-low.

Unfortunately for James, when the power of the English navy, wielded by Robert Blake, forced the French to accept Cromwell's alliance in 1655, he was specifically proscribed from continuing in his current role. It was not that Cromwell was averse to seeing the Prince in French service: just that he did not want James to do this in Flanders, where his deeds attracted attention in England. But while the future Charles II simply moved to Spanish-held Brussels, James was far less willing to acknowledge political realities. He eventually changed sides, joining the Spanish army but still retain-ing a loyalty to the French camp. He was quick to criticise his new employers, who did not match French standards. His personal courage was unsurpassed, but he remained politically naive, and he was not charged with any positions of real responsibility. His merits as a general remained untested. At the Battle of the Dunes in June 1658 James found himself in the unenviable situation of facing the Commonwealth troops, who were led by his former mentor, Marshal Turenne. When the English broke through the Spanish lines, James led two heroic cavalry charges, but nothing could stand in the way of the redcoats that day: the Spanish were heavily defeated. In the aftermath of defeat James behaved like a spoilt child, more concerned to preserve his own good name than to redeem the failure of his army. His obedience to his commanders was provisional and his assessment of the battle self-serving. After Cromwell's death, local risings against the government inspired him to organise an invasion, but the opportunity passed. Then in late 1659 the Peace of the Pyrenees ended his continental military career.

Yet even when all hope of restoration appeared to be at an end, James was not prepared to compromise with political groups in England. He clung to the old dream of imposing absolute rule by military power. At least his name had some international cachet, which brought him the post of High Admiral in Spain. But before he had reached Madrid, the situation in England had changed: George Monck's troops had ushered in a restoration without the Royalists even recognising the change in the wind.

Restoration

Upon the Restoration, James acquired an importance and rank for which his previous experience had hardly prepared him. From penniless exile to the second most powerful man in the state in a matter of days was a heady transformation. He married Anne Hyde (1637–71), a maid of honour to his sister the Princess of Orange and the daughter of Earl Clarendon, a prominent Royalist statesman. By the end of the decade it was clear that the King would have no legitimate offspring, and so James's succession became increasingly likely. Furthermore, James's daughters Mary and Anne had survived the dangers of childhood to secure the succession into the next generation. James emphasised his naval mission by naming one of his sons Edgar, after the West Saxon king who had united all England and was the first to claim his nation's maritime dominion. Sadly Prince Edgar, born in 1667, immediately after the Second

Dutch War, died in 1671; none of his legitimate brothers survived into adulthood. On such personal tragedies do the fate of dynasties turn.

James shared his brother's enthusiasm for the pleasures of the chase, keeping a succession of mistresses – notably Arabella Churchill, sister of the future Duke of Marlborough, and Frances Jennings, the sister of Marlborough's Duchess. These liaisons produced a number of 'natural' children: Arabella Churchill's son James Fitzjames, Duke of Berwick, proved to be a brilliant general. However, bastards were unimportant while James had legitimate offspring – and King Charles did not. The other great pleasure of James's mature years was hunting for deer or fox, a passion that he indulged at least twice a week, requiring him to maintain extensive stables and a pack of hounds. Hunting was still a good training for war, developing an eye for ground, a good seat on a horse and physical endurance. Hunting would outlast James's pursuits of the flesh by a decade, providing the last pleasure of his declining years. Almost to the end of his days James retained the lean, upright and athletic build of early adulthood, a key asset in an age when the royal image was at a premium. In Scotland he even took up golf, although it is hard to know which military skills or royal attributes this pastime flattered. He regularly attended races at Newmarket, though he did not gamble, and was remarkably sober. Even so, he lived in style and was perennially in debt – a problem that drove his interest in the expansion of overseas trade and a colonial empire. James viewed the world as an opportunity for his own profit and glory: national and personal interest were essentially one and the same. Furthermore, he was not overly interested in men's motives and ambitions, only their loyalty. This may explain why he showed little interest in science or culture, and positively loathed the theatre.

His domestic and official base was St James's Palace, with the old palace at Richmond serving as a country seat, conveniently placed for the Deer Park. He also had the use of the yacht *Anne*, this eight-gun vessel serving as a floating office during his visits to the fleet and the dockyards.[8]

Warrior Prince

By training and ambition a soldier, James understood the business of war at least as well as his Commonwealth predecessors. His military ambitions, sustained throughout the reign of Charles II, provided him with a major source of patronage, which he used to build a powerful personal following. Like most men of war he preferred simple patriotic loyalties, and even in exile could not restrain his admiration for the courage and military skill of his countrymen. At the Battle of the Dunes in 1658 he took real pleasure in the 'rash bravery' with which they drove his own cavalry before them; and again as he surveyed the blazing wreckage of his cousin's fleet on the beach at La Hougue in 1692, his last hope of recovering his kingdom, he could not resist crowing over the defeated French.[9] He constructed a warlike public image, using the military glory of his youth and the naval triumphs of his mature years to sustain a potent reputation: his portraits almost invariably feature body armour, often the full suit of a contemporary cavalryman. This image endured after his death, lending credence to those who saw James as an absolutist military ruler, rather than accepting his claim to be the ideal English warrior prince. But James did not understand that after the Civil War, men in armour were deeply unpopular. The decision to associate himself with themes of martial glory backfired monumentally when he converted to the Roman Catholic faith. Armoured heroes were acceptable in England, but only if they were Protestant. Conversion cost James his fame and reputation: nothing he might do thereafter on any battlefield, real or imagined, would redeem him in the eyes of his subjects.

There remained much of the soldier about James during his active life, and in retirement he turned to the simplest religious consolations. An athletic man of striking appearance, if not conventionally handsome, his blond wig and blue eyes contrasted with the darkly saturnine visage of his royal brother. Less appealingly, his political skills remained limited, his manner was abrupt and cold, and he could not take a joke.[10] But while James's human failings were significant, they did not disqualify him from holding high office. Royal birth and military experience would shape his career after 1660.

Lord High Admiral

As Lord High Admiral James provided effective, progressive and increasingly efficient leadership for the Royal Navy between 1660 and 1673, and sustained his connection through the trials and tribulations of the next decade before ascending the throne in 1685. His office went far beyond the administration of the navy to include control of Dover, Portsmouth and the Cinque Ports, the defensive keys of the kingdom. At this remove his contribution to the work of the Navy Board is hard to determine, even in the writings of that most industrious of chroniclers Samuel Pepys, one of his commissioners and a loyal supporter. The financial record is clearer: the percentage on prize judgements that had so handsomely rewarded Charles Howard provided a significant part of the Duke's income in wartime.[11]

At the Restoration, James's military reputation provided the monarchy with a counterweight to the armed might of the old regime, represented by George Monck and Edward Mountagu. On 16 May 1660 James was formally invested with the office of Lord High Admiral, taking overall command of the navy. He would have preferred to be Captain-General, but that office had been Monck's price for the support of the army. James began his term with a necessary programme of renaming all the warships with any hint of republican or Cromwellian references. The *Resolution* reverted to her old name of *Prince Royal*, while Charles II decreed that the *Naseby* should become the *Royal Charles*. The new first-rate *Richard*, named for that most inoffensive man Cromwell's son and successor, became the *Royal James*. The *Naseby*'s offensive figurehead of Oliver Cromwell was removed and ceremonially burnt. Warships that had terrorised all Europe for a decade under Blake's command simply disappeared and, as any seaman could have predicted, James's renaming policy did not end happily. All three of the renamed flagships would be captured or burnt by the Dutch. Among the lesser ships, West Country towns that had withstood a royal siege, including Blake's *Bridgewater*, were removed from the list.

Having dealt with the theatre of power James proceeded to address the substance. He dissolved the Interregnum naval administration on 4 July, replacing it with a version of the old royal system that would give him control. He opened new Admiralty Offices in the rambling Whitehall Palace, imposing a royal stamp on their meetings. Among his four 'Principal Officers', the Treasurer, Comptroller and Surveyor were old Stuart retainers with experience of naval administration and proven loyalty. Edward Mountagu's cousin Samuel Pepys was the only new man, beginning his naval career as Clerk of the Acts. James also called in key specialists to assist him as 'Extra Commissioners': Admiral Sir William Penn, shipbuilder Peter Pett and, after 1662, administrator William Coventry.[12] When new ship designs were produced, James normally referred them to the experts at Trinity House and exploited the bitter rivalries between the various designers, all desperate for orders and endorsements, to improve warship design. It helped that he himself possessed a sound understanding of ships, a yachtsman's eye for line and a sound grasp of the qualities required in an English warship – strength, firepower and good sailing.[13] When the new first-rate *Prince* proved unstable, he ordered her lower masts and yards to be reduced, which solved the problem.[14] He was also a capable navigator and mathematician. Indeed, Charles II and James II were the only English kings to be genuinely expert in naval matters, 'willing and able to transact much detailed and technical business themselves'. Uniquely, James was also a 'capable fleet commander'.[15] It was his ability to master every element of his post, exceptional among contemporary English admirals, that so impressed Pepys.[16]

In recruiting and employing naval officers James provided for returned Royalists, but when mobilising the fleet for the Second Dutch War he demonstrated a clear preference for the professional skill and experience of old republicans. The royal brothers worked hard to meld the two distinct streams of naval officers into a coherent, loyal and homogenous whole. When a junior dared to impugn the loyalty of his old Commonwealth seniors, James had him court-martialled.[17] He drew in the gentry, significantly increasing the social prestige of naval command because this was a vital step in binding the nation and the navy together. It also provided a major source of patronage for the Duke, who took an active role in officer selection. His integration of the new gentlemen officers and the 'tarpaulins' of the 1650s, with the addition of a powerful element of professionalism, was the defining feature of late Stuart naval development.

Not all his new men met the challenge, and it required further refinement after the Dutch wars to combine privilege with professionalism in the genesis of the modern naval officer corps. However, in drawing the gentry into the navy James was ensuring they understood the need to pay for the service: this was far more likely if they could see some personal connection and benefit. His memory of the gentry's revolt against 'Ship Money' may have been what prompted this tactic. Whatever his motives, he played a major role in ensuring that the political nation adopted the navy as an arm of the state, despite its very obvious 'royal' connections.

When the fleet mobilised in 1665 and 1672, scores of young gentlemen volunteered to serve.[18] James's navy had begun to achieve professional consensus between the disparate skills and claims of the hardbitten 'tarpaulin' officers and the 'gentlemen' who followed him into the service.[19] In 1677 he sat on the Admiralty Commission that required all future candidates for a commission to pass an examination and show certificates of competence from their captains.[20] Loyalty and a thirst for honour were great assets, but seamanship and navigation were vital.

From his commanding position James was able to play off the various factions that emerged, with Commonwealth officers looking to Monck, now Earl of Albemarle, and the Royalists to Rupert. His only rival as naval leader proved to be Blake's adept pupil Mountagu, now Earl of Sandwich, who possessed superior political and diplomatic skills and the prestige drawn from his successful sea commands. After the Second Dutch War, Sandwich could be safely ousted because James had secured the necessary naval glory to act alone. In the process Sandwich's followers, including Pepys, shifted their loyalties to the Duke.

After the Second Dutch War, James, supported by Pepys, reinforced the Navy Board, adding three auditors to oversee the major accounts.[21] When the First Test Act forced him to relinquish office, on 15 June 1673, James retained all his offices outside England, notably in Scotland and the colonies, and continued to play a major role from behind the scenes. As his nominees filled the higher ranks of the administration and the fleet, the new Admiralty Commission under Prince Rupert faced serious internal opposition, opposition that compromised the strategy of the Third Dutch War. Initially James also retained a seat on the Commission, which he used to ensure continuity. Although out of office, James retained his brother's confidence, and his ideas dominated the royal commands issued to Rupert. In effect, James retained much of the power of his office, acting through the King and key appointees like Pepys until he was forced into exile in 1678. His opponents attempted to remove his influence from the Admiralty, breaking up the Navy Board. Pepys and Treasurer Danby went to the Tower. A new Whig Admiralty Board was set up, and acted effectively until the Royalist resurgence of the early 1680s. However, the roots of James's Admiralty went deeper than his enemies realised, and as the cases against his servants collapsed for want of evidence, his networks began to reassemble. The King took more power into his own hands in 1681, and in 1684 James was back on the Privy Council and was the effective head of the Admiralty, although he still required the King's signature to circumvent the effect of the Test Acts.[22] The new regime now created the post of Secretary of the Marine; in part an imitation of the French model, which gave Pepys the authority to conduct the administration of the service with little obvious input from the Duke, the system was retained when James became king.[23]

For James, naval power, national interest and royal authority were necessarily exercised in harmony – by a warrior prince. Furthermore, this was simply too important a business to be left to professionals, be they sea officers, administrators or shipbuilders. He made it his business to master the key questions of Admiralty administration and naval warfare, and addressed the issue with the same energy and commitment he had demonstrated in his military career. The navy would be his contribution to the Stuart state, and he ensured it reflected his values. In 1660 Charles was already an enthusiastic yachtsman, and James, too, was quick to learn the art, providing the brothers with opportunities for friendly rivalry; they would sometimes wager a hundred pounds on a race, and when necessary they joined the crew in working the rig. In this way, James became a competent seaman.

His success as an administrator is less easy to account for: after all, seventeenth-century royalty did not lower themselves to function as office managers. The real contribution that a royal duke could make was to provide leadership, policy and energy. In this capacity, James proved to be an exemplary hands-on service chief. His yacht was often in service visiting the dockyards, naval works, sea defences and shipyards. Indeed, his love of detail stretched across all aspects of his portfolio – men, materials, tactics and strategy. And in everything James proved, somewhat surprisingly, willing to listen to advice from his experts, securing the funds they needed to execute policy and chairing their discussions with a combination of knowledge and authority. He took a particular delight in ships and shipbuilding, keeping a memo book of the fleet, welcoming shipbuilders and employing one to take a copy of a major new French warship, the *Superbe*, in 1672. He was anxious to learn about the construction programmes of rival powers, and used his knowledge to press for fresh programmes in Britain. One sign of his concern was a significant collection of books, maps and charts, ship draughts and models for his personal use and that of his Admiralty officials. Although a Fellow of his brother's new Royal Society, James was not an active member: he preferred more immediately useful knowledge, acquiring a sound grasp of navigational mathematics. Indeed, Pepys considered James, the King and Lord Sandwich 'the most mathematical Admirals England ever had'.[24] James also founded a navigation school at Greenwich in 1685.[25]

James's most important legacy was a passion for order, discipline and obedience in administration. The origins of such thinking were clear enough: royal authority, suitably restated through the medium of military discipline. He wanted to standardise navigation methods, the working of the Navy Board and the conduct of his captains in battle. The 1662 Instructions to the Navy Board provided the basis for a meritocratic administration in which able men like Pepys could advance. However, Stuart finances were weak, and corruption remained widespread: James only acted when the subject attracted public scrutiny – or when he could use the example to bring down his rival Sandwich.[26]

While James had no experience of naval warfare, his approach to his new career built on the important intellectual and practical legacy of his years in the French army. European armies were already producing drill books and tactical manuals, and as a staff officer under Turenne he had seen how such methods were used in battle. His familiarity with French practice extended to their naval regulations: he praised the *Ordonnance de Louis XIV pour les Armees navales et Arsenaux de Marine* as a model that improved on English and Dutch practice. In 1664 and 1666 James issued his own tactical manuals, or *Fighting Instructions*: in essence, he used the military and theoretical concepts of his erstwhile employers to impose control and order on a fleet that had already acquired extensive practical experience of naval combat.

The first set of *Instructions*, written when the fleet was assembling at Portsmouth in late 1664, built on the Commonwealth legacy of Blake, Monck and Deane, suitably amended to impose the necessary royal spirit. This was a major concession for James, who loathed republicans and all their works. His *Sailing Instructions* simply repeated the Commonwealth version, substituting 'admiral' for 'general'. The *Fighting Instructions*, too, were only slightly modified from their Commonwealth predecessor, displaying commendable pragmatism on the part of James. He was leading a fleet of old Commonwealth officers, and new Royalists, against a well-known and highly effective foe. He could not afford to let his captains learn their lessons the hard way. He provided them with a core doctrine, based on the most recent English experience, to limit the potential for mistakes and ensure all were acting to a common standard. His royal imprimatur ensured that the Royalists accepted the Commonwealth *Instructions*, and avoided the otherwise inevitable clash of doctrine between the two halves of the fleet. His reliance on Sir William Penn was reflected in the decision to adopt 'line of battle' tactics. Others favoured the more individualistic mêlée model or, like Rupert, didn't think it mattered particularly how the fleet went into battle.[27]

The modifications James introduced in 1664 stabilised the emphasis that had begun to emerge in the 1650s on linear combat and maintaining order. He refined the instruction to keep in line by stressing that they were also to keep their station in that line, and replaced an instruction for captured ships to be burnt, once the prisoners had been removed, with one that insisted that all ships able to sail were to maintain formation unless otherwise directed by the admiral. He then added two new instructions, one enabling the admiral to signal for a line ahead on the larboard or starboard tack, the other directing captains not to open fire 'until the ship be within distance to do good execution'. Failure to observe the latter was a court-martial offence. Well aware of the critical role of artillery in battle, James instituted regular gunnery practice.[28]

On 10 April 1665 James provided ten *Additional Fighting Instructions*, reinforcing the emphasis on using the line of battle to defeat the enemy and to maintain cohesion until the enemy had been broken and put to flight. On the 12th he added instructions for the captains and crew of fireships, encouraging them to defend their own fleet and to attack the enemy with promises of significant rewards. After his initial experience of handling the fleet at sea, James quickly added new signals to order the fleet to form a line and to detach squadrons to pursue the enemy.[29]

The pattern that emerges from James's first attempt to control his fleet, which eventually numbered slightly over a hundred ships, was the need to form a line, to engage at close range and to maintain cohesion until the enemy was broken by gunfire. There was nothing in this that a contemporary general would have found strange. Nor would an experienced officer of either service have been under any illusion as to the likelihood of this order being maintained in combat. James followed Blake and the generals in holding regular councils on board his flagship, but he used the occasion to impose an altogether more formal approach to the structure of the fleet.[30] The primacy of the line of battle, mutual support and obedience to the admiral's signals informed his approach, and it is highly significant that in his absence the Four Days' Battle of 1666 was fought without sense or system, Monck being no more able to control his hotheads than Rupert.

The second set of *Fighting Instructions* of 1666[31] demonstrated how much James had learnt in his first naval command and how well he could adapt military concepts to the naval environment. The dominant theme remained one of control: Monck and Rupert favoured initiative, but James and his ally Penn preferred discipline. The new orders imposed a centrally directed linear battle, on pain of severe penalties. In addition to core doctrine, James created a system that enabled the admiral to control and direct the fleet by signal, covering the essential tactical concepts that sailing warships could execute. These orders were developed and refined over the next century, but they remained the basis of naval mastery. A well-formed line of battle, composed of the heaviest ships, gave the English an advantage over all rivals. Only in the age of Nelson was it possible to dispense with such formalism, and only then because the enemy was significantly less competent.

The Second Dutch War

Having created a 'royal' navy at considerable expense, the newly restored monarchy was unable to resist the inevitable temptation to exploit its power. Neither Charles nor James had any love for the Dutch, while the whole country understood the value of commerce. In the short term the monarchy reimposed the Commonwealth Navigation Acts in 1660, refining them in 1663 to ensure trade was diverted from the Dutch to English ships and English harbours. Mercantilist thinking held that the trade of the world was finite and that any increase for England must be at the expense of the Dutch. Improved trade would increase customs revenue and enrich the King. The desire to strip the 'insolent Republican' Dutch of their trade was widely held: George Monck dismissed the various excuses, arguing 'What matter this or that reason? What we want is more of the trade the Dutch now have.'[32]

Encouraged by the optimism of old Commonwealth officers and his own military ambitions, James urged the King to strike while the navy was powerful and the Dutch appeared unprepared for the inevitable war. Such opportunistic arguments sit unevenly with James's passionate conviction that the English claim to 'sovereignty of the seas' rested on timeless and inalienable rights. The demand that all foreign vessels salute the English flag was the obvious indi-cation of this claim, along with the decision to name one of his sons Edgar. Enforcing the salute was a matter of honour, in which James would brook no compromise, court-martialling an officer who failed to make the demand to a superior Dutch fleet. Honour and prestige were not the least of his motivations in seeking war, although commercial ambition, notably in West Africa, and the need for ready money provided a more materialistic agenda. The lure was not land and an empire of settlement, but an empire of the oceans, based on trade and markets. The fact that colonial settlement would provide a vital element of the mature British Empire escaped James, who saw colonies merely as opportunities for profit. His leadership of the Royal Adventurers trading with Africa in the early 1660s cul-minated in a naval raid on rival Dutch settlements, which was swiftly repaid by de Ruyter. In America, meanwhile, James planned his infantry's swift, bloodless and decisive seizure of New Amsterdam – renamed New York – in 1664. The lure of gold soon faded, however, and a steady profit was drawn from slave trading, but this did not elicit the same level of interest.

James proved to be an efficient, popular Lord High Admiral, building a strong power base within the service and supporting the expansion of the fleet, and the funding on which it depended.[33] His administrative structure and his Admiralty officials were the backbone of the most powerful fleet in Europe, the instrument that significantly added to England's value in any potential alliance.

In November 1664 James watched the fleet mobilise at Portsmouth; in late March 1665 he took command of the fleet anchored off Harwich, anxious to prove that his military credentials were transferable to the ocean. In both Dutch wars the King frequently visited the fleet, dining on the flagship and sleeping on his yacht. After consulting his brother, James planned to scour the Channel and southern North Sea, seizing Dutch shipping in the hope that this would draw out the enemy for a decisive battle. While his vast collection of warships possessed more firepower than had ever been assembled before, it was altogether too large to be effectively directed by nine admirals with the existing limited flag- and gun-based signalling systems. While at sea, ships could be expected to follow their leader and to receive, albeit slowly, messages that were passed by flag or relayed by speaking trumpet. However, once they were engaged in a battle all semblance of control would disappear, and captains would look to the admiral for an example. Blake used discipline to ensure every officer followed his example on the day of battle; he paid less attention to the finer points of signalling. Cool courage and steely determination were enough in his early battles with the Dutch; only later did he acquire the skill and confidence to direct the fleet and rely on others.

Although the veteran Commonwealth admiral Sir William Penn stood at his elbow, James was desperately short of experience when the fleet dropped anchor on the Suffolk coast on 31 May. Despite his military reputation, he had never commanded anything larger than a squadron of cavalry, let alone a warship or a fleet at sea. In effect he had been promoted from cornet of horse to full admiral, and he would not have long to master the brief. The fleet was still at anchor the next day, waiting for supplies, when the Dutch appeared. After manoeuvring for advantage for two days, the Dutch secured the windward position, enabling them to control the battle.

Admiral van Obdam might have been a cavalryman by training, but he had commanded fleets in battle against the English and the Swedes. However, his fleet, riven by factional squabbles, proved a flawed instrument. Early on the 3rd, with the fleets off Lowestoft, the wind shifted to the south-west, giving the English the weather gauge. James immediately ordered an attack. The fleets engaged in a medium-range cannonade, twice passing on opposite courses. At the end of the first pass James tried to signal for the fleet to tack together and come to close quarters, but the flag hoist was delayed, and the opportunity was lost.[34]

Nothing decisive could come of such exchanges, so when Prince Rupert led the fleet round for a third pass he edged closer to the Dutch, the rest of the fleet following in his wake. Rupert's blood was up, for his flagship had already taken a battering. At this point the cohesion of the English fleet began to dissolve as clouds of gun smoke and the stunning cacophony of heavy cannon left every captain alone and confused. Even if the individual squadrons retained some sort of cohesion, the fleet was no longer a single line of battle. The new Dutch ships proved tougher opponents than those Blake had fought: they were larger, more heavily armed and stood and fought a linear battle for over an hour. Realising English firepower had not broken the enemy formation, James took the initiative, driving the *Royal Charles* into the heart of the Dutch fleet, supported by the *Royal Oak*. Their broadsides sank two Dutch ships, and the action quickly broke down into a series of ship and small squadron actions at point-blank range. When Sir John Lawson was killed, James sent one of his staff to take command of the *Royal Oak* and keep her in action. Inevitably the heaviest fighting centred on the flagships: Sandwich, commanding the rear, tried to engage Obdam's *Eendracht* but was immediately surrounded by Dutch ships, only escaping when James drove through the crowd to his rescue. With the enemy flagship in his sights, James had found the battle he desired: a Homeric engagement between admirals – man to man, nation to nation, winner takes all.

Having an opponent worthy of a royal prince, James pressed his flagship alongside the Dutchman and began a terrifying exchange of cannonballs, grapeshot and musketry. His staff were scythed down when a chain shot decapitated the King's favourite, Charles Berkeley, Earl of Falmouth, killed Lord Muskerry and Mr Boyle, and left James covered in blood and brains, with a piece of Falmouth's skull driven into his hand. James remained every inch the Prince: he did not flinch. He also behaved like an admiral, responding to the loss of close friends and key advisers without emotion. His dog was not made of such stern stuff, fleeing below to the safety of the hold.

Gradually the superior weight of fire and the superior elevation of the three-decked ship told: with Obdam dead and *Eendracht* reeling, a chance shot set off her magazine. All but five of her crew went to meet their maker in a catastrophic explosion that scattered huge chunks of timber across the battlefield. Tellingly, the Duke observed, 'Obdam was a brave man, but no seaman.'[35] Now leaderless, their second-in-command also dead, the Dutch began to waver. Catching a second wind after his relief by the Duke, Sandwich led his squadron through the middle of the Dutch fleet, completing the rout. With Rupert's squadron pressing their opponents hard, there were no reserves to parry Sandwich's move and no one with the authority to take command. Two rival Dutch admirals assumed they were now the senior officer, but neither could stem the rout. The Dutch had fought bravely, but they had no answer to the superior firepower of the English fleet. As the fighting came to an end, one admiral led his squadron towards the Texel, the other towards Rotterdam.

Once the ships came to close quarters, the linear constraints of the *Fighting Instructions* broke down: blinded, stunned and alone, some captains did their best, while others tried to hold back without being too obvious. Sandwich observed that many ships did not hold station even in the first pass, with the Dutch luffing up into the wind to find safety on the disengaged side of their own squadron, and compounding their crime by firing onto their own ships.[36]

In his first naval action James had achieved the holy grail of naval battle in the age of the sailing ship: he had a broken, fleeing enemy before him. If he could roll up the shattered remnants of the Dutch fleet, taking the bulk of their ships and men, he could settle the conflict in an afternoon. The war might be won as easily as the court optimists had hoped. However, as his Commonwealth predecessors had discovered, the transition from winning a battle to fully exploiting the victory was uncommonly difficult. First it was necessary to reassemble and repair the fleet, and as the flagships had been in the heaviest fighting, they would require the most work. Once his force was ready, James ordered a pursuit, with Sandwich leading the fleet. For three hours the English gained on the Dutch, but Sandwich had to surrender the lead when the main topsail yard of his flagship was shot to pieces.[37] This left James commanding the pursuit, just as the daylight began to fade. After eighteen hours of fighting and chasing, the Duke, who was only human, failed to issue clear instructions to continue the pursuit during the night. He intended to fight again at dawn but did not make this clear to his staff or his fleet; nor did Admiral Penn, his chief of staff and flag captain. Instead, James went to bed, and Penn followed his example. During the night a Gentleman of the Bedchamber, Henry Brouncker, ordered the fleet to break off the pursuit and overrode the authority of Captain Harman, the senior naval officer on deck. It is not known whether Brouncker was, as rumour had it, acting on the Duchess's instructions to keep the Duke safe or simply horrified by the carnage of the day, but once his signal went out the fleet shortened sail, allowing the men to get some much-needed rest. While it is easy to portray this as a glorious opportunity wasted, the difficulty of maintaining contact with a fleeing enemy through the night should not be underestimated; nor should the deeply partisan, factional manner in which the matter was discussed in the weeks and months that followed. The Restoration navy was a vicious, tribal collection of officers with complex links of patronage and loyalty.[38] Only truly royal leadership could rise above such internecine squabbling.

The next morning James, like many an admiral before and since, awoke to find the enemy had gone. As he saw it, his staff had failed him; his own failure to make his wishes clear did not trouble him. His line of reasoning was entirely justified: when he left the deck, the fleet was in hot pursuit of the enemy, and he had not issued any orders to the contrary. Therefore, any change of course was a clear violation of his wishes and should have been cleared with him before being executed. Brouncker had no authority to break off the pursuit, and richly deserved to be pilloried for his action. Had he been a commissioned officer, his fate might well have been worse. However, such reflections were moot. By the time James realised what had happened, the English had no hope of catching the Dutch before they entered the relative safety of their shallow coastal waters. But despite the incomplete nature of the success, the Battle of Lowestoft was a major victory: the English lost one ship and three hundred men, with another five hundred wounded, while the Dutch lost three admirals, had seventeen ships sunk and nine captured, and suffered around five thousand casualties. Only a foolish courtier prevented James from winning the Second Anglo-Dutch War at a stroke. Unfortunately for James, it was also his last battle in this war. His successors would be left to face the greatest fighting seaman of the seventeenth century, Michiel de Ruyter, a man with more skill and artifice in his little finger than the bold, blustering Obdam could muster in his by now much distressed carcass.

Lowestoft gave James what he most desired: an opportunity to live up to his heroic martial image. In his first sea battle he had smashed the enemy, while his conduct under fire had matched that of the finest commanders of the last war: even Blake himself had not shown more cool courage on the quarterdeck. It was his triumph. He sent the King Obdam's tattered flag, and received a parliamentary grant of £120,000 to reward his 'heroic courage', while the nation celebrated a glorious victory with pealing bells and days of thanksgiving.[39]

Unfortunately for the Duke, reports of his heroism, and more especially of his close proximity to random slaughter, persuaded the King that his only male heir was simply too precious to be risked in such viciously democratic warfare.[40] James was ordered ashore on 1 July, and the command passed to Sandwich.[41] By the end of the 1665 campaign, though, Sandwich had fallen from favour, and in 1666 the supreme command was held jointly by Rupert and Monck, now Lord Albemarle. Despite James's admonition to caution,[42] they managed to mishandle things so badly that de Ruyter found the English fleet divided. Although seriously outnumbered, Monck was too proud to retreat, and suffered heavy losses. Rupert put in a belated appearance, but his ill-disciplined squadron blundered into action and took a beating. The final judgement on the Four Days' Battle has to be one of heroic failure, heavily tainted by sheer amateurism. The contrast with James's command was clear, and a month later Monck had the fleet well in hand: the Duke's new *Fighting Instructions* had been thoroughly absorbed by the time he met and defeated de Ruyter in the St James's Day Battle.[43]

This success persuaded the Dutch to sue for terms. Confident the war was won, Charles decided not to fit out the fleet in 1667, despite the protests of his senior admirals. A combination of poverty and over-optimism provided the Dutch with an opportunity to reverse the result. John de Witt, the Chief Minister, prepared a plan to attack the main English naval base at Chatham, relying on English renegades and de Ruyter's skill. The Medway raid achieved all he had hoped, sinking and burning several important English warships and ensuring that the Treaty of Breda imposed little more than the *status quo ante*. Amid the chaos that descended on the dockyard, the *Royal Charles*, the Duke's flagship, was towed off to Amsterdam as a trophy of war.

James had ordered the building of a new fort at Sheerness and the installation of a boom at Gillingham to close the Medway, but in the event these proved inadequate. Only the old castle at Upnor prevented the Dutch reaching the dockyard itself. No one on the English side emerged from the Medway raid with much credit, but having opposed laying up the fleet and issued the necessary orders to secure the Medway, James had good reason to think himself blameless for the debacle. While he admitted the Dutch were superior in maritime skill,[44] he reckoned English sailors were braver and more numerous than those of France or Holland. He hoped to instil in officers and men alike something of the military discipline of the officers and men he so admired in the French fleet by increasing their pay.[45]

England failed to win this war because she lacked the finances and credit to wage war effectively for more than two years. While the Dutch spent £11 million, King Charles managed with less than half as much. As the humiliation of the Medway raid demonstrated, the mighty Royal Navy was too costly an instrument of national power for a fiscally weak nation to wield. It would require fundamental political reform, exchanging political rights for efficient taxation, to fund the fleet. Unwilling to make the necessary concessions, Charles took a bribe from his cousin Louis XIV in the 1670 Treaty of Dover, in return for alliance and vague promises that England would return to the Catholic Church. Charles knew that France was the real threat to England's interests, rather than Holland, but it would take another war to force that conclusion onto the political agenda.

Religion

Although born and raised in the Church of England, and ultimately to become its head, James's faith was challenged throughout his life. His mother, a French princess, remained a Catholic and actively tried to convert both James and his younger brother Henry during their exile in Paris. Although his exposure to Catholicism in the 1650s made James an advocate of religious tolerance, he remained a Protestant at the Restoration. He returned to a country still viscerally fearful of the Roman religion, Jesuits and continental tyranny. The English had long memories and a deep-rooted hatred of the Church of Rome. John Foxe's *Book of Martyrs*, the second most popular religious text after the Bible, was little more than a horrifying catalogue of Catholic brutality and conspiracy, and the national celebrations on 5 November were an annual reminder of the Catholic plot against James I. The Roman religion was feared and distrusted, associated with hostile foreign powers – most obviously Spain and France – and the suppression of political liberties. In truth James was tolerant of all religious views and an English patriot to the day he died, but his subjects would not see past his membership of the Roman communion.

Nor was James's conversion of the Pauline variety: he took his time and worked his way through the evidence to reach his conclusion. His experience in Europe convinced him that the English view of Catholicism was unwarranted, and he had become a proponent of toleration by the time he returned to England. When his wife examined the theological grounds of her Anglican faith, she ended up converting; James followed the same arguments, and after the Second Dutch War he had time and opportunity for study. He did not create a 'Catholic' party and did nothing to prepare his country for a return to Rome: he relied on persuasion and logical argument to overcome opposition. But in matters of faith few were open to logic or persuasion, even from a prince. Instead, his 'impolitic' personal move alienated his core support among the old Royalists, without garnering any new backing. By converting, James allowed his personal beliefs to damage his royal and political interests; he did so because he lacked the breadth of vision to see how personal choice might invalidate his divine right to rule. But having once made his decision, he was never going to change it.

In 1668–9 James was received into the faith of his mother, and thereafter never wavered in his belief, though it cost him his rank and titles, his popular reputation, another spell of exile, the support of his children, and ultimately his throne. Obstinate, wilful and foolish he might have been, but nothing so dignified the life of James Stuart as his constancy in religion. While his ancestor Henry of Navarre had famously declared 'Paris is worth a Mass', James Stuart refused to make a similar concession to the religious opinion of his people. But before his communion became an issue England was once more at war with the Dutch.

The Third Dutch War

The Third Anglo-Dutch War opened in much the same fashion as the second, with specious claims about Dutch ships not striking their flags and an unprovoked English attack on a Dutch convoy. But England waged this war in alliance with France, and Louis XIV sought the destruction of Holland. It was a war England could not afford to lose.

James took command of the fleet, scouring the southern North Sea and the Straits of Dover for Dutch shipping, hoping to draw out and destroy de Ruyter's fleet and pave the way for an Anglo-French invasion of Holland. He went to sea to dissipate factional squabbles in the English fleet and ensure the English commanded the allied fleet.[46] Once again, the shortage of English victuals forced him to abandon a commanding position on the Dutch coast for a rendezvous on the Suffolk shore. Never one to miss an opportunity, de Ruyter immediately put to sea, hoping a pre-emptive strike would cripple the Anglo-French fleet, preventing the allied amphibious assault. Early on 28 May 1672 he found his foes at anchor in Sole Bay, taking on food and ammunition. Had the easterly wind that brought him to the English coast not failed at the last moment, an all-out attack on the scattered allied warships might have achieved de Ruyter's aim. James was quick to raise anchor and get the fleet under way. His French van squadron was commanded by the Comte d'Estrées, while Sandwich commanded the rear. As the fleet sailed out on an ESE wind to meet the Dutch, James signalled for a starboard tack, heading north, which placed Sandwich's rear squadron in the lead. By ignorance, oversight or – it was darkly hinted – malice, d'Estrées headed south. James had not troubled himself to order the French to conform: he did not believe it was necessary when they could see perfectly well which way the admiral was heading. The two English squadrons continued north, and de Ruyter quickly detached a small force to engage the French at long range, while he led the fleet against the two English squadrons. Outnumbered two to one, the English faced a hot and hard day of fighting: this Dutch fleet would not break and run, and in de Ruyter they had an admiral they trusted.

The battle opened at 07.00 with a long-range cannonade, although de Ruyter was anxious to come to close quarters. By 08.00 de Ruyter, his second admiral van Nes and five other ships had surrounded James's flagship, the *Prince*. When the wind dropped, the rest of the squadron was unable to come to his support. James was in serious trouble: the unequal contest threatened to end in the disgrace of capture or the flaming shambles of a fireship attack. Undaunted by the danger, James went through the ship to inspire his crew, and pressed the captain to get as close as possible to the enemy. James trusted the power of his guns, and they proved to be his salvation. Unable or unwilling to face the *Prince*'s heavy cannon, the Dutch held off at musket shot, about a hundred yards, waiting for an opportunity to use fireships. It never came. The *Prince* proved too strong: her cannon and the musketry of a company of foot guards shattered the Dutch battleships and kept the fireships at a respectful distance. However, the human cost was high: Sir John Cox, the ship's captain, was killed by a heavy shot, and other members of the Duke's staff were hit. With her captain and two hundred men killed, the *Prince* was in danger of being overpowered. Ordering Captain Narborough to take command, James anxiously sought a wind to escape from his tormentors. Some time after 11.00 the main topmast was shot clean away; it fell onto the upper-deck battery, temporarily disabling many of her fast-firing light guns, and also fouled the mainsail. Seeing the *Prince* disabled and partially disarmed, the Dutch quickly sent two fireships to finish the job in spectacular fashion. Fortunately, the experienced Narborough had two boats tow the ship's bow round, until a breeze shook her headsails and she closed on the English ships to the north. No sooner had the danger passed than the foretopsail yard was shot away, leaving the ship crippled. There was no possibility that the damage could be repaired while the ship was still heavily engaged.

Narborough recorded the events of that day:

The Dutch finding us to ply our guns so fast, dare not venture to board us, although they had so great odds. His Royal Highness went fore and aft in the ship and cheered up the men to fight, which did encourage them very much. The Duke thought himself never near enough to the enemy, for he was ever calling for the quarter master which conned the ship to luff her nearer, giving me commands to forbear firing till we got up close to them. Between 9 and 10 o'clock Sir John Cox was slain with a great shot, being close by the Duke on the poop. Several gentlemen and others were slain and wounded on the poop and quarter deck on both sides of the Duke . . . I do absolutely believe no prince upon the whole earth can compare with His Royal Highness in gallant resolution in fighting his enemy, and with so great conduct and knowledge in navigation as never any general understood before him. He is better acquainted in these seas than many masters which are now in his fleet; he is general, soldier, pilot, master, seaman; to say all, he is everything that man can be, and most pleasant when the great shot are thundering about his ears.[47]

Unwilling to be carried out of the action on a crippled ship, or to wait while she was refitted, the Duke took a boat and shifted his standard to the *St Michael*, relieving the pressure on the shattered *Prince* and allowing him to rejoin the battle. Once James had hoisted his standard on the *St Michael*, the Dutch shifted their attention to the new target, and she was soon in the thick of the fighting. The chief pilot of the fleet was killed alongside the Duke on the new flagship. At this time the English fleet found itself pressed uncomfortably close to the inshore shoals. Narborough reported that the Duke and another twenty English ships were surrounded by the Dutch in the afternoon. By the evening the *St Michael* was a crippled wreck, and James shifted his flag onto the *London*. By keeping his flag flying in the middle of the fight, James inspired his outnumbered force to drive off the most determined and resolute Dutch attack ever seen by an English fleet.[48] The old rivalries and differences of the last wars had been forgotten: this Dutch fleet knew they were fighting for the very survival of their nation, assailed on land by massive French armies and at sea by a superior allied fleet.

It was a measure of the desperation of his enemies that the Duke came so close to disaster, not once but twice. De Ruyter knew that the key to English successes in previous wars had been the cohesion and leadership provided by their regulations and their admirals. If he could take out the admirals, it would break the English formation and give his fireships a chance. While James escaped, Lord Sandwich did not. Sandwich's flagship, the *Royal James*, was surrounded, isolated and, with the Dutch ship *Groot Hollandia* jammed under her bow, stationary. In this condition, she attracted a succession of fireships, but they were driven off or sunk by her heavy guns. Then, just as the *James* broke free, she succumbed to an incendiary attack, burning to the waterline and sinking. Sandwich tried to shift his flag, but he had become quite corpulent and drowned when his boat was sunk by a stray cannonball. When the errant French squadron, with their Dutch minders, finally appeared to the south, de Ruyter withdrew into the gathering gloom, well aware that the French could change the verdict of the day.

Holding the weather gauge, the Dutch chose not to renew the battle, and when the French finally rejoined his flag the next morning, James, having returned to the repaired *Prince*, set off after de Ruyter. Having brought his fleet to within two miles of the Dutch, and straining every nerve to renew the battle, a thick fog descended. When it lifted, James once more resolved to fight:

His Royal Highness went fore and aft cheering up the men, every man being very glad to fight. His Royal Highness commanded the flag of defiance [the red flag used to signal for battle] to be hoisted, which was presently done, and the whole ship's company gave three shouts for joy, to see it flying and we so near the enemy.

Within half an hour a storm blew up, ending any chance of further fighting.[49] Both sides lost two ships, with six to seven hundred killed and at least a thousand wounded. De Ruyter had spoiled the opening moves of the allied campaign, as he had hoped, but he had been denied a major victory by the resolute resistance of the outnumbered English ships, a performance dominated by the Duke's steely determination to hold his ground, ably supported by Sandwich and his captains. James recognised the Dutch admiral as 'the greatest that ever to that time was in the World',[50] a judgement that history has endorsed: de Ruyter had the skill, courage and human qualities that mark out all great leaders. With the Dutchman as his model, James would not go far wrong in naval command.

Indeed, Narborough's observations on the Duke's conduct were almost exactly mirrored by Dutch accounts of his adversary.[51] They were well matched in battle, the order and resolve of the Duke's English squadrons neutralising the impetuous zeal and agility of the Dutchmen. De Ruyter would save his country by outwitting the English, but after Sole Bay he understood that he could not defeat them. He spent the rest of the war fighting spoiling actions and exploiting local knowledge to embarrass the allies.

Many in England blamed the French: d'Estrées should have concentrated on the commander-in-chief, rather than acting as if he were in control. But the failure to develop an effective understanding between the allied squadrons was always going to cause problems. Furthermore, the French did not show much interest in fighting, avoiding close action with the Dutch throughout the war. D'Estrées was quick to pin blame on his subordinates; James, meanwhile, did not doubt the Frenchman's courage, but said nothing about his judgement. Sole Bay was an unsatisfactory engagement, but avoiding defeat when heavily outnumbered was nonetheless a great feat for a novice admiral in his second sea battle. No one would defeat de Ruyter in this war, even with far better odds. The Duke's performance had been decisive; his leadership and determination had saved the day.

Attempts to excuse d'Estrées and blame the Duke[52] for the failure of communication ignore the command relationship that joined them. As a junior flag officer, d'Estrées was obliged to follow the orders of his senior, and that included conforming to his movements. When the Duke settled on a course that reversed the order of sailing, he simply had to reverse his own order of sailing, falling into the wake of the Duke's squadron and changing places with Sandwich. He had no authority to impose the course of sailing on his senior officer, and an English admiral committing the same error would have been court-martialled for failing to give mutual support and for failing to obey his senior officer. Furthermore, the French *were* acting on orders to avoid close combat[53] – Louis XIV was happy to wait on the sidelines while the two Protestant navies annihilated one another.

After cruising on the Dutch coast and into the North Sea, James struck his flag on 18 September 1672, never to rehoist it. While the passage of the First Test Act ultimately forced James to resign as Lord High Admiral, he relinquished his command afloat to Rupert at the King's desire. Once again Charles was nervous about the succession.[54] James wanted to add some fresh military laurels to his naval collection, commanding the army that the allies planned to land on the coast of Holland.[55] The invasion was thwarted by de Ruyter. The 1673 campaign witnessed three more bloody exchanges between the English and Dutch fleets, the French consistently failing to engage. De Ruyter outwitted, and on occasion outfought, the allies, aided by French caution and Rupert's characteristic indiscipline. The Duke might not have been able to defeat de Ruyter at the Schooenveld or the Texel, but he would have done far better than Rupert.

In 1673 James issued a new set of printed *Sailing and Fighting Instructions*, which brought together the movements required and the signals used to control them in one compendium. It would be the basic model for all similar tactical books for more than a century – a codification of best practice, as developed during the Dutch wars. As Admiral Sir Charles Penrose observed a hundred and forty years later:

It is but justice to remark, that they displayed a very considerable degree of nautical skill, and must, at the time when they were first issued, have been a very superior code of tactics, highly creditable to their royal author, who was indeed a much better admiral than he proved to be a monarch.[56]

As a fleet commander James provided firm and effective leadership, and his success was remarkable, given how few opportunities he had to develop his methods. He commanded the fleet on only two occasions, and both times for little more than a month before major fleet battles took place. The only naval actions he ever witnessed were the two in which he held the supreme command. He made mistakes, and the results were inconclusive, but it is scarcely reasonable to judge him a failure as an admiral, as his latest biographer has, when he had so little opportunity to master the unique demands of naval warfare. The authoritarian streak that came all too naturally to a prince of his temper was a vital tool of command in the seventeenth century, as Robert Blake had demonstrated, while the heroic personal reputation James cultivated was a major asset for his service and his nation.[57] Admirals with a lifetime of experience rarely did better, and most significantly worse.

Any hope James had of keeping his conversion to the Catholic

Church quiet had been destroyed when he remarried in 1673. His bride, Mary of Modena, was a devout Catholic, and her arrival forced him to make his faith public. Fortunately, very few Englishmen realised that Louis XIV had paid Mary's dowry.[58] Unlike his pragmatic brother, James was not prepared to wait for his deathbed to admit his beliefs. While his personal morality in most other areas of public and private life was flexible, he held to his faith with the zeal of a convert, reinforced by the deathbed warnings of his first wife. While he could provide leadership and decision on the quarterdeck, James required absolute leadership in all other areas of his life. He had always sought someone he could defer to: Turenne, his brother and the ultimate in earthly certainty and authority, the Pope. This search for certainty was the key to his conversion.

With it, however, James was transformed from heroic admiral to political liability. When the King had to summon Parliament in 1673 to raise money for the Third Dutch War, the price he paid was the First Test Act, which barred Catholics from holding high office in the kingdom. At a stroke, James was forced out of the Admiralty and left struggling for dynastic survival. His faith also crushed popular support for the Dutch wars.[59] In the 'Exclusion Crisis' of 1679–82, the King proved to be a highly effective political operator, defeating Whig attempts to remove James from the succession. The exposure of the Rye House plot to murder both royal brothers in favour of Charles's ardently Protestant bastard the Duke of Monmouth led to a small amount of blood-letting and restored James to high office. He never profited from his brother's example of political skill, though; indeed, his occasional political successes were the result of overwhelming advantages rather than astute management. James proved more loyal than wise in his choice of followers and favourites. He was a man of absolutes: force and compulsion, rather than finesse, were his tools. But when his brother suddenly died, his position was secure and strong. He would be the last King of England able to rule without constant reference to Parliament.

King James II, 1685–8

On ascending the throne in early 1685, James was quick to overhaul the fabric of the navy.[60] In his first speech as king, he reminded Parliament of a basic truth: 'I must recommend to you, the care of the Navy, the Strength and Glory of this Nation that you will put it into such a condition as will make us considered and respected abroad.'[61] Parliament responded by providing a major increase in the naval vote.[62] With £400,000 a year and expert support from Pepys, James quickly rebuilt the fleet and demonstrated high standards of financial probity. The key issues were discipline, planning and the maintenance of accurate records afloat and ashore.

By 1685 English naval administration was efficient and honest, vital developments for the effectiveness of the ever larger, more powerful and more costly battle fleet. James had effective control over the fleet, and he did not share it with Parliament.[63]

With royal revenues boosted by a trade boom and reinforced by the parliamentary vote for the suppression of Monmouth's rebellion, James quickly built up a twenty-thousand-strong professional army. Then he began to undermine the opposition, breaking up local government structures that had survived war and revolution, and preparing to pack Parliament with his creatures. His object was religious tolerance and a Catholic Church establishment, which he expected would soon return many of his subjects to the true faith. But the sheer scale of his efforts destroyed his Royalist power base, without building an alternative among the dissenting sects he roped in to broaden the appeal of his pro-Catholic project for toleration. Even so, the country was prepared to tolerate him, as long as the throne passed to his Protestant daughter Mary. The birth of a prince in mid-1688 was the final straw, threatening to transform the eccentric rein of a middle-aged monarch into the dawn of a new Catholic dynasty. Mary's husband William of Orange, who needed the Royal Navy and the economic and military power of the English nation for his war with Louis XIV, reacted with alacrity when the opposition summoned him. He overthrew his uncle and father-in-law when James faltered, not as a warrior, but as a king. James had always needed guidance, and one suspects that behind his religious policies lay his wife, his confessor and fellow Catholics. He was a brave and honest man, but no one ever accused him of being clever. The absolute conviction with which he held to his politically disastrous faith summed up his qualities to perfection.

By 1688 the navy had a professional career structure for officers that limited the impact of political favouritism and provided admirals with access to a large and loyal body of seamen. This was the work of the last Stuart kings,[64] and James's personal touch was obvious. In 1687 he decided that the unfinished royal palace at Greenwich, begun by his brother, should 'be fitted for the service of impotent sea commanders and others'.[65] Here James followed Charles II, who had established the Military Hospital at Chelsea in 1682: both were almshouses for aged warriors.[66] The welfare and morale of the seamen was a standing concern.[67] Yet James's initiative, like so much else of his work for the navy, would soon be annexed to the credit of others. In 1691 his daughter Mary, now Queen, had the palace converted into a hospital for seamen, just in time for the decisive battle of La Hougue. It was fitting that the wounded from James's final battle should be housed in a Stuart palace, even if they had just ended his last hope of restoration.

James was denied his key role in the development of the Royal Navy because it did not suit the agendas of historians and politicians in the centuries that followed. They preferred the caricature villain, 'bad King James', who tried to overthrow that most uncertain and ill-defined thing: the English constitution. In the process, an accurate understanding of history was sacrificed, leaving a void in our comprehension of the Commonwealth foundations of the modern Royal Navy and of who sustained and directed the process. To avoid the politically awkward question of James II, historians were quick to elevate the role of Samuel Pepys from administrator and man of business to policy-maker and architect, a role that neither Charles II nor James II would have dreamt of giving him. Pepys executed royal policy, and for most of the period between 1660 and 1688 the chief policy-maker was James, as Lord High Admiral, Privy Councillor and King. For a navy based on battle-fleet fighting power, the ideas of Mr Pepys, who had no first-hand knowledge of battle, were necessarily of small moment.

In a brief reign of only three years, King James's inflexible commitment to the Catholic faith so alienated his subjects, and his navy, that soon after the birth of his son the nation welcomed the Dutch invasion and replaced James with his daughter and her Dutch husband. That his fleet failed to stop the Dutch was attributed to divine providence, but the real causes were more mundane. James did not lose his throne for want of power, or of a fleet, let alone of a horse.

He lost his throne because the same authoritarian leadership that worked so well for the Royal Navy proved altogether less successful when translated into the political arena. Even so, it took the issue of his faith, allied to the birth of a son and his own insensitivity, to prompt a Dutch invasion; and it took a failure of nerve to turn the invasion into a 'Glorious Revolution'. The combination of Catholicism and authoritarian rule broke the compact that bound ruler and ruled to share their interests. The birth of a prince was the final straw.

In his hour of need, James was failed by the Royal Navy, the mighty instrument he himself had created. Like the state it represented, the navy would not tolerate his absolutism and his pro-Catholic vision of religious tolerance. Even his own network of followers collapsed. The attempt to employ Catholic officers back-fired, as anyone with a grain of sense would have predicted. The sailors reacted violently to attempts to conduct Mass on board. The only Catholic senior officer was an arrogant ass, and while James's chosen admiral, the Earl of Dartmouth, was a Protestant, he lacked skill and authority. Then James sacked his most experienced admiral, Arthur Herbert, because he refused to compromise on the removal of religious disabilities. This was doubly foolish, for Herbert was notoriously immoral and lacked any profound principles. Further losses followed when Whig officers defected.

The defectors joined William of Orange, James's nephew and son-in-law, in his desperate attempt to seize the English throne and use the resources of the three kingdoms to defeat Louis XIV. William appointed Herbert to command his 460-ship invasion fleet. Carrying twenty thousand troops, William's fleet was twice the size of the Armada. However, he set off in October, and after a storm tried again in November, a time of the year when no sane man would take the battle fleet to sea. This time, fortune favoured the brave.[68]

The English fleet that faced the invasion in 1688 was an unhappy force, internally factionalised and well aware that several leading officers had joined William's fleet. Dartmouth proved unimaginative and indecisive, unable to deal with a fleet in turmoil or counter the endless swirl of rumours and propaganda. He anchored at the Gunfleet, believing the Dutch would land in the north. But this location proved disastrous when the enemy headed south-west down the Channel, leaving the English fleet impotently at anchor. James had urged Dartmouth to sail to the Dutch coast and seek battle, but the admiral's councils urged caution. Clearly Dartmouth could not hold a candle to his king as a seaman. If ever there was a moment to put on his armour and lead the fleet, it was in the autumn of 1688. Instead, James hesitated, dithered and allowed his support to ebb away. Eventually the wind shifted and Dartmouth put to sea, but as William's fleet dropped anchor off Brixham, Dartmouth had only made his way as far as Beachy Head. Here he hesitated, and was blown back to the east by a gale. Any enthusiasm for King James was evaporating, and Dartmouth lacked the personal authority to command.[69] James ordered Dartmouth to Torbay, but he arrived in foul weather and declined to engage. The fleet had failed: the Dutch were ashore, and James's position was crumbling.

In a bizarre failure of nerve, the warrior King James II did not wait for a military showdown but instead fled to France.[70] Here Louis XIV provided him with a palace, an income and opportunities to recover his throne. When Holland and England went to war with France, Louis recognised that William III was his most dangerous enemy and sent James to Ireland with French troops and money in 1689 to open a new front. From the start, James found himself caught between English patriotism and a desire to recover his throne. When a French squadron convoying his supplies drove off a few English ships, James was quick to tell the French officers that this was 'the first time' they had beaten his English fleet, and only then because the officers were still loyal to him.[71] Outnumbered and outwitted by a more experienced general, he lost the Battle of the Boyne in 1690 and retreated back to France. Weeks later the French won a major naval battle off Beachy Head. It seemed that James would soon be restored, but Louis did not act. It was not the least of the ironies of the occasion that the English fought the battle using a new edition of James's *Fighting Instructions* of 1673, and his name was still on the title page![72]

A King in Exile

The ultimate fate of the English throne remained uncertain, many taking an each-way bet on the ex-king while paying lip service to the new regime. The future of the country would depend on William's ability to consolidate his power and to secure vital military successes. Reinforcing the navy was his highest priority, once Ireland had been secured. Two years later King Louis decided to invade England: James was ready to recover his kingdom with an Irish army, conveyed in a French fleet. But 'his' Royal Navy, led by men he had trained, and their Dutch allies stood in his way. Off Cape Barfleur on 19 May 1692 the allies hammered a heavily outnumbered French Atlantic fleet: the Mediterranean squadron had been delayed by the weather, which forced it to retreat. Relentless pursuit turned the French retreat into a rout. Several heavily damaged French ships failed to weather the Normandy peninsula and were forced to shelter in the shallow tidal harbours of Cherbourg and La Hougue. On 22 May three ships at Cherbourg, including the French flagship *Soleil Royale*, were burnt by English boats and fireships. A dozen more arrived at La Hougue, where James's army was waiting to embark for England. James advised the French to keep the ships afloat and reinforce their crews with soldiers. This was sound advice from a successful admiral, but it was ignored, with Admiral Tourville declaring that it would be a dishonour to commit the defence of the ships to soldiers.[73] Stunned by the news from Cherbourg, and dismayed by the immense English force assembled to finish the job, the French sailors were already half beaten. On 23 and 24 May impetuous English sailors drove the demoralised Frenchmen from their ships; supporting fire from shallow-draught frigates kept the French shore batteries occupied, allowing fireships and boats to set the French ships ablaze.

On the first day some of the blazing, abandoned French ships opened fire as the flames touched off their guns. Several rounds smashed into a fort where James had been standing only moments before. Perhaps it would have been better for the warrior King if he had died there and then, killed by enemy fire, albeit in rather complex circumstances. While James attributed his safety to divine providence, later events suggested that he had been spared only in order to endure further torment.[74] As the Royal Navy made a bonfire of his earthly ambitions, James, every inch the English warrior King, could not stop himself cheering 'his' sailors on. 'Ah!' he declared to an assembly of French admirals, marshals and generals, 'none but my brave English could do so brave an action!'[75] When it came to naval warfare and religion, James preferred the truth to sparing the feelings of his fellows. Tact had never been his strong point. His audience were either too polite to comment or simply dumbstruck by such a singularly inappropriate comment.

When the sun went down on 24 May, all twelve of the stranded Bourbon giants had been burnt or blown up: with them went the naval dreams of Louis XIV and the personal ambition of James II. The troop transports beached inshore followed them onto the funeral pyre of La Hougue the next morning. Louis's navy, which had reached monstrous proportions by 1692, was destined to wither and collapse in a few short years after the catastrophe of La Hougue.[76] Louis would suffer many injuries at the hands of James Stuart's navy: it could not stop him conquering Europe, but it did ensure that the Stuart pretenders remained at St Germain-en-Laye far longer than he had hoped.

For several weeks James and his army remained on the Normandy coast, hoping against reason that another French fleet might be found to carry him home. Finally, in June, Louis ordered the camp to be broken up and sent the troops to Flanders. When the news of La Hougue reached England, James's closet sympathisers went the way of all flesh. England united behind the new regime, and France was the enemy.

After the shock had passed, James wrote to Louis, mortified that his cause had occasioned such a disaster for the French fleet:

I entreat you therefore to interest yourself no more for a prince so unfortunate, but permit me to withdraw, with my family, to some corner of the world, where I may cease to be an interruption to Your Majesty's wonted course of prosperity and glory.[77]

His self-confidence shattered beyond recovery, James abandoned earthly ambition for a life of religious introspection. Attributing his downfall to the withdrawal of God's favour, on account of his womanising, he abjured all earthly pleasures and subjected his flesh to the mortification of chains and scourges.[78] Had he possessed the self-knowledge to see the truth, he would have realised that his fall was caused by the foolhardy public avowal of a faith that his sailors and most of his people abhorred. Instead, James redirected his propaganda, replacing the image of an English warrior prince with that of a penitent saint seeking to redeem himself through his sacrifice and recover the throne for his son.[79]

Death and Legacy

After a series of strokes, James died at St Germain-en-Laye on 5 September 1701. Louis XIV recognised his son as the rightful King of England, sparking the second round of the Jacobite tragedy that would reach a denouement at Culloden forty-five years later. There were attempts to canonise the old king – which would have been a curious fate for an English admiral – but these faltered and James's name was left as a stark warning against royal absolutism and Catholic tyranny. In the process, his mighty achievements in naval warfare and administration were either ignored or credited to others. The distortion was part of the necessary Whig myth about the creation of the English constitution. Parliament forced William to accept a joint monarchy with his wife Mary and took control of the navy away from the King.

Never again would a monarch have the power and influence over the fleet that James II had possessed, and the navy would miss his expertise and long-term commitment. Under William III, Dutch methods changed the financial basis of British power: the National Debt and the Bank of England turned England from a short-winded country with a battle fleet, able to fight for two seasons, into a fiscal superpower with the endurance to break the French economy. That money, spent on the navy and on allies, purchased a world empire. Led by brave fighting men like George Rooke, Cloudisley Shovell, John Leake and George Byng, the Royal Navy became the arbiter of Europe.

James Stuart was a flawed human being and a poor king: he lacked self-awareness and sophistication, expecting the same immediate obedience from ambitious politicians that he could command from French soldiers in the 1650s and English sailors in the 1660s and 1670s. Yet he had few rivals as a naval administrator and a fighting admiral. His record as Lord High Admiral places him among the key figures in the history of the Royal Navy. His energetic long-term advocacy of naval development, together with his ability to secure the necessary funds and run a highly effective bureaucracy, created a force that could sustain the ferocious reputation built by Blake and would become a decisive factor in European power politics. It was James's own fleet that barred his return to his throne and ended the hegemonic ambitions of his cousin Louis. He laid the long-term foundations of naval power, finding consistent funding to pay for dockyards and shipbuilding, while royal patronage encouraged the upper ranks of society to send their sons into the fleet and to pay the necessary taxes. After the trauma of the Commonwealth, James, more than anyone else, made the Royal Navy into a national institution, one that commanded universal support. His lust for glory and prestige, the common currency of contemporary princes, added lustre and éclat to an otherwise rather plebeian institution.

James did not create the Royal Navy, but he directed a critical transformation in it – and his work would endure. He was the last admiral to command the English navy in battle on the basis of his social rank, army service or royal blood; and he was the architect of a professional career pattern for naval officers that ensured that all future leaders were drawn from the service, not imposed upon it. Future royal sailors needed to be professionals if they were to earn the respect of their peers.[80] While his political career was littered with errors and misjudgements, we should not condemn James's naval career because he failed as a king. The tasks are quite different. James, who lived and died an English patriot, reached his zenith the day he destroyed Obdam, his flagship and the Dutch fleet. He was a great admiral – pity about the rest.

4

SUPREME STRATEGIST

George Anson

1697–1762

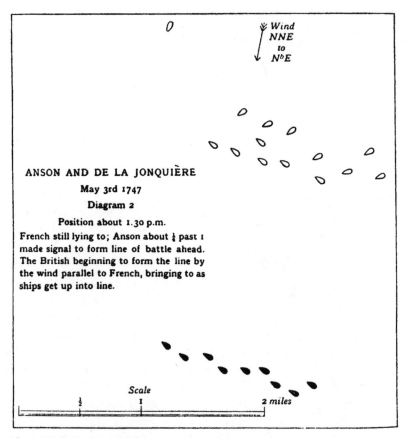

ANSON AND DE LA JONQUIÈRE

May 3rd 1747

Diagram 2

Position about 1.30 p.m.

French still lying to; Anson about ¼ past 1
made signal to form line of battle ahead.
The British beginning to form the line by
the wind parallel to French, bringing to as
ships get up into line.

Scale

½   1   2 miles

Wind
NNE
to
N^{b}E

Cape Finisterre was a classic encounter battle: Anson used the standard
line of battle to force the French to show their hand. They broke, and
he launched a dynamic pursuit

WHEN THE WARS OF LOUIS XIV ended in 1714, the Royal Navy was the undisputed master of the seas that washed the coasts of Europe. The French fleet had collapsed in 1704, the Dutch starved their navy to fund the land war, and the Spanish fleet was in ruins. The United Kingdom of Great Britain, established in 1707, possessed a mighty battle fleet that could discipline Spain and Russia in the same season without breaking sweat.

However, by the mid-eighteenth century Europe was only one of the continents on which the great powers struggled for dominance. The ability of the Royal Navy to influence events in America, Africa and Asia was limited by the design of its ships, its lack of overseas bases and the impact of diseases, whether tropical fevers or the humble but horrific mariner's complaint of scurvy. Moreover, the British did not want to rule the world, only to open its markets for trade. After 1714 British taxpayers funded an unrivalled battle fleet, but it did not develop into a global instrument. James, Duke of York had seen the need, but his horizons were limited. In the 1730s the temptation of making war on Spain in order to seize her trade finally got the better of Parliament. War was declared, ostensibly over the pickled ear of Richard Jenkins, a merchant ship captain who claimed that the appendage had been sliced off by Spanish coastguards in the West Indies. Having decided to go to war, Britain needed a global strategy to attack the Spaniards wherever their commerce could be redirected into British hands.

The business of naval command, as opposed to the far more complex business of seamanship, had not proved unduly difficult for Charles Howard, Robert Blake or James Stuart. Their main concern had been to secure sufficient authority to make the will of the admiral prevail. Tactics remained simple: it was largely a question of setting an example and ensuring it was followed – effective leadership based on human engagement. All three set their men a powerful example of aggression, courage and resolution. These were officerlike but not specifically 'naval' attributes. They expected to be followed, and used their authority, however derived, to secure this result. All three took a prominent role in the administration of the fleet, the appointment of officers, the provision of stores and the care of the seamen, the critical instrument in any successful navy.

James created a professional navy of career officers, with commissioned rank being determined by examination; promotion to captain by ability, favour or opportunity; and from captain to admiral by a combination of selection and seniority. In this service there were no openings for amateurs, however well connected. Instead, career officers jealously preserved their rights and privileges and developed their own patronage networks. Eighteenth-century carers were made or marred by patrons.

A New Career Path

George Anson was the first professional naval officer to rise to greatness through the new career structure. While earlier professionals proved brave and capable, he was the first to elevate the art of the admiral in British service to the strategic plane. He did so by mastering every aspect of the profession: after his first heroic achievement none could doubt his skill or his durability. He also understood that only by operating at the highest levels, in the Cabinet itself, could he hope to educate the politicians who directed the navy in war and funded it in peace.

Anson was born on 23 April 1697 in the county of Staffordshire. His great-grandfather was a barrister who had entered the rural elite by purchasing the manor of Shugborough, and the family retained powerful links with the law. Anson's uncle Thomas Parker, later the first Lord Macclesfield, was Lord Chief Justice and then Lord Chancellor between 1710 and 1725, the critical period of Anson's career. These posts gave Macclesfield Cabinet-level access to the political head of the navy. Macclesfield was also a prominent amateur astronomer, and his son George, Anson's exact contemporary, devoted his life to the subject, supporting the decision to abandon the old Julian calendar for the Gregorian in September 1752, thus bringing Britain into line with the rest of Europe, with the supposed sacrifice of eleven days.

How far this astronomical connection explains Anson's navigational skill is uncertain, but family ties were close. Another facet of the legal connection came when the Anson family committed their fortunes to the Hanoverian dynasty in 1714, unlike many of their Staffordshire neighbours, who favoured the Stuarts. The connection between loyalty, service and reward was clear: the winners prospered. As a second son, Anson entered the navy in 1712, but excellent political connections and ability ensured him almost continuous employment from 1714 onwards. Admiral Sir John Norris promoted him into a vacant lieutenancy in the Baltic in 1716, and he fought the Spanish at Cape Passaro in 1718 under Admiral Sir George Byng, who took him onto the flagship – a sure sign of solid connections.

In 1722 Anson received his first command, cruising in the North Sea against smugglers; in 1724 he became captain of the frigate *Scarborough*, a station ship on the coast of South Carolina, where he spent six years escorting convoys to the Bahamas, chasing pirates and protecting illegal British trade with Spanish Florida.[1] One local found Anson polite, well bred and astute enough to avoid taking sides in local squabbles. He loved music, but neither danced nor swore, which was somewhat surprising, given that 'he loves his bottle'.[2] His enthusiasm for alcohol may have helped to keep him alive on his most famous voyage; it may also have been responsible for his death at the age of sixty-five – not that heavy drinking was considered either unusual or reprehensible in the early eighteenth century. Nor did drink interfere with his career at the card table, where he played for high stakes, and with astonishing success. He used his winnings to fund extensive land purchases around Charleston and further afield, buying twelve thousand acres on his first tour in the colony. He gave his name to a street and a settlement that later become part of suburban Charleston. By investing his winnings, prize money and profits in local property and shipping, he built strong connections with the local elite.[3] At the same time, his local knowledge was valued back in Britain; after paying off his ship he returned to the Carolinas in 1732 in the *Squirrel*, spending another three years there and continuing to purchase land.⁴ It is revealing that in 1730 he gave his London address as the Middle Temple: lawyers and relatives were the bedrock of his career. Although Macclesfield had been impeached and driven from office in 1725, just after Anson's career had been made, family and professional links were sustained by his protégé Philip Yorke. Meanwhile, Macclesfield's nephew Sir Thomas Parker, Chief Baron of the Exchequer, would sustain the naval connection: his grandsons John Jervis and William Parker both feature in this book.

While other officers, like Byng's son John, spent their days on the flagship, relying on the admiral to make the decisions, Anson was out on his own from the age of twenty-seven, working on the frontier of Empire, where war, peace and piracy were the norm. Anson rose to the challenge while his mind and body were still flexible, and his American service equipped him for independent command: he had to make his own decisions and keep his ship in order for years on end. His success as a card sharp offers other insights into his character: the inscrutable, poker-faced exterior that he would show to the world clearly masked a shrewd, calculating intellect with an eye for the main chance. There was more than a hint of the lawyer about his public performance; later this reserve would become the 'mask of command' that defined his leadership. He went to war at the age of forty-three, demonstrating remarkable leadership in the face of an apparently endless succession of natural disasters and human failures. His cool determined presence was the key to the survival, let alone the success, of the expedition. By comparison, when John Byng was tested in command, he was found to be wanting, and paid the heaviest price for his failure.⁵

Anson knew what he wanted – land and wealth – and he seized every opportunity to secure them. After two years ashore, his first since joining the navy, Anson returned to sea in 1737 as captain of HMS *Centurion*, a sixty-gun ship protecting British trade on the coast of West Africa, before sailing for the West Indies and reaching England again in 1739. These were profitable but unglamorous posts, suggesting that Anson was a competent professional who preferred a lucrative peacetime side-show to half-pay or occasional fleet service. He also avoided lengthy service in the West Indies, quite literally the graveyard of many a promising naval career. He benefited from the patronage of Admiral Norris, the dominant sea officer of the era, and when the time came he found another prominent patron in his uncle's protégé Yorke, who would later become Lord Chancellor Hardwicke.[6]

Wartime Command

When war broke out in 1739, Anson's professionalism and effective networking was rewarded with a high-risk appointment, given by a Cabinet that included Lord Hardwicke. Anson seized the opportunity to secure fame, fortune and favour: he needed a 'good war', one that allowed him to advance onto the admirals' list in time to reap a golden harvest from the sea. War with Spain was about to be declared by a nation hungry for glory and profit and bored by endless years of peace and stability. Having adopted a simplistic quasi-Elizabethan strategy of large-scale, long-distance treasure raids into the Caribbean and the Pacific, the navy needed officers with experience of independent command. With the support of Norris and Hardwicke, the final piece of the jigsaw was provided by Admiral Sir Charles Wager, the First Sea Lord, who officially nominated him for the Pacific command. One of his ships was named *Wager*, and another was commanded by Norris's son. Anson was expected to equal the achievements of Drake, plundering the South American coast, capturing the Manila galleon and fomenting local risings against Spanish rule. This high-risk command required major feats of navigation, seamanship, endurance and, above all, leadership. Anson's eight-ship expedition circled the globe, often without reliable charts, in waters rarely traversed by Europeans. To make matters worse his five hundred 'troops' were either raw recruits or disabled veterans,[7] and long before the squadron left Spithead French intelligence had uncovered the plan and forewarned the Spanish.

The passage south was a trial: although Anson avoided the Spanish, typhus and dysentery, the common complaints of overcrowded, dirty ships filled with sick and dying soldiers quickly took hold. Because the squadron left England later than planned, it reached Cape Horn in the depths of winter, the worst possible moment for a passage to the west. It took Anson three months to beat a passage far enough west to enter the Pacific, his ships struggling against mountainous seas, a strong easterly current and ferocious winds that stripped the sails from their yards, snapped masts and strained every fibre of the men and ships to the absolute limit. In the midst of this elemental ordeal the men began to succumb to scurvy, the dread disease of the sea, brought on by vitamin C deficiency. Unable to understand, let alone prevent, this terrible enfeebling scourge, Anson could only watch as his men collapsed. Covered in ulcers, their teeth fell from rotten gums and old wounds reopened, before depression set in and they died, 'like so many rotten sheep'. The younger men, with larger natural stores of vitamin C, lasted longer,[8] but they were exhausted by endless work in freezing weather, unable to light their fires for hot food or dry clothes.

Logistical, elemental and infectious factors crippled Anson's force even as he entered the Pacific, but his determination seemed to reduce even the threat of scurvy. There was nothing on the circumnavigation that he had not seen before. By mid-June Anson and the *Centurion* reached the rendezvous at the Juan Fernandez Islands, better known as the haunt of Robinson Crusoe and his factual precursor Alexander Selkirk, with only the sloop *Tryal* in company. Later the storeship *Anna* and the fifty-gun *Gloucester* arrived, the latter so short of men that Anson's crew had to help her into the anchorage. Of the other three ships, the fifty-gun *Severn* and the forty-gun *Pearl* had turned back; the storeship *Wager* made it into the Pacific, only to be wrecked on the Chilean coast, depriving Anson of his field artillery and most of his 'soldiers'.

At this juncture Anson might have been forgiven for simply turning back: half his ships, and more than half the crew of the ships that remained, had been lost. With few soldiers and no field artillery he could not conduct any significant landing operations on the South American coast. However, his leadership had been proved: those ships that remained in company – and he had done all that was humanly possible to ensure that the squadron kept together – had fought their way through seemingly impossible circumstances to make it to the rendezvous. Once they lost contact with his pendant, the other ships seemed to lose the will to continue or the wit to act wisely.

Arriving at Juan Fernandez, Anson and his officers had to work alongside the crew to get the ships into the anchorage and the invalids ashore. Great leaders can let down the barriers of rank and dignity that are vital to the status of those who lack their natural authority. Having refreshed and restored his ships, and the 335 men who remained from the original 961, Anson headed for the Chilean coast, where he captured some unsuspecting Spanish vessels and sacked the small Peruvian town of Paita. Moving up to Acapulco, to attempt the Manila galleon, he was disappointed to find her already in port and the town far too strong for his depleted forces. With the voyage beginning to prosper, the men began to mutter about the distribution of prize money, expecting that Anson would act like the buccaneers of old and give them their share in cash. Hearing rumours of discontent, Anson called the men on deck and explained to them that in the navy things were done differently. Their rights were protected by an Act of Parliament, and all would get their fair share. At the same time, he made small but effective concessions to ensure that no one felt left out of the sudden treasure bonanza.[9]

After a second harrowing passage, this time across the Pacific, the *Centurion* arrived at the island of Tinian in late August 1742. She was alone: the other ships had been burnt and abandoned, lacking men even to sail them, let alone keep them seaworthy. Many more men had died, and the scurvy-stricken invalids once again had to be helped ashore by Anson and his officers; Anson himself took the lead in tending them. Fresh fruit and vegetables, fresh water and fresh meat restored most of the survivors to a semblance of health, but the ship too was showing signs of distress, and it would be difficult to effect repairs on a small island with so few men. Although afflicted with scorbutic symptoms himself, Anson tenaciously clung to his post on board ship while most of the men went ashore, and worked alongside his crew on vital repairs. Soon after he took his turn ashore, the ship was blown out of the anchorage and disappeared for nineteen days. Desperate attempts were made to rebuild a small Spanish vessel to carry the men, but the *Centurion* had survived, and Lieutenant Philip Saumarez and his tiny crew managed to bring her back. The sense of relief when she was sighted was overwhelming: 'For the first time Anson's famed reserve broke as he threw down his axe and rushed down to the water's edge with his men "in a kind of frenzy".'[10]

He soon recovered his composure, however, and resumed the mask of command. In early November the *Centurion* reached Macao, centre of the Portuguese China trade. Here he found the craftsmen to repair his leaky, battered ship and a chance to catch up on European news. To his consternation he found not one word from the Admiralty, nor a foot of rope for repairs. Although he maintained the dignity and composure expected of a commodore, both to reassure his men and to secure the necessary support from Chinese authorities who found a western warship both novel and frightening, Anson was desperately trying to salvage something from a disaster. If he returned home now, the trifling fund of prize stowed in the *Centurion*'s hold would appear ridiculous when set against the limitless expectations of those who sent him. His career would be over.

There was one chance to redeem the expedition. He would sail back to the Philippines and capture the legendary Acapulco galleon, loaded with silver and treasure that lubricated the Spanish end of the Chinese trade system. It was obvious to the Europeans at Canton that this option would be attractive to Anson: the French and Spanish bent their efforts to block his departure, while the English East India Company did little to help. However, the *Centurion*'s gun deck of twenty-four-pounders proved a persuasive diplomatic tool in discussions with the Chinese, who provided Anson with the food and craftsmen he needed. He also hired an international group of sailors to reinforce his feeble crew. Even with their help, however, he could muster no more than 227 men, a third of the ship's proper complement.

On 19 April 1743 the *Centurion* left Macao, Anson having done all he could to persuade the Chinese and the Europeans that he was going back to England. At Canton he had obtained vital intelligence on the Acapulco galleon from a drunken Englishman, once in Spanish pay. Expecting to meet two galleons, both with large crews, Anson was wagering his career on a battle. He gave his men the news in a characteristically short, factual speech. It was well received: the crew stood to become very rich, and having survived this catastrophic expedition must have believed themselves immortal. Once at sea Anson headed for Cape Espiritu Santo on the island of Samar, the galleon's regular landfall, and drilled the crew for battle. A month later *Nuestra Señora de Covadonga*, the 'prize of all the oceans', appeared. Unable to escape, the Spanish ship was forced to fight, but a merchant ship, however big, even with nearly three times as many men on board, could offer little effective resistance to a powerful sixty-gun warship. After ninety minutes of unequal combat, she surrendered, her officers mown down by musketry from the *Centurion*'s tops, her hull shattered by twenty-four-pounder shot.[11] By the close of 20 June Anson had 1.3 million Spanish pieces of eight, thirty-five thousand ounces of silver, and many other treasures. He had also gained one more opportunity to show his steely mien to the world: at the height of the action, a junior officer rushed onto the quarterdeck, breathless and panic-stricken, shouting that a fire had broken out below decks. Anson ignored this improper, rude outburst until he had finished giving orders to another officer. Then he rebuked the young man for failing to observe proper procedure, and only then ordered him below to put out the fire. Throughout the action Anson was in his proper place, standing calmly on the quarterdeck to direct the battle, in clear sight of friend and foe alike. Covered in half-burnt powder and smoke, Anson needed all his natural authority to overcome the disadvantage of looking like a chimney sweep.[12]

A month later Anson led his prize into Canton Roads. Exuding the confidence of a winner, he was prepared to stand on his dignity, riding roughshod over the local sensitivities that oiled the path of Eastern commerce. Even so, he experienced further problems with Chinese officials: it took five months to land his prisoners, sell the prize and store the *Centurion* for the passage home. She departed on 15 December 1743, arriving at Spithead on 15 June 1744. Anson was one of only 188 survivors from the original crew of the four ships that had reached Juan Fernandez, although a few officers had sailed home from Canton the previous year. The British sailors were assisted by seafarers from eighteen countries, ranging from Scandinavians to natives of Guam. This was leadership on a heroic scale.

Even the timing of Anson's return was fortunate: the navy desperately needed a success after a botched battle off Toulon, where Richard Norris, the original captain of the *Gloucester*, had disgraced himself, his venerable father and the service by his cowardice.[13] The political elite hurried to embrace Anson, but it was to Lord Hardwicke that he wrote the day before his arrival, explaining that much more might have been achieved if the squadron had reached the Pacific in good order; he hoped that he still enjoyed 'Your Lordship's favour and protection'.[14]

Establishing a Power Base

While it would be the political influence of the Pulteney dynasty that secured him a seat in Parliament for the Yorkshire constituency of Hedon in December 1744,[15] Anson was quick to link his fortunes with those of Hardwicke, who was politically astute and had the ear of the King. It was doubtless on Hardwicke's advice that Anson rebuffed an attempt by the government to curry his favour. Instead, he basked in the glory of a great procession that took thirty-two wagonloads of his treasure through the streets of London to the Tower, to be re-coined into shillings marked 'Lima'. Anson's share of the proceeds came to approximately £91,000; it is difficult to translate this into today's values, but for purposes of comparison his pay for the three-year command amounted to £719.[16] He had won the naval lottery.

Anson quickly used his money to create his own political power base – a vital step for any ambitious officer in an age when politics, preferment and profit were dominated by factional interests. He invested heavily in buying control of Lichfield, the nearest constituency to the family seat at Shugborough, and in 1747 nominated Captain Charles Saunders, but found his time so heavily taken up with the Staffordshire county election that the electorate did not follow his wishes. Instead, he used £20,000 of his own money to buy both seats at Hedon, and later secured his brother's return for Lichfield.[17]

Once he had used the political and financial rewards of success to build a power base, he resumed his true character: quiet, thoughtful and modest. Nothing he did after 1744 would match the notoriety of the circumnavigation, although almost everything he did far surpassed the voyage in real merit.

The circumnavigation spread Anson's fame throughout the country and beyond, and inevitably attracted immense public interest: narratives based on hearsay, survivors' tales and guesswork soon appeared to satisfy a sensation-starved market. Anson himself did not write an account of the voyage, instead hiring his chaplain Richard Walter to draft a book which appeared in 1748, after author Benjamin Robins 'had polished it into an acceptable form'. It became an instant bestseller, remaining in print to this day and helping to cement the image of an imperturbable Anson into the global consciousness as translations spread across the world. This was clearly the impression Anson wished to create, since he paid Robins £1,000 for his efforts. The book advocated further Pacific voyages to follow in Anson's footsteps, profiting from the evidence the text provided for would-be navigators of the great southern ocean. Yet the document conveyed only the public Anson: nothing emerged of the private human being, and even his officers did not penetrate the mask of command.[18]

Like any great leader, Anson was anxious to reward his followers: he had promoted many of the officers during the circumnavigation, and arrived home expecting the Admiralty to confirm his promotions.[19] He himself was promoted on his return to the rank of Rear Admiral, one of only twenty-one flag officers, yet when the Admiralty refused to confirm the promotion of Piercy Brett to captain, Anson showed his true worth as a leader, sending back the King's commission as something 'he could not accept with honour' while the promotions he had made were refused.[20]

This bold gesture told Anson's followers that he would sacrifice himself to serve their interests. They, in turn, would do their utmost to serve him, and their loyalty and courage would eventually make the task of command that much easier.[21] In the short term, however, he had put his career at risk: his commission was disallowed, and he was placed on half pay at the end of June 1744 by a Board of Admiralty that lacked the sense to acknowledge their error. Fortunately, leading political figures were wiser, assiduously courting Anson's support. When the government was reconstructed in December 1744, he joined the Duke of Bedford's Admiralty Board, and in April 1745 he received a belated double promotion to Rear Admiral of the White. By that stage, Anson had added political consequence to his portfolio, although he never troubled either the House of Commons or the House of Lords with his opinions in a parliamentary career spanning fifteen years.

Anson's true vindication came in 1745, when Piercy Brett defeated the squadron carrying the Jacobite 'Young Pretender', James II's grandson, to Scotland: while 'Bonnie Prince Charlie' had landed, he had done so without the bulk of his men and money. By advocating Brett's promotion, Anson was rewarding proven quality, not political convenience: he had rebuffed the government on a matter of professional principle, not personal pride. But he could afford to stand on principles because he was rich and had his own power base.

Upon joining the Admiralty Board, Anson immediately assumed a leading role. Bedford himself attended infrequently, although he expected to be kept informed, forcing a reluctant Anson to write.[22] Anson and Lord Sandwich, who was Bedford's deputy, soon formed a close and mutually beneficial partnership. Sandwich considered that Anson's expertise and his energy made 'a perfect union both in our private and public designs . . . and I have no doubt that he can [not] have any objection to acting with me in this capacity'.[23] Anson had indeed made it clear to Bedford that he would be happy to work under Sandwich.[24]

Return to Sea

Anson's partnership with Sandwich allowed him to leave the office secure in the knowledge that his patron would safeguard his interests. This was critical, for in the current political atmosphere only officers with powerful patrons could hope to hold their commands.[25] Anson combined a seat on the Board with command of naval forces in the English Channel, which he developed into the 'Western Squadron', the basis of British success in the French wars of the next seventy years. Because the prevailing winds in the western approaches to the English Channel come from the south-west and neither France nor Spain had a deep-water naval base inside the Channel, a powerful force stationed to the west of Cape Ushant and Cape Finisterre could intercept any invasion attempt aimed at England or Ireland, cover British shipping inbound and outbound, and attack hostile shipping. Anson did not initiate the process, but he drew it to a conclusion in July 1746, bringing the various Channel squadrons under his own command to carry it into effect.[26] His first sortie failed – a French convoy returning from Canada was warned of his presence – but he did not abandon the system, merely adding more frigates to the squadron to widen the sweep of his vision.

In spring 1747 Anson took the Western Squadron to sea with a clear remit:

Cruise on such station or stations you shall judge proper (according to the intelligence you have, or may receive) for intercepting and destroying the ships of the enemy, their convoys outward and homeward bound, and for suppressing their privateers, and annoying their trade, and for protecting the trade of His Majesty's subjects.[27]

That he had largely drafted the orders made their execution that much more certain. Anson had good intelligence of French plans, and put to sea a month before their convoys sailed, having cleaned the hulls of his own ships. He kept his fleet of fourteen battleships concentrated, ready for battle.

Aware that the existing tactical and signalling systems were ill-suited to the conduct of a fluid battle, Anson introduced additional signals to refine the ability to convey his orders to the fleet.[28] He used every day at sea to drill his ships and squadron, expecting high standards in combat. Nor was he entirely satisfied with the results. He also called his captains together for verbal briefings. Rear Admiral Peter Warren, his second-in-command, reported Anson giving 'directions [of] what he believed would be right for them to do, supposing they should not be able to see, or he to change his signals'.[29] In the event he abandoned the line, sacrosanct since the time of James, Duke of York, for the 'general chase' once the enemy broke and fled. This demonstrated an unusual degree of confidence in his subordinates and showed that he had learnt from the example of Cape Passaro. To ensure the battle was decisive, Anson insisted that his ships engage at very close range, his favourite distance being pistol shot, about twenty-five metres.

With fresh intelligence and a number of scouting frigates, Anson increased his chance of intercepting the enemy amid the vast, trackless wastes of the ocean. When the Marquis de la Jonquière's convoy was sighted off Cape Ortegal, soon after dawn on 3 May, the French commander elected to form a line of battle, adding his large East Indiamen to the warships to allow the convoys he was escorting time to scatter. By 13.00 the English were within three miles of the French line, which was patently inferior in size and firepower. Anson consulted Warren by speaking trumpet, but rejected his advice to launch an immediate attack without forming a line. Anson was not going to take any chances. Not only would it be improper to engage an enemy formed in a line of battle in any other formation, he could also see that the French were only putting on a bold front. Anson spent the next two hours forming a line, and his judgement proved to be sound: the French maintained a reasonable line while the English were disordered, but when Anson's line of battle bore down to attack, two of the Indiamen broke away, forcing de la Jonquière to abandon his pretence and flee after the convoy. Anson immediately hauled down the signal for the line of battle and hoisted one for a 'general chase'. The line of battle had served its purpose, breaking the enemy's mutually supportive formation. It could be replaced by individual pursuit, in which the faster ships were expected to catch and cripple the enemy vessels, before passing on to attack the next ahead. The slower vessels would finish off the disabled French ships. By 16.00 the leading English ships were in action, led by the *Centurion*. Initially they were outnumbered, but within the hour the numbers evened out. Soon the hindmost French ships began to surrender. Anson's confidence in his captains was well merited. By 18.00, when his sluggish flagship, the ninety-gun three-decker *Prince George* arrived on the scene, the battle was all but over.

At the end of the day, Anson had taken six warships and three large Indiamen. In a move that demonstrated his strategic maturity, he had detached two small ships and a sloop to keep contact with the convoy soon after the battle began. Confident he would win, Anson anticipated harvesting the fruits of success. Three more ships were detached once the battle finished, and the next day eighteen out of thirty-three French merchant ships were taken.[30] The French officers 'did their duty well, and lost their ships with honour, scarce any of them striking their colours till their ships were dismasted'.[31] They paid a heavy price, with over two hundred casualties on the two biggest ships. The French ships were richly laden, providing Anson with another prize windfall of £63,000.[32] Though Anson had been hampered by his sluggish flagship and was unable to lead the fleet in person, his reliance on flag signals, doctrine and training to ensure his orders were followed was highly successful, as Peter Warren told the Duke of Bedford:

In my life I never served with more pleasure, nor saw half such pains taken to discipline the fleet. While I have the honour to continue in it, I will endeavour to follow his example, however short I may fall of it, and could wish to be commanded by him rather than command myself.[33]

In truth Anson's tactics were essentially the same as those George Byng had used at Cape Passaro, but he had carefully refined the *Instructions and Signals*, trained his officers and laid the foundations for the mission-analysis style of command that favoured dynamic, aggressive forces. He did not let rules, precedent or the temptation of the safe option restrict the full development of the Royal Navy's fighting power. The decentralised, permissive tactical system he pioneered would be used to great effect by his successors, notably Edward Hawke. Both men knew how to balance the close-range fighting power of a well-handled line of battle with the open-order pursuit of a broken enemy.[34] It was in this second phase of battle that Anson translated tactical success into strategic effect. He knew that the purpose of battle was the destruction of the enemy fleet, and then the annihilation of any merchant shipping or military transports that it was escorting.

Anson's approach to the art of war was revealed a week after the battle, when he sat down in the cabin of the *Prince George* to report his success to the Duke of Bedford, First Lord of the Admiralty:

My Lord Duke,

I know your Grace will have great satisfaction in hearing that anything is done to the disadvantage of the enemy, and especially that it has fallen to the lot of one who has long been patronised and honoured with your friendship; and therefore the 3rd of May gave me the most sensible pleasure I ever felt, when I came up with a squadron of French ships, consisting of five ships of the line, and two frigates of 44 guns. They were going upon two expeditions, one to India, the other to America, and would have done much mischief to this country if they had succeeded, which is effectually prevented, having now in my possession the five largest men of war, and four of their richest India ships; and I am in great hopes that the *Yarmouth*, *Monmouth* and *Nottingham*, which I detached to pursue their transports and merchant ships, which are 30 in number, will destroy them all.

The enemy's ships behaved well; but I could plainly perceive that my ships made a much hotter fire, and much more regular than theirs, when they had a superior number, which they had in the beginning, before the ships in the rear could get up. Your Grace will be much concerned to hear that Captain Grenville died an hour after his leg was cut off above the knee: he was by much the cleverest officer I ever saw. Boscawen got a shot in the shoulder, but is almost well; his behaviour in the action pleased me, and I hope your Lordship will make him a rear admiral. As *Defiance* is vacant, I should be obliged to your Grace if you would give her to Captain Bentley, who has been my captain this cruise, and is very deserving of a cruising ship. How cordially I have cursed the Dutch, who, I find (by the French General Jonquière) prevented his whole fleet falling into my hands the last winter, when he came from Chibaton by one of their vessels informing him he was within 20 leagues of me, and must see me the next morning, upon which he altered his course, and steered for Rochfort. However I have caught him at the rebound, and ought to be satisfied, but wish he had had a little more strength, though this is the best strike that has been made upon the French since La Hougue; and I am pleased that something has been done by the fleet whilst your Grace has presided over us; and if you quit us, which I never think of without uneasiness, Lord Sandwich will come to a Board not quite sunk in its credit. He is the only person in the kingdom, after your Grace, that I will serve under: if he continues there seven years, and I live as long, I will never quit him, for I esteem him much. There was £200,000 in specie on board the French ships, and they say the equipping these expeditions cost a million and half sterling. The *Invincible* is a prodigious fine ship, and vastly larger; I think she is longer than any ship in our fleet, and quite new, having made only one voyage. I hope the Duchess is dismissed from her office of private secretary, and that you both enjoy as perfect health and happiness as is the wish of, & &

G. Anson.

P. S. If your Grace has no commands for me at Portsmouth, I should be glad to wait on you in town. I send my old acquaintance Captain Dennis express with these letters; he began the action in the *Centurion*, and behaved extremely well in it after his topmasts were shot away.[35]

For a man notoriously reluctant to put pen to paper this was a very full report. There was not one word about his own contribution to the success, how he located the French, the tactics he chose, or the role of his flagship in the battle: instead, we find a clear appreciation of why the English won ('a much hotter fire'), of the significance of the victory and the fact that he had ordered a pursuit. He also advanced the claims of his officers for promotion and preferment, and regretted the loss of an esteemed protégé, who also happened to be the younger brother of the Cabinet minister Richard, Earl Temple. Then he analysed French strategy and the merits of the largest of his prizes, a ship that would inspire major improvements in English design during his stewardship of the Admiralty. In all this, Anson's political loyalties shone through.

While Warren had been struck by his professional leadership, Anson found the experience pregnant with ideas for improvement. He requested that a mast of every size used by his squadron be kept in store, ready to install at Plymouth. The shortage of large sticks made this impossible.[36] He also lamented the slow proceedings of the yard: 'Tho' Mr. Warren and I are working from day light till it is dark the delays are such from the bad regulation of the Dock Yards, and the people that are worn out in Office there that it is impossible to do things with the dispatch I could wish.'[37] Soon afterwards the Admiralty Board took the revolutionary step of visiting the dockyards and inspecting the officers, workmen and procedures.

After the battle, Anson retuned to London in time to be ennobled as Baron Anson of Soberton in Hampshire, using the name of his new estate in the Meon Valley, north of Portsmouth. Having codified his combat experience into further signals and instructions, Anson left Warren and then the junior admiral Edward Hawke to command the squadron. Hawke used Anson's methods, systems and ships to win a second major convoy battle soon afterwards, adding to Anson's prize fund and wiping out the last remnants of the French ocean-going navy. In these two battles the Royal Navy took twenty-one French warships and a significant part of France's overseas shipping. The effect was ruinous for the French economy, helping to secure a tolerable peace for Britain in 1748.

Administrative Advances

In February 1748, with the war coming to an end, Bedford left the Admiralty. Sandwich became First Lord, and Anson was happy to serve a politician who shared many of his own concerns. They formed a powerful team, excelling in their distinct spheres of expertise and together offering perhaps the most effective naval leadership of the century. Although he accepted the authority of the politician, Anson was quick to assert his superior standing against the other naval lord, Vere Beauclerk, who did not long remain in post.[38] Much of Anson's work at the Admiralty involved upholding authority and improving procedures. He was not especially radical in his attitude, preferring to find solutions in changing personnel, rather than endlessly tinkering with regulations. He tightened up the rank structure and introduced an official uniform for officers in 1748, while the 1749 Navy Bill provided naval courts martial with fixed penalties for specific offences – a measure that would come back to haunt him a decade later. Recognising that the poor performance of the navy in the war thus far reflected badly on those admirals who had been employed, many of whom had reached an advanced age, Anson made it possible for the Admiralty to promote captains not required for flag rank into retirement and speed the advancement of able men. He also used the temporary rank of commodore to employ bright young captains in squadron command. Parliament was unwilling to go further than this towards reforming the careers of officers or creating a reserve of seamen.

While seeking to improve the lives of the navy's officers and men, the Admiralty also paid attention to the ships they served in. The basic concepts that informed the design of Royal Navy warships that were in service in 1740 had changed little since the time of James II. The ships were overcrowded with guns, short of space, not desperately seaworthy and found it difficult to open their lower-deck gunports in a seaway. A good investment for a fleet fighting between the Thames and Texel, they lacked the endurance, stowage, seaworthiness and speed for global conflict. Spanish and French ships of the line taken in battle were significantly larger, more weatherly and far less crowded. French frigates, cruising vessels not large enough for the line of battle, also possessed significant advantages over the old-fashioned English cruisers. Yet the English ships were tougher, more durable and more economical in service than their fragile adversaries. By combining the large, fine hull forms of the French ships with stout English construction methods, it should have been possible to produce a superior ship, but conservative design, restricted dimensions and the dead hand of precedent prevented such changes taking place in the lifetime of the old Surveyor of the Navy, Sir Jacob Acworth. In the meantime, Anson had secured a number of French prizes for inspection, and the example they provided began to revitalise the design process.

The fundamental stumbling block was that decisions on ship design resided with the Navy Board, which operated as a quasi-independent body on Tower Hill. When Acworth died in 1749, Sandwich effected a complete change at the Board, retiring the other old-stager, Controller Richard Haddock. Having reshaped the administrative body to reflect his ideas, Sandwich then revolutionised the way the Admiralty worked by taking the Board to the dockyards on a tour of inspection. The pretext for this innovation was the yards' slow execution of work, which he blamed on slack management or insufficient labour. Such visits ensured the Admiralty would no longer have to defer to the Navy Board's greater practical knowledge: they could respond from first-hand observation. The visits were instructive, revealing that the yards were not well managed: old officers and old workmen did not make for speed or zeal, and pay by the day provided no incentive for alacrity. However, the tense political relationship between the two Boards made it difficult to achieve immediate change: the Navy Board was able to obstruct, ignore or confound many of the Admiralty's plans. In the long run, this struggle for supremacy would end with the abolition of the junior Board, as politicians sought to exert ever greater control over the navy's expenditure. But Anson's agenda was less radical: he simply wanted to exert control, without having to manage the navy's day-to-day administration. While Sandwich's reforms would have reduced the Navy Board to a mere office of business, when Anson became First Lord he preferred to improve relations, changing a few key office-holders but dropping many of Sandwich's contentious ideas.

In every case, Anson's contribution to remodelling the navy reflected practical insight and first-hand knowledge. He patronised Benjamin Slade, the master shipwright at Plymouth dockyard, whom he had met when the Western Squadron was in port for repairs. In 1747 Anson requested Bedford, then still the First Lord, to have Slade take off the hull lines of a captured French privateer, the *Tyger*, and use them to build two frigates: he did so because 'all our frigates sail wretchedly'.[39] Slade's work on the French prizes, and his dialogue with Anson, ensured that British frigate design soon improved. Their next project, the classic seventy-four-gun battleship, appeared just in time for the next war.

The harrowing experience of his first command informed many of Anson's decisions at the Admiralty. In 1755 he established the Marines, to ensure that no more regiments of invalids would be sent to sea. Once he had control of the levers of patronage, he rewarded all his Pacific followers, and other officers of outstanding professional merit, with a marked preference given to those who had distinguished themselves in action. Although he served at the Board more than on the quarterdeck, he explained to Hardwicke that 'The Command of a squadron at sea has always been my principal object and passion.'[40] He relished the challenge of training ships and squadrons, of improving and simplifying tactics, of outwitting the enemy in the endless game of cat-and-mouse that could make or mar attempts to intercept ships travelling on the broad oceans. Yet his success ashore demonstrated that he also 'had a talent for politics without having the appearance and inclinations of a politician'.[41]

For all his professional merit, the key to his continuation in office lay in the familial and personal relationship with Hardwicke, who in turn offered his political loyalty to the Duke of Newcastle: 'Your Grace asks what Lord Anson thinks? You know his value in his profession. He is a man of strict probity and honour, and with a little cultivating, you may keep him thoroughly connected with you.'[42] This network of patronage would pay dividends three years later. When a new First Lord was required, Anson's stock was sufficiently high for him to be offered the post.

Between the Wars

After the end of the Austrian War, Anson's career continued to follow the same ballistic trajectory: a full admiral in May 1749, he was appointed Vice Admiral of Great Britain in 1750, in effect making him the head of the service. His political position had been further cemented by his marriage on 25 April 1748 to Lady Elizabeth Yorke, the eldest daughter of his patron Lord Hardwicke. The wedding was conducted at Hardwicke's London home by the Archbishop of Canterbury. The bride's portion was a suitably grand £12,000 – not that this was necessary, for George Anson was already prodigiously wealthy. The newly married couple lived for four years in one of Hardwicke's properties, Carshalton House in Surrey; in 1752 they moved to Moor Park in Hertfordshire, where they could indulge Anson's passion for gardening and floriculture. Lady Anson was twenty-eight years younger than her husband, a mature fellow of fifty-one when he finally entered the blessed state of matrimony, and enjoyed the full round of social activity. This must have been something of a trial for her reclusive husband, but he loved her deeply. Elizabeth was very much her father's daughter, taking a lively interest in politics and her husband's brilliant career. She conducted some of his correspondence, even on highly sensitive political issues.[43] Theirs was a relationship of mutual esteem based on intellectual equality. To their enormous regret, there were no children, so the estate – and the family estate, for Anson's elder brother was also childless – would pass to his sister's son.

The scurrilous diarist Horace Walpole observed:

Lord Anson was reserved and proud, and so ignorant of the world that Sir Charles Williams said 'he had been round it, but never in it.' Lady Townsend said he was in the same situation with regard to his wife. He had been strictly united with the Duke of Bedford and Lord Sandwich, but not having the same command of his ambition that he had of his other passions, he has not been able to refuse the offer of the chancellor's daughter, nor the direction of the Admiralty.[44]

For all his malice and scorn, Walpole was not without insight. He presented Anson as a cool, detached figure whose only weakness was the ambition to command the navy, but could not resist also making him the butt of a scandalous rumour. Whatever the truth of Lady Townsend's quip, the political value of Anson's marriage was obvious. He could lead the navy far more effectively from within Hardwicke's network than as an independent, constantly struggling to build a political power base. The Lord Chancellor combined a mighty legal intellect with acute political skills that made him the first name in any Cabinet for two decades, a position that made his son-in-law well-nigh invulnerable to naval or political rivals. His position was further strengthened on his appointment as First Lord in June 1751 by his clever decision to reduce the naval estimates to peacetime levels, thus neatly removing naval policy from Cabinet consideration.

After a decade of design disappointments, Anson appointed Thomas Slade Surveyor of the Navy in 1755. Slade was an inspired selection: the seventy-four-gun ships he designed to Anson's specification were still the backbone of the fleet fifty years later,[45] while his frigates transformed the performance of British cruising and scouting vessels.[46] Slade provided the navy with the ships for a global conflict: strong, capacious, durable and fast. The ultimate expression of this inspired partnership achieved a lasting fame far in excess of the men who created her. At the heart of Portsmouth dockyard, the navy has retained HMS *Victory*, the fastest and most effective first-rate warship of the eighteenth century. Forty-three years after Anson's death, she was Horatio Nelson's flagship in the climactic battle that ended the age of fighting sail and provided the ultimate expression of leadership and command at sea. Before that she had carried the flags of several distinguished officers, from Anson's pupils Keppel and Howe to Nelson's mentors Hood and Jervis.

Before the end of 1755 Anson also took effective control of the

Navy Board. After decades spent opposing new ship designs and domination by the Admiralty, this body was reduced to subordination by the appointment as Controller of Charles Saunders, one of the charmed circle of circumnavigators, who ensured that it followed Anson's lead.[47] With this appointment Anson set the administration of the navy on a secure footing for the inevitable conflict with France. He demonstrated little interest in deeper reforms, however: he preferred to expand the fleet for war by ordering ships from commercial shipyards, rather than reforming or enlarging the Royal Dockyards. His motives were financial: any dockyard expansion would necessarily be permanent, costing a fortune to maintain after the war ended.

War

While the Treaty of Aix-la-Chapelle in 1748 had ended the fighting in Europe, the situation in the rest of the world was very different. In North America the treaty had been no more than a truce of mutual exhaustion, settling little and providing endless scope for further quarrels in this area where English and French colonies shared an immense, unmarked, fluid boundary, thinly populated by bold settlers and Native Americans. Low-level fighting steadily escalated, and in 1754 ministers decided to send reinforcements under General Braddock to resolve the situation. They also ordered the fleet to intercept the French troop convoy heading for Canada, without being certain if they meant to use force or start a war. In 1755 Braddock was ambushed and killed, his force annihilated; Edward Boscawen's squadron intercepted the French convoy off Newfoundland, but took only two ships.

Thoroughly frightened by their folly, the ministers decided that war was inevitable, sending the Western Squadron out to seize French merchant ships. That autumn many of France's scarce ocean-going seafarers found themselves detained at the pleasure of His Britannic Majesty King George II. The French navy never recovered from this devastating blow.

Yet the strains of mobilisation also proved awkward for the Royal Navy: there were simply not enough seaworthy ships to equip all the squadrons required to protect Britain, her trade and her global interests. Anson had underestimated the scale of the task, although he did set clear priorities. The French were assembling two invasion forces – one for England, the other for the English base at Minorca in the Balearic Islands – but English security and English trade took priority over a small island in the Mediterranean. The King and the Cabinet agreed with the First Lord's analysis that absolute priority had to be given to the Western Squadron under Admiral Hawke: 'I think it would be a dangerous measure to part with your naval strength from this country, which cannot be recalled if wanted, when I am strongly of the opinion that whenever the French intend anything in earnest their attack will be against this country.'[48]

Though Anson's advice appeared sensible, it had consequences. The Mediterranean fleet, under Admiral John Byng, did not sail on time, nor was it particularly well manned or equipped. When he arrived at Gibraltar on 2 May 1756, Byng discovered the French had already landed an army on Minorca and laid siege to Fort St Philip. Lacking Anson's iron will or sufficient natural buoyancy to rise to the challenge, Byng was already half beaten before he left Gibraltar. On 18 May he fought an inconclusive battle with a French fleet of roughly equal size covering the invasion. His tactics were reasonable, and against a less skilful opponent might have achieved the desired result, but his attempt to concentrate his own line against part of the French fleet was thwarted. After the engagement, Byng quickly assembled a council of war to validate his decision to retreat, claiming that Gibraltar was in danger. He made no effort to renew the engagement, contact the garrison or throw in supplies and reinforcements. Had he but hung around and sought out the French transports, he could have paralysed the siege. Even before the news of Byng's pusillanimous retreat reached London, the dismal tone of his correspondence prompted the Admiralty to send Sir Edward Hawke to relieve him. Byng reached England in late July to find himself at the centre of a storm: fellow naval officers were convinced that the man who had brought such shame and discredit on their service must be a coward. In truth Byng was a brave man but lacked the moral courage to meet the challenges of high command in war. A competent captain, he was lost without the guidance of higher authority.

As public anger rose to the boil, the ministers ordered a court martial, anxious to avoid their share of the blame, only to find themselves before an unparalleled political storm that October.

Newcastle, Hardwicke and Anson were the high-profile casualties.[49] William Pitt's administration had no reason to punish Byng, and appointed a friendly president to the court. However, the twelfth article of Anson's 1749 regulations included the offence that if an officer had failed to do his utmost to defeat the enemy, through cowardice, negligence or disaffection, then he shall suffer death. Byng had not done enough – not from cowardice or disaffection, but from negligence. He was duly convicted. Anson's code provided only one penalty: death. Although the court recommended clemency, King George II, the last monarch to lead the British army into battle, had a simple soldier's contempt for cowardice. When the First Lord of the Admiralty and the French author Voltaire publicly intervened, they sealed the unfortunate man's fate. He met his end with great dignity, shot by firing squad on his own quarterdeck – sacrificed, as Voltaire observed, *'pour encourager les autres'*.

Command is a high-risk activity, and for every George Anson there are many John Byngs, commanders who lack the killer instinct to make a success of the ultimate opportunity. Navies are among the hardest environments for commanders because they provide so few opportunities to test them, yet the stakes for failure could not be higher. While John Jellicoe was the one man who could have lost the First World War in an afternoon, several of his precursors were in situations little less important.

Anson was, in part, responsible for the debacle. He had decided how many ships to send with Byng; he set the priorities between the Western Squadron and the Mediterranean fleet. Furthermore, he had appointed Byng, although there were no real alternatives and he had no reason to doubt Byng's competence. However, he was not in office during the trial or execution of the unfortunate officer. Anson had taken a major decision, and he had made a mistake. In a modern system he might never have had another chance, but eighteenth-century Britain was not the modern world, and George Anson had a powerful father-in-law. He had also created a mighty fleet, the largest Britain had ever taken to war, and it was in unusually good condition. A careful, economical service administrator in peacetime, he found the golden mean between undue cost and ruinous parsimony.

Cabinet Minister

The creation of the Pitt–Newcastle coalition in July 1757 proved to be the turning point in Britain's war effort, allying the energetic strategic thinking of Pitt with the astute behind-the-scenes political management of the Duke of Newcastle. Yet without an effective and well-led navy, the politicians could not hope to translate their vision into campaigns and battles. Even so, Anson had to be pushed into the Cabinet by Hardwicke: after Minorca his public reputation had all but evaporated, and there were other options. When the King demurred at Pitt's first candidate for the Admiralty, Hardwicke urged that something must be done for Anson, and George was happy to have him back, making Anson's appointment a *sine qua non* for any ministry that emerged from the political chaos.[50] His position was not perhaps as strong as it had previously been. The following month, when Newcastle tried to place a civilian on the Board, Anson pressed for Admiral Hawke and threatened to resign, but eventually he gave way.[51]

Nonetheless, Hardwicke's political power play proved to be a masterstroke. The war that had lurched into being in 1756 was always going to be a global struggle between the nascent British and French colonial empires, but unlike in the war of 1740–8 the European arena did not operate to Britain's disadvantage. At Aix-la-Chapelle Britain had relinquished colonial success to recover the Austrian Netherlands (Belgium) from France, an essential exchange given the strategic threat posed by a French fleet based at Antwerp. In 1756 Austria and France were allies, but Britain and Austria were not at war so France could not use Antwerp for an invasion attempt. To make matters even easier for the British, their ally Frederick II of Prussia, supported by a powerful British/Hanoverian army, fought the continental powers of France, Austria and Russia to a standstill. British strategy, once the alarms of 1756–7 had passed, quickly shifted to the offensive, using economic warfare, colonial conquest and the seizure of offshore islands to cripple France. While Pitt provided the overarching vision and energy, British success ultimately depended on Anson's unique ability to see the world as a strategic entity and to exploit his experience. His membership of the inner War Cabinet made him a key figure in the development of strategy and the management of national resources. The Cabinet left the business of the navy to Anson, only discussing operations and ship numbers.[52] Anson ordered many new ships at the outbreak of war, notably the vital seventy-fours. With a steady supply of improved ships coming into service, the only limit on British naval power would be the continuing nightmare of manning the fleet.[53] Little wonder Anson took a professional interest in the welfare of the men, dealing with individual cases despite the fact that the Royal Navy would get through over 184,000 of them over the course of the war. The scarcity of men was invariably his biggest problem.[54]

Anson's return to office was not followed by an immediate run of success: 1757 was not a glorious year. 'I wish I could send your Lordship any agreeable news, but there seems to be a fatality in everything we undertake and that nothing succeeds,' he confessed to Hardwicke, referring to the botched amphibious operation against Rochefort. His only crumb of comfort was that 'the fleet having done well and all in their power gives me satisfaction', but 'not one event from the beginning of the war has come before us, that has not been unfortunate'.[55] He was furious that after so much effort had been put into preparing this operation, Hawke had tamely accepted the general's decision to give up, in direct violation of Anson's instructions.

In addition to his role in developing policy and strategy, Anson used his intimate knowledge of his profession to appoint highly capable officers to key commands. The disgrace of Minorca was not repeated. He chose men he knew and trusted, so that he could discuss the operations he planned in confidence. Since many of them would be conducting major strategic operations of war half a world away, this mutual trust was essential. Men who had been round the world with Anson had little trouble understanding what he wanted, however infrequently he wrote. If the fleet was to be used to maximum effect, it had to be directed by the mind of the admiral, and this would require every ship to be well trained and well led. He despised officers who tried to avoid unhealthy or difficult assignments; he suspected the motives of those claiming to be ill and took great pride in promoting those who had proved their worth in battle. In an age of patronage he was prepared to bend a little before the breeze emanating from the Duke of Newcastle, who depended on such vulgar calculations to keep the government in office, but he knew that political expediency and naval efficiency were incompatible, and had the expertise to make his point. When Newcastle pressed him to appoint an officer on political grounds, Anson refused:

I must now beg your Grace will seriously consider what must be the condition of your Fleet if these borough recommendations, which must be frequent are to be complied with; I wish it did not at this moment bring to my mind the misery poor Pocock, that excellent officer, suffer'd from the misbehaviour of captains of that cast, which has done more mischief to the public (which I know is the most favourite point with you) than the loss of a vote in the House of Commons. My constant method since I have had the honour of serving the King in the station I am in, has been to promote the lieutenants to command, whose ships have been successfully engaged upon equal terms with the enemy, without having any friend or recommendation; and in preference to all others, and this I would recommend to my successors if they would have a Fleet to depend on.[56]

The logic of the argument, the clarity of the expression and the power of the example – all traits one would expect of a lawyer – were irresistible. Nor was Anson prepared to trifle with administrative appointments: he rejected an attempt to reward a political nominee with a commissionership at the Victualling Office: 'his Lordship might as well have asked to have had him made a Captain of a man of war, that branch always having been filled with a seaman, instead of adding to the useless people that are already in that office'.[57]

Anson's attitude to patronage and the demands of the political world was intelligent and realistic. He held office in large part because of his own political connections, and knew exactly how the world worked: the 'simple sailor man' image he liked to project was no more than a smokescreen. With the not inconsiderable patronage of the Admiralty at his disposal, and significant personal influence in three boroughs, Anson was a political ally of the Duke of Newcastle,[58] as well as a superb administrator and strategist. Five of his circumnavigators served as Members of Parliament, reflecting Anson's concern to have reliable friends in the House.

Anson was an active political operator working with and, when necessary, through Hardwicke.[59] It was significant that when Pitt wanted to exert influence at the Admiralty he tended to approach Hardwicke, rather than Anson.[60] Anson also helped to maintain ministerial harmony by smoothing tensions that occurred between the two leading ministers.[61] He recognised that other officers would be politically active, but unlike the politicians he was perfectly capable of keeping the professional and political spheres distinct. He promoted and employed officers who opposed both the government and his regime at the Admiralty if they were men of ability, but he would not countenance rewarding the hopeless and incompetent with naval patronage. That patronage was controlled by the Admiralty, and should be used to improve the navy. This was a high charge, and he did not bend to any man. When George III wanted to make his brother a rear admiral, Anson was ready to resign.[62] When Anson died, the Duke of Newcastle's anxiety to retain access to Admiralty patronage spoke volumes.[63]

Despite his horror of paperwork, the business of naval administration was conducted with dispatch. He had seen the consequences of slack procedures at first hand in 1740, and did all in his power to prevent a repetition. It would be wrong to conclude from his long years at the Admiralty Board that Anson had given up the sea for strategy and politics. He never considered labour at the Admiralty anything more than drudgery, and longed to resume command of the fleet. In 1755 he had suggested to Newcastle that he should command the Western Squadron, the basis of British strategy, but in response the Duke 'asked me what was then to become of the Admiralty, I cannot say I think it would be the better for my absence, but I am certain I sacrifice the thing that would give me the greatest pleasure by being obliged to continue at it'.[64]

A Final Campaign

His opportunity eventually came in early 1758. After two disappointing campaigns, Hawke resigned his command over a trifling matter.[65] Anxious to keep the post open while the hot-tempered admiral recovered his composure, Anson assumed command that summer, with Hawke as his second. He soon had the fleet drilling, manoeuvring, chasing and forming lines of battle. He was somewhat surprised to find the squadron rather rusty in all these areas; in fairness to Hawke it must be stressed that there had been significant changes in ships and captains over the winter, so this was not a reflection of Hawke's leadership.[66] Anson put the fleet through his favoured programme of exercise and developed a new signal which directed that if the admiral hauled down the signal for the line of battle, all ships were to attack or pursue the nearest enemy vessel and bring it to close action. This concept Hawke refined and used to great effect the following year.[67]

Although he was delighted to be back at sea, Anson knew that his place was at the Board. He trusted Hawke, an outstanding fleet commander, but there was no one else in the kingdom who could lead the Admiralty, as Pitt and Newcastle soon realised.[68] Although brief, his return to sea command had raised his stock with the politicians and refreshed his spirits.

Anson necessarily took a close interest in the wider strategic patterns of the conflict. From the first crisis in 1755 Anson had been concerned that the French would attempt to invade the British Isles – a fear that played a major role in the Minorca fiasco. He was not prepared to send too many ships abroad while this threat was unresolved, to the annoyance of Pitt. This necessarily delayed offensive operations in the extra-European world.

In 1759 a suitably chastened Hawke resumed his post, just as his freshly drilled fleet became the pivot of British strategy. The campaigns of 1757 and 1758 had knocked away the outer defences of French Canada, exposing the key position at Quebec. While General Wolfe commanded the amphibious operation, and secured all the glory, it was Admiral Charles Saunders, a circumnavigator, who delivered his army to the city. Saunders' fleet was led down the St Lawrence river by men like John Jervis and James Cook. Unable to meet the attack on Canada, the French attempted a counterstroke in Europe, and with Belgium neutralised this could only be a full-scale invasion of England. The assembly of invasion shipping and the attempt to link the Toulon and Brest fleets, repeating the plan used in the days of James II and La Hougue, gave the British ample warning. Anson deployed his forces with a masterful combination of purpose and flexibility, leaving his admirals ample scope to use their judgement within broad strategic directions. This confident, permissive leadership paid dividends across the globe. Officers had the confidence to act on their own initiative, trusting Anson to support them.[69]

Anson had absolute faith in Edward Boscawen, sending him to watch Toulon with orders to stop the French fleet leaving the Mediterranean; the details were left to his discretion.[70] Boscawen intercepted the French in the Straits of Gibraltar. When they sought sanctuary in neutral Portuguese waters off Lagos on 18 August, he annihilated them, ignoring the feeble protests of Britain's oldest ally. Diplomats would have to smooth the ruffled feathers of the court at Lisbon: this was total war, and legal niceties were swept aside by the imperative demands of *force majeure*.

With a large part of their naval force destroyed, the French could have been forgiven had they abandoned the invasion, but instead they pressed ahead, more in desperation than hope. The fleet at Brest would have to escort the invasion shipping to Britain. In previous wars the British blockade of Brest had been a half-hearted, temporary affair, inadequate ships, foul weather and poor victuals limiting the fleet's ability to keep station on the exposed western tip of the Breton peninsula. This time the seamanship of the fleet, the courage of the officers and the example of Hawke enabled the fleet to remain on station far longer, bending before the storms but immediately returning to station once the elements had done their worst. Alarmed by evidence of scurvy in the fleet in 1758, Anson had organised a new victualling system. From mid-August 1759 victualling ships sailed out to the fleet rendezvous off Cape Ushant with live cattle, fresh vegetables, water and beer – a 'healthful drink' that Anson believed prevented scurvy.[71] Instead of returning to port to replenish perishable foodstuffs, the ships could remain on station, resupplied by a steady procession of merchant transports. The preference for fresh food is not hard to understand, but the cost and complexity of afloat logistics was justified by strategic imperatives.[72] The effect on the men's health was immediate and profound. On the day of battle, Hawke's twenty ships had no more than one man per ship sick – a major reason why he was able to win a great victory. Little wonder that James Lind had dedicated his pioneering *Treatise of the Scurvy* of 1753 to Anson.[73]

Although they remained in harbour all summer, the French suffered far more from disease than the British: epidemics of typhus and dysentery swept through the town, further reducing the scarce pool of naval manpower, while the British blockade cut off vital Baltic naval stores. Nor could France afford to keep the fleet and army waiting: the country was bankrupt, and the war in Europe was going as badly as the war in America. While the French invasion shipping assembled in Quiberon Bay, Anson began a sustained effort to chart the wild and dangerous coast. The French fleet finally put to sea in late November, after a gale had driven Hawke's force off station. They headed south to collect their transports, but were quickly located by Hawke's frigates. With Hawke in command, Anson had no doubt of the outcome, if only he could catch the enemy: 'As to fighting him, which is given out by the French, my Lord Anson treats that as the idlest of all notions.'[74] He could afford to be confident – with two powerful British squadrons in the Bay of Biscay, the French could not escape.

On 20 November Hawke sighted Admiral Conflans. With the enemy in full flight, Hawke ordered the fleet to chase without forming a line. The French crowded on sail, racing into the dangerous shoal waters of Quiberon Bay, hoping to escape. But Hawke followed and destroyed the French fleet as a fighting force. The war at sea was over: Anson's men, his ships and his strategy had triumphed. This defeat finished the French navy: its financial credit was ruined, and French sailors, like their English counterparts, would not fight and die for promissory notes. Anson's Western Squadron had locked up many French sailors before the war began, cut French access to Baltic naval stores, and finally destroyed the fleet. The French made no further efforts at sea for the remainder of the war,[75] and the French global empire soon fell to the British: Canada in 1760, the West Indies in 1760–1, and the European island of Belleisle in 1762, this last taken as a *quid pro quo* for Minorca. In 1760 the Royal Navy possessed 301 ships and eighty-five thousand men: having annihilated France, Anson's navy was still growing.

But at the very height of his success, and without warning, Anson's world fell apart. The cool exterior that had preserved him from personal scrutiny through storms off Cape Horn, battle with a Spanish galleon and the trials of the Minorca affair finally cracked. Nothing in his professional life had ever unsettled him; his distress was private, personal and overwhelming when his beloved wife died of a malignant fever on 1 June 1760. Lord Hardwicke, who lost a much-loved daughter, observed: 'The storm and passion of his grief, and the impression of his loss far exceeded what I could have imagined, especially from him, who has naturally a certain firmness and composure.'[76] With Elizabeth's death, a light went out in Anson's life that would never be rekindled. No man could have a larger share of earthly glory and riches, but he had nothing left to live for. Yet in the months that remained, Anson would bring the art of command to a new level of sophistication and power. Weighed down by grief and failing health, he spurred himself to one last effort.

George II died suddenly on 25 October 1760, heralding the gradual dissolution of the Pitt–Newcastle coalition. As befitted an officer, Anson remained at his post: it was his duty, and he had nothing else to do.[77] It might have been of some comfort to him to know that 'the King put great store by Anson's views' and deferred to his objections.[78] In August 1761 Anson went to sea for the last time, as Admiral of the Fleet, commanding a squadron dispatched to Stade to bring home George III's bride, Princess Charlotte of Mecklenburg-Strelitz. Circumnavigator Peter Dennis commanded the Royal Yacht and, despite some rough weather in the North Sea, the voyage passed off without incident.[79] The same year Anson supported the first experimental use of copper sheathing to preserve ships against the dread ravages of the ship-boring mollusc *teredo navalis*. This had the valuable side-effect of deterring the growth of weeds and other organisms, preserving the ship's speed. While it was introduced too late to have any effect on the Seven Years War, copper sheathing would prove vital to the naval effort in the next conflict.

In late 1761 the Cabinet rejected Pitt's call for a pre-emptive declaration of war against Spain. Anson, Hardwicke and Bedford were among the majority who doubted the wisdom of such a measure. Anson considered his fleet, now reduced to 288 ships and eighty thousand men, was stretched to the limit by the French war. With Pitt gone, the Cabinet wanted to end the war, having secured all that could be desired from France. The task was to persuade France to accept defeat. However, Anson had listened to Pitt's warning. Writing to Saunders, now commanding in the Mediterranean, he shared his thoughts on Spain:

It is thought by some people here that Spain has an inclination to declare war against us, I own I am not of that opinion not seeing what advantage Spain can promise themselves from the measure, nor do I think their weight would be great though it was thrown into the scale of France in the present conjecture.

Even so, Saunders was to keep the fleet close by Gibraltar and investigate the possibility of an attack on the Spanish fleet at Cadiz, proposed by another of Anson's favourite officers, Lord Howe. 'It was certainly a gallant proposal, how fit and proper it may be to attempt if a war should happen, you must inform me, for I never was at Cadiz,' Anson responded. While the situation remained tense, he was anxious to avoid any rumour of such plans reaching the public: 'You see by this letter being written in my own scrawl, that I think it is necessary to be kept secret that I have not thought it right to trust it even to the Secretary's [*sic*] of the Admiralty.'[80]

To conduct a global war, Anson had to rely on his chosen officers to interpret intelligence on a variety of locations that he had never seen and of which the charts were invariably imperfect. A few weeks later, as war with Spain became inevitable, Anson approached the Chairman of the East India Company about a joint Company–Navy expedition to capture Manila. On 6 January 1762 the Cabinet discussed Manila, along with 'Lord Anson's project of attacking Havannah'.[81] Havana was the richest city in the New World, and the key to the Spanish American Empire. War had been declared two days earlier, and both plans were adopted unanimously.[82]

To attack Havana before the rainy season arrived, bringing a lethal cocktail of tropical diseases in its wake, the British had to move quickly, using resources already in the western hemisphere. Anson organised the whole with consummate skill, adding a singular flourish of his own by directing naval commander Sir George Pocock to approach the Cuban port via the rarely used Old Bahama Passage. The Spanish had charted the route along the north coast of Cuba, but considered it too dangerous for big ships; they had no idea the British knew of its existence, so the city was taken entirely by surprise when Pocock arrived on 6 June 1762.[83] Pocock recorded: 'We found Lord Anson's Spanish Chart of the Old Straits a very just one.'[84] Curiously, Anson had died that very day, still in harness, half a world away. One might wonder just how long he had owned the Spanish chart, and how he came by it.

After his last sea voyage, a sickly Anson had visited Bath, without improvement to his health, but despite his enfeebled state he continued in office. In June 1762 he was at Moor Park, walking in his beloved garden, when he suffered what seems to have been a heart attack: he took himself indoors, lay down on his bed and died on the 6th, as quietly as he had lived. His remains were interred in the family vault at Colwich in Staffordshire, where he had entered the world sixty-five years earlier. As the Duke of Newcastle observed a few days later, 'There never was a more able, a more upright, or a more useful servant to his King and country.'[85]

His final campaign culminated in the capture of Manila, four months after his death, and the capture of another Manila galleon. This stunning global strike was a fitting demonstration of Anson's genius: so effective were his plans that they could be conducted on the other side of the Atlantic, and the other side of the world, without his supervision. His expeditions placed the pearl of the Antilles and the jewel of the Orient in the hands of King George III. He went to his grave largely unlamented by the nation, and that, one suspects, is exactly how he would have wished it. He did his duty in order to serve his king and country, not to achieve public notoriety. When Anson died, the Seven Years War was already running down. Britain had triumphed beyond the dreams of avarice, the French Empire was in ruins, the Spanish would be held for ransom. Only his intimate circle, largely the Anson and Hardwicke families, knew his true worth. The glory of the war went to a politician, Pitt the Elder, and a mad general, James Wolfe; stout old desk warriors didn't merit a line. It was not until the early twentieth century that Anson was finally given a fair share of the credit, and another eighty years elapsed before his contribution was thoroughly appreciated.[86]

George Anson took control of the Royal Navy because he knew he could run it better than any man living. He did so for close on twenty years, fighting and winning the first global conflict and creating the British Empire. A man of few words, Anson transformed naval power into a global asset. As a strategist, tactician, trainer of fleets, naval politician and administrator he had no peer. He left a fleet well supplied with battle-winning officers, well-found ships, bases and funds. His navy gave Britain a world empire, and 150 years later his war was used to teach John Fisher's navy about strategy.[87]

Anson viewed the world with the detachment more commonly found in the lawyers who played such a vital role in his life and career. He presented himself to the world without a hint of braggadocio. Never entirely at ease in public, some considered him shy, others awkward. Horace Walpole preferred 'reserved and proud'.[88] But such comments missed the mark: Anson knew the world very well, and he preferred to keep it at arm's length. Austere and unsociable, Anson understood that silence was golden and should only be broken if it could be improved upon. He held his own counsel, wrote little and said no more, resisting the blandishments of society and politics. He did his duty, and he made sure the Royal Navy followed his example. He selected the best and brightest officers, giving them a uniform to reflect the pride they took in their calling. He built better ships so the fleet could operate around the world, and overhauled every aspect of the service. He made the Admiralty work as the co-ordinating body at the intersections of politics and professionalism, strategy and logistics, money and manpower. His judgements were sound, his status unquestioned. He put the navy above politics, defying two kings and countless ministers to uphold the primacy of professional merit.

Anson's example would endure throughout the eighteenth century, at first through his pupils, the circumnavigators who had shared his Pacific odyssey, and then through a constellation of captains who followed his star. As one recent historian has remarked, 'The stoicism and imperturbability shown by Anson under conditions of extreme stress were long remembered, and were soon incorporated into the evolving image of the British naval officer that was to reach iconic status in the age of Nelson.'[89] Another historian of the eighteenth-century Royal Navy observes: 'No one else ever so successfully combined the roles of political and professional head of the navy, for no politician ever knew so much about the service, and no admiral ever made so outstanding a political career, or turned it so much to the navy's advantage.'[90] As an administrator, Anson was content to work with the system largely created by the Duke of York: 'he simply made more efficient use of it', and he did so 'without fanfare'.[91]

The old idea that William Pitt the Elder won the Seven Years War single-handedly has long been overturned, and the most recent study pays due tribute to Anson:

Administratively, no minister made a greater contribution than Anson. Because of his endeavours before the war, the fleet was in an excellent condition and his continued supervision ensured that it undertook most of its assignments with an assured superiority. The good state of the Navy in

1755 was one of the points remembered at his death. So too was his judicious choice of officers.[92]

Among those 'judicious choices' were the best and brightest officers of the next war, the men who would lead the Royal Navy into the last and greatest of the French wars: John Jervis and Samuel Hood, both of whom had received their first ships from Anson.[93] His legacy was victory, and the *Victory*, the flagship of Empire for the next forty years, represented that success. George Anson was the first truly professional officer to put his stamp on the Royal Navy, leaving an example of command, leadership and management that has never been surpassed. That two of his relatives also rose to the highest ranks in the service suggests that the power of his example began close to home – but it did not end there.

5

PURSUIT AND PROFESSIONALISM

Samuel Hood (1724–1816) and John Jervis (1735–1823)

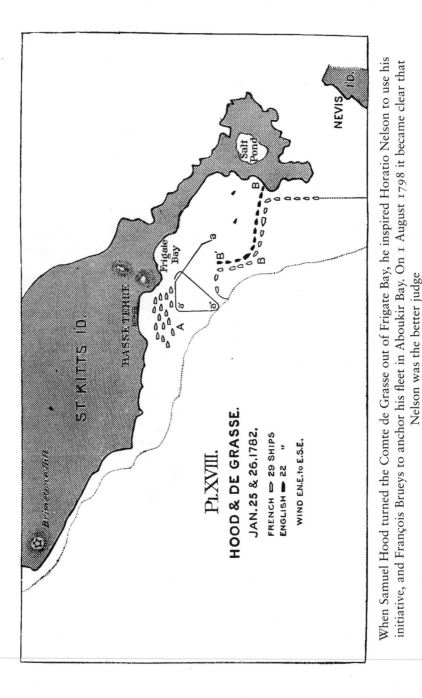

When Samuel Hood turned the Comte de Grasse out of Frigate Bay, he inspired Horatio Nelson to use his initiative, and François Brueys to anchor his fleet in Aboukir Bay. On 1 August 1798 it became clear that Nelson was the better judge

WHEN ANSON DIED, THE NAVY possessed many fine warriors and administrators, but he left no true successor. Hawke, Rodney and Howe won important battles, and developed the art of tactical command, with superior doctrine and improved signalling systems, but they missed the real point. Anson had used the Royal Navy to win wars, not battles, and for this Britain required complete command of the sea, such as she had achieved in 1747–8 and 1759–63, allowing her to break the French economy, seize her islands and annihilate her trade. This strategy required something more than tactical victory: only annihilation would suffice.

To achieve this end, the navy needed to be remade, developing Anson's methods to meet the ever greater demands of war as the eighteenth century turned into the nineteenth. The men who achieved this, Samuel Hood and John Jervis, produced a navy that, in the hands of an officer of genius, would annihilate Britain's enemies and build a world empire. Their navy met the challenge of twenty-two years of total war and destroyed the greatest empire of military conquest that Europe had ever seen. In 1815 Napoleon Bonaparte surrendered to a British battleship, and he acknowledged that it represented the ultimate cause of his downfall.[1]

Bonaparte had begun his war with the Royal Navy on the winning side, helping the republicans recapture Toulon from the British in 1793. But the man he defeated at Toulon would have his revenge: his protégé would be Bonaparte's nemesis. Among the officers who followed Anson, none recognised the strategic and political imperatives that drove naval warfare, or the tactical methods required to achieve them, more clearly than Samuel, Viscount Hood (1724–1816).[2]

Hood was the dominant intellectual influence on Nelson's professional career in the critical years that separated the American War of Independence from the French Revolution. A close similarity in outlook and method set these two great admirals apart from their contemporaries.

Born at Butleigh, Dorset, in 1724, Samuel Hood was the eldest son of a vicar, who, like many clerics across the country, hovered on the margins of gentry. Despite good local connections, the Reverend Hood lacked the income or occasion to place his sons in expensive careers, like the law or the army. The best he could hope for was that they might be bright enough for university and follow him into the Church, as one of them did. In 1740, just as Anson was assembling his fleet for the Pacific, Captain Thomas Smith RN stopped in the village and spent the night at the vicarage. As the navy was mobilising for war, Smith offered to take one of the vicar's sons into the service. Smith had local connections to the Grenville family, making the offer more a matter of patronage than politesse. With a Spanish war in progress, the navy suddenly looked like a good career opening for young gentlemen of limited means. The younger son, thirteen-year-old Alexander, was quick to accept Smith's offer; Samuel took his time and reflected on the options before following suit four months later. This may have been the last time he reflected over-long on anything. Sixteen was a late start for a trainee naval officer – he needed six years' sea service before he could be examined for a lieutenant's commission – but Hood's relatively advanced age paid dividends in other areas. The fact that he had acquired a significant education, and a degree of social refinement, helped make him an effective political admiral and allowed him to avoid the narrowly conceived professionalism of seamanship and tactics that bedevilled his generation. Hood would be the most thoughtful and the most discursive admiral of the age. Whereas the astute Anson kept his own counsel, Hood would be remarkably free with his opinions, able to sway his audience by force of argument and force of example. This intellectual power set Hood above his younger brother, who also rose to be an admiral.

It might be wondered why the navy took its officers so young, curtailing their schooling in favour of hard lessons on the quarterdeck. In truth the navy needed a large supply of capable officers for junior command, watch-keeping, managing the men and imposing order. It required relatively few captains to exercise the independent command of ships, and far fewer admirals to operate at the strategic level. Rather than overeducate those who would not rise beyond lieutenant, the navy took in boys and trained them for this specific rank, relying on chance and opportunity to select those who would become the next generation of leaders. The patronage system ensured that most of those promoted possessed the ability to reward and credit their patrons. When compared with other navies, British officers were markedly better seamen, better managers of their floating world, paying far more attention to health, hygiene and human resources and fighting far more aggressively. They were generally deficient in theoretical education, the arts and the sciences, and often in experience of society ashore. The navy did not make any provision for secondary or tertiary education, leaving such refinement entirely to the intellect and application of individuals. Officers who rose to the top of the service necessarily acquired a wide range of experience, and had opportunities to reflect upon it, but only a few, among whom Samuel Hood stands pre-eminent, combined education, social skills and political aptitude. Possessing 'a very real superiority of faculty', Hood was 'a thinking man'.[3]

In the war that raged between 1740 and 1748 Hood served under his patrons, Smith and Thomas Grenville, duly receiving his commission after six years' sea service. In the process he had seen some action, and Admiral Charles Watson rated him 'a very active good officer'.[4] When the war ended, Lieutenant Hood went on to half pay, marrying Susannah Linzee, daughter of a Portsmouth surgeon with strong local political connections, in 1749. When Edward Linzee became Mayor of Portsmouth, the Admiralty, which relied on mayoral support in parliamentary elections, appointed Hood to the Portsmouth guard ship. In 1754 the same links secured him his first ship, on the American station, although he found parting from his wife 'very severe'.[5] Hood was already at sea when the war with France resumed in 1756.

Management: The Divisional System

Hood had been fortunate in his patrons. Smith, Watson and, lastly, Commodore Holmes, who promoted him to captain in July 1756, were all able men who placed emphasis upon the professional qualities of honour, integrity and courage, the need to obey orders, attend to duty above personal profit and serve without regard to political connections. The eighteenth-century navy put many temptations in the way of its officers, and few escaped as lightly as Samuel Hood.

While he reached the rank of admiral, Thomas Smith did not win a great battle or leave a great name; his legacy was at once more subtle, and more durable. At the most basic level the task of naval officers was to lead and command their men at sea and in battle. Initially the rather relaxed, permissive methods drawn from commercial seafaring were employed, for want of anything more appropriate, in contrast to the unthinking obedience expected of contemporary soldiers. In a small ship, officers soon learnt the character of their men. However, on line-of-battle ships the large and constantly changing nature of the ship's company made it far harder for officers to know the crew. Smith solved the problem by introducing the 'divisional system', which remains the bedrock of leadership, command and management in the modern Royal Navy. On taking command of a squadron in 1755, Smith circulated his brother officers with a printed description of his system and a request for their opinions and advice. Smith's system made each officer and warrant officer responsible for the discipline and cleanliness of a specific division of men. Beginning with such simple concerns as clean hammocks and clothes, these responsibilities quickly broadened out into a general concern with the men's welfare, both as the vital resource of naval power and as human beings. Officers were encouraged to get to know the men as individuals, and this paid handsome dividends. The men were motivated by the officers' concern and identified their interests with those of the better officers, following them from ship to ship. The patronage of an officer could make a rating's career and ensure his promotion to petty officer. By 1763 the divisional system was widely used, and it became universal within two decades.[6] Samuel Hood understood Smith's system and its implications: he cared about his men, lent them money, bought them extra food and invariably took their side in arguments with the Admiralty over pay and conditions.

Captain Hood

Using his Grenville connections, Hood ensured that he was actively employed at sea. In 1759 he commanded the frigate *Vestal*, capturing a French frigate of the same force, *Bellona*, in a three-hour running battle. Such successes made an officer's name: Anson presented him to King George II. His next service was at the bombardment of the French invasion shipping at Le Havre under Commodore George Rodney. In 1760 he was sent, at his own request, to the Mediterranean, where he spent the rest of war on convoy service. After commanding the American station, his Portsmouth connections – his father-in-law was the city's mayor four times between 1771 and 1780 – kept his career tied to the local area. This enabled him to avoid becoming too closely identified with any one party, a particular advantage since the Grenville–Pitt clan were out of office for the entire decade. From 1771 to 1776 he commanded the Portsmouth Guard ship, although he lived ashore at Catherington House in Horndean, riding to work every morning.

While this comfortable existence sufficed for peacetime, Hood was consumed by a desire for active service. When the American war broke out in 1776, Hood was offered the post of Commissioner in the dockyard and Governor of the Naval Academy. At fifty-three it seemed that his active career was over and that he would spend the rest of his life in administration, running a dockyard and managing the navy's local political interests. He accepted the posts, but only after persuading Lord Sandwich, once again First Lord of the Admiralty, to retain him on the active list, eligible for an admiral's command. Hood began work in February 1778: when King George III visited the dockyard later that year, he was so impressed that he sent his third son, Prince William Henry, later William IV, into the navy under Hood's tutelage and made Hood a baronet.[7] At the 1779 Hampshire county election, Hood loyally served the ministry and then pressed for a command afloat, making sure that the prime minister, Lord North, knew that he was not a Grenville partisan. Hood got his chance in September 1780, when Sandwich needed a second-in-command for the abrasive George Rodney on the West Indies station. The choice smacked of desperation: half the officers in the navy refused to serve on political grounds, while the rest hated Rodney.

Loyalty, hard work and superior talents had not been enough: only the political divisions of the officer corps in the American war gave Samuel Hood the chance to be an admiral. Having served under Rodney in every grade from midshipman to captain, Hood was confident he could continue to work harmoniously with him. Even so, the belated opportunity for sea service came as something of a shock, and he initially refused the offer, citing poor health. Two days later he changed his mind, his bodily ailments having fled – given that he would live for another thirty-six years, one has to question quite how severe his ailments were! It may have been his concern to support the Linzee interest in Portsmouth that held him back: his father-in-law was returned as mayor in the brief interval between his initial refusal and his sudden change of heart.[8]

Admiral Sir Samuel Hood

Hood was promoted to rear admiral on 26 September 1780, and in mid-November he took eight battleships to join Rodney in the West Indies, with his flag in the recently coppered ninety-eight-gun three-decker *Barfleur*.[9] He had no experience of battle, little more of fleet handling, and had never served in the West Indies. If knowledge and experience were critical to success in command, then Hood seemed destined to fail. His first taste of independent command did not go well; left to blockade Martinique, he did not keep his ships fully stored and was caught out by local weather conditions when the French appeared. He soon realised why no one wanted to serve under Rodney, who ignored his advice and disallowed his promotions. The command relationship was not improved by the fact that the French had the upper hand. Frustrated by his failure, Hood let off steam about his commander-in-chief in acerbic, brilliant letters to well-placed friends at home.[10]

Rodney left for England in late July, when the hurricane season ended all major operations in the West Indies, sending Hood north to join Rear Admiral Thomas Graves' squadron on the American coast. De Grasse took the French fleet north to cooperate with George Washington's American army. Graves imposed the *Tactical Instructions and Signals* used by the North American station on the new arrivals, despite the fact that they outnumbered his own ships by four to one. Having no experience of fleet command or battle,

Graves did what most undistinguished men do in a crisis, falling back on the rule book. The North America signal book enshrined central direction and left no discretion to subordinates, even junior flag officers. The two fleets met at the entrance to Chesapeake Bay on 5 September 1781. When Graves appeared, the French were at anchor on the Virginia coast. De Grasse ordered his ships to cut their cables and head out to sea, a manoeuvre they conducted in haste and in no particular order. Graves was heading into the bay, on course to link up with the beleaguered army of Lord Cornwallis and complete his mission, but at the decisive moment he reversed course and tried to fight a linear action on a parallel course with the French. Such unimaginative formalism played into the hands of de Grasse, who had no desire to fight a decisive action: his mission was to support the American army and maintain the blockade of Yorktown.

Timing and aggression were vital, but Graves did not haul down the signal for the line, or hoist that for close action, until the battle was already under way. Consequently most ships were unable to read it; nor was Hood, who was anxiously looking for it! Graves also attempted to lead by example, turning the flagship onto a closing course with the French, but when the ship ahead luffed up and fired, he turned away to avoid a collision. After almost two hours of distant firing, with no more than half the ships of either fleet in action, Graves hoisted the signal for the line and broke off. Watching from the rear division, Hood realised that Graves' only hope lay in abandoning the line, signalling for a general chase and attacking the French van squadron while it was isolated. The *Tactical Instructions* in force did not allow him to use his initiative, and by the time Graves signalled for close action, the signal could not be read. But Graves' real failure came not during the battle, but beforehand.[11] Without well-briefed subordinates who understood the doctrine and had confidence in their leader, even a fleet of well-handled, aggressive ships would achieve little. Consequently the action was inconclusive. Hood lamented:

Yesterday the British fleet had a rich and most plentiful harvest of glory in view, but the means to gather it were omitted in more instances than one. I may begin with observing that the enemy's van was not very closely attacked as it came out of Lynn Haven Bay; which I think, might have been done with clear advantage, as they came out by no means in a regular and connected way.[12]

After the battle, Graves did not challenge de Grasse's control of Chesapeake Bay; he gave up and headed back to New York. His failure was decisive: Cornwallis was forced to capitulate on 19 October. The war for America was over.

Hood knew that superior British ship and squadron handling gave them a tighter battle line; they could bring more firepower to bear on a French formation of the same length. This was the pay-off for taking officers to sea at an early age and keeping them there: they were significantly better ship-handlers than the French. Skilful seamanship allowed British admirals to apply superior force against elements of the enemy fleet, meaning that a numerically inferior force could win. In Chesapeake Bay the French van was widely separated from the centre and rear divisions, and could have been cut off and destroyed. Hood realised that Graves lacked insight, understanding, speed of thought, aggressive instincts and courage to act. He was unfit for his place, and a danger to the Empire. Only after the battle did Graves ask for Hood's opinion – which he very properly declined to give.[13]

Hood had once again been given an example of how not to lead: while Rodney had kept silent and attended to his own interests, Graves simply lacked the necessary intelligence and skill to direct a battle. After a year of service, Hood had nothing to show for his efforts but failure. On the passage back to the West Indies he exercised his fleet of twenty-two battleships, turning hard-won experience to good effect. If he had the chance, he would make amends for the Chesapeake Bay fiasco: he requested the Admiralty Secretary Philip Stephens to 'assure their Lordships I will seek and give battle to the Count de Grasse, be his numbers as they may'.[14]

Hood's opportunity came when the French landed an army on the British island of St Kitts. Unlike John Byng, Hood would do his utmost to assist the troops. He planned a surprise attack on the supporting French fleet. Approaching the theatre of operations, Hood briefed his officers, conveying his doctrine at daily meetings. The planned attack was thwarted by a collision, which allowed de Grasse to put to sea with twenty-eight ships to Hood's twenty-two. Never one to despair, Hood looked to recover the initiative. The next morning he realised the French were a long way from their anchorage in Basse Terre Roads, and drew them further out. At the critical moment, when he reckoned he could race de Grasse into the anchorage, he hauled his wind and headed for Frigate Bay. A frigate passed detailed instructions to his leading captains to ensure they took up the correct positions as close to the shore as the depth of water would allow. He could not risk de Grasse doubling on his fleet to exploit his superior numbers. Captain Lord Robert Manners was in the rear division:

The taking possession of this road was well judged, well conducted, and well executed, though indeed the French had an opportunity – which they missed – of bringing our rear to a very severe account. The van and centre divisions brought to an anchor under the fire of the rear, which was engaged with the enemy's centre, and then, the centre being at an anchor and properly placed, covered us while we anchored, making, I think, the most masterly manoeuvre I ever saw.[15]

This was more than tactical skill: this was an example of the highest courage. In the absence of his commander-in-chief, Hood had taken responsibility for a high-risk operation upon which hung the fate of the West Indian empire. Had he lost, he would have been lucky to escape a hanging. His plan hinged on the arrival of a suitable naval reinforcement and the ability of the troops he was carrying to relieve the besieged fort on Brimstone Hill.

Temporarily stunned, de Grasse attacked the British fleet over the next two days, but Hood's ships, tightly anchored with springs on their cables to enable them to adjust their broadsides, easily beat him off. Having given the army a fighting chance, and sent as many troops as he could muster to support them, Hood found that the situation was beyond his control. Brimstone Hill surrendered on 13 February, leaving him trapped. Soon artillery would be placed on shore to drive him out of the anchorage, into the path of de Grasse's reinvigorated fleet of thirty-two battleships. As Captain Manners observed, 'Few situations could have been more unpleasing than ours,' but once again Hood had the answer.[16] On 14 February, he summoned his captains and lieutenants to the flagship for a detailed briefing, with a final meeting at 21.00 to synchronise watches. At 23.00 every ship cut its cable and stood out to sea without a signal or any significant noise. Once safely at sea, Hood court-martialled the watch-keeping officers of the two ships that had spoiled his original plan to attack at St Kitts: he never allowed slackness or inattention to pass unnoticed.

In the space of a month Hood had conducted two unprecedented operations in the face of a superior enemy. The French were mightily impressed: Lieutenant de Brueys would recall this episode sixteen years later, when he placed his fleet in Aboukir Bay. However, Brueys was not Hood's equal as a seaman, and his opponent was Hood's protégé. Hood's success reflected a remarkable intellect, quick, decisive, confident, clear and compelling, allied to the superior seamanship of his fleet. The fact that his ships were coppered gave him a crucial edge in speed, which he had fully exploited. As Manners reported:

If you give him half the credit the enemy does, Sir Samuel Hood will stand very high in the public estimation. Their sea officers say it was a bold and well-conducted attempt . . . they confess they cannot keep the line of battle with that precision we do, and manoeuvre with so much sail out without the danger of running aboard each other.[17]

Hood had drawn credit from a calamity: although St Kitts had fallen, the Royal Navy had recovered its reputation. Any officer with an ounce of spirit realised that the service had found an admiral. Hood had learnt another bitter lesson: the army, far less professional than the navy, was not to be relied upon. The defenders of Brimstone Hill had given him 'spirited and encouraging messages', only to surrender without even troubling to inform the fleet. To make matters worse, the fort had been demolished using the very weapons the army itself had landed on the island to reinforce their defences – the local planters had refused to assist in moving them up the hill![18] A decade later, such memories would influence Hood's handling of combined operations. He might also have reflected on the danger to which his overconfidence had exposed the fleet, but such introspection was the missing dimension of Hood's genius. His own errors and misjudgements rarely featured in his learning process.

He certainly appreciated the sustained hard work of his crews, however. When the fleet ran out of bread, the infamous 'hard tack', Hood bought local yams to supplement the remaining flour ration. Rather than issue this as a substitute, Hood turned it into a reward:

The men were under arms from the 25th last to the 15th instant, they performed their duty with that cheerfulness and good humour which charmed me. I therefore take the liberty humbly to propose to their Lordships that the yams should be a present upon this extraordinary occasion; it will show the poor fellows they are attended to, and will, I am persuaded be productive of very happy effects.[19]

He could 'propose' such a measure with confidence because he had made his mark as a commander, and the Board would be disposed to uphold his suggestion. And furthermore, even if they refused the news would not reach the fleet for months, long after the inevitable fleet action in which Hood anticipated the 'happy effects' of his generosity.

Early the next month Rodney rejoined the fleet, restoring a balance of forces with the French. De Grasse retired to Martinique to prepare for a Franco-Spanish invasion of Jamaica. This was common knowledge, and both fleets concentrated for the next move. Disturbed by Rodney's refusal to follow his advice on how to dispose the fleet, Hood feared that any success they might have would be a matter of luck rather than planning. When de Grasse's invasion force left Martinique on 8 April, heading for a rendezvous with the Spanish, they were seen by British frigates. The next day the fleets fought a partial action: Hood's van squadron was left to fight twice their number of French ships when the wind failed, 'but we handled them very roughly'.[20] Rodney shifted Hood's shattered force to the rear and continued.

Finally, on 12 April 1782 the two fleets met off Les Saintes on passing courses. De Grasse's plans had been delayed by a series of collisions, caused by poor ship-handling, which reduced his force to thirty battleships. Rodney, despite the rickety state of some of his ships, still had all thirty-six in company. When one of the collision-prone French seventy-fours fell astern, de Grasse put about to rescue it, giving Rodney a chance to force an action. The engagement was framed by the Saintes passage and the regular shift of the wind round from north to south during the day. The battle opened with de Grasse heading due south. He intended reversing course, but with a close-range battle raging, this proved impossible. With the fleet closely engaged, the wind shifted to the south, forcing the French ships to starboard, and this, in combination with battle damage and the thick pall of smoke that hung over the fleets, opened large gaps in the French line. The British drove through the gaps in three places, with Rodney's flagship leading in the centre. Hood's division was quick to follow suit. With their line in tatters the French captains were left to make their own decisions, and most chose flight over fight. Neither they nor their men had any stomach for close-range action. Rodney's physician observed that when the ships came to point-blank action, the French gun crews ran below, well aware that British gunnery was faster and far more effective.

From his position at the rear, Hood watched the battle unfold, and as soon as Rodney hauled down the signal for the line of battle, just as his flagship passed the last ship of the French van, he pushed through the gap between the two French divisions, forcing the French centre to veer further off to starboard. The *Barfleur* was heavily engaged, taking the surrender of the French flagship, the mighty *Ville de Paris*, after a furious close-range battle. When British officers boarded her, they were startled to find blood swilling across her decks and over their shoes; de Grasse was the only man on the quarterdeck to escape death or injury. Anson's copper sheathing had allowed the Royal Navy to catch the French, and the new short-range, rapid-fire, heavy-calibre carronades gave them a decisive firepower superiority: 'His Majesty's fleet had given such beating to the one of France as no great fleet ever received before.'[21]

Although five French ships had been taken, Hood knew that only annihilation would secure the British interest in the West Indies and the wider war. He pressed Rodney to pursue the beaten and demoralised enemy, confident that twenty enemy ships would have been taken that day if Rodney had only signalled for a general chase, as Anson had off Cape Finisterre. Having completed the hardest part of war, destroying the cohesion of the enemy force, Rodney failed the supreme test: conducting an effective pursuit to transform hard-won tactical success into strategic triumph. Only by annihilating the enemy could he influence the course of war, and this he failed to attempt. Hood declared:

I am confident not more than three of the line could have escaped had they been properly pursued, which would most effectually, and substantially, have retrieved all the misfortunes of poor old England, have set her on tip-toe, and have humbled France in the extreme. It is truly mortifying to think what a glorious turn might have been given to our royal and most gracious masters' affairs, not only in this country, but at home, with only common exertion and management; and how shamefully was the opportunity neglected.

The following morning, while the enemy could easily have been caught, Hood boarded Rodney's flagship to urge a pursuit. But Rodney lamely declared, 'Come, we have done very handsomely as it is.'[22] Hood was convinced that the moment the French flagship surrendered, Rodney lost interest in everything other than taking his prize back to England.[23] William Cornwallis, one of the captains who fought under Hood at Basse Terre Roads, dismissed Rodney's offer of the *Ville de Paris* with scarcely veiled contempt. He knew that more should have been done, and saw Rodney's behaviour as a tacit confession that the old admiral knew as much.[24] Years later Rodney confessed the fact to his physician.[25] It would be from Cornwallis that Nelson took the view that the Saintes was 'the greatest victory, if it had been followed up, that our country ever saw'.[26]

Hood was right: enough has never been done until all the enemy's ships have been taken, sunk, burnt or otherwise destroyed. That sentiment would inspire the navy of 1793–1815 to the height of glory. He was the godfather of genius. His insight and judgement earned him the admiration of an entire generation, while William Cornwallis and Horatio Nelson adopted the battle of annihilation as their *leitmotif.*[27]

In Rodney's defence it should be said that he was tired and did not want to run any more risks. He finally released his anxious subordinate on 17 April, and Hood nearly intercepted the French fleet. Instead, he had to be content with the lesser reward of two straggling battleships, a frigate and a sloop. Buoyed up by success, Hood's letters home became ever more startling, serving as a vital outlet for tensions that might otherwise have overwhelmed him. When Rodney was relieved by the inexperienced Admiral Hugh Pigot, Hood once again tried to be a loyal second, but the attempt was doomed. His contempt soon turned to abject pity for a man so utterly out of his depth: Pigot's appointment was a blatantly political choice by the new Whig ministry. The Saintes made the appointment ridiculous, while Pigot's lack of energy and inattention demonstrated just how much Hood missed Rodney's flair for fleet command.

In truth Hood was simply too intelligent, clear-eyed and ambitious to be second to anyone, however capable. It was a failing he shared with a bright young officer who boarded the *Barfleur* later that year. Nelson picked Hood to be his mentor because Hood had about him the charisma of greatness. On reading his 1780–2 correspondence, the pioneering naval analyst Captain Alfred Mahan 'was particularly struck by what seemed to me a strong similarity of *professional* temperament between him and Nelson'. Mahan was quick to elevate Hood to second place in his list of all-time naval worthies, second only to Nelson, supplanting Admiral Sir John Jervis, Earl St Vincent.[28] Little wonder he attributed the opening of Nelson's great career to the patronage of Hood.[29]

By the time Pigot led the fleet to New York that autumn men were dying by the dozen from scurvy, and Hood's temper was not improved by illness. He took the necessary precautions to ensure fresh food was ready when they arrived: 'If the commander-in-chief of a great fleet does not upon every occasion look forward, the crews of it will be often disappointed of what they stand in need of, are entitled to, and might have.'[30] While Hood was not the commander-in-chief, he, unlike the nominal head, thought like one. His attention to fleet logistics and the needs of his men was as professional as his concern with ship-handling, seamanship and attention to orders.

Hood's success in 1782 saw him ennobled. Already entrusted with the seagoing education of Prince William, he was now described by his king as 'the most brilliant Officer of this war'. The compliment was well earned. Having become a national figure everyone wanted to exploit Hood's name and fame. In 1782 his son withdrew his name from a contested election, much to the father's relief:

I shall ever most carefully and studiously steer clear, as far as I am able, of all suspicion of being *a party man*, for if once I show myself of that complexion . . . I must from that moment expect to lose every degree of consideration in the line of my profession, which has been, and ever will be, the first and greatest object of my wishes . . . even if I had abilities equal to the undertaking, I think it an employment derogatory to the true character of a sea officer, whose highest ambition is to stand fair in the good opinion of his Sovereign and fellow subjects.[31]

However, such a clear, simple division between the two spheres of activity was a counsel of perfection in 1780: the link between politics and naval service would endure for another century. Hood's own principles, meanwhile, were altered by events. When his father-in-law died, his Portsmouth political power base collapsed; a chance to compensate for this came when he returned to Britain to find the parliamentary seat of Westminster waiting for him. He fought and won an election in 1784 as a follower of Prime Minister William Pitt the Younger, and by extension in the King's interest. The latter was the clinching argument. His speeches in the House of Commons (where he was entitled to sit as an Irish peer) were as opinionated and direct as his letters and made him few friends outside his new political family. In 1788 he was appointed senior naval lord on an Admiralty Board headed by the Earl of Chatham, Pitt's elder brother, a position he held until 1795. He complained that his political career ruined his finances, which was at least partially true. Hood made little money from his naval career, insisting that duty came first. His relationship with Rodney never recovered from the realisation that his superior was bending theatre strategy to defend a rich haul of prize money.

Much as he disliked politics, Hood's close relationship with the Pitt family ensured that he was the obvious choice whenever a senior admiral was required. In 1791 war with Russia appeared imminent: Hood took command of a Baltic fleet. His preparations were so thorough that ten years later they were hastily dusted down for the Copenhagen campaign. That war was avoided, but in early 1793 the French revolutionary war broke out, and Hood took the Mediterranean fleet – a command of immense complexity, ideally suited to his talents. Admiral Lord Howe commanded the Channel fleet, in close touch with London, with the relatively simple mission of destroying or blockading the French fleet at Brest, while protecting British trade and annihilating that of France. Hood was responsible for the overall direction of the British war effort inside the Straits of Gibraltar. In addition to the obvious naval tasks, he would oversee British diplomacy, deal with foreign rulers and convoy a large, dispersed and valuable commerce. For a man of Hood's imperious will and powerful intellect, these were opportunities: he was not oppressed by responsibility and did not hesitate to act as he thought fit, confident that the Pitt brothers would support him.

Mediterranean Command

When Hood set sail from Portsmouth on board HMS *Victory* on 22 May 1793, his orders were to defeat the French fleet and secure the navigation of the Mediterranean for the King's subjects and those of his allies. This would be a theatre command: war, politics, diplomacy, commerce and, above all, endless correspondence. While the military position was relatively simple – the demoralised, leaderless French fleet was unlikely to give battle – the real problems lay elsewhere. He would have to work with a collection of difficult allies: the Spanish, who resented the very presence of the British fleet and the continuing occupation of Gibraltar; the kingdoms of Sardinia and of the Two Sicilies, who were mortally afraid of France; while Austria looked for naval support, but was remarkably unwilling to offer military assistance. The North African corsair regencies threatened British commerce, and their relations with the Iberian powers complicated the picture. Nor were the problems of fleet logistics and maintenance any easier. The nearest dry dock for his fleet was at Plymouth, while he was responsible for securing local sources of food, water and naval supplies.

Hood selected his senior officers from his own patronage network, and included numerous relatives. The admirals he selected, from second-in-command William Hotham to his in-laws Linzee and Goodall, were not of the first rank. Hood wanted loyal subordinates, not talented colleagues. The captains were equally undistinguished. We should not confuse the fact that many of them would achieve greatness with their merits on appointment. Captain Horatio Nelson's career was effectively over after his failure in the West Indies a decade before: Hood only pardoned him because he needed experienced men. Younger officers would rise through this fleet, inspired by Hood's example, but for every Nelson, Thomas Fremantle and George Cockburn, at least as many failed the test of war.

In 1793 and 1794 Nelson would learn the art of the admiral by watching a master at work. The critical point he learnt was the absolute, overriding importance of political courage. Arriving off Toulon, the main French base, Hood was greeted by local envoys from Marseilles and Toulon. Both towns were controlled by moderate republicans, in mortal terror of the Jacobin government in Paris. In return for British protection they were prepared to adopt the constitutional monarchy of 1789–91 and hand over the forts and fleet at Toulon. This was way beyond anything anticipated in Hood's orders and did not accord with stated British war aims and policy towards France. Hood knew all of this, and he knew the importance of time. If he waited for instructions from home, both towns would fall to the Jacobins, and the greatest prize in naval warfare – the enemy's fleet and arsenal – would be lost.

On 23 August Hood issued a declaration that Britain and the allies were at war to restore the French monarchy, and that they accepted the 1791 constitution and promised to return the French warships after the conflict. He was only just in time: Marseilles fell on the 25th, but on the 27th he landed fifteen hundred men from the fleet to occupy the forts that controlled Toulon harbour. Some five thousand radical Breton sailors who opposed the British occupation were allowed to sail home in four old ships. When the British war minister reminded him that British war aims were restricted to resisting French aggression, Hood observed that he had known as much, but acted in haste because 'all might be lost by the delay of a few hours'.[32] The ministers quickly sent out a political commissioner to represent them in Toulon, but they did not disavow Hood's policy. He had taken a mighty fortress, twenty-two battleships and a dockyard with the stroke of a pen. On the day he took control Hood observed: 'Had I 5000 or 6000 good troops with me, the war would soon be at an end' – but the government had planned to attack Toulon in 1794, and was caught out by this dramatic turn of events.[33] Prime Minister Pitt saw Toulon as key to victory, but failed to deliver the manpower and the alliance effort needed to hold the base. The disposable British army had been dispatched to conquer the French West Indian islands, while the allied powers quibbled and procrastinated. By December Hood's garrison was still no more than seventeen thousand men, from six nations. Dealing with dilatory, hesitant allies did not improve Hood's temper. His commentary was as sharp as ever, which did not enhance cooperation with British or allied troops.

For a man of seventy, Hood possessed prodigious energy and determination, and he used every ounce of both to secure Toulon. He stuck to his belief that the town could be held throughout the siege, and never allowed the failings of others to depress his spirits. It was vital for those under his command that he showed no fear and no doubt. Despite his age and profession, Hood was always at the point of danger: his tall, angular frame and that stark spare face, rendered unforgettable by a truly majestic nose, were enough to inspire tired and hungry men. The only reliable foreign contingents were the Sardinians and the Neapolitan Grenadiers; the Neapolitan line infantry, the Spanish and the various French royalists were all prone to sudden flight when attacked. The better-disciplined, professional allied soldiers won most of the battles, but they lacked the numbers to turn tactical success into decisive results.[34] When the troops were used for counter-attacks, Hood sent sailors ashore to man the defences, but even here he was short of manpower.

Hood needed every resource: he faced a ruthless and determined enemy who would ultimately assemble over fifty thousand men and had no hesitation in expending its human capital. However, raw soldiers fired with revolutionary zeal were never going to capture Toulon from regular troops. To capture the fortress, the French needed professional officers who understood siege warfare. They found their man when artillery lieutenant Napoleon Bonaparte arrived on 16 September. Bonaparte immediately set to work, building batteries to drive the British ships away from his siege works. He realised that the high ground controlled by the newly built Fort Mulgrave was the key to the city. If he could take the fort, the allies would be forced to evacuate. Hood was quick to sense the presence of a superior intellect in the enemy camp, something that shook his hitherto untroubled confidence.[35] The allies did not have any officers with the same understanding of siege warfare, as their extemporised defences demonstrated.

The optimism of Hood and General Lord Mulgrave, while essential to sustaining the garrison and controlling the disparate elements in the town, had misled the government at home into thinking the town was safe. By the time warnings from Toulon convinced them that more resources were needed, there was little time to spare, and further days would be wasted in dilatory proceedings at Gibraltar.[36] Mulgrave was replaced by General David Dundas, an experienced and able officer, but temperamentally despondent. Dundas advocated preparing for an evacuation, and was angry when Hood rejected his counsels of despair: the admiral was hanging on for the promised five thousand Austrian and ten thousand Sardinian troops, along with British reinforcements.[37] Any one of these detachments would have been enough. Late in November Hood learnt that British troops were coming, and rushed to tell the Civil Commissioner. Sir Gilbert Elliot observed, 'I never saw a man more delighted than Lord Hood. He came skipping into my room, out of breath with hurry and joy.' British soldiers arrived ten days after the fortress had fallen.[38]

Throughout the siege, Hood had continued to disperse the fleet across the Mediterranean to conduct the full range of missions covered by his instructions; as a result, Nelson took no part in the siege. When the French launched their decisive attack, Hood had less than a third of his fleet in harbour. This meant that he had too few disposable men for an effective counter-attack or to ensure the dockyard and the fleet were completely destroyed. The French ships could have been moved earlier, but that would have been a sign of despair that he could not afford with morale already fragile. He preferred to hope, and was still grimly hanging on when the last attack came. In the event it was touch and go, but he lost. On 15–16 December Bonaparte opened a heavy fire on Fort Mulgrave from eight well-placed batteries, and early on the 17th the fort fell to an assault. Having taken the high ground, the French could fire down into the harbour, rendering the town and dockyard untenable. With his British and Sardinian troops exhausted and no relief in sight, Hood could not counter-attack. Once he accepted the town was lost, he launched a full-scale evacuation. In two days he managed to retrieve all of his soldiers and sailors, along with many French refugees.

In the chaos and horror of the evacuation, with a vengeful, murderous republican army storming through the town, thirteen French battleships were taken or destroyed, although the Spanish proved less enthusiastic about torching French ships than the British. Even so, it was a massive blow: a fifth of the French navy had been wiped out. Among the ships that survived were nine battleships that Nelson would destroy at the Nile in 1798. This campaign did more damage to the French fleet than all the naval battles before the Nile put together. It also ruined the arsenal, largely by stripping away the workforce,[39] and destroyed the bond of trust between the Toulonese and the government in Paris.

Hood's outstanding abilities were most obvious at the highest level of strategic and political direction. His analytical approach to war provided a solid base for a truly remarkable confidence in his own judgement. Offered the keys to Toulon in 1793, he immediately seized an opportunity that would have terrified his contemporaries. He read the situation clearly, weighed the options, and took a wise decision. The ultimate failure of the operation did not detract from its merit: 'No blame can attach to the British Fleet. Hood's conduct of the naval operations erred, if at all, by excess of energy in several parts of the Mediterranean at once.' Indeed, without Hood's 'indomitable spirit Toulon would not have been held for a month', and he handled the evacuation with great skill.[40] The project was ultimately doomed by the political failure of the royalist cause – the Toulonese were unwilling to fight for the crown – and the half-hearted response of the allied governments.

Throughout the 1793–4 Mediterranean campaign Hood worked tirelessly to impress 'the strength and power of Great Britain' upon the local states,[41] promote the national interest and cripple the French fleet. Despite the failure at Toulon, he was far from downcast – that was not his way, at least not when he held the supreme command. Having landed the French refugees in Italy, he decided to invade Corsica. Corsican nationalists under Pasquale Paoli had risen against the French government, pinning down the republican troops in a handful of coastal towns. From a base in Corsica Hood could keep a close watch on Toulon, isolating the French fleet from the rest of the Mediterranean while turning the large supply of timber and other naval stores they had been taking from the island to his own account. This would ease his critical problem of matching resources to the sheer scale of the theatre. He landed the British troops evacuated from Toulon at Mortella Bay and San Fiorenzo in February, urging General Dundas to push on and attack the capital, Bastia. Once again he met with asinine obstinacy that contrasted with his own boundless self-confidence: where Hood could never see any reason for inaction, Dundas could always see a good reason for doing nothing. Little wonder they disagreed.[42] Nothing daunted, Hood landed his marines and sailors to build batteries and bombard Bastia, while applying a close blockade. After seven weeks of starvation and bombardment, the belated, half-hearted appearance of the army secured a result the general had publicly declared to be impossible. Hood was openly contemptuous: a dignified silence might have served the national interest rather better, but it would have required a saint to hold his tongue under such provocation. His constant activity, energy and example inspired those around him, as Nelson testified when reporting the fall of Bastia to his old friend Cornwallis: 'We, who know his judgement, which no affected fears can warp, will not be surprised that success is the consequence.'[43]

The last French fortress, at Calvi on the west coast, was quickly subjected to a similar combined siege and blockade, surrendering eight weeks later on 10 August. In both operations, Hood employed naval officers to command land batteries; Nelson lost the sight of his right eye in a battery before Calvi.

While the soldiers and their biographers have criticised Hood's imperious manner, they have missed the critical point. He needed Corsica as a base, and he needed it quickly. The main resources being tied down, ships, guns and men were his, and the army had no other task in view. The urgency of his mission became clear in early June, when a French squadron of seven battleships put out from Toulon. Admiral Hotham retreated when he had enough force to engage, and it was only on 10 June that Hood, rushing north from Calvi with thirteen sail, sighted and pursued the French. On the 11th Admiral Martin scuttled into nearby Gourjean Bay. Hood quickly planned an attack that reversed the position he had taken at St Kitts: he would sail in and anchor two ships against each French vessel to ensure the battle would be over quickly and limit British casualties. This action would complete the work begun at Toulon, wiping out the French fleet to secure undisputed command of the sea. The elements were against him, however: for two days a flat calm precluded any attack, and the French took the chance to improvise shore defences and reinforce their ships with gunboats. Hood had to forgo his battle – the French ships would not be annihilated until four years later at the Nile.

Leaving Hotham to blockade the French, Hood went back to oversee the siege of Calvi and begin the process of setting up a dockyard to repair and refit his ships. The capture of Corsica was a wonderful demonstration of Hood's talent at all levels of war – although no advertisement for inter-service cooperation. By the end of the campaign season in November Hood was exhausted, and in the fashion of eighteenth-century warfare, he decided to go home and recover his health at Bath. The ministers accepted his request; Hood fully expected to return refreshed and reinforced to resume his responsibilities. However, the political scene in Britain had changed in his absence, and Lord Chatham, the indolent elder brother of the prime minister, was no longer First Lord.

Pitt had rebuilt the Cabinet by taking in moderate Whigs, and had given one new recruit, Earl Spencer, the post of First Lord of the Admiralty. Hood's imperious manner and reliance on the Pitt family quickly alienated the new First Lord: Spencer removed him from the Board of Admiralty, where he had been the senior officer. He was replaced by Admiral Sir Charles Middleton, who had been a friend and colleague years before. However, Middleton owed his place to a family connection with Henry Dundas, and backed his kinsman's West Indies strategy at the expense of the Mediterranean theatre. Nor was Hood satisfied with the Board's efforts to reinforce his fleet: intemperate private letters to Pitt and Spencer demanded more ships and seamen. Finally, on the very eve of his departure for the Mediterranean, he condemned the projected reinforcement of the fleet as inadequate and unsafe in a public letter to the Board. As the French had sent reinforcements into the Mediterranean, he considered the British force 'very unequal to that of the enemy, and the various Services committed to my charge, but although I have not the slightest shadow of prospect of being able to add Lustre to the Arms of His Majesty I entreat to have credit, for doing my utmost, that they are not disgraced'.[44] Recognising their culpability, the Admiralty immediately sacked Hood – in effect for publicly drawing attention to their failure, though Spencer argued to the King that it was a question of 'discipline and subordination'.[45]

Cornwallis would not have been surprised to learn that Hood's absence could not be supplied by any other flag officer. After his dismissal, the French were caught at sea and allowed to escape with only a skirmish: as Nelson rightly said, 'To say how much we wanted Lord Hood at that time, is to say will you have all the French fleet or none at all.'[46] He elaborated in other correspondence: 'Oh, miserable Board of Admiralty. They have forced the first officer in our service away from his Command.' 'This fleet must regret the loss of Lord Hood, the best Officer, take him altogether, that England has to boast of. Lord Howe certainly is a great Officer in the management of a Fleet, but that is all, Lord Hood is equally great in all situations which an Admiral can be placed in.'[47]

The utter folly of sacking the first officer in the service for a minor act of insubordination, on the eve of his return to a theatre he understood better than anyone, hardly needs stressing. It was an act of petty, narrow-minded stupidity that defies comprehension. The war was going badly, the Mediterranean fleet was under strength, and they had no one to replace Hood – certainly no one with half his ability. Furthermore, the Board had already given his temporary relief Admiral Hotham permission to return to England for his health.[48] As they had no suitable successor to hand, the Board had to keep Hotham in place for a further five months, despite his repeated desire to stand down.[49] Pitt, a long-time supporter of Hood, regretted his loss, but meekly acquiesced in this folly.[50]

After his climactic sacking, Hood never again held a sea command, although he was briefly considered for the post of First Lord in the crisis of 1805: that honour eventually fell to Middleton, who, it must be admitted, acquitted himself very well. The Pitt connection did see Hood promoted to the English peerage and secure the highest honour the navy could offer a retired sea officer: the governorship of the Greenwich Hospital. This provided a dignified but deeply unsatisfactory end to a stellar career. The fact that Hood needed the post demonstrated how little attention he had paid to prize money.[51] However, he was not quite as careless as his biographers have implied: while he viewed prize as a distraction, he left the settlement and collection of such monies to his agents. The same disinterest would characterise his greatest follower, the man who lay in state in Hood's hospital before his elevation to the pantheon of the immortals. Hood remained governor of the hospital until his death in January 1816, having outlived his wife and an entire generation.

Samuel Hood taught the Royal Navy to annihilate the enemy. He also taught it to be as bold politically as it was tactically. As the world in which British fleets operated grew ever larger, and the pace of warfare accelerated, admirals had to make big decisions at the grand strategic level. This was where John Byng had failed: he did not have the ability or the confidence to make such decisions. Samuel Hood did, and this was the most important asset that he imparted to the only admiral to surpass him.

Hood was a bold and decisive commander with the confidence and courage to carry out the most complex and dangerous plans in the face of the enemy. His quickness of thought and penetration of the enemy's intentions – stemming in large part from sea sense and informed reflection, probably aided by good eyesight – enabled him to exploit the transient opportunities of naval engagement, especially those that occurred as the fleets closed to contact. His perspective on war was invariably offensive: he was anxious to engage the enemy wherever encountered, and without hesitation. The Nile was the ultimate expression of Hood's style: a well-briefed squadron launched into battle without a thought for the line, or an order of sailing, because the situation warranted such action. Concentration of force two against one, as in the plan he proposed at Gourjean Bay in 1794,[52] could be managed by a man with the foresight to anticipate enemy failings and the practical skill to put lanterns in the rigging for identification in a night engagement. Hood understood that a battle was only part of a campaign, and that it should be exploited to the fullest extent. His greatest achievements at sea, off St Kitts, in Frigate Bay and the Saintes, only hinted at the rich vein of insight and acumen that informed his judgement.

While Hood was 'apt to be censorious, and impulsiveness often led him into exaggeration . . . his warm heartedness and cheeriness won him the devotion of subordinates, and carried him through difficulties insuperable to mediocre or desponding natures'.[53] His direct leadership, concern for drill and discussion with his subordinates provided a model for his most famous protégé.[54] His plans were carefully explained, and he always thought ahead, often picking up points of detail that made operations run more smoothly. He was always in the post of honour and danger, never more so than during the siege of Toulon, where he served on shore and rallied the troops, despite his advanced age.[55] His fleets were in good order because he inspired his officers by example, rather than harsh measures. But once his leadership was removed, his fleet quickly fell into disorder and confusion. It was an eighteenth-century approach, personal, unique and quite irreplaceable. The endless needs of total war ultimately made such idiosyncratic methods unacceptable; the navy needed a generation of leaders, not a single great man.

Even in defeat, at Toulon, Hood never lost his optimism or his ability to think through the problems. These qualities, which in large part reflected force of character, were complemented by outstanding communication skills. Nelson famously observed, 'He is certainly the best Officer I ever saw. Everything from him is so clear, it is impossible to misunderstand him.'[56] Nelson realised that Hood took responsibility for the actions of his subordinates, possessed the mind and activity of a much younger man, and never gave way to despair.

This last was an essential quality when he was campaigning in Corsica with British generals who lacked his drive and commitment. Dealing with the vast demands of the Mediterranean theatre, where diplomacy, politics, alliance warfare and logistics required constant attention, was as much as any officer could handle. Hood was equally effective in using intelligence and other assets to further his aims. Above all, he was a man who never wasted time, constantly trying to keep the enemy off-balance.

As a fleet commander, his concern was to ensure his ideas were simple and easily understood, and that he could convey the key points. He added a signal for breaking the line after the Saintes, and directed his secretary to codify the new signal book of Lord Howe to ensure all officers could use it. He was undoubtedly a great admiral.

So why does Hood not deserve a chapter to himself? The simple answer is that he lacked the sustained professional application required for the wars of the French Revolution and Empire. His brilliance was that of the eighteenth century, and as his pupils discovered, required some updating to be truly effective in the new circumstances. He tended to take on too much himself and did not delegate enough, a habit reinforced by the relative poverty of talent among the flag officers and senior captains he selected in 1793. While Nelson, Fremantle and others rose to the top, Linzee, Goodall, Gell and Hotham were at best capable seconds. When he left the Mediterranean, everything began to fail: his success was personal and did not survive his departure. He did not build a system and did not bother to pass on his confidential orders to Hotham when he sailed home in November 1794.

Moreover, he had personal failings that sometimes undermined his judgement. That 'crushing condescension' he used as a management tool, conveyed in tones of 'acrimonious contempt', proved to be a weakness: it did not reconcile and conciliate, but rather alienated and disgusted.[57] When Nelson failed him in the 1780s, Hood withdrew his support, and only slowly restored it in 1793. He never supported those who failed: he was quick to judge and hasty to punish, as if to shift the blame from himself. Nelson himself, by contrast, tended to the other extreme in this respect, protecting those who had failed where he believed them capable or unfortunate. Hood chose competent second-rate men to serve under him and kept the big decisions in his own hands because he had no faith in others.

While Hood was a brilliant analyst and critic of other men's errors, he lacked the reflection and capacity to be an effective critic of his own performance. This was the flip side of his boundless confidence and constant analysis of the moves of others. Yet despite his flaws, Samuel Hood remains a study in genius: the architect of annihilation.

The Professional

While Samuel Hood applied his unique genius within an eighteenth-century concept of war, with summer campaigns that permitted elderly officers to take the waters at Bath and resume their endeavours the following spring, John Jervis was made of sterner stuff. While Jervis lacked Hood's quickness of thought, tactical penetration and political courage, he provided the navy with the determination, seamanship and logistics to impose a close blockade like the one Lord Anson had used to cripple the Brest fleet in 1759 as the basis of national strategy. His school of officers – seamen to the core, professional and courageous – was the backbone of the navy's glory. It would be ships from his fleet that annihilated Bonaparte's dreams of an Alexandrine empire at the Nile, although the vital spark came from Hood's greatest pupil.

Jervis's navy – and he ran it as a reforming First Lord for three years – was a very modern affair: hard-nosed, aggressive and prepared to take big decisions. Jervis fortunately understood that he himself lacked the genius to turn his resources to best account, so when war came again in 1803, he chose Hood's pupils, Cornwallis and Nelson, to command his two big fleets. As a politician he proved partisan, narrow and inflexible; but as the creator of the professional navy that was vital to British success against Napoleon he was equalled only by Nelson.

Jervis raised the art of war at sea to a new level of professionalism: he kept ships at sea and took risks with wind and tide that earlier generations would have considered insane. His close blockade system was the ultimate test of command under sail, and his chosen followers met and exceeded that test in every ocean of the world between 1797 and 1815.

Making a Career

John Jervis entered the extensive Parker legal dynasty at Meaford in Staffordshire in 1735, with a useful if distant connection to Lord Anson. He was intended for the bar, not the sea.[58] His father evidently saw an opening for the boy in his own profession; indeed, his talents would have made him a worthy grandson of Chief Baron Sir Thomas Parker. However, Anson's patronage provided Swynfen Jervis with a position as Auditor of Greenwich Hospital, complete with accommodation, and in 1747 the family moved to the riverside palace. The proximity to mighty ships, old sailors and fabulous stories clearly worked the usual magic on an impressionable thirteen-year-old. That his kinsman Anson had made his name and fortune at sea was proof positive that a wartime naval career had potential.

Jervis's father seems to have been a lacklustre and irresolute fellow, overbearing and mean-spirited besides. In 1748, while his father was travelling on legal business, Jervis and a school friend stowed away on a ship at Woolwich, only to be forced home by hunger. The boy refused to return to school, so the hospital governor's wife found him a naval patron – hardly difficult for a boy with such connections. This stubborn and wilful streak would resurface throughout Jervis's adult life, often with less positive results. In January 1749 he entered HMS *Gloucester*, the flagship of Commodore George Townshend. After five years in the West Indies, he returned to England a lieutenant, having supported himself on his pay, with an initial gift of only twenty pounds from his mean father. From the start Jervis took a distinctly self-righteous pride in his dedication to his profession and learnt the importance of fresh food for maintaining health, though his resistance to the temptations of sea life proved imperfect.

When war broke out in 1756, Jervis was taken on board the flagship of Admiral Sir Charles Saunders, one of Anson's elite circumnavigators and a colleague of Swynfen Jervis at Greenwich. From Saunders' quarterdeck he progressed to his own command, the appropriately named sloop *Porcupine*, in May 1759. Saunders commanded the fleet that took James Wolfe's army to Quebec, and Jervis earned the eccentric young general's commendation for his quick and decisive conduct. On 13 October 1760, when Jervis was promoted to captain, his career was made. The rest of the war proved to be an active but unremarkable anticlimax, largely occupied with convoy duty.

He was held in high regard by Saunders, while the Admiralty gave him command of the first ship to be copper-sheathed, the frigate *Alarm*. Peacetime service was always a sure sign of merit and good connections; so was being sent with a cargo of bullion to the Mediterranean in 1769, earning a valuable freight commission. While unloading the cash at Genoa, two Turkish slaves escaped from a Genoese galley onto the *Alarm*'s boat. Genoese officials forcibly removed the slaves, but Jervis demanded their return, on pain of retaliation. The Genoese handed back the slaves and arrested the officials. Like any good professional, Jervis knew his precedents, telling his father that he had taken 'an opportunity of carrying the dignity of the British flag as high as a Blake'.[59] The *Alarm* returned to the Mediterranean in 1771, as the holiday transport of a royal duke.

Jervis spent 1772 in France, learning the language of the enemy and absorbing the latest theoretical writing on naval signalling and tactics. A visit to the Baltic and the Russian arsenal at Cronstadt in 1773 widened his knowledge of other navies, while a cruise off the west coast of France in 1775 widened his store of useful knowledge. In 1775 Jervis took command of the Portsmouth guardship HMS *Foudroyant*, an eighty-gun battleship, which he took to war in 1778. He fought in the indecisive battle off Cape Ushant that year and backed his admiral, Anson's protégé Augustus Keppel, at the subsequent court martial. On 19 April 1782 he captured the French seventy-four *Pègase* off Brest in a one-sided action that lasted less than an hour. Jervis was one of only five men wounded, while the French ship suffered severely. Single-ship glory earned him a knighthood and public fame. He took the opportunity of peace to marry his first cousin Martha Parker in June 1783. The marriage produced no children.

Public fame was swiftly converted into a political career, under the guidance of his patron the Earl of Shelburne, whose agenda of moderate political reform and significant administrative improvement he shared. Jervis was a long-time critic of the waste and inefficiency of naval administration, from the Admiralty Board to the royal dockyards. In 1786 he made a forceful speech in Parliament on the need for root-and-branch reform, while later efforts resulted in improved treatment for superannuated officers and seamen. Shelburne was initially a supporter of William Pitt the Younger, but by the early 1790s the two had moved apart over the looming war with revolutionary France. Despite Shelburne's opposition to the war, Jervis put his name forward and was given the naval command of a joint expedition to the West Indies, with fellow Whig general Sir Charles Grey, in the autumn of 1793. The following spring he resigned his seat in Parliament, and never stood again.

With Grey's son serving as flag captain and the general often living on board, their close friendship proved a vital command tool for joint operations. The 1794 West Indies campaign opened well, taking Martinique, Guadeloupe and St Lucia, but French reinforcements, fired with republican zeal, recovered Guadeloupe while the British army wasted away from tropical disease. By the time Jervis left that November, the tide of success had ebbed to reveal some unpleasantly old-fashioned conduct over prizes, profits and preferment. Jervis and Grey had exceeded their authority in disposing of prize goods through their own *ad hoc* courts, alienating French royalists, providing a propaganda coup for the republicans and harassing neutral carriers. A motion of censure on the two commanders was defeated in the House of Commons in May 1795, but few doubted they were guilty.[60] John Jervis's matchless probity had failed, and not for the last time.

Mediterranean Command

The Whig First Lord, Earl Spencer, desperately needed an officer of merit to replace Hood, whom he had unceremoniously sacked; once Jervis's name had been cleared in the House of Commons, largely by Whig votes, the appointment was made. Arriving in Corsica at the end of November 1795, Jervis hoisted his flag on HMS *Victory* and found a fleet full of aggressive, ambitious warrior captains, led by uninspired flag officers lacking the skill and resilience for the task. The admirals went home, and in their stead Jervis used senior captains like Nelson and Thomas Troubridge. His energy and determination infused every aspect of the fleet: he made it clear from the outset that any officer who went home for 'health' or 'private affairs' should not come back. Nelson, who had planned to follow Hood home, quickly understood that the nature of service had changed: he would stay with Jervis until forced home by serious wounds. With little more than an open roadstead for a base, and few stores, Jervis made his fleet refit with any resources they could find. By holding station and keeping up appearances, Jervis dominated the enemy, ensuring they never came to sea. However, Britain's fragile hold on the Mediterranean evaporated once Spain joined the French in October. Outnumbered and friendless, Jervis was ordered to retreat to Lisbon. This last point is critical: Jervis obeyed his orders with skill and determination, but rarely took the initiative at the highest level. He lacked the confidence and decision that informed Hood's actions at Toulon or Corsica.

Jervis entrusted the evacuation of Corsica to Nelson, his best captain. With the fleet safely outside the Mediterranean, he sent Nelson back to evacuate the garrison of Elba. Once again Nelson succeeded brilliantly, and on the return voyage he reconnoitred Toulon, which was empty, and Cartegena, which was equally bare. Realising the enemy was at sea, Nelson hurried south with this vital intelligence to rejoin Jervis in the Straits of Gibraltar. The French fleet, led by Pierre de Villeneuve, passed the Straits and reached Brest, but the Spanish had been delayed. When Admiral Cordoba finally got to sea, under enormous political pressure, he was also charged with assisting the siege of Gibraltar and escorting four vital mercury ships to Cadiz, before heading for Brest to support an invasion of England. Attempting two tasks on one cruise was always going to be problematic; to set three for a fleet as inexperienced as Cordoba's was a recipe for disaster. The British had no such problem. Their fleet was far better prepared, and their object far simpler. Jervis knew that defeating the Spanish fleet would break the enemy's strategy.

Cordoba encountered heavy weather off Cadiz and but for the mercury ships could have sailed for Brest without a fight. Instead, he rode out the storm in the Atlantic approaches, in plain view. By late December Jervis had lost two seventy-fours, while two more had to be sent home and another ship was seriously damaged. By the beginning of February he had only nine battleships. Having taken station off Cape St Vincent on 6 February, he gleaned enough information to know the Spanish were still near Cadiz. Nelson rejoined early on the 13th, having passed right through the Spanish fleet the night before and bearing fresh information on the enemy ships. By the end of the day Jervis knew the enemy's strength and that they lay to the south-east, heading for Cadiz. All he had to do to force a battle was to place his fleet in their path. The mood that evening was infectious, for the fleet had just been reinforced. Jervis commanded fifteen battleships: six powerful three-decked ships, eight standard seventy-fours and a single sixty-four. Cordoba had twenty-three: seven three-deckers, two eighty-fours and the rest seventy-fours; the four mercury transports, big armed ships, could be mistaken for ships of the line, but only at a distance. Four Spanish battleships had been detached and took no part in the fighting. In all respects other than numbers of ships, the forces were very unequal. The Spanish were short of time at sea, seamen and combat experience, while the combat-hardened British had been at sea for years: five ships freshly arrived from the Channel fleet would perform as well as Jervis's veterans. Both sides knew there was a major difference in quality, and this knowledge would play a key part in the battle.

When the two fleets came in sight at daybreak on 14 February, Cordoba believed that Jervis still had only nine ships and decided to push through to Cadiz. Forming a line of battle and fighting an inconclusive action was his only hope in the face of a more skilful and resolute opponent. Realising the British were more numerous than he had anticipated, Cordoba reversed course to cover his merchant ships, and in the process a gap opened between the main body and the escort force. This was all the encouragement Jervis required. His tactics had been set long before: he was going to drive through the enemy fleet, divide it and then destroy one of the sections, an idea he had been discussing with Nelson for over a year. Despite the significant disparity in force, he employed tactics better suited to a battle between equal fleets. He sent six ships to chase, and then at 10.57 signalled for the fleet to form a line of battle in the shortest time on a bearing set by the flagship. At 11.26 he advised the fleet that he meant to pass through the gap in the Spanish fleet. For a man of Nelson's penetration, either signal would have been a delight; together they confirmed all the hopes he had placed in his admiral. Jervis had abandoned eighteenth-century formalism and was now doing what he believed should have been done on many previous occasions. The most significant precedent for his tactics – one that he must have discussed with Nelson, Troubridge and other captains

– was the example provided by Captain Edward Hawke in 1744, when he left the line of battle off Toulon to close with and capture an enemy ship.

Cordoba was unsettled by Jervis's move and by the remarkable seamanship and celerity of the British ships as they formed a fighting line. If Jervis had not moved so quickly, the Spanish would have been able to reunite their force; instead, Troubridge's *Culloden* led the line through the gap, forcing the Spanish three-decker leading the detached portion of the fleet to sheer off with two double-shotted broadsides. At 12.08 Jervis, having divided the Spanish, ordered his own fleet to tack in succession to engage their main body. Brave attempts by the detached force to block Jervis's move were beaten off, but this caused a gap to open between the five ships led by Troubridge and the rest of the British force. Furthermore, the wind had shifted, increasing the distance between the two parts of the fleet. Anxious to get a better view of the situation, Jervis climbed onto the poop deck, only for a round of shot to take the head of the marine standing beside him, leaving the admiral splattered with blood and brains. Assuring his staff that he was uninjured, he called for an orange to rinse his mouth.

Anxious to keep up the tempo of the attack and to support the five leading ships, Jervis wanted the rear division to reinforce the van by tacking into their wake, while the centre division engaged on the opposite quarter, placing the Spanish between two forces. He wanted Troubridge to be joined by Admiral Thompson in the *Britannia*, leading the rear division. To Jervis's mounting displeasure Thompson failed to take in either the signal made at 12.50 to 'tack in succession' or the following one to 'take suitable station and engage'. The gap between the five advanced ships and the rest of the fleet was growing with every minute; the admiral's hastily modified plans had failed.

Throughout the opening phases of the battle, Nelson, on board the *Captain*, had been watching in admiration as Jervis's plans unfolded. Stationed near the rear of the British line, he had a good viewpoint, which he enhanced by shifting to a course parallel with the British line in order to clear his view of the admiral's signals from gunsmoke. As a commodore with a captain to command the ship, he had ample opportunity to watch and think. He was conscious of Troubridge's exposed position and read the signals that Thompson failed to note. More significantly, he had an excellent view of Cordoba's flagship, the unique four-decked *Santissima Trinidad*, which began to signal furiously. The fleets having passed on opposite courses, the Spanish now overlapped the British rear, and Cordoba saw the chance to alter course, pass astern of the British line and reform his fleet. When a group of Spanish ships began to move in that direction, Nelson decided to act. Jervis was too far away to see, and Thompson was not answering the signal to tack in succession, which had now been overtaken by events.

Nelson acted because he had the utmost confidence in his own judgement and because he knew his commander-in-chief. He did not expect to be rebuked for abandoning the line or using the initiative that Jervis had pointedly given him only twelve months earlier. Nelson wore his ship, rather than tacked – a quicker manoeuvre, although less suitable for a squadron than a ship – then cut back through the British line and took station ahead of Troubridge's *Culloden*. The two ships quickly turned the Spanish fleet back onto their old course. The *Captain* was engaged by many Spanish ships, but Nelson, who had recent knowledge of Spanish gunnery, knew the risk was acceptable.

The speed of the British move surprised the inexperienced Spanish ships, and their line collapsed, leaving Cordoba under attack with only five other ships in company. Jervis finally managed to get his rear division into battle, and soon two lines of British ships were chasing the Spanish: one astern, the other on the starboard quarter. Both were closing quickly. At 14.05 Jervis signalled for close action and for Cuthbert Collingwood's *Excellent* to pass through the enemy fleet. Collingwood was no sooner bid than he raced into action, his finely honed gun crews shattering the four rearmost Spanish ships. Each time he passed on to engage new targets. Jervis had ordered him into action to relieve the *Culloden* and the *Captain*, now closely engaged with several Spanish ships. The *Captain* was effectively disabled by the time Jervis flew the signal 'Engage the Enemy More Closely', which Nelson so admired. The superior speed and accuracy of British gunnery enabled British seventy-fours to master Spanish 112-gun three-deckers. After forcing two ships to surrender, Collingwood ran between Nelson and his opponents, pouring in rapid broadsides at pistol shot. The two Spanish ships collided, while *Excellent* set off after Cordoba in the *Santissima*, the ultimate prize.

Nelson, Troubridge and Collingwood had broken the back of the Spanish fleet, leaving four ships crippled and the rest fleeing in disorder. The eighty-four-gun *San Nicolas* and the 112-gun *San Josef* had collided, stunned by Collingwood's fire, and remained entangled. With his ship crippled, Nelson could take no further part in the battle: he ordered the *Captain* alongside the *San Nicolas* and boarded the two ships, one after the other. Two more ships were taken, while the *Santissima* hauled down her colours, but Jervis called off the attack shortly after 16.00, before a British ship could take possession.[61] While the British secured their prizes and repaired their ships, the Spanish crept away.

In truth, the result was little better than Rodney achieved at the Saintes: Jervis had allowed a beaten enemy to escape, and did not attempt to pursue and destroy. The Spanish formation had collapsed and there was still time for an effective pursuit. By the morning they might have recovered their composure and their formation. Jervis lacked Hood's absolute obsession with annihilation. Nelson had been in no position to pursue: his ship was the most heavily damaged of all, and he had cashed in his chips to win undying fame by boarding. He did not reflect on the missed opportunities of 14 February 1797 because he would make the very best of his own. That evening Nelson boarded the *Victory*, where Jervis greeted his grimy and battered commodore with public thanks and a professional appreciation of his merits. After a brief stand-off the following day with the reinforced and reformed Spanish fleet, Jervis allowed Cordoba to withdraw back to Cadiz. He then took his own squadron into Lagos Bay to refit.

Jervis's brief public report avoided singling out anyone for praise, but a private letter to the First Lord praised Troubridge, Collingwood and especially Nelson, 'who contributed very much to the fortune of the day'. He was understandably anxious to remove Admiral Thompson. Nelson produced his own account of the battle, which his wife was quick to show to Hood, who was in raptures. After St Vincent, Jervis was ordered to blockade the Spanish fleet in Cadiz, although he was equally anxious to intercept a Spanish treasure convoy. This was a matter of national importance: the length and cost of the war was making unprecedented demands on the British economy, demands that even the fiscal expert William Pitt struggled to meet. In the wake of failed peace negotiations in late 1796, the evacuation of the Mediterranean and the landing at Fishguard in February 1797, there was a run on the banks. Money was in short supply, and in order to meet the problem, Pitt suspended bank payments in gold and silver, introduced paper money and issued captured Spanish silver dollars as legal tender from March 1797. When Jervis sent Nelson to attack Tenerife, then, his object was to raise cash at a time of severe shortage at home.[62] A successful attack would secure 'six or seven million pounds sterling . . . thrown into circulation in England, it would ensure an honourable peace'.[63] It would also, of course, knock Spain out of the war. It was for these stakes that Jervis gambled the lives of Nelson and his followers. Though his object was national salvation, his personal share would also be welcome, for John Jervis was never slow in claiming his rewards. In the event, Nelson's attack on Tenerife was an abject failure: the landing force suffered heavy casualties, Nelson was lucky to escape with his life after his right arm was shattered, and there were no dollars.

On 23 June 1797 Jervis was created Baron Meaford and Earl of St Vincent, with a life annuity of £3,000. The title was chosen by the King, despite Jervis's concern that it might appear arrogant to adopt the name of his victory. However, he had more important matters to attend to, for the after-effects of the 1797 Spithead and Nore mutinies had reached the Mediterranean fleet. Here the political and social strains of war met the immovable rock of Earl St Vincent's discipline. He stepped up inspections by officers, segregated the Royal Marines from the seamen, banned the use of the Irish language and kept his jaundiced, unsleeping eye on every new ship that arrived. When two men were convicted of mutiny one Saturday, he had them hung the next morning, despite one admiral protesting that he was profaning the Sabbath; St Vincent had him recalled. When the men of HMS *Marlborough* refused to hang a mutineer, St Vincent sent armed boats to surround the ship and prepare to fire; the *Marlborough*'s men hauled their shipmate up to meet his maker at the end of the yard arm. The ferocity of Jervis's discipline was carefully calculated to meet the demands of the moment: Britain was facing an ideological as well as a military threat, and those who spread subversion and indiscipline were a fundamental threat to the state. Even Nelson, who took a far more modern view of his men, backed the admiral on this occasion.

When a hastily repaired Nelson rejoined the fleet in the spring of 1798, St Vincent had weathered the crisis of the naval war through hard work, harsh discipline and high standards. In the process, he had welded the best units of his fleet into the elite 'inshore squadron' that had kept up the blockade of Cadiz: these were the best ships in the Royal or any other navy. It was this force that St Vincent entrusted to Nelson when the Admiralty ordered him into the Mediterranean to take, sink, burn or otherwise destroy the menacing French armada that Napoleon had assembled. St Vincent's role in the Nile campaign was to support Nelson. Several flag officers protested that their superior rank entitled them to the opportunity, but Jervis sent home the ringleader, Sir John Orde. Though the Admiralty considered that the earl had gone too far this time, it did not reverse his decision. When St Vincent heard that Nelson had annihilated the French fleet in Aboukir Bay, he detached Commodore John Duckworth to seize Minorca, the best base in the western Mediterranean.

By this stage the earl was exhausted and ill, effectively commanding from ashore at Gibraltar. Nelson's prizes were refitted at the newly energised dockyard and victualling base, with remarkable results. On the basis of this brief, small-scale experience St Vincent would attempt to overhaul the royal dockyards, the largest industrial enterprise in eighteenth-century Europe. Although too sick to remain afloat for any length of time, St Vincent fancied himself irreplaceable, and with the tide turning in Britain's favour there was a rush of rich prizes, so he decided to hang on to his command. Only the sudden, dramatic appearance of a French squadron from Brest took him back to sea, where his health failed. Finally, in June 1799, he had to hand the command to Admiral Lord Keith and go home – his reason for delay had been to secure additional prize income. In the years that followed, he sued Nelson for the commander-in-chief's share of the prize money earned while he had not been on the station, but he lost the case in 1802. The squalid pursuit of other men's rewards ruined his private relationship with Nelson, although both men were sufficiently professional to ensure the public service did not suffer.[64] However, St Vincent's occasional slighting references to Nelson should be read in the light of this dispute.

The Channel Fleet and the Admiralty

After spending eight months recuperating from rheumatism and dropsy at his country seat, Rochetts in Essex, St Vincent was begged to assume command of the Channel fleet. This was the pinnacle of his ambition, and he took with him a handful of Mediterranean captains like Troubridge and James de Saumarez to ensure that his ideas of discipline were adopted. The Channel fleet had been run with a light touch by Lord Howe and Lord Bridport for the first five years of the war, and few expressed any enthusiasm for the new regime. St Vincent imposed new levels of discipline so that he could carry out a different strategy. He imposed common-sense professional rules for officers' conduct, banning them from sleeping ashore when in England, for example, so that the ships would always be ready to sail. Many officers had moved their wives close to the anchorage at Torbay and deeply resented being made to show an example to their men, who were not allowed any such opportunity. With a major concentration of French and Spanish battleships at Brest, it was essential to prevent the enemy getting to sea, and St Vincent swiftly adopted the 'inshore squadron' concept used off Cadiz. With a small force close to the enemy base, in visual range, and the main fleet lying in more secure waters out to sea, he could keep the enemy bottled up. This was the blockade system used by Anson and Hawke in 1759; now it was the key to the survival of the British Empire.

The standard of seamanship required on this station laid the foundations for the success of the Royal Navy. Defeating the French in battle was child's play after a winter off the Black Rock. Logistics were improved to sustain the fleet with food, water, clothes and other essentials; St Vincent's personal physician ensured that lemon juice and fresh food were available to prevent scurvy; and improved treatment for the sick ensured that most recovered. The 1800 campaign was a remarkable display of sustained blockade and exemplary health, and in the event the Royal Navy had little trouble living up to the standards St Vincent set, for they were good practice, common sense and received wisdom, distilled with an admixture of pure vitriol.

Over the winter of 1800–1 St Vincent was forced ashore by his health, handing the fleet over to Admiral Sir William Cornwallis, who maintained the blockade without the acidic commentary. A

disciple of Hood and a veteran of the Saintes, Cornwallis was a better fleet commander for the day of battle[65] – not that the enemy had
any intention of putting to sea in the face of such opponents. Nor
had the earl forgotten the shore establishments, writing to the First
Lord: 'Nothing short of a radical sweep in the dockyards can cure
the enormous evils and corruptions in them; and this cannot be
attempted until we have peace.'[66]

In early 1801 Prime Minister William Pitt resigned, and his successor Henry Addington persuaded St Vincent to accept office as
First Lord of the Admiralty. He faced an immediate crisis: the
'Armed Neutrality' of the Baltic powers, Russia, Prussia, Sweden
and Denmark, demanded that Britain abandon its rigorous interpretation of belligerent rights at sea with regard to neutral shippers,
or else face war. When the dockyard workmen used the occasion to
go on strike, they found 'old Jarvie' in no mood to be trifled with.
He sacked every man who took a significant part in the strike; the
rest went back to work, fitting out a Baltic fleet in time for the Battle
of Copenhagen. Nelson's brilliant stroke crushed the Armed
Neutrality and highlighted the utter folly of the administration sending the feeble Sir Hyde Parker as his superior. When Nelson
returned, St Vincent immediately sent him to watch the threatened
French invasion, more to calm the nerves of the frightened populace
than because of any real threat.

When peace negotiations with France opened in October 1801,
the earl prepared for a shattering assault on the administration of
the navy. The Peace of Amiens, signed in March 1802, allowed him
to commence reforms that reflected his long-harboured hatred of
inefficiency, corruption, mismanagement and waste. Many realised
that the peace was only a brief truce between two exhausted com-
batants in a life-and-death struggle for survival, but such concerns
did not trouble the earl: in his anxiety to implement radical change,
he was prepared to tear down the whole structure. His own experience of shoreside administration and management was limited, and
he made no effort to consult those who were better placed. He visited the naval bases, and was horrified: 'Chatham dockyard appears
. . . a viler sink of corruption than any imagination ever formed.
Portsmouth was bad enough but this beggars all description.'[67]

Instead of cooperating with the Navy Board, he treated the
Controller, a senior naval officer with extensive administrative expe-

rience, with contempt and viewed the Board itself as a festering source of corruption. In part the object was to reduce the Navy Board to proper subordination, but it was also ideologically driven monomania. Penetrating enquiries rooted out all manner of petty malfeasance, graft and folly, but St Vincent's ultimate object – to prosecute the offenders and replace them with his nominees – was thwarted. This was fortunate, for St Vincent had little understanding of the complex business and was too quick to impute dishonesty, while his lieutenants, the ever-zealous Troubridge and Captain John Markham, were attack dogs rather than advisers.

Inevitably the morale of the naval administration collapsed, while the much-maligned timber suppliers and shipbuilders refused to contract. When the war with France resumed in 1803, St Vincent's administration of the navy was the principal complaint of the opposition and the government's main weakness. Little wonder: the dockyards were short-handed, the timber piles reduced to matchsticks, the goodwill of contractors and workmen alike entirely withdrawn. By January 1804 even St Vincent's own Admiralty secretary had been driven to resign. In May 1804 the government was dissolved, but the navy took a long time to recover from St Vincent's ill-advised reforms.

Fortunately St Vincent did far better as a strategist. When war resumed in 1803, he had selected Cornwallis for the Channel fleet, Nelson for the Mediterranean, and Lord Keith for the North Sea, placing the three best senior officers in situations that suited their talents. Cornwallis and Keith placed an impenetrable wooden wall between France and Britain, leaving Nelson free to act as the sharp sword of state, ready to annihilate any French fleet that put to sea. Trafalgar was the culmination of St Vincent's strategy, as interpreted by Nelson and Cornwallis, men whose genius acted on a higher plane than his own. Although personally estranged from Nelson since 1801, St Vincent was stunned by his death.

Despite the entreaties of the King and the returning prime minister, St Vincent refused to resume the Channel command unless Pitt apologised for criticising his administration.[68] At a time of national emergency this was mean-minded, partisan and pathetic. Only in 1806, when his Whig friends returned to office, did St Vincent take up the command again, though once again his health failed and he stood down in March 1807. It was his last public office. In retirement he occasionally spoke in the House of Lords, opposing the

Copenhagen expedition of 1807 as dishonourable, applying old-fashioned notions of national integrity to a crisis that threatened the very survival of the British state. He remained a bitter partisan to the end, refusing to allow the honours and rewards of a distinguished old age to still his venomous pen. In 1821 he was especially promoted to the rank of Admiral of the Fleet, attending King George IV at Greenwich in August the following year in a unique ceremony. Yet such honours did not temper his hatred of the Navy Board. When the government reduced the dockyard labour force a month later, he wrote to a close friend:

I agree with you in toto as to the rapid ruin of the British Navy; instead of discharging valuable and experienced men, of all descriptions, from the dockyards, the commissioners and secretaries of all the boards ought to be reduced to the lowest number they ever stood at, and the old system resorted to: one of the projectors of the present diabolical measures should be gibbeted opposite the Deptford Yard, and the other opposite to Woolwich Yard, on the Isle of sad Dogs.[69]

He died at home on 13 March 1823.

Admiral of the Fleet

John Jervis was the ideal foil for Samuel Hood: his dedication, commitment and professionalism complemented the older man's insight, genius and dynamism. Together they moulded an officer corps that would defeat all comers and establish a century of unchallenged naval mastery. Jervis failed as the political head of the service, however, and it is highly significant that no sea officer has held the post of First Lord since 1806. His ideological imperative came closer to ruining the Royal Navy than anything Napoleon Bonaparte ever attempted, and the country was only saved from the consequences of such intemperate folly by his strategic judgement and the brilliance of the two great admirals he employed to carry it into effect. Nor was he an inspired fleet commander. His attempt to control the fleet during the battle of Cape St Vincent proved the existing signalling system to be remarkably opaque, both in conveying meaning and in effecting communication once the guns began to fire. Only Nelson took in the vital signal, and only Nelson fully understood what he was trying to achieve. This was the result of discussion and the exchange of ideas between admiral and captain. Had

Jervis briefed all of his captains and adopted a more permissive doc-trine, the battle could have been more decisive. Similarly the failure to pursue was, if perfectly understandable, hardly in line with cur-rent best practice. The Spanish fleet was broken and demoralised, so even a partial pursuit might have paid dividends. Instead, Jervis took care of his valuable prizes, and his cripples, and several of the Spanish ships lived to fight another day – a day on which Nelson would finish what he had begun that afternoon. In 1805 Sir Robert Calder, Captain of the Fleet at Cape St Vincent, fought a battle in the same fashion, only to be court-martialled and censured.

As an enabler, motivator and hard driver Jervis succeeded: he picked out talented men, adopted the best practice from the past and the present to mould a more professional service, and did so just in time to meet the life-and-death challenge of the Napoleonic wars. Brave and cool under pressure, he was not given to reflection, and does not seem to have changed his mind about anything. This was a major flaw. A closer examination of his record as a theatre com-mander reveals a striking lack of initiative: he acted on orders, and acted well, but he waited to be told what to do. There was nothing proactive or forward-thinking about his leadership.

For all his talents Jervis was a divisive figure: he lacked the human warmth to build a following throughout the service, beyond a small circle of privileged officers. Nor was he any better at conciliating the feelings of the lower deck. He cared greatly for the welfare and health of his men, but his hard-edged professionalism was rarely tempered by any indulgence. Instead, he exacerbated his crews' sense of an entrenched, antagonistic 'us and them' mentality in which class-based divisions were upheld by armed marines. His pri-vate generosity was no substitute for simple human consideration in his public conduct; he upset many men, not all of them fools or crooks, and did more harm than good at the Admiralty. Further-more, there was always a hint of hypocrisy and the whiff of cor-ruption about him – he never forgot his penurious beginnings.

St Vincent completed Nelson's education by teaching him the supreme importance of absolute dedication, high professional stan-dards and attention to detail. When Nelson took command of squadrons and fleets, he adopted St Vincent's Standing Orders, thus using the management tools of one great officer while applying the command concepts of another, moulded together by his own unique approach to leadership. While Nelson had admired fine seamen and brave warriors like Captain William Locker, Hood and Jervis taught him the art of the admiral. Speaking in the House of Lords on 30 October 1801, Nelson seconded a motion by St Vincent, then First Lord of the Admiralty, that the thanks of the House be given to Admiral Sir James de Saumarez for his brilliant action off Algeciras. After describing the action in a manner that enabled the noble but largely land-bound peers to understand it, Nelson then placed it in context. He declared that the unsurpassed merit of the achievement 'would be less wondered at, when the school in which he was educated was considered by their Lordships. He was educated at first under Lord Hood, and afterwards under the Noble Earl near him' (by whom he meant St Vincent).[70] The speech earned Nelson generous applause, but it was no mere courtesy to the other naval peers in the chamber. Nor were the benefits of this 'education' restricted to de Saumarez. In truth Nelson was speaking about himself: he too had consciously sought the patronage of Hood, the leading strategist and tactician in the service in 1782, shifting his ambition to the more durable figure of Jervis in 1796. By doing so, he had neatly changed his methods and sensibilities to match the new age, and his appreciation that war had reached a new level. These two men provided him with the inspired education and advanced practical training that enabled him to reach the heights of genius, meet the demands of total war and become the national icon.

After Trafalgar, the Royal Navy had another ten years of hard work before the final victory, but it did not require a Nelson to carry the war to a conclusion. Instead, this situation produced a host of talented, hard-working professionals. While Nelson's protégé William Hoste was the closest to his exemplar in talent, it was Jervis's nephew, another of Nelson's frigate captains, who bore the load of post-war command. After Trafalgar, there would be very few opportunities for a classic main fleet battle: the Royal Navy has only fought one such action in the past two centuries, and that proved tactically inconclusive. Rather, command, management and leadership have been vital to the effective use of naval power, in diplomacy, deterrence, power projection, technology, strategy, human resources and hydrography. Little wonder that 'Old Jarvie' has been such a powerful presence in the service.

6

DIPLOMACY AND DETERRENCE
William Parker
1781–1866

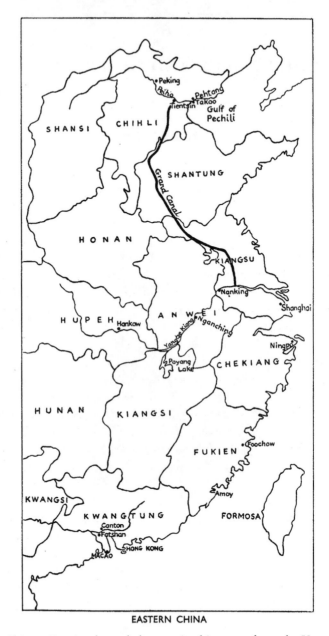

EASTERN CHINA

The Chinese Empire depended on grain shipments from the Yangtze to feed the population of Peking. When the British cut the Grand Canal, they defeated the most populous nation on earth – with a surgical strike

Admiral sir william parker was a man of firm principles.[1] He did not permit the filthy habit of smoking on his flagship, and would not appoint officers who smoked.[2] However, his decision was based on sound professional concerns: the 'pernicious practice of smoking', he observed, 'tends to confuse many, otherwise clear-headed, men – produces in some habits of intemperance – it is, at best, a very expensive indulgence, and sometimes fraught with danger'.[3] He was equally firm with the enemies of the state.

Born on 1 December 1781 at Almington in Staffordshire, William Parker joined a family with powerful legal connections, but he was always destined for a naval career. He would follow in the footsteps of John Jervis, his father's cousin and brother-in-law, and his aunt's husband. As the younger son of a landed family, he needed a career free from the taint of 'trade', socially equal with the army and the law. These careers were costly, and his father had more children than his limited income could provide for. Only the navy offered status and pay – but it required application and professionalism. Jervis tried to dissuade William's father from sending his son to sea, on account of 'the small probability . . . of any warfare happening in my time'.[4] Six months later, however, Britain and France were at war and would remain so for most of the next twenty-two years. War made naval careers very attractive, promising rapid promotion and rich prizes for those who survived the lottery of disease, shipwreck and battle.

His relationship with Jervis gave the young Parker a distinct advantage: it enabled him to join the seventy-four-gun battleship HMS *Orion* just as war broke out, under the watchful eye of

Captain John Duckworth, one of Jervis's followers. Jervis was inevitably a powerful example for William, but he was also inspired by the gift his father gave him when he left home of Anson's first commission, inscribed as follows: 'Lord Anson, our relation by marriage, set out without the least patronage, and worked his own way to a peerage and the First Commissioner of the Admiralty, an example of encouragement worthy of your attention.'[5] The commission was in Parker's desk at his death, among his most prized possessions.

After a cruise to the West Indies, *Orion* joined the Channel fleet and fought in Lord Howe's victory on 'The Glorious First of June', 1794. When the ship returned to harbour, Duckworth was distressed to find some of the men drunk and mutinous. Although they repented when the sober Duckworth punished most of them, it was a lesson in man management that Parker never forgot. He excelled at exams, passing navigation in first place. In 1795 Parker followed Duckworth into the *Leviathan*, which went to the West Indies, where he remained until 1800. Duckworth used his privilege as acting commander-in-chief to appoint the fifteen-year-old boy as acting lieutenant of HMS *Magicienne*, a ship commanded by his relative William Henry Ricketts, Earl St Vincent's nephew and heir. This was no coincidence. From October 1796 Parker was a watch-keeping officer on a successful cruiser in a station full of prizes and privateers. For all his ability and enthusiasm, the boy was still three years short of his proper sea time. Despite his connection, the standards set in the days of James, Duke of York were upheld: it was not until March 1799, after six years' service, that Parker was finally commissioned.

However, the exigencies of war ensured that long before this Parker was the acting commander of a twenty-four-gun ship. At this impressionable age he witnessed the execution of several mutineers from HMS *Hermione*, men who had butchered their officers and handed their ship to the Spanish.[6] Unlike the sadistic Captain Pigot, he maintained strict discipline but applied it fairly and without severity. At the age of eighteen, Parker took command of the sloop *Stork*, continuing a successful career as a cruiser captain. He had learnt his business from excellent officers, and collected enough prize money to make his parents an allowance. The support of his relatives, the Earl of Macclesfield and Earl St Vincent, ensured his promotion to commander in October 1799.

In 1800 Parker returned to England and joined his uncle's Channel fleet. He dined with Nelson, 'who is very pleasant at table, and chatted a good deal about his intention of giving the Danes and Swedes a thrashing'.[7] Zeal and bold seamanship secured Parker many prizes, although he pushed his ship to the limits. Despite his youth, he was already a fine judge of officers and men and an attentive patron. He had a number of prime seamen and petty officers on his list, and the beginnings of a quarterdeck following. By the time Parker became a post-captain in October 1801, no one could deny that he had earned it, although patronage had ensured his merits were recognised. Nor did he take his privileged position for granted: 'I must consider myself one of the luckiest young men in the Service,' he admitted, attributing his success to St Vincent and Sir William Cornwallis.[8] Both men independently decided to move him into a small frigate, ensuring he reached the post list before the end of hostilities. Characteristically, Cornwallis responded to the thanks of Parker's father by stressing that 'every attention paid to him by me has been in consequence of his merit'.[9] The greatest officers in the service saw star quality in William Parker. He was an outstanding cruiser commander with a wonderful record of captures and an ability to maintain both firm discipline and a harmonious atmosphere on board ship. Nor did he lack outside interests: he found relaxation in music, begging his sister for some violin scores and taking lessons from a professional player when he came ashore in 1802.[10]

Star Captain

For as long as his uncle remained First Lord of the Admiralty, Parker would not be forgotten. He even shared a house with St Vincent's private secretary, his brother. In consequence, he received a scarce peacetime commission, taking the frigate *Alarm*, the very ship that Anson had chosen for the experiment with copper sheathing and which Jervis had commanded thirty years earlier. The history lesson ended with his transfer to the larger frigate *Amazon* in November 1802.[11] This class of frigate, a fifth-rate armed with eighteen-pounder guns, was the standard heavy cruiser of the era, used for fleet scouting, commerce protection and detached operations. The independence of frigate command contrasted with the more regulated existence of the battleship captain, allowing greater scope for initiative and individual skill. Parker was soon enamoured of his 'wife', which was hardly surprising: she was fast and powerful under sail, although a challenge to maintain in good trim and prone to roll. These 'thoroughbred' qualities tested his seamanship, and he took enormous pride in making his ship 'the admiration of everyone'.[12]

Throughout this command Parker continued his education: 'whenever opportunities permitted he read substantial books; and his excellent memory enabled him to retain the knowledge acquired through them'. His wide range of interests may have helped develop an enlightened approach to naval command: 'A lover of discipline and order, he abominated every species of cruelty and unnecessary harshness.'[13] But his leadership also reflected an understanding of the crew: he knew who could be trusted with shore leave, and in which ports. After 1803 *Amazon*'s muster books record only one desertion, and in a career lasting over sixty years he never took an officer or man before a court martial. Yet his ship was rightly considered all but perfect. His Standing Orders provided simple, clear directions for both officers and the men. The men were to do their duty in silence, to keep themselves and the ship clean and tidy; the officers were not to disturb the men at their dinner other than for emergencies, and he directed that marine officers inspect their own men. His object was to generate mutual respect, though he was aware that the men he led were no angels: he reminded them that 'Contempt to an officer; drunkenness; fighting; and quarrelling will not be forgiven.'[14] Even so, this was 'a very enlightened culture of command', which he had developed from existing models through his own extensive experience.[15]

With his uncle at the Admiralty, Parker received some choice tasks. He brought the Duke of Kent home from Gibraltar, opening a useful patronage connection with Queen Victoria's father and his brother, the Duke of Sussex. When war broke out in 1803, he was given a 'good cruise' in the Atlantic approaches, where he took a powerful French privateer[16] – the first of twenty-one such craft captured over the next decade – and followed this with a profitable freight of diamonds from Lisbon. Finally, on Christmas Eve 1803, *Amazon* joined Nelson's Mediterranean fleet at anchor on the Sardinian coast: 'All the Captains and officers of the squadron are delighted with his Lordship, and I think I have a good prospect of being very happy under his command.'[17]

Nelson's Favourite

After *Amazon* had chased a French frigate back into Toulon, Nelson was quick to commend Parker's 'spirit' and all-round professionalism to St Vincent: 'I every day see new and excellent traits in him. Hardy is his great pattern about his ship, and a better he could not have.'[18] Parker often cruised off Toulon, watching for any sign of movement by the enemy fleet. Frigates were also used for less glamorous tasks, such as collecting fresh food. On one such mission Parker astonished Nelson by returning with sixty bullocks and thirty sheep, a remarkable feat that turned his gun deck into a farmyard but also earned him the next 'good' cruise. Typically, this involved a complex task: he had to take Nelson's dispatches through the newly established command of Sir John Orde in the Mediterranean approaches without revealing his mission. Parker slipped through Orde's fleet at night, only to be spotted by Captain William Hoste, Nelson's brilliant protégé. Hoste boarded the *Amazon*, but on reading Nelson's orders kept silent about the meeting.[19] Both men recognised a higher duty than mere obedience.

Parker's reward for his skilful actions, once he had seen the dispatches safely on their way from Lisbon, was a cruise off Cape St Vincent, where he took the Spanish ship *Gravina* on 27 January 1805. The prize had a fine cargo of colonial produce and 330,000 silver dollars. Parker had hit the jackpot: his prize share was £18,000 for the cash and another £6,000 for the ship. This was enough to set up his parents in some style, despite their objections, as well as forming the basis of his own fortune.

Rejoining Nelson in March, *Amazon* was immediately sent to Malta with dispatches to convoy the storeships back into the anchorage off Sardinia. Once the fleet had been replenished it put to sea, searching for the French. Parker picked up intelligence that Villeneuve had passed the Straits of Gibraltar: *Amazon* was detached to Lisbon for news. When he learnt that the enemy was sailing for the West Indies, Parker raced back to rejoin Nelson. It was the ability to think for himself, not just obey orders, that earned Parker the respect of the greatest admiral. This advanced understanding, based on shared professionalism and close attention to the ideas and methods of his superior, enabled Parker to exceed the expectations of a genius. Little wonder Nelson held him in the highest regard, treating him like a son.

The *Amazon* was one of the ships that Nelson led across the Atlantic in hot pursuit. Knowing he faced an enemy almost twice his strength, Nelson used the voyage to prepare for every eventuality. On 15 May he selected Parker to convey his tactical instructions to the fleet. Anxious to catch the enemy, who had a month's head start, Nelson refused to slow down while the message was delivered. Instead, Parker sailed ahead of the fleet and dropped his boat on the weather bow of each ship; a junior officer delivered the written memorandum and then reboarded the boat, which was recovered by the *Amazon* from the battleships' lee quarter.[20] Outstanding seamanship like this helped Nelson halve Villeneuve's advantage by the time he reached Barbados.

Having chased the enemy out of the West Indies, Nelson sent Parker ahead to locate them, finding out whether they had sailed for Cadiz or the Mediterranean. Villeneuve had in fact taken a more northerly route, putting into Ferrol. Proceeding north towards Cape Finisterre, Parker picked up intelligence that Villeneuve was heading south, and followed his instructions to take this information to Cork. Here two priceless convoys were waiting, one with troops to capture the Cape of Good Hope, the other carrying that season's East India Company trade. Then he joined Cornwallis, who was once more commanding the Channel fleet off Ushant, to repeat the message. It was brilliant, initiative-driven cruiser work such as this that destroyed Napoleon's plans in 1805: such scouting usually enabled British fleets to be in the right place at the right time, to the consternation of their opponents.[21]

Cornwallis had already heard the news, but he was still highly impressed, detaching *Amazon* to scout the Channel approaches for three weeks for a French squadron that had put to sea from Rochefort, as well as covering the incoming Jamaica convoy. The French proved elusive, but on 13 September Parker took a large Spanish privateer, saving many a merchant ship in the process. He came into Portsmouth harbour two weeks after Nelson had sailed to command the fleet off Cadiz. The Battle of Trafalgar was fought while *Amazon* underwent a much-needed refit: when the battered

Victory returned to Spithead, *Amazon* was just completing for sea, and Parker hastened on board to hear the details from his friend, Thomas Hardy. While the nation mourned the loss of their war god and talisman, Parker lamented the death of a friend and inspiration.

After Trafalgar

Amazon joined Admiral Sir John Borlase Warren's squadron, hunting for French detachments. Their targets proved elusive – Duckworth annihilated one in the West Indies and the other crept home – but Warren was a lucky commander. Late on 13 March 1806, cruising about six hundred miles west of the Canary Islands, one of his ships gave chase to two French warships. At daybreak, approximately 05.30, HMS *London* engaged the eighty-four-gun *Marengo*, flagship of Admiral Linois. As the only frigate in the squadron, Parker hurried after Linois's supporting frigate. The superior sailing of the *Amazon* enabled him to close on his opponent, ignoring the French battleship, although he did exchange long-range broadsides, losing his cutter in the process. Once past the *Marengo*, he sent the men to breakfast, well aware that English sailors fought better on a full stomach. By 09.00 he was in action with the frigate *Belle Poule*, a ship of almost identical size and firepower containing three hundred and forty men to the *Amazon*'s three hundred. The French captain did everything in his power to avoid coming to close quarters and only surrendered two hours later, when the *Marengo* hauled down her flag. Parker's exemplary seamanship and skill ensured that *Amazon* lost only three killed and nine wounded, only a third of her opponent's losses. The *Belle Poule* was purchased for the Royal Navy and served out the war.[22]

Warren was quick to congratulate St Vincent on his nephew's gallantry and skill. The old earl wrote of his 'inexpressible satisfaction; and it is not less fortunate than true, that he has merited the esteem and regard of every officer he has served under – many of them men of eminence in the profession'.[23] Parker would earn the esteem of many more great men before his career was over. There were also more tangible rewards: he 'liberated' a grey parrot for his mother and a pipe of wine for his father from the prize.

After this cruise, Parker spent the rest of his war on the Channel station, often on the north coast of Spain. The Peninsular war pro-

vided many opportunities for power projection, laying the foundations of his later career as an amphibious commander. In June 1809
he landed at the head of sailors and marines to occupy Corunna and
dismantle the coastal defences, working under Captain Sir Henry
Hotham, another outstanding officer. There were still opportunities
to take prizes, although by 1811 most were American merchant
ships trying to break the blockade of France, leavened with a few
privateers. In May 1810 Parker took three months' leave, passing
Amazon to an acting captain while he married Frances Anne
Biddulph, daughter of a Warwickshire landowner. Two sons and six
daughters of the marriage survived to adulthood. When his leave
was up, captain and ship were reunited for another eighteen months
on the Spanish coast and off Brest, sometimes in company with the
Shannon under its captain, Philip Broke.[24] When the *Amazon*
returned to Plymouth for a refit in December 1811, the shipwrights
decided that she was past economic repair, and the following month
she was paid off. Convinced the war was almost over, Parker took
a well-earned rest from the sea.[25]

Parker was indisputably one of the finest captains ever to serve the
Royal Navy, but that distinction did not necessarily guarantee similar success as an admiral. He was one of the elite 'star captains' who
captured an enemy frigate and significant numbers of enemy privateers, operated effectively as a scouting vessel for the main fleets, sustained the blockade in difficult circumstances, carried out
amphibious operations and commanded frigate squadrons.[26] In ten
years commanding the *Amazon* Parker captured a frigate, twenty-
one privateers and fifty-eight merchant ships. Had his career ended
in January 1812, Parker would still be remembered as a great captain: a brilliant seaman, leader and cruiser commander in a navy
filled to the brim with outstanding officers. This reputation was
earned purely on merit: Parker himself did nothing to promote his
public reputation. While many of his contemporaries commissioned
paintings of themselves, their ships and their victories, Parker did
not. Instead, he put his money into Shenstone Lodge in Staffordshire, a house that his parents had once hoped to buy. He decorated
its gateposts with two immense stone shot that had been fired at the
British fleet near the Dardanelles in 1807, under his old commander
Sir John Duckworth.

Parker's prize fortune enabled him to enjoy the life of a country gentleman for the next fifteen years. It would be in the saddle that he suffered his only serious wound, losing the sight of an eye while fox-hunting. He also entered local politics, as Deputy County Lieutenant, in the Whig interest that his family had always espoused. Parker's post-war career prospects were severely limited by a decade of Tory government, but nonetheless, the benefits of an extended opportunity to move in polite and political society would be obvious when he returned to sea. Admiral Parker displayed a breadth of understanding in war, peace and diplomacy that marked him out from his salt-horse contemporaries.

Admiral Parker

George Canning's Conservative–Whig coalition government of 1827 included the Duke of Clarence, an old friend of Nelson, as Lord High Admiral. Clarence offered Parker command of the Cape of Good Hope station as a commodore – a temporary rank that allowed senior captains to command small squadrons. Citing his uncle's opinion, Parker requested a battleship command before he received his flag. In October he took command of HMS *Warspite*, a seventy-four-gun ship already part-way through her three-year commission. It was revealing that he relieved twenty-eight-year-old Captain Richard Dundas, who had joined the navy as a boy after Parker had come ashore in 1812 but received rapid promotion because his father had been First Lord between 1812 and 1827.

Parker joined *Warspite* at Lisbon, and proceeded to the Mediterranean. He was struck by a marked decline in discipline: ship and crew were too relaxed for his taste, and he reintroduced the strict attention to orders that had characterised his time on the *Amazon*. Since 1815 few ships had been employed and fewer still had seen any action, but that was about to change. The navy would need to smarten up if it was to retain the distinction it had earned under Nelson. *Warspite* joined the fleet of Admiral Sir Edward Codrington, a well-connected Whig Trafalgar veteran widely regarded as the most gifted fleet commander of his generation. As Parker was sailing east, Codrington's squadron, with French and Russian support, had wiped out a Turco-Egyptian fleet in Navarino Bay, effectively securing the independence of Greece after five centuries of Turkish rule.

When he reached Malta, Codrington's battered flagship and most of the Russian squadron underwent repairs in Grand Harbour. For the next twelve months, *Warspite* operated on the Greek coast, supporting the new government, blockading the remaining Egyptian troops and dealing with pirates. There would be little drama: Parker fired on an Egyptian vessel attempting to break the blockade and conducted a smart piece of seamanship to avoid being wrecked on the Cretan coast, but these were isolated incidents. By contrast, there were many opportunities for a senior captain to demonstrate his competence in a complex, sensitive context. Parker's analysis of the Greek situation was acute and perceptive, honest but not censorious. He had enough classical learning to appreciate his surroundings and to see the absurdity of philhellene notions that these warring bandit chiefs were the descendants of Pericles, Alexander and Aristotle. He also assessed the French and Russian ships, which were often in company, sizing up the second and third largest navies as potential rivals. The Russian seventy-four *Azoff* was well disciplined, but her captain had served four years in the Royal Navy.

At the end of the year *Warspite* was recalled, and Parker took the admiral home. Codrington had been dismissed by the Duke of Wellington's government, which declared the battle of Navarino 'an untoward event' and found an excuse to sack him. Codrington nonetheless publicly praised Parker's 'energy . . . zeal and ability', a judgement shared by the Board of Admiralty. As war with Russia began to seem likely in early 1829, *Warspite* was recommissioned, enabling Parker to reappoint the first lieutenant of the *Amazon* – a typically thoughtful piece of patronage. Parker's care for his followers was as noteworthy as Anson's, and for exactly the same reason: he rewarded success and surrounded himself with ability. He also thanked Clarence for his own appointment and his support of the naval profession. Clarence, soon to become king, was delighted by the compliment: 'In peace I thought it my bounden duty to employ the best officers in His Majesty's service, and I therefore conferred on you the command of the *Warspite*. I know . . . how well and meritoriously you have executed your various orders.'[27] The newly restored Board of Admiralty had also noted Parker for flag service, giving him the sinecure command of a royal yacht. Parker knew that he owed this honour to Admiral Sir George Cockburn, another of Nelson's protégés and now the leading naval officer on the Board.

However, the real work of 1829 was a Navy Board committee revising the Rigging Warrants and Sea Store Establishments, 'under Sir T. Hardy, unquestionably the best seaman, and most understanding on the points to be under consideration, in the service'.[28] Parker was one of five noted seamen helping Hardy to ensure that ships fitting for sea had the best selection of spare sails, ropes and spars to keep them in service without recourse to dockyard assistance. This was just one part of a wide-ranging attempt to reduce the lessons of the long war with France to doctrine and make it available to a navy whose officers increasingly lacked wartime experience. This work prepared Parker for his role in naval administration and fleet management.

With the Navy List full of excellent officers, Parker waited a long time to become an admiral. Only on 22 July 1830 was it his turn to join the flag list. Having become a captain at only twenty-one, it had taken a further twenty-nine years to become an admiral!

Operations Other than War

Rear Admiral Parker was appointed second-in-command to Codrington in a very Whig Channel fleet in mid-1831. This selection was hardly surprising: his friend Hardy was the senior naval lord and the right-hand man of First Lord Sir James Graham. The Whig Reform ministry that took office in December 1830 had Parker's full support, and he was anxious for it to continue.[29] But while the politics of his new squadron were to his taste, its seamanship and command left a lot to be desired. Codrington stretched his rusty, imperfect pupils until they cracked: collisions and chaos followed his more demanding signals, signals that several captains had not troubled themselves to master. Flying his flag in the massive 120-gun three-decker *Prince Regent*, Parker found his patience tested by Captain James Whitely Deans Dundas. Despite impeccable Whig connections, Dundas presided over a severe disciplinary regime, keeping the ship neat at the expense of efficiency. During the trials Parker was quick to observe the improved sailing qualities of the new ship designs of Captain William Symonds, who was a distant relative. The introduction of steamships also promised to improve the conduct of operations, but as yet they were limited to towing and carrying messages.

In early September Parker was detached from the fleet and sent post-haste to the Tagus with two battleships. The European situation was deteriorating rapidly. There were revolutions in France, Belgium, Poland and Italy, an absolutist *coup d'état* in Portugal and the threat of a civil war in Spain as soon as the disreputable life of Ferdinand VII came to its end. The Royal Navy would have to uphold the peace of Europe and sustain British interests across the globe. Where Captain Parker had made his name with gun and sword, Admiral Parker would earn fresh laurels with the pen.

Lisbon was a critical post: Portugal was an old ally and a valuable trading partner, while a neutral Lisbon was essential to ensure the safe use of the Atlantic by British commerce in wartime. With the active support of the Pope, Spain and Austria, Prince Dom Miguel had overthrown the constitutional regime of his niece, the underage Queen Maria, to whom he was ostensibly betrothed. Although cruel, cowardly and vulgar, Miguel had the backing of the clergy and the peasantry for a campaign of sequestration against merchants and persecution of the liberal intelligentsia. His regime was a dictatorship disguised only by the threadbare dignity of a stolen throne: his rule promised only chaos and collapse. Britain refused to recognise his government but could not leave the field clear for other powers to interfere. Furthermore, if Miguel succeeded, there was every prospect that another absolutist coup would be staged by Ferdinand VII's younger brother Don Carlos, returning the Iberian peninsula to medieval darkness and bigotry. While British liberals bleated about 'human rights', British merchants reminded the Foreign Office just how much trade the country stood to lose. The threat to the British-owned Oporto wine trade was especially serious. Miguel was bad for business and really ought to go, but the trick would be to get rid of him without any overt British action. Parker was instructed to cooperate with the local diplomatic agent, a low-ranking consul; to maintain strict neutrality; and to protect the lives and property of the British community, merchants to a man. Relying on Hardy's judgement, Graham wrote: 'I can place implicit reliance on your judgement and cool discretion in every circumstance of difficulty.'[30] The two ships dropped anchor off Lisbon on 22 September.

Cool and discreet he might have been, but Parker would not tolerate slackness, disobedience or amateurish conduct. Dundas infuriated him by banning his guests from going below decks, an order that he considered 'objectionable'. Forced to rescind his order, Dundas decided to leave. This suited Parker very well, since he had already found an ideal flag captain in Peter Richards – the very guest Dundas had ordered off the gun deck. Furthermore, Dundas had shown a marked predilection for the usurper – curiously, given his Whig politics – and had embarrassed his own government in the process.[31]

The *Prince Regent* had other problems besides Dundas's behaviour: a serious outbreak of erisypelas had killed several of her crew, and it was with some relief that Parker turned over to the smaller but altogether healthier eighty-four-gun two-decker *Asia* in January 1832, with Richards as his captain. Without causing any undue commotion, Parker had got his way: this was typical of his public behaviour. If he was to meet the expectations of the ministers, Parker needed a well-run ship so that he could concentrate on command, and with Dundas that was simply not possible. The introduction of a fortnightly steam packet service from Falmouth speeded up communications between London and Lisbon, reducing the extent to which Parker would have to anticipate the wishes of his political masters. This process would gather pace in the century that followed, as first telegraph cables and then wireless successively reduced the scope for admirals to use their discretion.

Miguel's main problem was that the young queen was not in his power: her father, his brother Dom Pedro, had just arrived in the Azores with a small army and a useful war chest borrowed from British and French sources. He also had a fleet commanded by ex-Royal Navy officers. While Britain would have liked nothing better than for Pedro to overthrow Miguel, they would not move an official muscle to help. Parker was singularly unimpressed by Miguel and his regime, but he was too professional to allow his preferences to be known, let alone to act on them. His official reports were models of lucid, intelligent analysis, providing London with the latest assessment of local conditions. Well might Graham take pleasure in knowing 'that an officer of your talent, sound judgement, and tried experience is now in command of the Lisbon squadron'.[32] Prime Minister Earl Grey agreed: 'It is a fortunate thing that we have an Admiral there who is so entirely to be trusted.'[33] That trust was both political and operational: the ministers were comfortable with

Parker because he shared their politics and would not divulge sensitive information, and Hardy had vouched for his operational skills.

In July 1832 Pedro's forces captured Oporto. Privately the British government applauded; publicly they used the crisis to reinforce Parker with two more battleships and remove him from the Tagus, hoping the war would soon be over. With serious fighting under way, Parker had to plan for every eventuality, from evacuating Dom Pedro to forcing his way back up to Lisbon. He promised 'to adopt a moderate but firm tone, which I hope may have the desired effect with the Portuguese Government'.[34] The same rules applied to the fleet. Observing that the sails of the *Revenge* had not been furled to his satisfaction, he directed that they be lowered and refurled. Captain Mackay had the temerity to signal back: 'Of a different Opinion'. He was summoned to the quarterdeck of the flagship and obliged to apologise in public in writing, on pain of court martial. He did not remain with Parker much longer. Absolute obedience was vital because, as Parker explained to another officer, one wrong move by a British ship could start a European war:

... which our ministers wish to avert, and we have only to *obey* their orders to the best of our ability, leaving on them the responsibility and the odium of any measure that may be unpopular or otherwise with the *people of England*. As servants of the Crown we must be governed by this principle, or their wisest plans may be defeated; but where discretion is left, let the honour and interest of our country, under the exercise of humanity, be our guide.[35]

He was equally firm with Lord William Russell, the envoy sent to Lisbon with a dormant commission to become minister when Queen Maria was restored in his pocket. Arriving in June 1833, Russell's initial pleasure at finding that Parker was not acting in a partisan manner turned to contempt as his own sympathies became ever more constitutional: 'our poor Admiral', he observed, 'from taking neither side has not a friend'.[36] Russell considered that Parker took too strict a view of neutrality, and wanted him to intervene; Parker was very clear where his duty lay, and unlike the envoy did not let his sympathies override that duty. While Parker was at sea, Russell's coachman was murdered and he ordered the remaining ships to enter the Tagus. In a public letter to Captain Hillyar, Russell implied that the admiral's orders were too restrictive, and effectively requested him to ignore them. Hillyar did no such thing. Parker was furious – such correspondence was destructive of subordination and discipline – but he conveyed his opinion in calm, measured tones: 'I have been trained in the school of obedience; at the same time a due regard for my profession requires me to uphold properly the station which I fill.' After such a potent lesson, Russell was quick to apologise, restoring relations to the state that public service required: frank, honest and open.[37] The Admiralty 'entirely approved' his conduct, and after it had been debated in Cabinet Russell's brother, a Cabinet minister, reminded the enthusiastic diplomat: 'Parker is rather punctilious, but as a servant of Government he is in the right.'[38] Russell hastened to renew the relationship: 'Parker is a well meaning man, and we are the best of friends.'[39] A year later he concluded: 'The old Admiral, on further acquaintance, I have found true & honest as a British sailor, with the soundest judgement & great firmness.'[40] It was a lesson that others would also have to learn.

Having resumed its station in the Tagus on rather dubious grounds, the unfortunate coachman being a Spanish citizen, the government adopted a more bullish position on British rights, as advocated by the interventionist Foreign Secretary Lord Palmerston. Portuguese affairs were politically divisive at home, and the Tory opposition loudly condemned the government for stretching the concept of British neutrality; Parker compared his situation to being inside 'a complete nest of hornets'.[41] By mid-1833 a solution was at hand: the Portuguese Constitutional Party had secured enough funds to hire another fleet, the first having failed, and a remarkable naval officer to take command.

Captain Charles Napier (1786–1860) had earned a brilliant reputation in the Napoleonic wars, combining seamanship, daring and initiative in the best Royal Navy tradition with a mastery of coastal and amphibious warfare. His quickness of perception and extensive study, allied to intuitive understanding and coolness under fire, revealed a true 'genius' for war. Napier's overriding attraction for his new employers was the bold, immediate course of action he proposed: embarking a Constitutional army from Oporto to attack Lisbon from the sea. With the Constitutional forces pinned down in Oporto, Napier's proposal was attractive, and he was initially promised twelve steamships and seven thousand troops – typically unrealistic figures. Napier advised that if a smaller force were used, it should be sent to attack other coastal areas: 'the command of the sea is an enormous advantage, and it ought to be used'.[42] Little wonder Parker was excited. He had been secretly supplying Napier's predecessor with intelligence but knew Napier was a far abler man – 'as courageous as he is shrewd', and understanding 'more of the strategy of war' than any man he had ever met.[43] Parker provided Napier with details of the state and movements of the Absolutist ships, his flagship having a ringside view of their arsenal.[44] Nor was this his only intelligence source: Parker was also reading most of the Miguelite telegraph messages. 'We are masters of many of the secret keys,' he told Graham, 'and feel confidence, therefore, in the greater part of these communications.'[45] Lord William Russell explained that the telegraph cypher was constantly changed, 'but always bought for a few crowns'.[46]

Parker recognised that the crisis was at hand. He trusted that Napier, although heavily outnumbered, would 'achieve everything that is practicable'.[47] With battle 'inevitable', he prepared his ships to deal with the consequences.[48] For the next fortnight British representatives in Lisbon followed the progress of the Constitutional forces from the Absolutist telegraph.[49] When Napier landed a Constitutional army in the Algarve, the Absolutists sent their squadron to sea. On 5 July the fleets met off Cape St Vincent, and Napier reported, 'I have got the Miguelite fleet'[50] – he had captured the entire enemy fleet and decided the war. Parker was delighted, congratulating Napier on a 'most brilliant victory',[51] before joining Russell to convey the happy tidings to Miguel's foreign minister: 'The morning after we heard of it Admiral Parker and myself called on Viscount Santarem, and told him that, in our opinion the issue of the contest was decided by this blow.' For good measure they delivered the same message to Miguel's main supporter, the Spanish minister.[52] Napier urged Palmerston to recognise Donna Maria.[53] His victory was particularly welcome at the Admiralty, which was under severe pressure to find the ships to support British foreign policy in many places without having to go back to Parliament for more money. Graham admitted that it was Palmerston's triumph: he had enabled this remarkable officer to settle the war, solving a major diplomatic problem in the process.[54] The Absolutists evacuated Lisbon on 24 July, just before Napier's fleet arrived, driven out by a liberal rising. Finally free to show his true feelings, Parker signalled the news to Napier as the Constitutional fleet beat upriver.[55]

Parker received high praise for his adroit handling of the transfer of power. Palmerston and William IV agreed that the occupation of Lisbon by the Queen's forces, and the fact that 'the whole of the naval force of Portugal is now serving under her flag', justified renewing diplomatic relations. Parker had been right: Napier understood more of war than any man alive. In a month he had settled a conflict that had been running for years. For the next two decades these two officers would be the right and left hands of Palmerston's diplomacy. Napier provided swift incisive strikes; Parker the careful diplomacy of armed might.

Although Earl Grey considered moving Parker to the Mediterranean command,[56] the Portuguese crisis took longer to resolve than he anticipated, and Parker's task continued after the decisive blow. Initially stunned and demoralised, the Absolutists regrouped and tried to recover Lisbon in August. Once the British had recognised Queen Donna Maria, however, Parker could provide more support, although still without participating in the conflict. It was left to Parker and Russell to protect British interests, advising the new regime to ameliorate the inevitable tensions left behind by years of ideological strife. Parker endured another eleven months' hard labour in the Tagus: for as long as Dom Miguel and the Spanish pretender Don Carlos remained at large, the Iberian peninsula would not be at peace. The British government hoped to remove Miguel, and his equally unstable brother Pedro, without upsetting the balance in Spain.

By October the Queen's army had driven Miguel's forces into the mountains, at which point the Admiralty began to reduce Parker's effective strength. The crisis centre had shifted to the eastern Mediterranean, where the fate of Turkey hung in the balance. By early 1834 the threat of war over Belgium prompted Graham to prepare Parker to shift his squadron for Channel service.[57] Once that danger had passed, Graham decided to employ the admiral ashore, to relieve Hardy:

Impressed with a deep sense of the exemplary manner in which you have conducted a difficult service, I have not hesitated to recommend you to His Majesty, and to my colleagues, as an officer, in my judgement peculiarly fitted to discharge the important duty of a Lord of the Admiralty.

Needless to say, King William concurred, awarding him the KCB at the same time.[58] Flattered and gratified by the honour and the offer, Parker was characteristically modest, declaring himself willing to serve, but 'unacquainted . . . with the details of such important duties, and diffident of my powers to discharge them with the ability which I feel is essentially necessary, I will frankly confess that I have never ambitioned this high and responsible station'.[59]

Such diffidence was not altogether unwarranted: the major reform of naval administration pushed through in 1832 had, as his friends on the Board would have told him, made a major difference to the post. The Navy Board had now been abolished, loading responsibility for the civil branch of the service onto individual Admiralty lords. Previously the Admiralty had been a political and operational centre; now it carried an administrative burden that required altogether more professional and dedicated admirals. But while Parker waited for his relief, Graham resigned from the Cabinet on an unrelated issue. Parker told Graham's successor Lord Auckland that he did not consider Graham's offer binding, but Auckland was just as anxious as his predecessor to secure the admiral's services.

The delay ensured that Parker was still in place when Miguel agreed to leave the country and abandon his cause, a decision that saw him conveyed to Genoa by HMS *Stag* in early June. Don Carlos was also removed, leaving Parker to conclude that 'Everything here has terminated as satisfactorily as I could have wished, and it has been no small satisfaction to me to send the two Doms on their travels before my departure.'[60] Graham praised Parker's diplomacy warmly: 'The merit and praise in my humble judgement are principally due to you'; 'your conduct has been marked by that sound judgement, nice sense of honour, and exemplary firmness, which, when happily united in a British Admiral with naval skills, make him at once the terror and the admiration of foreign nations'.[61] Such praise was well deserved after three years serving the interests of the state and maintaining the peace with unrelenting watchfulness and exemplary management. If the glory went to the mercurial Napier, the honour was Parker's. His conduct had been so judicious, discreet and well balanced that he was roundly abused by both sides in the conflict! He left the Tagus with the thanks of the British commercial community ringing in his ears.[62] Parker's Portuguese service set the pattern for the rest of his career: it had earned him the absolute trust of his political masters.

Second Naval Lord

On 10 July 1834 HMS *Asia* cast anchor at Spithead; a fortnight later Parker was gazetted Second Naval Lord on Lord Auckland's Whig Admiralty Board. It was a brief sojourn: the government fell in December, and the incoming Conservative ministry replaced the naval lords. Graham thought that Parker should have been retained on professional grounds, but it would be another eighteen years before a naval lord survived the change of ministry. Although a confirmed Whig, Parker steadfastly refused to take a seat in Parliament. His seat on the Board reflected professional merit; lesser men secured theirs by taking a seat in Parliament at their own expense. In April 1835 the Whigs returned to office, and Parker began a six-year term as Second Naval Lord. Lord Auckland soon departed for India, to be replaced by Lord Minto. Parker kept in close contact with Graham, the one front-rank politician with a serious interest in the navy. In a relationship lasting more than twenty years, they would solve the age-old problem of manning the fleet at the outbreak of war without impressment. Parker did all he could to sustain Graham's reforming impulse at the Board – and the two men also promoted each other's sons and relations whenever they had the chance!

Desperate to maintain a bare majority in Parliament, despite attacks from Radicals and Conservatives, the government exploited Admiralty patronage to secure votes. In October 1839 Parker approached Codrington about becoming commander-in-chief at Portsmouth, on the condition that he resign his parliamentary seat at Devonport. Codrington was furious, but Parker, the one officer on the Board he trusted,[63] resolved the issue.[64] When Codrington complained that this rule did not apply to captains in full pay, Parker replied:

I confess *I* should be very glad to see the regulation extended, not only to *Captains* but to *every Naval and Military* officer in *actual employment* as I think it would ensure their Professional duties being *better performed* & prevent *much jobbery.*[65]

That said, Codrington's seat was very conveniently taken by Lord

Minto's private secretary, who was soon transferred to the Treasury. In reality, Parker's opposition to 'jobbery' was relative, rather than absolute.

Although crippled by painfully low naval estimates – the lowest of the century – and decidedly partisan, the Minto Board still effected a number of important reforms in ship design, technology and, above all, personnel, Parker's area of responsibility. As Second Naval Lord he was responsible for the appointment of lieutenants, midshipmen, mates, masters, clerks, boatswains and carpenters, and could recommend all but the first group for promotion. Because these men were critical to the quality of a new ship's company, Parker required captains to provide confidential reports on them when paying off. Using this information, Parker provided the backbone of a new crew, and no captain was ever disappointed. His business habits were those of a busy flag officer, learnt in the years off Lisbon. He answered letters by return, entering the details of every item in a journal. Despite having only one sighted eye, he spent long hours working by candlelight, supervising the storekeeper's department at Somerset House. His nineteenth-century biographer, despite the luxury of a massive archive and two thousand pages to lay out his case, seriously undervalued Parker's work at the Admiralty, as if it were unworthy of notice. He focused instead on the finer points of naval diplomacy and squadron handling: though these were important aspects of his achievement, they only represent part of the picture.[66]

Despite tight financial limits, the Board was under constant pressure to provide more ships, initially to meet the general crisis of the 1830s, but latterly to sustain Lord Palmerston's energetic diplomacy. Capital ships were needed in the Mediterranean and at home, while cruisers were spread across the globe, dealing with pirates, slave traders and failing states. To make ends meet, the Board cut back vital shipbuilding programmes. The economic pressure was so serious that when radical alarmists drew attention to the size of the Russian Baltic fleet, Lord Minto could only beg the Permanent Secretary to rebut the critics in print![67] In early 1839 six new battleships were ordered. Only in 1840 did the estimates rise, to fight two wars and rebuild the battle fleet. By early 1841 the Royal Navy had twenty-six battleships in commission, the largest number since 1815, and they had served their purpose, driving the Egyptians out of Syria and deterring France.

Parker was an exemplary naval lord. He was the only admiral left in London when Parliament rose, and in harness with Admiralty Secretary Charles Wood he supported Palmerston's adroit handling of the Syrian campaign. He also kept up a remarkable correspondence with Napier, second-in-command on the Syrian coast. As professional seamen there was little to separate the two men, but they were very different characters: one as wild, free and brilliant as the other was calm, cautious and reserved.[68]

As the most experienced seaman on the Board, Parker had a significant input into ship design, favouring the radical hull form of Captain Symonds, the Surveyor of the Navy. Graham had consulted him in 1831 before appointing Symonds, and he admired the speed and seaworthiness of his ships. They offered a solution to the great problem of the war years: how to catch flying French ships and fleets and force them to fight? Speed, and the skill to use it, would be major professional desiderata for the next twenty years. Parker ensured that the service had the high-quality personnel necessary to operate these vessels: the astonishing performance that they coaxed out of what were essentially gigantic floating fortresses excited the admiration of the nation and terrified potential rivals.

The Opium War: An Affair of Honour?

On 12 May 1841 Parker was nominated to command the East Indies station. An intermittent, awkward war with China, sparked by questions of trade and dignity, had been under way for two years and was becoming a serious embarrassment for the ministry. The first admiral they sent had died, and the second had fallen ill, neither having achieved anything. Ministers desperately needed someone they could trust. As Lord Palmerston explained to trade superintendent Captain Charles Elliot RN:

It is the duty of an Officer of the Crown on a foreign Station to take no important steps without Instructions; and to obey promptly and punctually the Instructions which he may receive; and the greater the distance which separates the Officer from England, the more incumbent upon him it is, to attend to these Rules; because so much longer will be the interval of time which must elapse before the Government at home can repair any inconvenience which may be produced by his unauthorised acts, or by his neglect to execute his Instructions.[69]

Elliot's actions had turned a local trade dispute over illegal imports of opium to China, which a reforming administration was trying to stamp out, into an affair that compromised the honour and dignity of the British flag.[70] Because the cash-strapped ministers lacked the money to uphold British prestige by force, they were acutely sensitive to such insults. Caught between radical supporters, many of whom had links with trade and backed a dynamic China policy, and a Conservative opposition who found the spectacle degrading and damaging to British interests, ministers compromised. The initial policy, which all agreed was illegal and morally reprehensible – trying to save money and having nothing to do with the opium trade – collapsed when Elliot made the government responsible for £2-million worth of opium that he had taken from the British traders and handed over to the Chinese authorities. As Parliament would not provide compensation, the ministers decided the Chinese would have to pay.

Palmerston was confident that a small naval force could blockade the Chinese coast, cut off vital trade and secure redress. At all events national honour had to be upheld, and it was this last point, rather than grubby commercial concerns, that led to war.[71] In the context of a war caused by insubordinate officers and fought to retrieve national honour, Parker's appointment made perfect sense. He had been collecting intelligence on the region since October 1839, when the government decided to go to war.[72] By the time he reached China, Parker was an expert on contemporary Anglo-Chinese relations.[73]

Very much a creature of habit, Parker selected Peter Richards as captain for the flagship, the Indian-built seventy-four-gun battleship HMS *Cornwallis*. Although named after the former Governor General of India, the man who had surrendered at Yorktown, Parker would have appreciated the link with his friend the admiral. This was the biggest ship that could operate effectively in the largely uncharted Chinese coastal waters and major rivers. Furthermore, with no significant hostile warships in the theatre, it would provide all the firepower the Royal Navy would need. With the housekeeping in order, Parker and the new Plenipotentiary Sir Henry Pottinger set off on a record-breaking global circuit. By using steamships and the overland Suez link they reached Macao on 9 August, a journey of only sixty-seven days, of which ten were spent ashore at Bombay.

After the embarrassment and failure of the past three years, the ministers provided detailed instructions and delegated 'local' control to the Governor General of India, Lord Auckland. In China, Pottinger would be responsible for political decisions, Parker for strategy and logistics, and General Sir Hugh Gough for shore operations.[74] As all three men were competent professionals, this joint command worked well enough, although some friction was inevitable. The ministerial plan was deceptively simple: British and Indian forces would enter the Yangtze River, capture key cities and proceed inland to the intersection of the river and Grand Canal, which intelligence suggested was the vital supply artery carrying rice from the southern provinces to Beijing. Cutting the rice supply should force the Emperor to talk peace, which Pottinger was empowered to conclude. The key to success would be the Indian navy's steamships, including the novel iron-hulled shallow-draught *Nemesis* and *Phlegethon*. These were a new experience for Parker, but not one that posed him any difficulties. Steamers would tow sailing ships upriver and land the troops. They were the prime movers of the campaign, and by a stroke of fate local Chinese coal worked well in their hungry boilers. The 'army' initially consisted of only two thousand British and Indian troops drawn from the Indian garrison. Inevitably the main problems were disease; soldiers and sailors were prostrated by a series of debilitating or lethal complaints and the lack of accurate charts. Clean ships and skilled surveying officers provided effective answers, although deaths from disease greatly exceeded the minimal casualties suffered in the war itself.[75]

On 21 August Parker led his force to sea: twenty-two transports, two battleships, seven smaller sailing warships, a survey vessel and four steamers carrying some 2,700 troops.[76] On the 26th Amoy was captured. After a massive close-range naval bombardment lasting some two hours, the army occupied an almost deserted city. In the previous year the Chinese had thrown up massive artillery batteries and earthworks, mounting ninety-six guns, but they were poorly sited. British steamers soon exposed the lack of any flanking protection, driving the half-trained Chinese gunners from their posts with rapid, well-directed broadsides of shot and shell. A small garrison was left on the offshore island of Koolongso, where it remained until the final peace treaty was executed. On 1 October the British repeated the operation on the island of Chusan, where a brand-new two-hundred-gun battery protected the harbour. Nothing daunted, the British simply landed troops and guns outside the harbour, took up commanding positions on the exposed flanks of the new batteries and drove the defenders out. The attack depended on an accurate chart made the previous year by Commander Richard Collinson.[77] Leaving another garrison, the expedition pressed on the mainland city of Ningpo, which was occupied after demolishing extensive defences at Chinhai in a skilful operation that exploited all the advantages of steam and disciplined troops to overcome formidable earthworks, forts and numerous enemy soldiers. Commanding mandarin Yukien had issued blood-curdling threats, but the Chinese army was comprehensively out-manoeuvred by Gough, while Parker pounded the citadel into silence with two seventy-four-gun battleships. Then the marines landed, with Parker at their head, to drive out the Chinese garrison. Yukien committed suicide, at the second attempt, by swallowing opium.[78] Ningpo surrendered without a fight on 13 October, becoming the winter base for the army.

British casualties for the entire operation were fewer than twenty killed and forty wounded; the Chinese, who fought with suicidal bravery, lost several thousand. A handful of 'barbarians' had defeated the Celestial Empire. Tightly disciplined troops firing volleys with modern muskets, professionally directed heavy artillery and steamships had shattered the illusion of power that had sustained Chinese national pride for half a millennium. Unaccustomed to war and weapons, and lacking any sense of national purpose, the populace offered no resistance. Centuries of hierarchical, regimented social behaviour had turned the Chinese people into serfs, perfectly happy to serve new masters. While Parker and Gough used naval firepower and mobility to great effect, the Chinese showed no interest in naval operations. Chinese officials had studied British naval technology, but the Emperor was unimpressed by their reports of steamships and other innovations, believing that the proper place for fighting was on land.[79]

After capturing Ningpo, Parker led a reconnaissance upriver, but Gough had too few troops left for further operations, while the river proved too shallow for the fleet. The sea approaches to Hangchow, the southern terminus of the Grand Canal, were equally difficult, so a small army of seven hundred effectives was left to winter at Ningpo. Meanwhile, in November Parker was elevated to the rank of vice admiral – a promotion of which he would have been aware before the 1842 campaign opened. Of more immediate significance, Lord Auckland provided major reinforcements: eight thousand troops and ten more steamers which arrived with Parker's flagship. There was also a new government to deal with, since the Conservatives had come to power in September 1841, in time to settle the strategy of the new campaign. The new ministry persisted with the concept of a decisive strike into the interior, cutting the Grand Canal where it crossed the Yangtze River: 'to control the internal commerce of the Chinese Empire, and thus render the moral pressure upon the Court of Pekin irresistible'.[80] Palmerston had doubted the efficacy of this operation and preferred attacking Beijing via the Peiho River and Tientsin. The new ministers gradually came to share his analysis,[81] but they were saved from potential embarrassment by Lord Ellenborough, the wilful and decisive new Governor General of India, who used his local authority to restore the original Grand Canal plan.[82] This proved wise: the Peiho was too shallow for effective fleet operations and proved a dead end for naval forces in 1900. Ellenborough's initiative saved the local commanders from an awkward shift of strategic focus just as the new season opened. However, he left the final decision to them, and made it clear that he would back their judgement.[83] Parker was in no doubt that Ellenborough, who became a close colleague, was right, observing that the Peiho route would limit naval cooperation with the land forces, for offence or evacuation.[84] Gough depended on large-scale naval support for his army, which would be impossible if he moved on Beijing.

The troops at Ningpo had spent a fraught winter, facing unpleasant weather and a series of small-scale attacks. Finally, on 10 March a large assault penetrated the city wall, but the swift, decisive use of grapeshot and canister rounds scythed down the Chinese troops in the narrow streets. Five days later, steamers destroyed the Chinese camp with trifling losses. The river proved too shallow and the current too strong for the expedition to attack the regional capital at Hangchow, so Ningpo was evacuated and the troops joined the latest reinforcements on the coast off Chinhai.

On 17 May the coastal city of Chapu was captured through an

expert amphibious operation, combining heavy naval fire with skil-fully placed guns on a commanding hill overlooking the town. This time the British faced Manchu or 'Tartar' troops, representing the alien dynasty that ruled China. After a day of heavy fighting, the garrison slaughtered their families and then committed suicide. The following day some fifteen hundred corpses were left for burial, of which only nine were British. Chapu had been taken as the base for an attack on Hangchow, but, in view of the navigational difficulties, this proved impossible and on the 28th the focus of operations shifted north to the Yangtze River.

On 13 June Parker led the fleet towards Woosung. This time the steamers were lashed alongside the heavy sailing ships, producing a curious hermaphrodite vessel, half steam and spray, half potent broad-side. This time the Chinese batteries scored a few hits on their attack-ers as they took up position, but two hours of sustained fire from a battleship, a frigate and two corvettes overpowered the Chinese gun-ners and demolished their works. The marines and soldiers who fol-lowed up the bombardment needed little time to clear out the last remnants of a demoralised garrison: a hundred and seventy-five guns were taken. News of the fall of Woosung on 16 June ensured that Shanghai was taken without a fight on 19 June with a combined land and sea attack: some troops marched overland from Woosung, while others were landed by the steamers. At both places powerful batteries were outflanked and overpowered by skilful British seamen, steamers and charts. Parker pushed further up the River Hwangpu, but Gough was anxious to head for Nanking now that the reinforcements from India were arriving in force. On the 23rd Shanghai was evacuated, but not before the commercial opportunities had been noted and approaches charted.

The next target for the invaders was Nanking, the ancient capital of China, some 170 miles up the Yangtze. Surveyors had been at work in the river in 1840, and after a skilful reconnaissance by Commanders Collinson and Kellett, who rejoined the fleet on 5 July, Parker was ready.[85] The survey showed that the battleships could make the passage, although the fleet would have to be led by survey ships, which often anchored over the shoals, so the ten-mile-long armada of ships could pass in safety. The expedition consisted of ten regiments of British and Indian troops, five batteries of artillery and three companies of engineers on forty-five transports escorted by three battleships, seven smaller sailing warships, ten war steamers and the two survey vessels. The deep-draught battleships were a problem, frequently running aground, but Parker and Gough were unwilling to operate without their overwhelming firepower.

At daybreak the following morning the fleet weighed anchor, launching the most astonishing operation of war yet undertaken by a western nation in Asia. While the surveyors pioneered the route, Parker was careful to maintain his supply line back to Woosung, leaving nothing to chance. After nine days without sighting the enemy, a solitary battery was encountered a few miles short of Chinkiang, but a few well-placed round shot persuaded the Chinese to abandon their position. They had reached the target, for the Grand Canal ran through the suburbs of Chinkiang. Seventy-three ships had moved 170 miles upriver, ably piloted by the surveying officers from a chart drawn in 1840. Many ships ran aground, 'but the bottom was everywhere of soft mud, and fortunately no damage resulted'.

When Parker and Gough inspected the defences of Chinkiang from the deck of a steamer, it appeared abandoned. Despite this, they took proper precautions, anchoring the *Cornwallis* close to the city walls a day before the fleet arrived. The prospect from a nearby hill revealed nothing more than some camps in the distance. On the 21st the army landed, broke open the gates and found 2,600 Chinese troops, half of them elite Manchu units. This time the fighting took place at close quarters in a heavily built-up area, without naval gunfire support. Despite the stifling heat and the suicidal courage of the Manchu, the enemy was steadily driven back by Anglo-Indian soldiers. Parker accompanied Gough ashore, flag captain Peter Richards led a storming party, and other naval personnel were heavily engaged. Even so, casualties were light: the army lost nineteen men in battle and sixteen to sunstroke, with the marines losing a further two – scarcely surprising when temperatures regularly exceeded 90° Fahrenheit.[86] When all further resistance was useless, the Manchu troops repeated the horrific ritual first encountered at Chapu, slaughtering their families and then themselves: their general set the example, committing suicide on a hastily thrown-up funeral pyre. These troops, heirs of a great tradition, had been left by the arrogance of their politicians to fight with outdated weapons and tactics: the manner of the soldiers' death may have preserved their honour, but it shamed their masters. The Chinese government refused to make any concession to the military prowess of the outer barbarians, despite having ample opportunity to learn. Throughout the war the Chinese constantly tried to exploit surprise and ambush, an obvious response from the descendants of Sun Tzu, but without modern weapons and tactics their efforts proved little more than a cerebral prelude to mass suicide.

With Chinkiang taken, the Grand Canal had been cut, and within days over seven hundred junks had been seized. With a frigate already lying off Woosung to cut the coastal traffic via Shanghai, the effect was immediate. Pottinger insisted that Gough and Parker adopt the hard-line policy of destroying all river traffic to speed the move to peace. He knew that if the Chinese were allowed to negotiate before they were utterly defeated, he had little chance of securing a quick settlement.[87] The Chinese authorities knew they were beaten: without the free movement of food the Empire would collapse. On 2 August, as Parker prepared to advance on Nanking, the surveying officers had already begun to chart the way. A week later *Cornwallis* lay off the walls of the ancient city, waiting for the rest of the fleet to arrive. The attack planned for the 15th proved unnecessary; the threatening position of the powerful seventy-four was a negotiating tactic, not an operational manoeuvre. Finally the Emperor understood that his realm was in danger. Late on the 14th a message reached the flagship: the Chinese would treat for peace. After the elaborate ceremony of diplomacy had been completed, the commissioners met on the 26th, and British terms were accepted after a few hours of polite discussion. Three days later the Emperor authorised his representatives to sign the treaty. Imperial ratification arrived on 15 September, and the news was sent to London by steamship and the overland Suez route.

The Treaty of Nanking overturned the Chinese world, replacing arrogant complacency with the alarming prospect of domination by heavily armed western imperialists. The British acquired Hong Kong in perpetuity – the return of the colony in 1999 reflected the hundred-year lease taken on the New Territories, not the original acquisition of the island – while the ports of Canton, Foochow, Ningpo Shanghai and Nanking were opened for trade, with resident British consuls. China paid a war indemnity of £4.25 million in silver, the old merchant system was abolished, and British and Chinese officials of equal rank were to have equal status.[88] However, the Chinese translation of the treaty did not make the final point clear, and it would take another war before the real issues – status and honour – were finally resolved.[89] The Chinese Empire would suffer more grievous losses in the process.

Once the treaty had been ratified and indemnity payments made, Parker took his unwieldy fleet back downriver. This proved at least as difficult as the upriver voyage, not least because the Chinese had removed the buoys. Fortunately the muddy river bed was yielding, and no serious damage was suffered. Local coal kept the steamers running, while outstanding surveying officers like Henry Kellett and Richard Collinson limited the danger.[90] By late October the fleet was assembling off Chusan, concluding an unprecedented feat of amphibious warfare. Ten thousand British imperial troops, operating on the other side of the world, had defeated the most populous country on the planet in a single campaign. Even so, Parker was in no doubt that a significant force would continue to be required on the Chinese coast to uphold British interests and ensure the Chinese did not forget 1842.[91]

Rewards always follow success, and Parker received the Grand Cross of the Order of the Bath, with a baronetcy to follow at the end of his command. It was the least he could have expected. What would have pleased him far more was the acclaim of his professional peers and political masters. Graham declared, 'Great skill and great powers of command have been evinced by you in the midst of difficulties; and the Captain of the *Amazon* and the favourite of Nelson, has proved himself capable of leading a fleet to victory.' Lord Haddington, First Lord of the Admiralty, reflected on the 'singular' nature of the warfare he had conducted, and the 'great and essential benefits' that his 'skill, talent, and energy' had given to the British people.[92]

With the treaty in force, Parker found the easy business of war superseded by the altogether more complex task of dealing with British civil authority. Having been an interested spectator of the war, Sir Henry Pottinger took the opportunity of peace to assert an entirely improper control over the movements of the fleet. Pottinger was authorised to request naval aid, but responsibility for delivering it lay with Parker. It was his command and he was careful to maintain his authority: 'Be careful not to entrench on matters beyond your province, but at the same time be mindful of the dignity and proper position of your profession.'[93] Pottinger's demands, he stressed, would reduce him 'to a mere cypher' and 'subject me to humiliations inconsistent with the rank and station which I have the honour to hold'.[94] They were also 'altogether contrary to the regulations and customs of Her Majesty's naval service'.[95] While Parker could not persuade Pottinger that he had exceeded his authority, the government backed him, praising the remarkable manner in which he had kept his temper and continued to cooperate with the presumptive plenipotentiary. This judgement necessarily took time to reach China, but even when it did Pottinger seemed oblivious, and he was still causing problems when Parker left for home.

Parker also had to deal with officers who did not meet his standards of behaviour. Captain Edward Belcher, so useful in charting the Douro during Parker's last command, proved equally capable in China, but he was also a nit-picking, bullying martinet who sent every one of his officers before a court martial. Parker told him, 'A skilful navigator and a clever seaman you may be, but a great officer you can never be, with that narrow mind.'[96] When a younger officer came before Parker charged with being drunk on duty, the problem was compounded by the fact that he had recently been promoted, on Parker's nomination, and the admiral knew his family. He didn't mince his words. 'I hold this vice in such detestation that you must expect no . . . favour from me', he declared:

Let me admonish you to beware against committing yourself by any recurrence of the unofficer-like, ungentleman-like, and hateful failing of intemperance, for I would much sooner see you deprived of your commission than endure the mortification of finding that I had been accessory to saddling the country with a half-pay *sot*.[97]

Unlike his uncle, a partisan bigot who judged men on their politics, Parker reserved his ire for moral failings. He had a high notion of what it meant to be a gentleman and no patience with those who did not match his standards.

The flagship finally departed Hong Kong on 4 December 1843. Parker stretched across his vast station, calling at Manila before heading west to visit Lord Ellenborough at Calcutta. Honours continued to flow: a Good Service Pension in May, and the promised baronetcy in October. By then, HMS *Cornwallis* had sailed for home, departing Trincomalee in July. A 112-day passage home, broken at the Cape and Ascension Island, ended at Spithead, where Parker struck his flag on 5 November 1844. He used his leisure to argue for the promotion of deserving officers, many of whom went on to have brilliant naval careers. The creation of a personal following remained critical to the transmission of an admiral's professional legacy. Not that Parker had much time to rest and contemplate this. The Conservative government immediately selected him for the premier seagoing appointment, the Mediterranean fleet, despite his Whig politics. This was a tribute to his ability, as well as to the fact that there were no other vice admirals fit to serve. Parker's health had held up remarkably well in China, a station that had killed several senior officers: his abstemious, non-smoking regime, combined with ample exercise, undoubtedly helped prolong his career.

Mediterranean Command

The Mediterranean fleet that Parker was going to command was not the mighty force of Nelson's day. There would be only one battleship, the flagship, and it required some serious negotiating with the Foreign Office before he was allowed to hoist his flag in a three-decked first-rate, the *Hibernia*. The foreign secretary, more in hope than wisdom, allowed a brief Anglo-French entente to dictate the size of the fleet. The feeble Orleans dynasty would prove a broken reed, betraying Lord Aberdeen's trust within a year, and would be overthrown in a revolution in 1848. Parker was left to deal with the consequences, and he would require a rather larger fleet to do the job. He observed that the French were annoyed when his fleet was heavily reinforced: 'This is as it should be; the presence of our large ships has had the desired effect, and I am quite sure that nothing will tend more to keep our neighbours quiet than a liberal display of three-deckers.'[98] It was just as well that the French could be kept quiet by a display of naval might, for the Mediterranean would soon be convulsed by civil strife, revolution and war, while Parker would be called on to serve outside his station. As the dominant sea officer of the age, his opinion was sought on every issue by his political masters and his naval colleagues at the Admiralty.

From the start, Parker put his faith in officers from the

Cornwallis, led by Peter Richards. With the flagship in good hands, he could impose his own brand of discipline on the fleet. His approach was essentially unchanged from the *Amazon* Standing Orders. Efficiency was best served by ensuring that every man acted in proper subordination to his superiors; he discouraged any familiarity across ranks and classes as invariably tending to breach discipline. He expected sobriety, decorum of act and word, and unwavering enthusiasm for the service from all. His example, and that of his flagship, provided the model for officers and ships alike. The need for discipline and order was, if anything, more important in peace than in war.

Hibernia sailed for the Mediterranean in July 1845, where Parker relieved Vice Admiral Sir Edward Owen. A star frigate captain in the Napoleonic wars, Owen's later career did not compare with Parker's. His relaxed discipline was soon overturned:

I find the ships here all desirous of being perfect in training to arms of all kinds, but I cannot help perceiving that they are in some instances declining into the old habit of not getting everything on deck as if for action, and avoiding to move things that will disturb *paintwork*, or dirty their white decks.[99]

At the end of the year the new First Lord of the Admiralty, the Earl of Ellenborough, offered Parker a seat on the Admiralty Board, but he declined, feeling the impaired sight of his remaining eye was unequal to winter work by candlelight. For much of the first year of his command the flagship lay at anchor in Malta harbour. With no fleet to exercise there was no point going to sea. Instead, he kept watch on the theatre through the eyes and ears of British ministers, governors and consuls. He also supervised the retrieval of antiquities from the mausoleum at Halicarnassus, embarking from Bodrum for delivery by warship to the British Museum.[100] When the minister at Istanbul, who had secured the export permit, requested a visit, Parker decided to travel in the flagship, despite very clear stipulations in the 1841 Straits Convention that no heavy warships were allowed to enter the Dardanelles. This fact had to be pointed out after he had passed the entrance: it would not be the last time he made a mistake in these classical waters.[101]

In May 1846 Ellenborough ordered Parker to leave his station and take command of a Squadron of Evolution in the Western

Approaches. This was a remarkable testament to his standing in the service, not least because the object was to test the controversial ships designed by Sir William Symonds and largely ordered during Parker's time at the Admiralty. By the time he reported, the Whigs had returned to office, with his old friend Lord Auckland at the Admiralty. Auckland and other ministers urged him to accept the post of First Naval Lord: 'in so doing you will render an essential service to the country, and particularly to the Navy'. Once again he declined, citing the state of his eyesight.[102]

The Squadron of Evolution took Parker as far north as Cork, where he tested ten big ships and the first screw steam warship before heading south for Lisbon, where renewed civil strife placed the Crown on the brink of catastrophe. The sudden appearance of a powerful fleet in the Tagus helped to stabilise the situation. This time Parker was in no doubt how to act; his labours a decade earlier had given him a sure grasp of Portuguese politics, and he acted without waiting for orders from London. With Portugal in crisis, Parker had to remain in the Tagus, detaching several ships into the Mediterranean, to forestall the possibility that France might secure control of the Balearic Islands from Spain, as part of the disgraceful 'Spanish marriages' deal that ruined Anglo-French relations. Although he considered war inevitable, Parker did his best to avoid a rupture on this occasion, refusing to respond to newspaper reports of French occupation and waiting for official news. Once again his judgement was sure: the rumours were unfounded.

Back in Portugal Parker learnt that British policy, as he expected, was to reconcile the two sides in the conflict and restore the constitution with as little loss of life as possible. With weary resignation, he recognised that the efficiency of the fleet would be sacrificed to political necessity; preparation for war would be compromised by prolonged detention at anchor. Furthermore, such static service encouraged:

. . . gallivanting and picnics, instead of sea-practice, which is so essential to enable us to preserve the pre-eminence which our Navy has ever held, and in which foreigners are now endeavouring to surpass us. Moreover, it brings us into closer communion with them than is desirable: it teaches them a system which they are too ready to imitate, and offers no corresponding benefit to ourselves. It is far, very far, from my wish that the officers and men should not have reasonable recreation and amusement; on the contrary, I like to see them enjoy themselves; but this should not be their principal pursuit, and the mischief produced by being perpetually at anchor is incalculable. Six or eight months in Portsmouth or Devonport is enough to ruin any set of officers or men. Malta is almost as bad, and we must beware of extending this evil.[103]

The answer lay in an early, complete resolution of the Portuguese crisis. This time there was no Charles Napier at hand: he had to act on his own. After consulting Sir Hamilton Seymour, the British minister, Parker decided it was time to exceed his orders. When four thousand insurgent troops put to sea from Oporto on 31 May, Parker's ships seized them, relying on overwhelming force to ensure there was no loss of life. The insurgent vessels were taken without a shot being fired. Two weeks later Parker hoisted his flag on the steamer HMS *Sidon* and led a small force of British, French and Spanish ships to anchor off the insurgent stronghold of Setuval, which quickly surrendered.[104]

In two weeks Parker had solved a problem that was crippling the effective development of British policy in southern Europe, without firing a shot or taking a life. Not surprisingly, the government was delighted, and anticipated that he would soon return to his proper station 'with a confirmed character for ability, judgement, and discretion in the conduct of difficult affairs, and for wisdom and decision in the application of the force under your command'.[105] Once again he was offered the post of First Naval Lord, on the retirement of his old colleague Sir Charles Adam; once again he refused. But this time he did not escape so lightly. The new First Sea Lord, Rear Admiral James Dundas, Parker's unsatisfactory flag captain in 1831–2, had never commanded a squadron at sea. Consequently both Dundas and Lord Auckland treated Parker as the government's principal adviser on naval policy.[106]

The *Hibernia* finally left Tagus on 19 August, having secured a dynasty and received an elegant expression of the Queen's thanks. The foreign secretary, Lord Palmerston, observed that a pro-British Portugal provided great advantages:

Those advantages are many, great, and obvious; commercial, political, military, and naval, and if we were thus to lose them, some of them would not be mere loss, but would become formidable weapons of attack against us in the hands of a hostile power. For instance, the naval position of the Tagus ought never to be in the hands of any power, whether French or Spanish,

1 Admiral Charles Howard against a backdrop of the English defeating the Spanish Armada in 1588. In this battle and the capture of Cadiz in 1596, Howard created the role of the admiral and made England a naval nation.

2 The English and Dutch fleets fighting the Battle of the Gabbard, 1653, which marked a turning point in the art of the Admiral. Robert Blake's decisive, determined leadership helped to secure a decisive victory over the Dutch.

3 Destruction of the *Soleil Royal* at the Battle of La Hogue, 23 May 1692.

4 James, Duke of York painted as Mars, after his great naval victory at Sole Bay
in 1672. His professionalism established the rules of Fleet Command for the next
century, but his arrogance would cause his downfall as a king and a man. His final
chance to regain the English throne was dashed when English boats boarded and
burned the great ships of his cousin Louis XIV's navy (left, plate 3) marking the end
of the Battle of La Hogue in 1692. As the Royal Navy made a bonfire of his earthly
ambitions, he could not resist cheering 'his' English sailors on.

5 Lord Anson used the crushing superiority of British ships and men to annihilate a French naval squadron and merchant convoy off Cape Finisterre on 3 May 1747, crippling the French economy and hastening the end of the War of Austrian Succession.

6 The Admiral in battle: while Lord Howe is represented fighting the Glorious First of June 1794 in full dress uniform he actually wore common sailor's clothes – and like the rest of his staff ended the day blackened by gun smoke.

7 A strategist and tactician of genius, Lord Hood exemplified the art of naval command: his vision, courage and speed of thought were only equalled by his star pupil, Nelson.

8 Brave and cool under pressure, Earl St Vincent created a new, professional fighting navy to meet the challenges of Revolutionary War – he won a key battle, suppressed a serious mutiny and taught Nelson the business of war.

Ashore setting fire to Chymer China, Octr 1 1841

9 The capture of the Chinese city of Chusan in 1841, in which William Parker demonstrated his mastery of coasted operations and diplomacy. Parker re-defined the art of the admiral in the decades after Trafalgar.

10 'Masters of the Sea'. The power, speed and majesty of Beatty's Battle Cruiser Fleet made it the cutting edge of British seapower in 1914.

11 The forecabin of HMS *Elizabeth*, as David Beatty accepts the German surrender of the High Seas Fleet – a broken remnant of the Kaiser's once-mighty force. The victory was a striking endorsement of Beatty's maverick style of leadership.

12 Andrew Cunningham's battleships bombard the Italian coast – a major factor in the success of the Allied Landings in 1943. A throwback to the age of heroic naval command, Cunningham was magnificent in victory, unbreakable in defeat.

which might become hostile to England, and it is only by maintaining Portugal in its separate state of alliance with England, that we can be sure of having the Tagus as a friendly instead of its being a hostile naval station.[107]

Once back on station, Parker prepared his heavily reinforced fleet to meet the crises that afflicted every European state on the Mediterranean littoral, from Spain to Greece. His attention was occasionally diverted by the effects of modern habits on the service. Too many junior officers were 'flippant and conceited', reflecting a lack of due subordination that did not auger well for military efficiency in the next war.[108] Then the seamen of HMS *Superb* mutinied. They had been refused permission to smoke because of the dirt and disorder caused by spitting on deck. Given Parker's opinion of smoking the outcome was predictable: the ringleader received fifty lashes.[109] Old-fashioned discipline quickly brought the fleet up to the highest standards of seamanship and drill.

If 1846 and 1847 had been busy years, 1848 would surpass them. The many and various states that occupied the Italian peninsula, ruled by the Pope, two kings, Austrian archdukes and other princes, were in ferment. The nationalist idea had taken hold in some regions, while in Sicily separatist agendas were at work. British concern to preserve peace, stability and commerce would be tested as never before. The Sicilians ejected the King of Naples' troops in January, seeking a return to a quasi-independent status with their own constitution, then in February the French King was overthrown and a republic proclaimed, inciting fresh uprisings. Parker kept a close eye on the powerful French fleet, relying on the British consul at Marseilles for the latest information.[110]

The Second Term

British ministers despised the King of Naples and sympathised with the Sicilian cause, but they had no occasion to interfere. Consequently Palmerston advised Parker that he 'should not act, but only look as if he might do so'.[111] However, Parker was not afraid to interpret his orders with insight and latitude, secure in the knowledge that he had the absolute confidence of his political masters. On 23 August the prime minister, Lord John Russell, told the House of Commons: 'Sir William Parker was an officer of the greatest prudence and discretion;

and he thought both the Government and Parliament might fairly trust him to take any future proceedings he might think right.'[112] The endorsement was a comfort, as the soundness of his judgement, and that of his captains, was frequently put to the test. Parker always supported his officers, and in most cases they met his expectations, showing firmness, decision, humanity and commendable consideration for the sensitivities of other nations.

In September 1848 Neapolitan troops began bombarding Messina, but when the French Admiral Baudin, an officer Parker admired, decided that it was time to intervene, demanding the contestants accept an armistice in the interests of humanity, Parker was quick to join the démarche. While he had exceeded his orders, preserving the unity of action between Britain and France was essential – little wonder the Admiralty decided to extend his period of service. The sudden death of Lord Auckland at the end of the year ended an effective partnership that dated back to 1834. Parker spoke of his loss as 'a national misfortune, and almost irreparable to the Navy, for where are we now to find his equal in experience, sound judgement, and impartial administration of his office?'[113] The similarity of these men's professional and political outlooks, allied to their calm, reflective temperaments, had made them ideal partners in command. Auckland had readily accepted Parker's advice on the major policy questions that faced his Board, from ship design and tactics to manpower and reform. He was replaced by Sir Francis Baring, a competent First Lord but never a personal friend of Parker.

In March 1849 a Neapolitan army landed at Messina and launched a furious attack on the town. Having rejected the King's concession, the Sicilians failed to prepare their defences. Within days they had surrendered, and were reintegrated into the Neapolitan kingdom. Although he regretted the manner in which the crisis had ended, Parker was relieved that he could withdraw his ships from the various ports where they had been protecting British lives and property. That summer he assembled a fleet to defend against the possible risk of Russia attacking Ottoman Turkey and sailed eastward to the Ionian Islands, where his new flagship HMS *Queen* joined at the end of September. He had been anxious to man the new flagship with as many officers and men from the *Hibernia* as wished to serve, making the transition easy. The advantages of flying his flag in the fastest ship in the fleet – instead of the slowest – were immediately apparent.

The British minister at Istanbul, Sir Stratford Canning, had summoned the squadron to Turkish waters in great haste. When a Hungarian rebellion against Austrian rule collapsed, the rebel leaders escaped to Turkey. Austria and Russia demanded that they be handed over, and mobilised troops. Parker had been expecting the summons, making a rapid passage through the Aegean archipelago in October. The timely appearance of a powerful fleet at Besika Bay, just outside the Dardanelles, stiffened the Sultan's resolve and the Austro-Russian demands were soon withdrawn. However, Besika Bay was not a safe anchorage so late in the year: it was exposed to frequent gales and offered only poor holding ground for anchors. The government wanted the fleet to remain on station, to back British diplomacy or if necessary defend Istanbul against a Russian attack. While the French supported Britain, the French fleet only arrived after the work had been done.

As it still took months to communicate between London and Istanbul, the government left Canning and Parker with considerable authority. On 1 November Parker took the fleet from Besika to a secure anchorage inside the Dardanelles, with the full concurrence of the Turkish government. He had consulted the local British consul, whose advice proved inaccurate. Canning had emphasised the need to study the Straits Convention, but Parker misunderstood the stipulations.[114] However, he was absolutely correct in his seamanship: no sooner had he entered the Dardanelles than the weather broke, rendering Besika utterly untenable. To have sailed away from the Turkish coast at this critical period would have sent the wrong signal to St Petersburg, Vienna and Istanbul.

While no one could dispute Parker's professional judgement that the safety of his fleet required entering the Dardanelles – 'I would not willingly anchor the line of battle ships beyond a few days in a position so unsheltered as Besika Bay at this season'[115] – it was a highly sensitive political act. Canning declared that the move gained 'an immense moral advantage'.[116] Russia, with good reason, took offence at this clear violation of a convention that expressly forbade the passage of battleships inside the Dardanelles in time of peace. In the event the Russians dropped their demands on Turkey, well aware they could not be enforced while the British fleet was in the area, while the British government publicly 'regretted' the entrance of the fleet. In private, though, they thanked both minister and admiral. Parker's merits were not in doubt.

By the end of the month the crisis had passed, and Parker's fleet was sent to Athens to support British demands for the settlement of several outstanding complaints against the Greek government. King Otho, the compromise choice of the great powers for the new kingdom in 1830, had proved a poor investment. Palmerston was openly contemptuous of Otho, who treated Greece like a petty German principality. Although he expected that seven battleships and five large steam frigates would secure the necessary concessions, the foreign secretary gave Parker wide latitude to seize Greek warships, impound merchant shipping and blockade the country until outstanding debts, which were not large, had been settled. The largest single item was the settlement of a claim for damages and loss by a British citizen of Portuguese Jewish ancestry. Don Pacifico claimed that his house had been wrecked and looted in an anti-Semitic riot during an Athenian Easter parade, when valuable documents detailing his claims on the Portuguese government were destroyed. His valuation of the papers was seemingly inflated, but the British had little option but to uphold his estimate. Although many, including Parker, doubted his honesty, Pacifico had served the British state since the Peninsular war. He had earned his naturalisation, and the right to protection.

Parker arrived in Salamis Bay on 11 January 1850, but the King rejected the British demands, and Parker began seizing warships on the 18th. The French minister, abetted by his Russian colleague, encouraged the King in his obstinacy. By the end of the month Parker had seized a small armada of warships and merchant craft while blockading the harbour. The tact and professionalism the Royal Navy displayed in executing this disagreeable duty reflected the admiral's long experience of operations other than war and the effect of his leadership on the fleet. Although petty debt-collecting was unworthy of them, the men of the fleet behaved well. Aside from their pathetic king and his cronies, the Greeks were equally restrained, recognising that the fault lay with their government. When the Greek Parliament met, it accepted the British terms, and despite French efforts, the government caved in on 27 April. The embargo was lifted and the ships returned. As Palmerston had already told his minister: 'Nothing can be better than the manner in which you and Sir William Parker have conducted the affair . . . You have . . . combined firmness, decision, and promptitude with all moderation, forbearance, and courtesy compatible with the execution of your instructions.'[117]

During the hundred days it took to settle the affair, French opposition had prompted many in Parliament to attack Palmerston for causing a crisis by backing the apparently unworthy claims of Don Pacifico.[118] One politician dared to impugn Parker's integrity, but he was sternly rebuked by the prime minister, who declared, 'Sir William Parker is a man who may be believed on his own statement.'[119] Palmerston finished the crisis with the greatest speech of his parliamentary career, comparing his defence of British citizens abroad with the policy of imperial Rome. The House of Commons was persuaded, his critics silenced.

After cleansing King Otho's Augean stable, Parker returned to Malta, where he reformed the fleet before touring the anchorages Nelson had used when the continent of Europe was closed to the Royal Navy in 1803–5. The voyage combined homage, nostalgia and precaution – war with France seemed imminent. Finally, Parker's unprecedented term of almost seven years commanding the Mediterranean fleet drew to a close. The fact that he was replaced by Rear Admiral Sir James Dundas suggested the service had fallen on hard times: Dundas had no experience of fleet command when he replaced the master in this most complex and demanding art. A week later Parker sailed for home, paying off his flagship at Spithead on 22 April 1852.

Home at Last, but not to Rest

Only two months later Parker was appointed to chair a committee on future naval manning requirements. His committee, which included his long-serving flag captain Peter Richards, agreed that the age-old system of recruiting men on a ship-by-ship basis for the length of the commission, which had served every admiral since Lord Howard, must be replaced by continuous general service for an agreed number of years. From this decision emerged the modern naval rating. The final report was submitted to the First Lord, a post once again taken up by Sir James Graham, and adopted by an Order in Council of 1 April 1853. By the time the navy went to war against Russia in March 1854, some seven thousand men had accepted the new scheme.

In October 1853 a fresh crisis over the future of Ottoman Turkey loomed, prompting Graham to offer Parker command of a projected Baltic fleet. However, there was a span to all human things. Feeling unequal to the demands of working up a new force, entering a new theatre and conducting large-scale operations, the seventy-three-year-old admiral declined, 'in justice to my country'.[120] Instead, he took the shore command at Plymouth, where he served throughout the Crimean War (1854–6). He was also consulted on the viability of Lord Cochrane's plan to capture Sebastopol with poison gas, a proposal that was ultimately declined on humanitarian grounds.

In 1863 Sir William became Admiral of the Fleet, the ultimate tribute to a life of service. As one old colleague declared, 'he stood indisputably first in his profession'.[121] That pre-eminence survived him: men who were raised in his school led the navy into the twentieth century. Parker died of bronchitis at Shenstone Lodge on 13 November 1866. He was buried without pomp or ceremony at the local church.

Sir William Parker was an admiral's admiral, the ultimate professional: hugely competent, consistent, calm and quiet. Modelling himself on Thomas Hardy, he never achieved the public profile of Charles Napier and Lord Cochrane; he cared nothing for popular headlines, but he held the affection and loyalty of an entire service for three decades. Although Nelson had admired the seamanship, insight and commitment of Captain Parker, it was his less obviously heroic post-war service that earned him a place among the great admirals. His later career also indicated the value of a mid-career break: Parker came ashore as a brilliant young captain, returning as a highly effective flag officer fifteen years later, just as the demand for naval force began to grow.

When Parker returned to sea, he reintroduced the navy to the standards of seamanship, discipline and initiative that had been the hallmark of the fleets led by Jervis, Nelson and Anson. Under his leadership, the Royal Navy recovered its unquestioned pre-eminence: Parker's fleets were the envy of every other navy, the ultimate sailing battle fleets. In his first independent command, monitoring the com-

plex politics of the Portuguese Civil War, he protected British interests and appeared even-handed, while ensuring the 'right' side won.
This made him a favourite at the Foreign Office and ensured he was
employed almost constantly thereafter. After half a decade in naval
administration, he was sent to settle an embarrassing little war in
China that had already floored several admirals. His triumph combined age-old naval skills with inspired use of steam navigation and
the latest hydrographic intelligence to defeat a regime that simply did
not understand British power. Finally, the long years he spent maintaining peace and stability in the Mediterranean made a priceless
contribution to the maintenance of British interests.

Despite his own political convictions, Parker was the first truly
professional admiral, serving both parties with unwavering loyalty.
He knew when to obey, and when to use his initiative. He made very
few mistakes. He worked well with civil and military colleagues, and
upheld the honour of the flag without undue fuss. Parker served the
complex agendas of central government to perfection, his dignified,
firm leadership bringing the fleet to a pitch of perfection. The potent
theatre of a British fleet at exercise, with its precise, silent drill and
effortless seamanship, struck fear into the hearts of rivals. Because
the Royal Navy was credited with enormous power, the security of
the British Empire was maintained for a pittance. Parker helped to
sustain the theatre of deterrence and prepared the way for the
resumption of real naval might in the last decades of the century.
Superior seamanship, discipline and training gave the British an
edge, while Parker's resolute leadership and unequalled skill invested
his command with a Nelsonian aura. His mastery of the admiral's
art was unrivalled in his era.

Between 1827 and 1856 Parker was hard at work at an age when
modern admirals have taken up other occupations. When he hauled
down his flag for the last time, he would, in today's terms, have qualified for a free television licence. Parker left the navy with a large
body of able officers, experienced in sail and steam, diplomacy and
war. It was fitting that his last contribution was the creation of the
modern naval rating, and the admission of a young John Fisher into
the service.

7

THE EMBODIMENT OF THE VICTORIAN NAVY

Geoffrey Hornby

1825–95

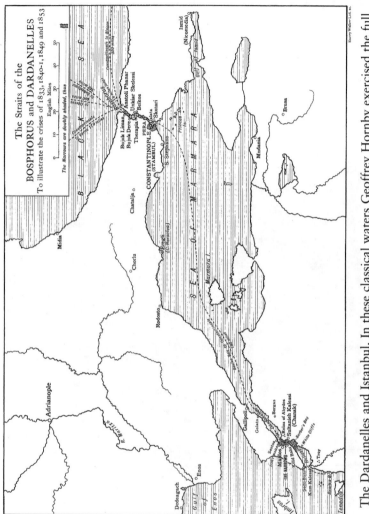

The Straits of the
BOSPHORUS and DARDANELLES
To illustrate the crises of 1833, 1840-1, 1849 and 1853

English Miles

The Narrows are doubly shaded, thus

BLACK SEA

Midia

Chatalja

Chorlu

Adrianople

R. Maritza

R. Ergene

Dedeagach

Enos

Gulf of Enos

Tenedos

Imbros

Troy

White Cliffs

Kum Kalessi

Sedd Bahr

Sultanieh Kalessi
(Chanak)

Ruins of Abydos

THE NARROWS

Maidos

Bergas

Galata

Gallipoli

Rodosto

Ernekli
(O. Marmara)

Marmara I.

SEA OF MARMARA

Princes Is.

Scutari

Galata
PERA
CONSTANTINOPLE
(STANBUL)

S. Stephano

Bujuk Liman
Bujuk Dere
Therapia

Anatoli Phanar
Unkiar Skelessi
Beikos

Mudania

Brusa

Mudania

Ismid
(Nicomedia)

Gulf of Ismid

BOSPHORUS

Dardanelles in 81 hours

The Dardanelles and Istanbul. In these classical waters Geoffrey Hornby exercised the full
weight of sea power and command. His masterclass in armed diplomacy averted war, saved
Turkey and secured the British Empire

WHILE WILLIAM PARKER BESTRODE HIS ERA with the calm assurance of a man with a stellar war record and the admiration of the greatest sea officer of all, the next great admiral would hear guns fired in anger only once, while still a child. Geoffrey Hornby's career was propelled not by experience in battle but by patronage, family and favour, yet here, as with Nelson, was a case of merit justifying patronage. As a commander of ships, squadrons and fleets, as a naval lord and reformer, as a political agitator, tactical pioneer and as the very embodiment of the service for the last two decades of his life, Hornby embodied British global power. He created the steam-powered iron-clad navy, developing the drill and signal systems that would govern the use of navies in combat for as long as heavy artillery remained the principal weapon. His example was universally copied – but never surpassed.[1]

Geoffrey Thomas Phipps Hornby was born at Winwick, Lancashire, on 20 February 1825, the sixth child and second son in a large family. His father, Captain Sir Phipps Hornby RN, was related by blood and marriage to the local Stanley dynasty, the earls of Derby. His wife, Sophia Maria Burgoyne, had been brought up in the Stanley household, along with her brother, Field Marshal Sir John Burgoyne. If his mother's anecdotes are to be relied on, the red-headed Geoffrey was a determined little boy who learnt to master his temper and acquired the classic early Victorian qualities of honesty, integrity, faith and duty. The family often joined large gatherings of the clan at Knowsley, Lord Derby's ancestral home. Hornby began his schooling at Winwick Grammar School, but in 1832 his father was appointed Captain Superintendent of the Naval Hospital and Victualling Yard at Devonport. The official residence lay at the heart of the naval base, surrounded by ships and sailors. The boys were dispatched to Mr Southdown's school in Plymouth, noted for excellent tuition in mathematics. Maths was essential for a naval career, and there was no better opening for young Hornby. While his elder brother followed uncle Burgoyne into the Royal Engineers, Geoffrey entered the navy in March 1837 as a first-class volunteer on board HMS *Princess Charlotte*. The 104-gun copy of Nelson's *Victory* was to be Admiral Sir Robert Stopford's flagship in the Mediterranean.

This prime opening reflected the close personal ties between senior Tory officers. On board Stopford's flagship, Hornby joined other hand-picked young gentlemen who shared his politics and social mores, including William Peel, son of the prime minister, who died young after heroic service in the Crimean War and the Indian Mutiny.[2] Hornby's connections with his admiral went beyond service: his favourite sister would marry Sir Robert's son. He also learnt the skills and accomplishments expected of a contemporary naval officer from the chaplain and instructor chosen by Captain Arthur Fanshawe, one of Stopford's nephews. His precocious mastery of French proved useful on a visit to Toulon and made his name with the admiral. He shared a lifelong predisposition to sea-sickness with Nelson, but it never interfered with the performance of his duties. Despite its modern aspects, the navy Hornby joined retained much eighteenth-century practice in the routines of fitting out and taking leave, with the sailor's last day in port marked by bacchanalian revels. All this would come to an end long before Hornby completed his career, for the easy-going reign of William IV ended that June, and he would see out his life in the navy of Queen Victoria.

An Early Battle

While the peacetime routine of cruising, harbour visits and refits in the Mediterranean provided a gentle introduction to naval service, the commission ended with a bang. In 1840 Mehemet Ali, Pasha of Egypt, asserted his independence from his nominal master, the Ottoman Sultan. Britain, in concert with Austria and Russia, decided to restore him to his proper place by force. In a swift amphibious campaign along the coasts of modern Lebanon and Israel, then simply called 'Syria', the Egyptians were driven from every town and fortress save the old crusader castle of Acre, the place where Napoleon's advance into Asia had been halted back in 1798. Acre had been rebuilt by European engineers and armed with numerous modern cannon. However, winter storms would soon break on the coast, ending all operations. On the advice of Commodore Charles Napier, the foreign secretary, Palmerston, ordered a reluctant Stopford to capture the place.

On 3 November the fleet, supported by a few Austrian and Turkish ships, attacked the two sea faces of the old fortress, with *Princess Charlotte* at the heart of the operation. The fleet engaged at ranges of well under half a mile. After two hours of heavy firing, a British shell detonated the main magazine inside the fortress, killing over a thousand men and countless mules. The demoralised garrison evacuated the city that night, and Turkish soldiers and British and Austrian marines were ashore before daybreak. The fleet suffered only eighteen killed and forty-one wounded, which, together with the loss of a few spars, some rope and the expenditure of forty-eight thousand rounds, made it a very cheap victory. The Syrian crisis was over, and so was Sir Robert Stopford's command – he returned home the following spring. Hornby acquired a medal for Acre, but it would be his only experience of war, acquired at the age of just sixteen.

The *Princess Charlotte* paid off in August, and Hornby spent the next six months at Woolwich dockyard, where his father was Captain Superintendent. Woolwich was the home of the steam navy, and Hornby had seen how useful steamships were on the Syrian coast. However, his next appointment was to a sailing frigate, HMS *Winchester*, fitting for the flag of Admiral Sir Josceline Percy at the Cape of Good Hope. Percy's brother was the Duke of Northumberland, and his appointment reflected the fact that a Tory government had taken office in 1841.

For the second time in his career, Hornby sailed out to his new station on a flagship crowded with the admiral's family, including three daughters. He recorded his impressions of the voyage, including a classic account of 'Crossing the Equator' with 'King Neptune', for Admiral Stopford.[3] As an experienced midshipman Hornby was stationed in the main top and took command of the admiral's barge. Greatly admired by the younger midshipmen for his leadership and good humour, he was also the best cricketer on board. There was, however, a deeper purpose to his time in the *Winchester*: having been stuck on the captains' list himself for decades, Hornby's father knew the importance of early promotion. He ensured that his son would master his profession so that he could secure the first opportunity for promotion that emerged. On distant stations, admirals were allowed to fill vacancies occurring through death from among their own officers, and in June 1844 Hornby was promoted to lieutenant in just such a vacancy because the admiral's own son was still too young. Joining the frigate HMS *Cleopatra*, Lieutenant Hornby moved to the East African anti-slavery patrol.[4] Here he commanded boats serving inshore before returning to the Cape in charge of a vessel taken off Mozambique in mid-1846. By this time, the newly promoted Admiral Hornby was anxious to bring his son home, having found another opportunity to advance his career.

While waiting for a ship at the Cape, Hornby spent some time with Anthony Hoskins, another *Winchester* midshipman. Years later, Hoskins recalled a conversation during which Hornby, in addition to discussing the essential professional skills, stressed the importance of upholding the dignity and discipline of the service.[5] Hornby's vision of a well-conducted fleet, presided over by cultured gentlemen, would be central to his career, but beneath the drill and formality lay an iron resolve and an unequalled commitment to the highest professional standards. There was nothing amateur about Geoffrey Hornby: gentlemanly conduct was an essential tool of leadership and command in the Victorian navy. After 1815 the officer corps became essentially aristocratic in character, due both to the social origins of many new recruits and the manners that all affected. Hornby belonged to this new elite, advancing along the twin streams of aristocratic and professional patronage.

Return to Shore

After five years at the Cape, Hornby returned home lean, energetic and fully grown, at about five feet ten inches. He passed the examination for lieutenant and rejoined his family at Knowsley. Admiral Hornby was offered the Pacific station, and accepted the assignation in order to advance his son's career. If Geoffrey served as flag lieutenant, he would benefit from the 'haul down' promotion that flag officers were awarded at the end of their commissions. As the flag captain of HMS *Asia*, the admiral chose Robert Stopford, soon to become his son-in-law, in part because Mrs Hornby, her three daughters and the admiral's widowed sister also joined the ship. While the family would live ashore at Valparaiso, they joined some of the less demanding cruises.

Geoffrey Hornby's logbooks from this period reveal his consistent attention to detail. Initially he noted the navigational features and holding ground of every harbour visited, with the sources of food, water and firewood; the latter observations were soon replaced with notes on the availability and cost of coal and local lighters.[6] The station, essentially the entire west coast of the American continents, was relatively quiet, but two deaths changed Hornby's situation. His elder brother Phipps died suddenly in Canada, making him heir to the family estate. Then a death vacancy secured his promotion to commander on 19 February 1850, the day before his twenty-fifth birthday. The flagship paid off at Portsmouth in June 1851.

On his return, Admiral Hornby moved into a house he had inherited at Littlegreen, only sixteen miles from Portsmouth. Hornby did not have long to rest. His cousin Edward, Lord Stanley, heir to the fourteenth Earl of Derby, invited him to India, leaving London in late July 1851. They travelled across France by rail and coach, then by steamship to Alexandria, by river to Cairo and across the desert by camel wagon to Suez to join the P & O steamer to Ceylon (now Sri Lanka). Here Hornby was taken ill with abscesses of the liver, and he retraced his outward voyage as an invalid. He arrived home, much recovered, shortly before Lord Derby formed a government. Admiral Hornby joined the Board of Admiralty 'chiefly in the hope of being able to help his son'.[7] Hornby spent the year studying steam engineering at Woolwich. When the government fell, both Admiral Sir Hyde Parker, the senior naval lord, and Phipps Hornby had their sons promoted to captain, effective from 18 December 1852. As his father retained office in the new ministry, Captain Parker, another youngster from *Winchester*'s gunroom, received a command. Tragically he was killed early in the Crimean War, attacking Russian batteries in the Danube. Hornby avoided this fate by spending the only major war of the century ashore and unemployed. As the son of an avowed Tory and nephew of the last prime minister, he was ignored by the Liberal ministries of Lord Aberdeen and Lord

Palmerston. However, he remained the youngest captain in the service, outranking many officers promoted for Crimean service.

Though his enforced idleness was frustrating, Hornby was due some time ashore after three long commissions. With a useful increase in pay and time on his hands, he married Emily Coles of nearby Ditcham Park on 27 April 1853. Later the couple settled at Lordington, a cottage on his father's estate, where four children were born. Sir Phipps' good fortune continued when an uncle and cousin died, leaving him further funds to add to the freight money (a percentage paid on any precious metals of coins carried home by warships) from the Pacific command and a four-thousand-acre property on the Hampshire–Sussex border. Geoffrey took to the life of a farmer: he ran the estate and began to sign himself Phipps Hornby, in honour of the man who had left the estate to his father. His scientific approach to life extended to advanced agricultural methods, and he took particular pleasure in tree planting, little realising that the days of the wooden warship were over. Professional studies, mathematics and science occupied him indoors, while hunting, shooting and fishing provided outdoor amusement. However, his continuing commitment to the navy was reflected by his decision to spend a year studying at the Royal Naval College, Portsmouth, between August 1857 and June 1858. As heir to an estate, many men would have found a higher duty at home, but Hornby had other ambitions. When Lord Derby formed his second administration, he pressed for a ship, and did not have to wait long. On 16 August he was ordered to join HMS *Tribune*, a steam frigate on the China station.[8] The ship had been ordered to carry 150 spare Royal Marines to Vancouver, where a gold rush had caused considerable unrest. With improved communications he managed the passage to Hong Kong in forty-five days! This was a choice command for a young captain, but Hornby did not rest on his laurels. On arrival he discovered the ship badly needed a refit: the first lieutenant, 'who is very young', had only kept up appearances. Nor was the station's discipline to his taste. Admiral Sir Michael Seymour operated a relaxed regime in the sultry heat of south China. Hornby was horrified to find that once the ship was ready for sea after the refit, it took four hours to bend and furl all the sails, and the captains of tops were ignorant of their duties. There was a complete lack of that man-of-war discipline he considered essential.[9] After a rough and frustrating passage to Nagasaki, Hornby found the ship's company much improved on the second leg, putting in some impressive ocean sailing to reach Esquimault dockyard in early February. Here the tail end of the gold rush prompted some desertions, while the ship's rotten mainmast was replaced from a local forest.

Although the original crisis was over and the admiral had departed, Hornby's arrival was timely. A dispute blew up with the United States in July over the title to San Juan Island, which lay between Vancouver and the mainland. American troops occupied the island, but the British governor sent the magistrate to demand they leave, and directed Hornby to prevent any reinforcements from landing. Confident the American government would disavow their local commander, the British decided to keep quiet until instructions arrived from Washington. As the senior officer on station, Hornby found himself as acting admiral, and demonstrated his superior understanding of issues far beyond seamanship and smart sail handling. When the American commander rejected his proposed compromise, Hornby was quick to make his point:

I have told him that he and his Government must be responsible for whatever happens hereafter, and also that I land directly if I conceive that the honour or interests of England require it. As we are fortunately here in much superior force to him [the American commander], we can afford to be forbearing without danger of our motives being misunderstood, while I hold it would be impolitic to land except some of our people are absolutely interfered with.[10]

When the governor suggested that Hornby recapture the island, on his own responsibility, Hornby wisely refused. The Victorian empire was secured by such quiet, confident and assured diplomacy, very much in the mould of Sir William Parker. The local engineer commander wrote to Hornby's uncle, Field Marshal Sir John Burgoyne, praising the young man's judgement: 'He will avert war to the last moment without in any degree periling the proper dignity of England.'[11] On his return Admiral Baynes concurred, his official letter to the Admiralty attributing the preservation of peace to Hornby's tact and judgement.[12]

The *Tribune* was not fated to remain long at Vancouver. That autumn symptoms of serious dry rot were discovered in her stern, a common fault with early wooden-hulled screw steamers, and she was ordered home via Valparaiso and Cape Horn. After an involuntary stop in the Straits of Magellan to recaulk her leaky stern, the *Tribune* proceeded by way of Rio de Janeiro without further adventures.

It was a mark of Hornby's enhanced standing in the service that he was soon offered another ship, this time by a Liberal government. The new vessel was the steam battleship HMS *Neptune* on the Mediterranean station, which had been manned in 1859, when war with France seemed imminent, with men raised by the offer of a £10 bounty. Two captains had failed to make their mark on the ship's company, and Hornby inherited a rough-looking set of men and a scruffy ship that performed badly at basic sail and gun drill. Furthermore, new regulations restricted the use of summary corporal punishment. This was a serious test of his leadership. He had to impose his authority on a badly manned ship – without the aid of the lash. The more he saw of them, the less he liked his 'shameful riff-raff'. Within a month the inevitable explosion occurred: the starboard watch refused to hoist the main topsail, and a fortnight later he found that many ropes in the running rigging had been cut during the night. He called up the entire crew and asked if they had any grievances. They complained about being made to scrub their hammocks every week and being drilled after dinner. Marine sentries were placed on the ropes thereafter, but the culprits were never discovered. As Lieutenant Edmund Fremantle observed, these men were quite unlike the regular man-of-war sailors, who valued order, consistency and the odd indulgence.[13]

Commander-in-Chief Admiral Sir William Martin, another old-fashioned Tory, lacked the political insight and broad concept of duty that Hornby had displayed at Vancouver. Martin complained bitterly whenever the government directed his ships to support diplomacy, to the detriment of squadron exercises and ship drill. But despite the unpromising circumstances, this was Hornby's first period of commissioned service in a major fleet, and he had much to learn about the seamanship of a close-ordered line of battle. Martin proved to be an inspiring, if not a particularly engaging, tutor. That summer Hornby began to handle the squadron under steam, following theoretical attempts to devise suitable tactics. He was initially dismissive of paper exercises and ridiculed the admiral's efforts to test them with rowing boats, fearing full-scale exercises would end in collisions. However, Martin took the sensible precaution of discussing his ideas with his captains before and after each exercise. In three days the squadron made rapid strides in steam-powered ship-handling.

Hornby, however, had seen the future – and it did not look like the one Martin was advocating. Nor was he backward in letting Martin know what he thought. His father provided an ideal sounding board:

It is no use fancying that steam-ships can only form as sailing ships used to do; and by adhering to those ideas, instead of following the new systems, which have been shown to be possible under most circumstances, we are throwing away the advantages that steam has given us.[14]

He agreed with Martin's basic point that endless practice in complex and demanding manoeuvres would bring the fleet to a level of expertise where simple movements could be made safely under fire.

When Martin needed a new flag captain, he approached Hornby unofficially, but Hornby refused, citing disagreements on professional issues and his promise to return home shortly.[15] The ideas that had their genesis in the Mediterranean would be the basis of his fleet management and tactical development until he stood at the head of his profession. Although inspired by Martin's initial efforts, the outcome was quite different. Where Martin saw tightly controlled, signal-driven squadron evolutions as an end product, Hornby used such exercises to instil in officers and men the basic skills necessary for combat and to ensure that a common doctrine informed their decisions in battle.

In the meantime, he had an opportunity to assess the competition. Attending the arrival of King Victor Emmanuel at Naples in April 1862, he found eight French battleships in harbour. They were well painted and appeared to be in good order. But Hornby was quick to note that they had difficulty taking up their berths, and their sailing evolutions were nowhere near as smart as those of the British ships. The prospect of war only two years earlier and the continuing high-tempo rivalry between the two powers gave these apparently friendly meetings a certain frisson, in which the ability to put on a superior display of seamanship gave the British officers considerable personal satisfaction, and no small degree of confidence.

Such reflections were soon disturbed by Admiral Martin.

Believing his duty lay in denying his officers any personal pleasure in their work, Martin deliberately moved ships from their stations to break up any prospect of family life. When he peremptorily ordered Hornby away from Naples, where he had been acting as senior officer, he received an unexpected but potent complaint in the official acknowledgement. Hornby considered the order a rebuke, one that he had done nothing to warrant. Suitably chastened by a full and frank exposition of Hornby's opinions, Martin swiftly reversed his position. That autumn the *Neptune*'s time was up, and she sailed home in November. A chance encounter with the Channel fleet at Gibraltar gave Hornby the sight of his first ironclad: HMS *Black Prince*, sister of the pioneer iron monster HMS *Warrior*.

Flag Captain

In March 1863 Rear Admiral Sir Sidney Dacres asked Hornby to be his flag captain in the Channel fleet, in the new steam battleship HMS *Edgar*. The two men had formed a good working relationship in the Mediterranean, where Dacres had been Martin's flag captain. Hornby accepted – an unusual move for a senior captain at a time when the pace of promotion was increasing – but made sure that Dacres understood that he could look forward to a good appointment in the near future, 'especially if there is a change of ministry'.[16]

As flag captain Hornby would be responsible for the flagship and for fleet manoeuvres. His new ship was a far better sailing ship than the old *Neptune*, a thirty-year-old sailing battleship converted into a steamer. The crew was also an improvement, but the men required some serious drill before they handled the sails and yards to Hornby's satisfaction. The squadron consisted of the *Edgar*, five ironclads – *Warrior, Black Prince, Defence, Resistance* and *Royal Oak* – the wooden steam frigates *Liverpool* and *Emerald*, and the dispatch vessel *Trinculo*. The variety of ships posed serious problems for squadron manoeuvres: the last three ironclads were poor performers under sail, while the *Warrior* and *Black Prince* were downright dangerous in close company. Maintaining station required constant juggling of the sails, and once steam was employed speeds differed wildly. Before much progress could be made, the fleet was dispatched on a round-Britain tour, visiting a number of ports where the ships were open to the public and local

dignitaries were entertained. While the admiral handled public relations, Hornby was responsible for the safe arrival of the squadron,
a task that kept him busy juggling the sails and boilers of his diverse
assembly. This initially proved so stressful that his liver complaint
returned, but he had recovered by the time they reached Glasgow.
Here he saw the answer to the problem. The shipyards were full of
iron steamships, both warships and blockade runners for the
American Civil War, which made no attempt to carry a full sailing
rig. Hornby was no reactionary: he wanted to exploit to the full the
opportunities offered by steam and iron, and was willing to cast out
traditional methods in order to achieve this. The following year the
first steam signal book appeared, but Hornby considered it beneath
contempt. Unfortunately his own fleet had little time for tactical
exercises, though it had at least been brought into an orderly and
hygienic state. Spending the autumn at Portland, with only a few
brief exercises to undertake, allowed Hornby to assist his brother-
in-law Captain Cowper Coles in his long-running dispute with the
Admiralty over the use of his turret system. Coles' concept of low-
freeboard armoured ships, equipped with a small number of very
heavy guns in revolving armoured mountings, was the way ahead,
but the transition would take time and cost lives. Hornby helped
Coles with his correspondence and primed the Tory spokesmen Lord
Stanley and Sir John Pakington to ask awkward questions in the
House of Commons. The Admiralty gave in, ordering two first-class
turret ships, one of which was designed by Coles. Hornby had managed to make a significant contribution to the turret-ship debate
without publicly taking a position.

Despite Hornby's progressive outlook, he would not let the old
order pass without a flourish: on 27 March 1865 he took *Edgar* out
of Portsmouth harbour under sail, the last time a battleship performed the manoeuvre without steam. Sail was now finished as a
force in battle, although it would serve as an economy measure and
a useful drill system for another decade and more. After a ceremonial visit to Lisbon, the fleet spent much of the summer exercising
out of Portland, with Hornby anxious to keep his motley collection
from colliding. Inspired by the very different handling characteristics of the ships in the squadron, Hornby and Dacres developed the
system of equal-speed manoeuvres, in which safety was ensured by
requiring ships to execute helm orders together, and at the same

speed. This facilitated far closer station-keeping and introduced an element of the parade ground into fleet exercises.[17] It was at this time that younger officers began to refer to Hornby as 'Uncle Geoff', although one suspects only behind his back. In August the fleet marked the end of a decade of heightened Anglo-French tension by exchanging visits with the French fleet at Cherbourg. France had lost the naval arms race in 1862, and with it her hopes of relegating Britain to the role of junior partner in her European designs. By maintaining naval mastery and upgrading her defences, Britain had avoided compromising her vital interests and helped to preserve peace.[18]

The visit to Cherbourg confirmed what Hornby had seen at Naples half a decade before: the French ships were remarkably clean and well organised, much of their equipment was better designed, and they had solved the problem of ventilating ironclads. Yet he was never one to be despondent:

Thank God, we are young and strong, and we must grind till we beat them. But we shall have plenty to do to beat them, for they are active intelligent men, and have got a start which they mean to keep. Admiral Dacres tells me the Minister of Marine is immensely struck with the *Royal Sovereign*.[19]

The *Royal Sovereign*, the first of Cowper Coles' warships, was a wooden steam battleship that had been cut down, armoured and fitted with four turrets. The French minister was impressed because she had been designed to attack a major naval base such as Cherbourg. When the fleet reached Brest, Hornby enjoyed showing off its ability to come into harbour under steam and sail. The mystery of the well-ordered French squadron at Cherbourg was explained, meanwhile, by the fact that it had hardly been at sea. The French Mediterranean fleet that lay at Brest was nowhere near as neat as the British ships.

African Command

Hornby's hopes for a dockyard appointment had faded between 1859 and 1865 as Lord Palmerston's Liberal government continued to hold office. Just before the fleet left for France in 1865, however, he was offered the command of the squadron on the west coast of Africa: as a first-class commodore, he would go in one move from being a flag captain himself to having one serving underneath him!

Though he disliked the thought of leaving his wife and family – the African coast was no place for women or children – he realised that the new post would ultimately benefit them: 'it brings me so much to the front that it cannot but eventually be a help to those dear boys'.[20] With the support of his wife and Dacres, Hornby took up the post once the Anglo-French visits had finished.

For much of the previous fifty years the African station had been the front line of the Royal Navy's campaign against the slave trade: it was well known as the most dangerous place for warships to cruise, as they frequently suffered terrible losses from yellow fever and other tropical diseases. Hornby's father was well aware of this vile reputation and pleaded with his son not to go; ironically, it was Sir Phipps himself who would not live to see the squadron's return, dying on 18 March 1867. Hornby's flagship, the steam frigate HMS *Bristol*, arrived at the end of 1865 and immediately lost twenty-two men from a working party of 104 sent to move an infected depot ship: a harsh lesson in local morbidity.

The trade which the squadron was sent to drive out was almost finished by the time Hornby arrived. The American Civil War had closed down the last significant market for slaves, while Spanish Cuba, where the practice was still legal, was no longer importing. Only in East Africa was slaving still big business. The squadron, therefore, was ripe for reduction. Hornby quickly mastered the Foreign and Colonial Office correspondence on the slave trade, visited the ports and assessed the options. The last stronghold of the trade in West Africa was a stretch of coast some 220 miles east of the River Volta, where the local king, a devotee of human sacrifice, depended on slaves as a source of revenue. Hornby proposed breaking down the region into separate coastal trading communities, bolstering the power of local chiefs so that the rule of the King could be overturned and supporting legitimate trade from which the chiefs could draw revenue.[21] Such strategic issues were only part of Hornby's concern on this commission: his time passed in a steady procession between different trading posts and offshore islands, the daily regime of exercise and maths punctuated by violent bouts of diarrhoea.

After another round of inspections, Hornby wrote to the Admiralty urging it to relax the blockade, which was killing officers and men for no good purpose, now the slave trade had ended. He advocated a reduction of the squadron, amalgamating the station with the force based at the Cape – something eventually achieved in 1870. When a smaller ship was selected to relieve the unreliable *Bristol*, he requested his own recall after two years' service. He arrived home in early 1868, showing symptoms of nervous and physical exhaustion. To make matters worse, his properties had been let: he ended up living in Dresden until Lordington became vacant. Various charges on the larger property at Littlegreen would require some years to pay off, but before he could enlarge the cottage Hornby was back in service.

A New Squadron

On 1 January 1869 Hornby was promoted to the rank of rear admiral. Although he had been a captain for the past sixteen years, he was still only forty-four, making him the navy's youngest flag officer. Almost immediately he was appointed to command the new Flying Squadron, a formation intended to show the flag to the widely dispersed British colonies and dominions where no fleets were stationed. In reality this was an economy measure on the part of the new Liberal prime minister, William Ewart Gladstone: thanks to the growing global network of telegraph cables, forces could now be rapidly summoned rapidly from long distances, allowing the numbers stationed locally to be reduced. The new squadron would additionally serve as a training formation. The fact that a Liberal government should choose Hornby for this important position reflected his unrivalled record as a seaman, the political acumen he had shown as far back as the San Juan Island affair – and the appointment of Admiral Dacres as First Naval Lord a few days earlier.[22]

Once he received his commission, Hornby began drafting standing orders that turned the Flying Squadron into a masterclass in contemporary seamanship. Though these covered everything from men's clothing to the economical use of coal, their prime object was to convey the principles of squadron sailing:

Precision under sail will lead to precision under steam, which otherwise cannot be learnt without great expense.

I am myself anxious to learn – always ready to discuss all questions – my own orders as much as anything else – with captains, and wish to give every information. But my great wish is that we may be able to do the country good service by training a large body of young officers in a good school.[23]

With four steam frigates and two corvettes, Hornby had enough ships to exercise, and took great delight in inspecting them at sea, whatever the weather. On the outward leg of the voyage the squadron called at Madeira, Bahia, Rio, Montevideo, Cape Town, Melbourne and Sydney. The Australian ports offered a wonderfully egalitarian reception to the officers and men of the squadron; Hornby repaid the hospitality by opening the ships to the public and taking numerous guests to sea for evolutions. Such openness had its dangers: some two hundred sailors deserted the squadron for the goldfields, and despite Hornby warning the local authorities that such losses would prevent future visits, none was returned. After stopping at Hobart, the squadron crossed the Tasman Sea to call at Lyttleton, Wellington and Auckland: Hornby found New Zealand more British than the other colonies.

The long passage across the Pacific to Japan that followed these visits demonstrated the value of the cruise: the ships were much better handled, easily outdistancing large merchant clippers. Two Japanese cadets joined the fleet, but one, finding his studies difficult, committed suicide. The squadron then retraced *Tribune*'s route to Vancouver, before stopping at Honolulu, refitting from the Royal Navy depot at Valparaiso and hastening home on hearing that war had broken out between France and Prussia. A final stop at Bahia was followed by another high-speed run to Plymouth, where the squadron anchored on 15 November, exactly as Hornby had predicted.

The Flying Squadron had circumnavigated the globe with far less fuss than Anson's ships 130 years before. Touching at a succession of British or friendly bases, it was greeted by rapturous crowds, fresh food, stores, coal and water. The cruise provided a body of officers and men – most of them long-serving regulars – with an unrivalled expertise in ship and squadron handling, taught by a strict but encouraging admiral. Hornby characteristically concluded his report by praising his officers and men. Having revived the art of seamanship under sail and brought it to a pitch of perfection, Hornby would reconstruct the very nature of seamanship for the steam age.

On 7 September, while Hornby's squadron rounded Cape Horn, the ultimate test of seamanship, Coles' HMS *Captain*, the turret battleship designed to combine sail with steam, armour and low-freeboard gun mountings, had capsized in a gale in the Bay of Biscay. She went down with almost all her crew, including Coles. While the loss of a much-loved brother-in-law was a personal tragedy for Hornby, the disaster caused a serious loss of confidence in the navy, all the more shocking because it occurred in the middle of a major continental war. The navy desperately needed leadership but possessed remarkably few men of the right calibre. Hornby soon became a focus for the hopes and ideas of talented younger officers, building a following across the service. In turn, 'Uncle Geoff' set about remaking the navy in his own image: he encouraged his protégés to think about the future and picked out the most promising from the pack.[24]

Within weeks Hornby was sitting on a committee of admirals and engineers to consider warship designs, chaired by Lord Dufferin. The committee met many times over the next six months, and agreed that masts and sails were not required on first-class battleships, although battleships and cruisers with sails were still essential for the trackless wastes that Hornby had recently visited. Only in the 1880s, with the triple expansion engines, would warships acquire the economy and reliability necessary to cross the Pacific under steam. Hornby had little to say in these discussions, and unlike his colleagues he was not cross-examined by the committee: his over-riding concerns were the shape the future navy would take and the men that would comprise it, rather than the materials they would use.[25]

More pressing services awaited, meanwhile: less than a year after the *Captain* catastrophe Hornby took command of the Channel squadron, in an appointment designed to build the fleet's confidence. On 2 September he hoisted his flag on the awe-inspiring five-masted ironclad HMS *Minotaur*, commanding a squadron of seven first-class full-rigged ironclad battleships. No sooner had he put to sea than the fleet was conducting tactical exercises under steam. Although the ships could spread vast amounts of canvas, they could not sail, reinforcing Hornby's conviction that steam seamanship was the basis of future service. Much of his work involved teaching basic skills to ensure that simple evolutions could be conducted accurately under fire. The exercises nonetheless required good judgement by the officers of each ship, and became more complex and demanding in the second year: Hornby was well aware that the transition from sail to steam had witnessed a marked falling-off in standards of seamanship, squadron navigation and tactical drill. Few officers shared William Martin's zeal, and coal was expensive. Such slack proceedings would not be allowed for much longer.

Inevitably, political pressures made it difficult to sustain a purely professional focus. In 1873 the fleet had to embark the lately abdicated ex-King of Spain, watch over the affairs of Portugal and stand an inspection by the Shah of Persia. The last provided an occasion for the type of high-profile display in which Hornby's fleets always excelled, as did a voyage carrying the Duke of Connaught to Sweden for the coronation of King Oscar II. On his return the Queen sent Hornby a signed photograph that remained among his most prized possessions.

Once such duties had been performed, Hornby returned to the serious business of the future of the battleship. 1873 saw the arrival in the Channel fleet of the brand-new, low-freeboard, mastless battleship HMS *Devastation*. Designed before the *Captain* tragedy, many believed her unsafe, though the 1871 committee considered her the ideal fighting ship. Someone had to test her seaworthiness, and there was no one better qualified than Hornby. He sailed from Portland on 13 August, and placed the new ship abeam of his flagship to observe how she rode in a heavy sea. Initially the *Devastation* plunged heavily into the short, steep swell, shipping large quantities of green water onto her foredeck, and seemed almost borne down by the sheer weight of water. As the swell became longer, however, she made better progress. Once two hundred tons of coal had been burnt, she rode the ocean well and, despite being in the very unseamanlike condition of having her decks awash from stem to stern, neither her buoyancy nor her stability were in any way compromised. The new design had been thoroughly vindicated. In mid-September Hornby took a passage on board the ship. In heavy weather off the Irish coast, 'green seas were at times two-thirds of the way up the jack-staff. It seemed incredible that she could live with so much water on her, yet she rose without effort.'[26] In essence, as long as the ship was watertight, she was in no danger. Even so, Hornby was not yet prepared to declare her perfectly safe, and she spent the winter undergoing modifications. Meanwhile, the fleet steadily improved the standard of steam evolutions, although they did not quite reach the standard Hornby desired: 'absolute precision and safety at 11 or 12 knots'.

When Disraeli formed a Conservative government in February 1874, Hornby was immediately offered the post of Second Naval Lord, but as his price for coming to Whitehall he demanded a naval officer as secretary to handle routine business and an enquiry into the state of the service. Refused the naval secretary, he declined office: he did not need the post, and did not believe the current Admiralty system sufficiently robust or effective to oversee the transformation in the service that rapid advances in technology and manpower concerns had made necessary. As a man with a modest private income, he could afford to be selective, and he had seen more service in the past four decades than any officer alive – though he would ultimately accept the post, probably against his better judgement, the following January. At one stage he was even persuaded to stand for Parliament as well, but this plan was later shelved, and instead Hornby completed his three-year term with another round-Britain cruise, paying off in September 1874.

He lived for the next three months at his family house, Littlegreen, the only period of his life that he would spend there. He loved the estate and the life of a country gentleman, and spent the short months before duty called rearranging the grounds, his personal effects and 'his beloved books'.[27] For all his success at sea, Hornby was by instinct a bookish intellectual rather than a man of action. One officer who served under him listed his qualities in order: he was 'a brilliant officer, a well read, clever man, and a good sailor'. Admiral Fremantle credited Hornby's success in the higher reaches of his profession to the amount of time he spent ashore in the 1850s, his formative years:

Given, of course, sound grounding in naval matters, a man's mind was enlarged, and he was a more capable officer through mixing with civil life . . . for in the higher ranks especially, our best officers are those who have spent much of their time on shore, always assuming they have kept closely in touch with the naval service.[28]

The intellectual lives of nineteenth-century admirals have rarely been an object of study: it is generally assumed that their public duties required minds as stiff as their collars and as straight as their swords. But Hornby possessed an unusually open, enquiring mind. If his faith and his politics were not open for debate, his thoughts on other matters – science and technology, social reform, the development of his profession – underwent constant development. He took a close interest in international affairs and studied naval history diligently, well aware that his profession could learn from the experience of the past. The quality of his mind was obvious to the leading naval intellectuals of the age: Professor Sir John Knox Laughton, Sir William Laird Clowes and Captain Alfred T. Mahan USN. Laughton, who knew him very well at Greenwich in the early 1880s, considered him the finest sea officer of the age because he combined intellectual facility with the highest professional standards, while Clowes observed:

He was a great student of professional history; he had a wonderfully clear head and a scientific mind; he was a natural diplomatist, and an unrivalled tactician; and, to a singular independence and uprightness of character, he added a mastery of technical detail, and a familiarity with contemporary thought and progress that were unusual in those days among officers of his standing.[29]

Mahan met him at a dinner in 1894, and asked who he considered second among British admirals, assuming that Nelson's pre-eminence was unquestioned. He was rather surprised to be told: '"St. Vincent, if second." I gathered that he thought Nelson erratic.'[30]

Hornby's intellectual attainments enabled him to place his professional activity in context, a critical asset for any admiral. In 1859 he demonstrated a degree of political sophistication that few contemporary flag officers could have equalled, and he passed a far harder test in his final command.

Admiralty Service and Mediterranean Command

In January 1875 Hornby was promoted to vice admiral and began his only period of duty at the Admiralty, as Second Naval Lord. It proved to be as uncongenial to his health and temper as he had feared. Hours confined to a stuffy office, the lack of opportunity for exercise and the inevitable pressures caused by the need to reconcile political agendas with professional concerns left him 'seedy' and prone to headaches: beneath the calm professional exterior Hornby was highly strung, prone to anxiety and obsessive. His lean, weather-beaten face and taut frame mirrored the iron self-discipline he displayed in command. Ill health and occasional irritability were the most obvious signs of the immense strain to which he subjected himself. He served because it was his duty, he excelled because he could – and he paid a heavy price for the effort.

The work was doubly uncongenial because it offered little opportunity to improve the quality or war-readiness of the service. While the fleet was desperately short of new ships, and struggling to keep those in service effective, the ministry would not consider a substantial new shipbuilding effort: no one was sufficiently alarmed to act, and the big domestic priority was tax reduction. The demands of routine administration and bureaucratic oversight denied Hornby the opportunity to achieve anything substantial and made him long for the promised day when he would be released to command the Mediterranean fleet. Offered the post of First Naval Lord in July 1876, he preferred the seagoing appointment because he could not reform the Admiralty sufficiently to give the naval lords a significant role in policy-making.[31]

His journal for 13 January 1877 recorded his frustrations: 'I left the Admiralty today with less regret and more pleasure than any work with which I have hitherto been so long connected.' He blamed this on the absence of a strong naval staff – the very thing he had called for in 1874 – to deal with matters of detail: the naval lords were smothered with purely routine business, to the exclusion of major policy questions. The situation was exacerbated by frequent changes of personnel, both political and naval, and the lack of consistent rules on personnel, deployment and promotion. In essence the Admiralty was trying to run the navy along political rather than professional lines.[32] The abolition of the Navy Board in 1832 had thrown the routine administration of a massive, complex and costly service onto the Admiralty, hitherto a political and policy-making headquarters. First Lord George Ward-Hunt admitted the office was inefficient, blaming the House of Commons for constantly checking the details of naval administration.[33] While the navy was held accountable for every penny, its role in ensuring national security was neglected.

By contrast, Hornby would suffer no shortage of opportunity for high-level strategic thinking on the Mediterranean command: this fleet was the showcase of British power throughout the nineteenth century, deployed in a region where political instability seemed endemic, while British strategic, commercial and humanitarian interests were legion. Rarely did a three-year term in command pass without a major crisis or a stream of lesser problems. Sir William Parker had been kept very busy, and Hornby would find the time for professional training severely restricted. He could have been under no illusions: the situation that faced him as he prepared to take up his post was unusually threatening. The Sultan was widely rumoured to be insane, his regime incapable of reform, while Russia was playing on pan-Slavic and Orthodox Christian alliances to stir up trouble over the unsavoury character of Turkish rule in Bulgaria. In this she seemed to have German support. As if the international complications were not serious enough, Gladstone, who had stood down as Liberal leader two years earlier, published a pamphlet on the so-called 'Bulgarian Atrocities' in September 1876. This document combined righteous indignation with graphic accounts of the barbarous cruelties practised by Muslim against Christian, and its success helped return him to party leadership. His moral crusade caught the mood of the moment. After a fortnight of mass meetings, domestic enthusiasm for Bulgaria began to abate, but the subject did not disappear: events in Turkey would excite uncommon interest throughout Hornby's Mediterranean command. Disraeli's ministry initially prepared for war in 1876, Hornby planning the necessary fleet concentration.

While the nation went mad over Bulgaria, Hornby's flagship was completing for sea. HMS *Alexandra*, the last fully rigged battleship, had been named for the Princess of Wales, who sent her down the slipway in 1875. She packed twelve heavy guns, 674 crew, 680 tons of coal and armour protection up to a foot thick into an overall weight of less than 10,000 tons. Unlike the first generation of iron-clads, *Alexandra* was an economical steamer, equipped with power-ful compound engines. However, the design had lost the elegant simplicity of the older ships, and Hornby considered her 'too com-plicated'. Her bluff hull made no concession to style or speed. Hornby was nonetheless determined that the *Alexandra* would be the smartest ship in the service: she was commissioned on 2 January 1877 with hand-picked officers and men, intended to set an exam-ple for the squadron.

Before he left England, Hornby called on his cousin Edward, now fifteenth Earl of Derby and Disraeli's foreign secretary. Having stressed the need to avoid war with Russia, Derby noted: 'the only point on which he pressed me was not to order or allow the squadron to be separated if it could be helped . . . I shall bear in mind what he says, for his judgement is good and sound.'[34] Hornby pressed for reinforcements, but the ministers were unwilling to move before Russia showed her hand. He visited the Queen before heading for his station in March, arriving at Malta on the 18th. While on passage he tried the ship under sail, and found her so slow – no more than six knots – that the experiment was only ever repeated as an exercise.

Warned by Captain John Fisher that the fleet had no idea of steam evolutions and one or two perfectly inefficient captains,[35] Hornby spent five weeks at Malta inspecting ships, stores, the dockyard and the administration of the station. Then he ordered that the admiral's residence should be overhauled in preparation for his family's arrival, and put to sea. He was directed to cruise to the east, heading for Corfu. Once at sea, the long anticipated equal-speed steam evolutions commenced, following a schedule sent ahead to the captains. Hornby required more than the precise execution of orders: looking for the next generation of admirals, he expected intelligent responses from his officers. His command system had a Nelsonian quality, bringing the fleet to a level of tactical proficiency where he could expect captains to display initiative within the parameters of a clearly understood doctrine. This reflected hard-won practical experience in handling squadrons under steam and a mastery of the professional literature, ancient and modern. Hornby understood that in certain circumstances the fleet needed to be controlled by signal and that on other occasions it would follow the initiative of junior admirals and captains. By imparting a consistent, effective doctrine through extensive drill, he ensured that the fleet could function as a team at the highest tempo.

Over the next six months a combination of increasingly complex evolutions, lectures, briefings and consultations with captains and lieutenants brought the fleet to a pitch of perfection. After mid-September 1877, Hornby rarely mentioned the conduct of exercises in his journal. The development of the fleet went on against a threatening backdrop of conflict in the Balkans and Russian pressure on Turkey. Well aware that he faced months waiting on diplomatic moves, Hornby kept the ships at sea for eight to ten days a month – essential if the efficiency of ships, men and machinery were to be preserved. However, Hornby also faced a problem that had never troubled Nelson. The boilers of many ships were worn out, but could only be replaced in a British dockyard. As the ministers would not commission new ships, or increase the estimates, Hornby was left with ships that might fail when called on for hard service – and the small problem of establishing a reliable wartime coal supply.

While the captains soon buckled down to their lessons, some of the men gave vent to their feelings about the new disciplinary regime with minor acts of insubordination. Hornby blamed the rapid turnover of crew and the loss of many senior ratings every year into the reserve. After a court martial on the *Achilles*, the seamen understood their situation rather better and gave no further trouble.

While the fleet was lying at Athens in late June, news arrived that the Russian army had crossed the Danube into Turkish Bulgaria: the two countries were at war. A week later, the fleet was ordered to Besika Bay – the nearest anchorage to the Dardanelles, the usual location for a British fleet supporting the independence of Turkey. Hornby boarded the dispatch vessel *Helicon* to visit Istanbul and confer with the British ambassador, Austen Henry Layard, famous for his rediscovery of the ancient cities of Assyria in the 1840s.[36]

Before leaving England, Hornby had requested Rear Admiral Sir Edmund Commerell VC be sent as second-in-command if war became likely, and Commerell duly arrived with two more battleships. While Hornby hoped the Turks could block a Russian advance on Istanbul, he knew that if the city fell it was highly likely Britain would declare war. He did not want to repeat Sir John Duckworth's experience of 1807, retreating down the Dardanelles under heavy fire. While the fleet could get through, relying on speed and armour, essential supplies of coal, ammunition and food could be stopped by a few well-placed guns on the Gallipoli shore. He requested ten thousand troops to secure the Bulair lines, built by Anglo-French forces at the outbreak of the Crimean War in 1854, to hold the peninsula against the Russians. This was a step too far for the ministers, who found themselves under attack at home for backing the Turks and short of friends abroad to help resist Russia.

Fortunately for Turkey, her armies proved far better than anyone had expected. Hornby recognised the quality of the troops but had less faith in the officers. At Plevna in the Balkan mountains, well-armed Turkish soldiers in strong earthworks beat off a succession of Russian attacks, each bloody repulse buying time for European diplomacy to resolve the crisis. The British government was divided, sending confused messages to friend and foe alike, to the consternation of the admiral, whose fleet was the primary symbol of British power.

Hornby kept the fleet busy exercising boats and the new locomotive torpedoes, while ships were detached for shore leave in Athens or maintenance at Malta. He was not amused, though, when enterprising Greek merchants set up tavernas at Besika, and they were summarily removed. The war began to go against the Turks in the winter, but by late November the exposed anchorage at Besika was becoming untenable. While Ambassador Layard wanted the fleet closer, the ministry sent it south to Vourla, near Smyrna (Izmir). Once the essential telegraph cable connection to the outside world had been established, Hornby went to Malta, only to be ordered back to the fleet a week later when Plevna fell. After outlining the state of the fleet, he advised the First Lord of the Admiralty, W. H. Smith, that 'the further I can be informed of your views, consistently with State secrets, the more I believe I should be able to prepare to carry them out, as for instance, in two subjects . . . coaling and the moving of troops'.[37] But the deeply divided government could not provide this information: Hornby would have to use his own judgement, at a time when war with Russia could start at any moment.

Back at Vourla on 17 January, Hornby found that Commerell had established a base; he also removed another unwelcome taverna. But he had more pressing problems: Layard warned him that the Russians were about to occupy Adrianople, and war seemed inevitable. Orders arrived on the 23rd: the fleet would sail to Istanbul to keep open the Dardanelles and protect British life and property. Hornby feared they were too late, since having failed to secure the Bulair lines he could not keep the waterway open. Even so, he sailed immediately, organising a five-hundred-man naval brigade to hold the lines at Bulair until troops from Malta and Britain could arrive. With the Gallipoli peninsula in British hands, the fleet could operate effectively in the Sea of Marmora, and potentially in the Black Sea, to cut Russian communications and support the Turkish Asiatic front. A dispatch vessel confirmed that the Turkish forts at Chanak had orders to allow the fleet through, but just as the vessel was about to rejoin the fleet on the 24th, a British telegram ordered it back to Besika Bay. Hornby was not amused.

Back in London, the Cabinet was in turmoil. In his anxiety to preserve peace, Lord Derby placed a wholly unwarranted faith in Russian assurances. Prime Minister Disraeli favoured more belligerent solutions, pushed on by the Queen and significant elements of public opinion. Disraeli's unofficial correspondence with Layard only added to the confusion in Istanbul and on board the *Alexandra*. On 23 January the Cabinet ordered the fleet to enter the straits, aware that Derby would resign. On the 24th they reversed their position when news arrived that the Sultan had accepted peace proposals from Russia.[38]

This sudden reversal of policy demoralised the Turks, who had anticipated British support, and encouraged the Russians, who feared the arrival of the fleet. It left Britain looking irresolute and incompetent, especially when the policy was reversed once more on 9 February. In effect, the Russians had bamboozled the Cabinet by holding out vague promises. The contrast between the clear and certain statement conveyed by the movement of the fleet and the dishonest wordplay of Russian ministers had escaped Derby, who did not share his cousin's concern for simplicity and clarity. When Layard telegraphed that the Russians had occupied Istanbul, opposition to active measures collapsed, both in the Cabinet and on the floor of the House of Commons. Layard's communication was erroneous, though perhaps deliberately so: the Russians never occupied the city. On 8 February the government secured a large vote of credit to fund preparations for war and ordered Hornby to enter the straits, ostensibly to protect British life and property. It was late in the day for such moves to have any effect, and Layard telegraphed home to oppose the attempt.

In the interim, the opportunity to occupy the vital lines at Bulair had been lost, and there was little chance it could be recovered. When Hornby arrived off Chanak for a second time on the 10th, he found that far from welcoming the fleet, the Turks protested against his passage. Clearly the situation in Istanbul had altered radically in the intervening fortnight. Nor had Layard sent any instructions.

Hurriedly taking advantage of the darkness to reverse course before anyone ashore saw the fleet, Hornby waited outside the straits for a few hours before putting back to Besika. The Turkish position was easily explained: the Russians had threatened to occupy Istanbul if the fleet entered the Dardanelles. On the 12th fresh orders arrived to enter the Sea of Marmora without waiting for permission, but the forts were only to be engaged if they hit the ships.

After two false alarms, the fleet was roused for another early start on the 13th. The six ironclads, their masts lowered and cleared for action, reached the entrance to the straits with a north-easterly snowstorm blowing directly into their teeth. Hornby took no chances, assigning each ship a target if the Turkish forts opened fire. He understood that the minefield had been destroyed by the winter storms. When the dispatch vessel *Salamis* reached Chanak, her commander observed that the Turks were not prepared for battle. After hearing Hornby's declaration of intent, the governor pointedly refrained from firing, supposedly in the interests of humanity, although his motives may have been patriotic. While the Turkish guns remained silent, the fleet did not make the passage unscathed. In blinding weather, the flagship ran aground just below Chanak; Hornby quickly shifted his flag and ordered the squadron on to Gallipoli. With the assistance of HMS *Sultan*, the *Alexandra* floated off unscathed four hours later, rejoining the fleet the next morning.

Predictably the arrival of the fleet alarmed the Russians. Grand Duke Nicholas demanded that if the Turkish fleet was not surrendered he would occupy Istanbul, but his demand was curtly rejected by the Sultan. The Russians were in no position to make such demands, since their troops were still twelve miles short of the lines at Bulair, where the Turks were reinforcing the defences. Leaving Commerell with two battleships to watch the lines, Hornby sent the *Salamis* to open telegraph links with London and brief the ambassador. He followed with four battleships the next day, 15 February. With the front line at San Stefano, the Turks still held Istanbul. Ever since the fall of the Byzantine Empire, Russian rulers had dreamt of restoring the city to Orthodox Christianity, of reconsecrating the Agia Sophia and of making themselves masters of the strategic hub of Eurasian land mass. But with Hornby's fleet on the Bosphorus, the Russians did not dare to seize the greatest prize that their army had ever laid eyes on.

They had good reason not to move: while Hornby's four ships represented the Mediterranean fleet, the Channel fleet had been ordered to Malta and a third fleet was mobilising to attack St Petersburg. Once the right arm of the British Empire flexed, Russia was paralysed. For all her military manpower and vast lands, Russia could not compete with British naval, economic and industrial power. Having secured the Bulair lines and replaced the local governor with a more reliable officer, Hornby could support any diplomatic demands the government chose to make:[39]

I look on that peninsula [Gallipoli] and the Dardanelles as the key to the naval position . . . If we lose it the Fleet would be of no use – and we should go as far west as Salonica to find a base, and that a less influential one for any military operations.[40]

The Admiralty immediately authorised him to resist any Russian attempt to land on the Gallipoli peninsula.[41] The government was not prepared to land marines or a naval brigade to strengthen the lines. Instead, Hornby warned Commerell to resist any Russian attempt to land on the peninsula by force and instructed him to ensure his ships were well placed to support the Turkish defenders. As the main roads to the city of Istanbul were easily commanded from the sea, Hornby was confident he could prevent the Russians from moving heavy artillery. He also planned to operate in the Black Sea, receiving the latest intelligence on Russian naval forces, restricted to a few crude torpedo boats and merchant steamers. As Lord Derby put it on 22 February: 'Telegram from Layard: he and Hornby seem prepared to take on themselves the responsibility of resisting the transfer of the Turkish fleet.'[42] The following day the Russians gave up that demand. Hornby's actions allowed Disraeli to tell the Queen on 8 March that 'we are in a commanding position'.[43]

Little wonder that the Russian commander Grand Duke Nicholas was refused a state audience with the Sultan. To avoid needlessly humiliating the Russians, the fleet was not brought into the Golden Horn, but the *Salamis* lay there, her name recalling the first great triumph of sea power over eastern tyranny, and the White Ensign flew at her masthead. It was enough. The preliminaries of peace were signed on 4 March, allowing Hornby to move his ships to a healthier location. Lord Derby resigned from the Cabinet on 27 March; Disraeli then mobilised the reserves, moved ten thousand Indian troops to the

Mediterranean, and occupied an advanced base in Cyprus to recover British 'prestige'. Derby was replaced by Lord Salisbury, making the government's diplomatic position clearer and, from Hornby's perspective, more effective.[44] Commerell was authorised to secure the lines at Bulair by any means, including paying the Turkish troops.

With the fighting over, the British focused on securing a European congress to revise the terms Russia had imposed on Turkey, with considerable success. While the fleet was at anchor maintaining the peace, Hornby prepared for operations in the Black Sea, urging the Admiralty to send cruisers, stores and, if possible, a small force of troops to hold a key position.[45] Concerned the Russians might try a surprise torpedo attack, he kept the fleet on high alert until the European congress met in Berlin. In reality, such military concerns were increasingly out of step with the diplomatic course being pursued, but the government, to Hornby's evident displeasure, did not choose to confide in him. Even in late April Smith suggested to Hornby that serious preparations were still in progress: 'we are pressing forward the fitting out of another fleet and I hope in less than a month to have a formidable force assembled . . . available either for service in the Mediterranean or the Baltic'.[46]

As late as May Hornby remained on watch, convinced Russia would try to seize Istanbul. But her army was utterly spent – short of men, horses, food and stores – while the country had been bankrupted by the cost of the conflict. Hornby's fleet could block any local advance, and Russia was in no position to fight Britain. His insistence on being kept informed of government policy and tendency to frighten ministers did not make him any friends in the Cabinet, but like many an admiral before and since, he found the political process imprecise, irresolute and interminable. If his complaints seemed rather tetchy to those sitting comfortably at home, they reflected the immense strain of a complex and demanding task.[47] Armed peace was far harder to sustain than open war: he had to be ready at a moment's notice, and respond to a variety of potential scenarios, ranging from a declaration of war to rapid withdrawal. Hornby was far too intelligent to sit back and wait for orders: he was constantly trying to anticipate the next move in the military and diplomatic crisis, sifting the facts from a mass of rumours and disinformation. His task was greatly complicated by the confusion in London.

On 8 July the island of Cyprus was ceded to Britain and occupied by forces landed from the Channel fleet, then under Hornby's orders. Hornby joined the Board of Admiralty at Famagusta in November, finding the anchorage deeper than expected and easily developed into a base for ironclads.[48] Just in case the message was not thoroughly clear, ten thousand Indian troops arrived via the Suez Canal. Once the peace congress opened, however, Anglo-Russian tension relaxed. On 13 July the Congress of Berlin concluded with major reductions in the Russian gains from Turkey and a much smaller Bulgarian state.

On 6 August Hornby was awarded the KCB, a fitting tribute to the remarkable leadership that had kept the fleet in hand throughout a long and complex diplomatic struggle, without firing a shot. But the honour meant less to him than the wholehearted support of his officers and men, whose claims he urged on the government. Throughout the crisis the ships were constantly exercised and always ready for action. The intimate connection between the fleet and the preservation of British interests was evident when the Russian army moved back from their advanced position at San Stefano in September; the fleet withdrew from the vicinity of Istanbul the following day. However, the foreign secretary kept Hornby's force in the Sea of Marmora until the Russians had withdrawn from all Turkish territory.[49] Lord Salisbury had no faith in Russian promises, preferring the potent security of an ironclad battle fleet to the word of a diplomat. Although anxious to return to his cruising ground, Hornby kept up the drill of the fleet until the Russians left.

Once the crisis passed, Hornby, anxious to improve conditions for his long-suffering men, moved to a more salubrious anchorage off Ismid. The following day, 2 January 1879, the fleet suffered its only serious casualties of the crisis. The battleship HMS *Thunderer* was firing practice broadsides when one of the two guns in the forward turret burst, killing eleven and wounding thirty-five. Although the ship's crew and the rest of the fleet responded to the disaster with customary professionalism, it was essential that the men did not lose faith in their weapons. Hornby praised the initiative of two captains: Tryon and Heneage ceased firing to send medical teams, but then resumed target practice with renewed vigour to demonstrate the safety of the guns.[50] After further inspection, it transpired that the muzzle-loading thirty-eight-ton gun had been double-loaded, the first charge having misfired. This was only possible because it was a muzzle-loader. The noise and shock of the other guns being fired having overwhelmed the senses of all involved, the misfire was not noted. Shortly after this accident the Admiralty adopted breech-loading guns.

In March 1879 the Russians left Turkey. The fleet withdrew through the Dardanelles on the 19th, after thirteen months in the Sea of Marmora. Despite occasionally letting off steam in private correspondence, Hornby's public conduct had been strikingly suc-cessful. His calm, determined demeanour and immense reputation, combined with the constant readiness of the fleet, did more to avert a major European war than all the tortured efforts of politicians and diplomats. After passing the Dardanelles, Hornby anchored at Besika, and the Admiralty dispersed the squadron to visit various parts of the station. By mid-April the flagship was at anchor in Grand Harbour, Malta. The normal peacetime routine had been resumed – just before Hornby's promotion to full admiral on 15 June. He spent the summer cruising the Aegean, examining poten-tial advanced coaling bases in case the Russians came out of the Dardanelles. Otherwise the regime of exercises, consultations and steam evolutions continued, and it was a testament to the skill of the officers concerned that the elephantine dance of these unwieldy war-ships, each possessing very different power and handling character-istics, concluded with nothing worse than a single broadside-to-broadside contact between the flagship and the *Achilles*. Nor were the latest technical developments ignored: Hornby commenced experiments on the defence of anchorages against torpedo boats.

Between January and June 1879 John Fisher commanded one of Hornby's battleships, his first experience of serious fleet evolutions. The experience left him awestruck:

That great man was the finest Admiral afloat since Nelson . . . He was astounding. He would tell you what you were going to do wrong before you did it; and you couldn't say you weren't going to do it because you had put your helm over and the ship had begun to move the wrong way . . . He couldn't bear a fool, so of course he had many enemies. There never lived a more noble character or a greater seaman. He was incomparable.[51]

Meeting Hornby's high standards was an achievement, his praise a prize beyond purchase. The corollary was that fools and failures received short shrift. When HMS *Invincible* joined the fleet in 1878,

Hornby was particularly unimpressed by Captain Lindsay Brine. In early 1879 *Invincible* blundered badly during squadron exercises: Hornby immediately placed Brine under arrest and had the ship handled by the commander. Court-martialled for hazarding two ships, Brine was acquitted. However, the ship went home and Brine was relieved by Edmund Fremantle.[52] *Invincible* returned to the Mediterranean in poor order, and Hornby followed up a damning report by dismissing two of the senior executive officers. Suitably chastened, her new captain soon had the ship in first-class order: he had served under Hornby before and knew what was expected. For Hornby, the smart and efficient condition of a ship, and her ability to execute orders with precision and celerity, were the bedrock of naval professionalism: officers who failed that test were never forgiven. This struck some as harsh, but the service had fallen into bad habits and required a major overhaul if it was going to meet the test of war. By this time Hornby's views were well known, and some officers preferred to go ashore rather than face his wrath.[53]

After the fleet had the luxury of wintering at Malta in 1879–80, Hornby's relief, Sir Beauchamp Seymour, arrived in March. Hornby departed on the 12th, universally regretted.

Influence at Home

Hornby had stamped his character on the showpiece fleet of the Empire, raised the tactical skill of the force to a high pitch and played a critical role in deterring war. The Admiralty commended the 'zeal, ability and good judgement with which you had carried out the instructions of the H. M. Government, and so ably supported H. M. Ambassador at Constantinople in upholding the dignity and honour of this country'.[54] Sadly, Gladstone's new Liberal administration did not back up their fine words by promoting his officers, the customary mark of their Lordships' satisfaction. Hornby would not have been surprised. After two years at the Admiralty he was anxious to reform and reinforce the professional naval aspects of the office. Well aware that politicians of both parties were unwilling to relax their tight control over the Admiralty, which set the annual budget and made highly sensitive appointments, he tried to mobilise the leading officers in the service to adopt a programme of reform and refused to take the post of First Naval Lord until it was adopted. For man of private means, like Hornby, the sacrifice of refusing office on a matter of principle was not difficult, especially when the alternative was arduous and uncongenial labour.

Although Hornby couched his demands in terms of staff and intelligence functions, the real object was to complete the work of detaching naval administration from party politics, a process that had occupied much of the nineteenth century. It was still the case that when a government fell, the entire Board of Admiralty resigned with it. Hornby considered this wrong in principle, as well as a serious waste of time and effort. Only by establishing a thoroughly professional naval board, on which the lords would remain for a fixed term, could the office become an efficient policy-making body. In view of the rapid technological changes of the past two decades, politicians were no longer equipped to resolve the major policy questions. They would require a new type of First Naval Lord, an admiral with a wide experience of technology, administration and operations who had the confidence of the entire service and was not considered to be politically partisan. The ability to direct operations around the globe by telegraph gave this post an added importance, and Hornby was pressing for the establishment of an intelligence staff to ensure the naval lords could advise politicians. Though Hornby would have made a powerful First Naval Lord, and was only fifty-five when he returned home – younger than many men of lower rank – he was tied to the past by the very family connections and party politics that had helped him move so swiftly through the service.

Hornby had refused the post of First Naval Lord in 1876, hoping to secure reforms and believing that only three officers were serious contenders for the position: Sir Astley Cooper Key, Sir Beauchamp Seymour and himself. He proposed that the three of them agree on the necessary reforms, and that they should all refuse office unless they were conceded. His ploy was frustrated, however, by the appointment of Admiral Yelverton, an undistinguished officer content to follow the political lead. When Yelverton fell ill, George Wellesley was appointed, an officer with no obvious merits other than malleability; then in June 1879 Key took the post without pressing for the reforms he had agreed in 1876.[55] Unlike Hornby, Key had little or no income apart from his service pay and had recently remarried, which made the attraction of a fine residence and five years on full pay hard to refuse. But as a consequence, reforms over the next five years were limited and piecemeal.

Having failed to secure a fundamental overhaul of naval administration, Hornby would devote the rest of his life to gradually improving the service. He was not long unemployed: in early 1881 he became President of the Royal Naval College at Greenwich, the navy's officer-education establishment, whose curriculum and personnel required attention. The Board was equally anxious to have his advice, and he was frequently called to Whitehall. At Greenwich, Hornby planted two rows of trees at either end of the estate, which still provide much-needed shade, and encouraged officers to take more interest in the social life of the college. Above all, he infused the academic programme with his own vitality and hard-earned wisdom. He attended lectures and took an active role in setting the examinations, making sure the courses were well delivered and the tests both fair and resistant to last-minute cramming. He ensured the courses met the navy's needs and developed a close relationship with Professor John Knox Laughton, the pioneer of modern naval history. Although his primary duty was teaching maths, meteorology and astronomy, Laughton had demonstrated that a sound appreciation of past experience could equip the officer of today to face the problems of the future. In 1886 he published an edition of Nelson's correspondence for the benefit of students, which he dedicated to Hornby.[56] The admiral regularly attended Laughton's courses, contributing three lectures on contemporary fleet tactics. These were great events. He later refined them and published them privately, bringing his arguments against formal tactical systems to a wider audience:

It is often asked what is to be our fighting formation in future? None has been prescribed: it is to be hoped that none will be prescribed. To prescribe any would be exceedingly foolish and in a high degree presumptuous. Foolish; for all our past history shows us the evil of having a prescribed formation for fighting in; it needed the genius of Nelson to disentangle us from the mess. Foolish; for, unless perhaps the state of his enemy's bunkers, there are few things an admiral would give more to know beforehand than the formation in which his enemy was going to fight. Presumptuous; because in the present day, we have no business to speak with authority.

Hornby was the first admiral to conceive of the modern fleet, combining battleships, cruisers and flotilla craft for mutual support.

[279]

The prospect of fighting a Russian force largely composed of torpedo boats and armed merchant cruisers in the Bosphorus or Black Sea in 1878 only reinforced his appreciation of the need to escort the battleships against torpedoes and rams.

In November 1882 Hornby became Commander-in-Chief Portsmouth, one of the greatest honours that the service could bestow on a distinguished officer. The job was largely concerned with dignified supervision and occasional prestige visits. At least he was near his beloved estate and could get away to hunt. The command confirmed him as the master of his profession, his immaculately uniformed, athletic frame immediately recognisable.

In April 1885 a fresh crisis with Russia blew up after a Russian army crossed the Afghan frontier at Penjdeh and defeated the local garrison. Many anticipated an invasion of India. Portsmouth played host to a stream of bright young officers on their way to war commands, while ships were refitted and commissioned. Although Hornby doubted his fitness for command, he was willing to return to the Dardanelles if required. However, Key, the First Naval Lord, intended him for the Baltic, the main theatre. The combination of a powerful fleet and a well-known name was too much for the Russians, and the crisis passed quickly.[57] In June Hornby took the 'Baltic' fleet to sea, with Captain John Fisher as his chief-of-staff, to conduct a series of exercises. With his flag once more in the *Minotaur*, Hornby took a mixed bag of warships old and new, large and small, to Berehaven on the southern coast of Ireland. Under the supervision of Fisher, the navy's expert on mines and torpedoes, the fleet prepared to attack an anchorage protected by minefields and an extensive boom. The exercise reached a suitably dramatic climax when the armoured torpedo cruiser HMS *Polyphemus* smashed through the boom as if it had been made of matchsticks. The Royal Navy was ready to pass any defences and sink enemy fleets in harbour. After extensive trials of cruiser dispositions, Hornby skilfully escaped the 'British' cruisers that were trying to blockade his battleships in Berehaven, took his fleet to sea and arrived off Glasgow without being located.[58] A lifetime of operational skill and the leadership of an admiral who took his officers into his confidence quickly and ensured they met his high standards exploded the complacent basis of contemporary British strategic thinking. The fleet as it existed was too small, slow and unseaworthy to blockade an

Atlantic naval base like Brest, and once the enemy put to sea they could inflict massive losses on British shipping and coastal cities. This was the first of the new annual exercises in which the tactical and strategic concepts that underpinned British war planning would be tested. The exercises enabled the service to profit from the wisdom of its leading officer, prompted improved ship designs that emphasised seaworthiness and endurance, and secured enlarged orders. They also attracted considerable attention from the press and public.[59]

Hornby's squadron paid off at the end of July, and in late November 1885 he hauled down his flag at Portsmouth. He would remain on the active list until he reached seventy, but there were no peacetime posts for a man of his rank and authority. Not that he was going to retire. At a farewell dinner on 27 November Hornby praised the officers and men of the service, the best he had ever seen, credited Greenwich with improving the character and intellect of the officers, and rounded on successive ministries for their parsimony. He blamed their failure on the reformed Admiralty structure adopted in 1869 by the first Gladstone government, which 'tended to make the naval element subordinate to the government of the service, and which made it more difficult to get the naval voice heard'. Hornby gave every indication he would solve the latter problem himself.[60] Nor was the award of the GCB in December going to purchase his silence. In January he became the Queen's principal naval ADC and contributed to new official handbooks on signals and manoeuvres.

Hornby had already made a powerful contribution to the naval debate the previous year, albeit not under his own name. In 1884 a remarkable series of articles appeared in the *Pall Mall Gazette* under the title 'The Truth about the Navy'. They had been written by the editor, W. T. Stead, with copious support from Captain John Fisher, discreetly backed by Hornby and his old shipmate Sir Anthony Hoskins.[61] Within weeks a new naval programme was launched, adding several ironclads, cruisers and torpedo boats to the fleet. It was an experience that Hornby, and Fisher, would never forget.

An Active Retirement

Although he must have expected to see out his final years in the house at Littlegreen, Hornby would be sorely disappointed. The agricultural recession had halved estate income, forcing him to let the house and live in the overgrown cottage at Lordington. While his financial embarrassment was only relative – he kept a horse for the local hunt and a shoot – it was unpleasant and reinforced his aversion for populist politics, Radical politicians and newspapers of every description. He preferred to deal with the problems of the country at a local level, taking a paternalistic concern for the lives of his tenants, providing work, food and outdoor relief for the elderly. Administering the estate kept him busy, and like many sailors he took great pleasure in the countryside. His habits remained austere: he never smoked, rarely took a drink and only ate in moderation.

While maintaining contact with the best and brightest officers, Hornby gradually widened his sphere of activity. Although his politics remained Conservative, he refused the invitation to stand as the party's candidate for Portsmouth Dockyard, where his election must have been certain. This was wise: his name was too important to become the property of a political party. The nation needed his example, and the navy his advice. His opinions would be sought, cited and repeated for the rest of his life. The success of the 1884 agitation provided a model and many allies within the service: Fisher continued to provide him with confidential information from inside the Admiralty, while Lord Charles Beresford's high-profile resignation from the Board over the need for a staff helped to ignite a public debate.

The events of 1884 prompted W. H. Smith, who had been the Conservative First Lord of the Admiralty between 1878 and 1880, to develop a party-political 'big navy' campaign. Hoping to recruit the City of London to the cause, Smith appeared at a City meeting in April 1885, at the height of the Russian war scare, calling for naval increases. This caused a dramatic fall in stock prices. Suitably roused, the City decided the issue was national, not political. City groups lobbied the new Conservative government for a stronger navy. This agitation provided Admiral of the Fleet Sir Geoffrey Hornby with the ideal platform. Smith could see which way the wind was blowing, and in 1887 moved to neutralise Hornby with the offer of a peerage. Hornby refused, and prepared for battle. Smith knew that where 'Uncle Geoff' led, most would follow. In 1888 Hornby took centre stage as the leading figure in the emerging 'big navy' agitation, writing to *The Times* and speaking on public platforms. He argued that the navy had too few battleships and far too few cruisers to blockade and destroy the French fleet, the only certain method of securing the oceanic commerce on which the empire depended.[62] His speech on 'The Defence of Merchant Ships in Case of War' at a London Chamber of Commerce meeting on 28 May was a skilfully targeted triumph: a resolution was passed calling for a large increase in the navy, effectively derailing Conservative attempts to control the debate. Within a week the Admiralty had announced a supplementary vote to increase the fleet, a move which Hornby commended at a second public lecture in the City, before a serious bout of hepatitis temporarily halted his campaign. The final outcome was the Naval Defence Act of February 1889, committing £21.5 million to construct ten battleships, thirty-seven cruisers and numerous torpedo boats over five years.[63] At a stroke, the 'Two-Power Standard' of 1817 had been re-established.

Hornby's short-term concern at the inadequate size and strength of the fleet for the defence of British overseas commerce had been addressed. He had found new allies among the commercial classes, exploiting his status as *the* admiral to kick-start a major campaign for naval improvement, one that was supported by the Queen and large sections of the press. Although Hornby was prone to exaggeration, often issuing uncomfortably large estimates of the size of fleet he considered necessary, his lead was greatly appreciated by younger officers. Captain Lord Charles Beresford, the chief public advocate for reform, was a committed supporter, but others joined the applause. In the decade that followed Hornby's retirement the estimates increased from £12 million to £18 million, and the number of men in service from fifty-eight to eighty-eight thousand. Much of this increase was occasioned by the large cruiser programmes, the very thing Hornby had called for.[64] The lean mid-Victorian years of minimal naval expenditure, obsolescent ships and under-strength crews were over; the Royal Navy would expand almost continuously down to 1914. Hornby provided his followers, notably John Fisher, with a model of how well-handled pro-naval agitation could change government policy.

In 1889 Hornby was sent to Cowes to greet the young German Emperor Wilhelm II, the Queen's grandson, beginning a remarkable friendship that was renewed whenever the Emperor visited England. In 1890 the Kaiser requested his attendance at the German army and navy manoeuvres, and gave him a jewelled snuff box complete with imperial portrait. Hornby treasured the box, along with his father's Gold Medal for Lissa and the signed portrait of the Queen. He did not live to see the collapse of the Anglo-German relationship, never suspecting that his charming young host had plans for German naval power. In turn, the Kaiser treasured his connection with the glory of the sea. This remarkable man made the Kaiser proud to wear the uniform of a British Admiral of the Fleet.[65]

Hornby responded to the Naval Defence Act by renewing his call for a more professional Admiralty, reinforcing the naval element and reducing the influence of politicians. While they jealously guarded the estimates, for which the government was responsible, the politicians had also usurped the role of policy-making, which rightly belonged to the professionals, and he agreed with Beresford in wishing to place the opinion of the naval lords before the public through Parliament.[66] He found the solution in Germany. Like most intellectual warriors, Hornby was an early convert to the concept of a naval general staff, along the lines of the German general staff, which had become famous through successful wars against Austria and France.[67] He contributed articles to the reformist, pro-staff *United Service Magazine*, which began publishing in 1890.[68] He also supported the Navy Records Society, founded by his friend Professor Laughton in 1893 as an unofficial naval historical section for the Admiralty. Hornby observed, 'I fancy our forefathers were more careful than we are about telling the truth, and therefore the more we can retain of what they recorded, the better.'[69]

In 1891 Hornby was thrown out of his carriage and left unconscious with a fractured skull. He recovered consciousness after three weeks and recalled a dream that he had commanded the fleet in the Baltic, reflecting his regret that there had never been an opportunity to exercise the classic function of an admiral. Although he seemed to make a good recovery, the deaths of his favourite sister and then his wife in early 1892 were severe blows. He nonetheless carried on his public life in the stoical manner characteristic of the Victorians, but 1893 was another bad year. On 22 June the flagship of the Mediterranean fleet, HMS *Victoria*, was rammed by HMS *Camperdown* and sank with heavy loss of life. Among those who found a watery grave was the commander-in-chief, Sir George Tryon, once a brilliant captain in Hornby's Mediterranean fleet. When the question of responsibility came before a court martial, Hornby found himself in the uncomfortable position of knowing all those involved. While Tryon had ordered a manoeuvre that was impossible to execute, he was confident that had he himself done the same, none of his captains would have had the least hesitation in ignoring it, apart from Tryon, who would have sheered off at the last opportunity to show that he understood the nature of the test. Yet he joined Charles Beresford in a statement endorsing unquestioning obedience to orders, whatever their merit.[70] He was not going to let the details of this case override the wider interests of the service. The delicate balance between subordination and initiative was a matter of judgement, not rule. He had always expected complete obedience, but never hesitated to praise those who used their initiative. He was, after all, a lifelong student of Nelson. When Admiral Sir Michael Culme-Seymour went to replace Tryon, Hornby advised him, 'You will have to catch a good hold of each [captain] and put them through the goose-step for a long time before you can trust them.'[71] He did not need to say 'trust them to use their initiative'.

In June 1894 Hornby had the unusual experience of giving evidence in a libel case, the defendant being his old friend Professor Laughton. Laughton had written a very severe review of a nasty little book attacking the navy by a disgraced ex-Paymaster. After hearing Hornby speak for the defence, prosecuting counsel declined to cross-examine him and the case was dismissed with costs: Hornby was so honest, upright and direct that his word required no corroboration, his opinion no second.[72] Later that year he dined with the famous American naval writer Captain Mahan, whose books he greatly admired, and proposed a toast to the American squadron in which Mahan served. It was appropriate: Hornby was a grandson of General Burgoyne of Saratoga. In late 1894 he became chairman of the Defence Committee of the London Chambers of Commerce, and in early 1895 he took the chair of the newly formed Navy League, whose objects of naval reform and reinforcement were so close to his own heart. The Navy League combined a public-relations agenda with concerns for the planning process and the size of the fleet; it called for a naval staff led by 'a single professional advisor, responsible to the Cabinet, upon the maritime defences of the Empire, who shall hold office for a term of years, and whose opinion as to the sufficiency of the preparations covered by the Estimates shall be communicated to Parliament'.[73]

It would have been hard to find a more effective summation of Hornby's views or a cause more likely to elicit his active support. He agreed with Navy League founder Spenser Wilkinson that the Cabinet was ill served by the current system, in which the advice of the experts was at a discount.[74] The close connection between the League and the City was a source of real satisfaction, for it was only through the City that the ministers could be persuaded to act. His final victory came in 1894, when Gladstone resigned rather than adopt the enlarged naval estimates forced on his government by Hornby's imperious call for additional naval expenditure. Sadly, he did not live long enough to savour his greatest triumph: on 3 March 1895 he succumbed to influenza. He was just seventy but worn out by a life of service, his dedication and commitment equalled only by his professionalism and skill. He was cremated on 9 March and buried in the small village churchyard of Compton in Sussex, alongside his beloved wife and close to the sea. The Kaiser's representative took a prominent place at the funeral.

Hornby left little by way of earthly riches – his will was proved at £27,339 – but his professional legacy was immense. He led the transformation of the sailing navy of his youth into a steam fleet, harmonising the standards and traditions of Nelson's day with the technology and opportunities that emerged in his years of high command. He picked out the best men of the next generation, men who led the service into the next century and defeated the fleet built by his young German admirer. He was a man of reverent faith, remarkable intellect and unsurpassed character.

While many of Queen Victoria's admirals brought seamanship, dignity and character to the office, Hornby was unique. His intellectual attainments provided a breadth of understanding that placed his role in the widest context, be it matching his actions to the demands of high-risk diplomacy or redressing the undue subordination of enduring naval concerns to short-term political expe-

[286]

diency. By the time he died the key post in the British navy was no longer the command of the Mediterranean fleet: now the First Naval Lord was the head of the service. As John Fisher observed in 1893, Hornby was 'our greatest Admiral since Nelson, a man of iron nerves and extraordinary gifts as Commander of a fleet'.[75] On the surface he appeared to be the very embodiment of the Victorian navy, stiff with his own dignity and power; but behind the facade lay a mind utterly dedicated to the improvement of the fleet and prepared to use any trick in the book to defeat the enemies of the state – 'Little Englanders', Gladstonian Liberals and fort-building soldiers.

8

RADICAL REFORM
John Fisher
1841–1920

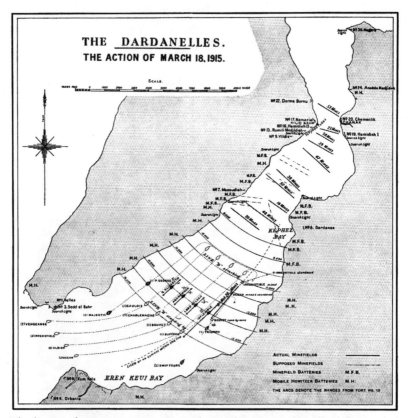

The limits of sea power. Despite Fisher's objections, the Allied fleet sailed into the Dardanelles Straits on 18 March 1915 and ran into a minefield. After that, Churchill's vision of winning the war at a stroke crumbled into the dust at Gallipoli

JOHN FISHER WAS A CURIOUS naval officer. He did not like being at sea, spending his career mastering new technology and cultivating the powerful. Ruthlessly ambitious and utterly dedicated, he possessed a mercurial intellectual brilliance that far outshone his contemporaries. He used the press to push his name forward, persuading his silent service contemporaries that he was mad and more than a little devious. He spent his life persuading others to do his bidding, be they old admirals, British ministers or German emperors. He did so because he loathed war, having seen it up close and personal. Because Britain controlled the world, he knew it made sense to deter conflict. As First Sea Lord between 1904 and 1910 he transformed the Royal Navy into a modern fighting force, in order to maintain peace. When the war broke out in 1914, he was recalled to service at the age of seventy-three because he was the only man for the job!

Fisher's career has been examined many times, but most authors have followed the great man's own estimation of his life.[1] Because he lived long enough to compile his memoirs, Fisher consciously created his own past. Nelson was always his model.[2] He cited Nelson's motto about reward and merit in 1860.[3] In 1880 he read the seven-volume edition of Nelson's correspondence and the latest biography, finding fresh inspiration and a heightened appreciation of the hero's talents.[4] The Nelson model required Fisher to be a self-made man, writing his family and connections out of his rise to prominence – but stressing the link with Sir William Parker, the last of Nelson's captains.[5] Nelson would occupy a significant place in Fisher's thoughts for the rest of his life.[6]

Formative Years: The Education of a Strategist

Born at Rambodde in Ceylon (Sri Lanka) on 23 January 1841, John Fisher was the eldest son of an impecunious army officer turned coffee-planter. Relative poverty meant that Fisher only scraped into the navy through distant relatives, a link with Sir William Parker and the outbreak of the Crimean War. After dining with Parker and entering the service on board the *Victory*, Fisher was set for a career in the time-honoured tradition. But such prospects soon withered. In his first five years of service he witnessed four battles that shaped his view of naval power. The first was the bombardment of Sweaborg, the fortress/arsenal complex outside Helsinki, in August 1855. The attack was the high point of the Baltic campaign and a major demonstration of naval firepower.[7] While Fisher's ship, HMS *Calcutta*, was not engaged, she was close enough to hear the three-day attack. Using the latest technology and overwhelming firepower, the allies suppressed Russian defensive fire and destroyed the naval arsenal without fatal casualties. This Baltic operation was a masterclass in naval power projection; it was a role and a sea that would feature prominently in his career.[8]

On his next ship, HMS *Highflyer*, Fisher met one of the navy's leading intellects, Captain Charles Shadwell FRS. Serving on the China station, Shadwell taught him navigation, astronomy and advanced mathematics. This was the making of Fisher, who had already displayed a fine intellect, outstanding powers of application and a talent for exposition. He could master new subjects, convey their meaning and command an audience. Between 1856 and 1860 Fisher took part in three battles during the Second Anglo-Chinese War. At Fatshan Creek his boat was up with the leaders at the destruction of the Chinese flotilla. This operation was the antithesis of Sweaborg, a foolhardy and costly, if heroic, close-quarters boat attack. After the capture of Canton, he was present at the second attack on Taku Forts in 1859, when Sir James Hope's overconfident combined operation ran into well-organised Chinese defences and suffered the navy's worst defeat of the nineteenth century. The following year a chastened Hope succeeded with a much better-planned operation. After his baptism of fire, Fisher was commissioned: now well aware of the limits of naval power, he waited twenty-two more years to see his last battle.

Fisher's lack of social connections meant that if he wanted to secure early promotion, he needed to demonstrate excellence and impress senior naval officers. From the start he demonstrated a remarkable ability to charm admirals. Sir Astley Cooper Key, pioneer of the technology-driven career path, would be one role model, but Fisher was careful to cultivate other admirals too.[9] He both earned his opportunities and exploited them to the full. Not content to follow an obvious career path, Fisher pioneered a new area of expertise, that of underwater warfare. This choice of specialisation allowed him to make his reputation far sooner than other bright junior officers. Along the way, he became a strategist and policymaker with the ideas, confidence and opportunity to remodel the service.

Fisher was clearly smarter than the great majority of his fellow officers, more determined than anyone else and prepared to play the political games necessary to rise to the top. He was an astute observer of shifts in power within the service, and having achieved a degree of national notoriety, he broadened his support by cultivating politicians, the press and the monarch. Just because Fisher wrote and said rather more than the average naval officer, however, we should not presume that he revealed his true intentions. From the beginning of his career his utterances were calculated and targeted performances, not the random effusions that passed for wisdom in some of his contemporaries.[10]

Fisher made his career in shore postings. After receiving his commission in November 1861, suitably backdated to reward record-breaking examination results, he went to HMS *Excellent,* the floating gunnery training ship in Portsmouth harbour. Already an elite establishment, *Excellent* was closely linked to the Royal Naval College at Portsmouth, providing the core technical, scientific and educational establishment of the service.[11] The future leaders of the service were educated men with enquiring minds: they worked hard to keep abreast of technical changes and to integrate new weapons and systems into their concept of naval operations, and they published their ideas widely. Fisher was part of an intellectual renaissance at Portsmouth, and he also met his future wife there, Katherine Delves-Broughton. They married in 1866, relatively early for an impecunious naval officer. After a period of intense religious introspection, Fisher's marriage provided him with the stable home life that he craved. The union produced four children, a son and three daughters, two of whom would marry naval officers.[12]

Fisher thrived in shore posts, profiting from his service under Charles Shadwell. Like his exemplar, Key, Fisher found a new subject to make his own. Key emphasised gunnery; Fisher made his way in gunnery before finding an opening in mines and electricity. He spent a year on HMS *Warrior*, the first modern warship, ending his tour as gunnery lieutenant, before going back to his spiritual home at HMS *Excellent* in 1864. Now he commanded a gunboat and worked on mines.

Growing naval interest in underwater weapons, sparked by their use in the Crimean and American Civil Wars, enabled Fisher to make his name while still only a lieutenant. When writing the official book on mines and electricity, Fisher exploited the work of others and synthesised the latest thinking. He condensed experimental ideas into a subject suitable for classroom instruction and prepared the navy for ever more sophisticated underwater weapons. His sound grasp of the principles and attention to detail were fundamental. Mines were a reality by the late 1860s, as were spar torpedoes. Robert Whitehead's locomotive torpedo worked, but it would not be proven in action for another two decades. The navy's interest was limited to two areas: the use of mines to protect temporary bases, and mine countermeasures to facilitate coastal power projection.

In 1869 Fisher inspected German underwater warfare establishments. The very thorough report he produced did nothing to hamper his early promotion to commander that year. Even so, he had no desire to go back to sea, seeking an Admiralty appointment for 'a lift in the service', but Captain Beauchamp Seymour, later Lord Alcester, the First Lord's private secretary, knew better.[13] Fisher was woefully short of sea time for a future service leader, so Seymour appointed him commander of the China station flagship. After getting the ship into first-class order, Fisher affected to find the rest of the commission a sore trial: he complained to his friend George Tryon that 'I am getting horribly tired of being a sort of upper housemaid, devoting severe thought to the cleaning of paintwork.'[14] But the same letter enclosed pamphlets on naval tactics, torpedoes and ship organisation, which Tryon was requested to pass on to Geoffrey Hornby, the one officer for whom Fisher retained an unquestioning admiration. Hornby, who had a discerning eye for talent, was sufficiently impressed to write back. Fisher had used his time at sea to open another avenue of patronage.

In fact, Fisher did rather more than keep HMS *Ocean*'s paintwork tidy. He installed his own system of centrally controlled electric firing for the broadside and a new concentration sight to replace the existing service model. He also built and tried his own version of the Harvey towed torpedo.[15] There were also opportunities to hone his deft political skills, the admiral confiding in him to the exclusion of the flag captain. Fisher used the relative leisure of a sea passage home to continue studies that demonstrated just how closely involved he was in the contemporary naval intellectual renaissance. He knew the work of all the key players, and if his own work was not at the cutting edge of naval opinion, it was solidly grounded in practical experience.

From the other side of the world Fisher used his best efforts to secure the patronage of the leading men of the service: Key, Hornby and Seymour. The ability to win friends in high places was a talent that he never lost. His messianic zeal for his subject and talent for persuasion were soon in action when he rejoined the *Excellent* in 1872 as commander for torpedo duties: 'I have told them very distinctly that I am not going to do anything which takes me off the main line of the profession,' he noted.[16] Fisher soon secured his own separate establishment, HMS *Vernon*, to provide training and trials; another visit to Germany and committee work cemented his name in this area. Promotion to captain in 1874 would hardly seem surprising for such a high-profile officer, until we recall that since becoming a commissioned officer, he had seen no action and taken part in no heroic enterprises. He had exploited the new technological career path, and his promotion followed the visit of an Admiralty lord to one of his lectures.[17]

Following this promotion, Fisher demonstrated remarkable acumen by stepping aside from the technical work that had made his name. Captains needed to be all-rounders, employing technical experts: he had no intention of becoming a narrow specialist on underwater weapons, effortlessly avoiding an order to compile the next torpedo manual, which could have typecast him.

In 1876 Fisher went back to sea, and after a relief post became Key's flag captain in the West Indies in 1877. Once again he excelled, and retained his position when Key was selected to commission the

Particular Service Squadron, or Baltic fleet, in 1878. The Russo-Turkish crisis passed, and the fleet got no further than Spithead, but the lesson in deterrence and the problems of mobilisation were not lost. Joining Hornby's flag in the Mediterranean the following year would be only his second period of service in a major fleet, a remarkable record for a future service chief. The Mediterranean commission was all too brief: Key, now First Sea Lord, sent Fisher back to the West Indies as flag captain to Arctic hero Sir Leopold McClintock. By now Fisher's name was public property, and many influences, not least royal, were behind his appointment in 1881 to command the latest monster battleship, HMS *Inflexible*. The new ship was the most complex piece of machinery yet assembled, requiring a remarkable officer to make her efficient. As an expert on electricity and an outstanding commander, Fisher was the ideal choice. But for all the kudos of this great ship, Fisher was anxious for a shore post and offered to exchange her for Pembroke dockyard![18] *Inflexible* went to the Mediterranean, where Beauchamp Seymour was in command. Here Fisher took part in his last battle, Seymour's bombardment of Alexandria on 11 July 1882. The bankrupt Egyptian regime was in chaos, the nationalists were about to assume power, and British bond-holders would lose out. Finally Gladstone, a prominent bond-holder himself, ordered the fleet to act. If the popular press noted the hero-ics of Irish aristocrat Captain Lord Charles Beresford, professionals were more impressed by the accurate shooting of the *Inflexible*.

However, Fisher's post-action reflections were dominated by the pathetic performance of service fuses, which were the responsibility of an army-led Board of Ordnance.[19] After the bombardment, Fisher and Arthur Wilson, a friend from the 1860s, went ashore, where they built and operated an armoured train. While his ship had performed well, Fisher was struck by the higher trial speed of her Italian counterpart, condemning the mania for tactical handiness that resulted in British battleships being short and slow.[20]

Struck down by dysentery and forced to give up his ship, Fisher found the Queen and Prince of Wales among his well-wishers. A mere twelve and a half years of his career before promotion to flag rank had been spent at sea. Sea service was a relatively insignificant element in his career, just a task that he had to pass with credit to ensure his career progressed smoothly. Unlike many of his predecessors, Fisher was not in love with the sea: his correspondence contains no poetic rhapsodies on the ocean. For him the sea was a place for work, not an emotional playground. He looked to Key for a good shore post.[21]

He got what he wanted, command of HMS *Excellent*, in 1883. Suddenly Fisher was as zealous for gunnery as he had once been for torpedoes. He recruited members of a future brains trust and began an important connection with the Armstrong Company which would pay many dividends, including the estate Josiah Vavasseur left to Fisher's son Cecil.

He also began to work the press, acting as W. T. Stead's main source for the 'Truth about the Navy' campaign in the *Pall Mall Gazette*. That the naval leadership found it necessary to use the press to circumvent the economic and domestic agendas of post-Reform Act governments showed how far the political consensus on defence had shifted since the 1850s. The agitation was highly effective. Lord Northbrook's board, which had given Fisher so much, trimmed its sails to a Fleet Street gale, finding £5.5 million for ships, docks and coal supplies. For another decade Fisher provided Hornby with evidence for his high-profile 'big navy' campaigns. While acting as Hornby's right-hand man, he acquired those skills that were used to sell his own programmes.

In the mid-1880s, as Key's term as First Sea Lord was coming to a close, Fisher shifted effortlessly to the patronage network of 'Uncle Geoff' Hornby. Fisher knew how to make friends and secure patrons; he also knew when to break off a relationship that might hamper his career. Having cut his mother and siblings out of his life, he was hardly going to keep up contact with a retired officer who, having done so much to make his career, was no longer in a position to help. This ruthless streak reflected his determination to excel: he simply could not afford to invest time and effort in extinct volcanoes.

He had one last opportunity to serve with Hornby: as flag captain of the 1885 Particular Service Squadron, once again destined for the Baltic. Fisher's expertise on gunnery, torpedoes and mines remained critical for any Baltic operations, which would have involved the attack of defended anchorages and sea fortresses. When Russia backed down, he planned large-scale exercises at Berehaven to examine the attack and defence of anchorages, and a second series at Weymouth later in the year.[22]

By sheer hard work and conspicuous attention to patrons, Fisher forced his way to the top of the navy, always with an eye on the highest posts ashore. It is unclear whether he had already set his course for 1904 when he went to the Admiralty as Director of Naval Ordnance in November 1886, but there is no doubt where his ambitions and interests lay. Arms races and deterrence were already strengths, and the attack of coastal positions had been his study since childhood. The army's inability to defend the British Empire was a truism: it would be used to secure the strategic bases from which the navy would dominate the world and to apply British power to the weakest points of any nation so foolish as to make war on Britain. But this would be the last resort: Fisher preferred the non-violent approaches because he recognised there were no logical limits to the application of violence in war. Fisher entered his years of command a convinced proponent of peace through deterrence, and bent his policy to securing the necessary appearance of strength.

The Nature of War

To understand how Fisher thought about war, we have to remember that his formative experiences, like those of the younger generation of naval officers today, were of asymmetrical warfare. While officers discussed fleet combat, the Royal Navy faced no significant threat at sea. Instead, it policed the oceans and projected power against a broad range of foes, from slave stations to Russian fortresses. In the 1850s and 1860s France built powerful fleets, but their purpose was to secure diplomatic leverage rather than to fight, and they were easily bettered in arms races.[23] Both imperial Russia and the United States relied on coastal ironclads and wooden cruisers. This left the Royal Navy to secure Britain's global empire of trade based on market access and communications dominance. Both the Second China War and the occupation of Egypt arose out of commercial interests. By contrast, the Russian war scares of 1878 and 1885 demonstrated Britain's ability to secure vital interests by mobilising a fleet to threaten St Petersburg. Victorian Britain adopted a unique strategy, exploiting superior communications and the ubiquity of naval command to counter-attack at a point where British power would be most effective and the aggressor most vulnerable. India and Turkey would be defended in the Baltic, Canada in New York Harbour, and much of Africa at the northern end of the Cotentin peninsula. The fact that the same ships could be used for each mission, and the strategy extended to embrace new foes such as imperial Germany, allowed the British to function on minimal levels of defence spending. The proof of the system lay in the fact that it was never tested: any foreign naval build-up that challenged Britain's freedom of action in European politics would inevitably be defeated in an arms race. Deterrence was the strategic system that dominated Fisher's formative years: unique, economic and highly effective. The proof of this success is to be found on the coasts of every major power of the nineteenth century, where the remains of massive coastal fortress systems provide mute testimony to the impact of British strategy. Only skilled, confident strategists like John Fisher could operate this system.

The financial resources of the British Empire, allied to a dominant shipbuilding industry, facilitated a reactive global strategy based on the use of competitive arms races, while communications dominance enabled centrally directed forces to secure oceanic trade, global possessions and key strategic interests by deterrence, from Belgium and the Dardanelles to Afghanistan and Vancouver. Clear warnings of Britain's capabilities, usually signalled by the movement of battleships, backed up British diplomacy. By the early 1870s Fisher had recognised that there was no logical reason for restraint in war, a Clausewitzian insight that ensured he would do all he could to avoid conflict, through the possession of overwhelming strength.

During Fisher's term as Director of Naval Ordnance, he secured control of naval gun procurement from the army and hastened the introduction of modern guns. His links with Josiah Vavasseur at Armstrong's produced quick-firing medium-calibre weapons with hydraulic mountings. He reached flag rank on 2 August 1890. Although his career would run for another twenty years, only five of them would be spent at sea. Remaining as DNO, he addressed the strategic problems caused by the proliferation of French torpedo boat stations on the Channel coast.[24] He proposed new torpedo boat destroyers: larger, faster and more seaworthy than French torpedo boats and armed with Vavasseur's quick-firing guns. From this proposal grew the ubiquitous destroyer, an all-purpose offensive/defensive flotilla vessel.[25] The logic and clarity were typical.

Fisher next spent a year as superintendent of Portsmouth dockyard. He arrived at an auspicious moment, profiting from the reorganisation of the yards begun in 1885 by the Director of Naval Construction, Sir William White. His energetic leadership helped Portsmouth complete the Naval Defence Act battleship HMS *Royal Sovereign* in less than three years, the fastest such construction process for two decades and far better than any foreign navy could manage. After this useful experience, Fisher returned to the Admiralty as Controller and a member of the Board in February 1892. Over the next five years he oversaw the introduction of the destroyer, helped secure a second major naval programme – the Spencer Programme of 1894, which prompted Gladstone's final resignation – and pushed the navy into using new, more efficient water-tube boilers. His willingness to take large risks with novel technologies reflected a close professional alliance with White.

Fisher's projects were not always an unqualified success. Though his destroyers ended the French threat, they proved somewhat fragile.[26] The boilers, too, suffered from technical problems. Though his decisions on new technology were usually right in principle, his timing could be out by a significant degree. His talents were effectively displayed, however, during the debate over the Spencer Programme, where he did battle with the Chancellor of the Exchequer as well as any officer in the succeeding years: he showed not only a mastery of technical issues, but also a talent for verbal argument that his senior colleagues lacked, not least Earl Spencer, the First Lord. Although he was a junior member of the team, his colleagues appreciated his appetite for work and awarded him the KCB. Up to this point the bombastic, domineering side of his character had been held in check by the prospect of promotion. Fisher had been a wonderful servant, but the day when he became master came closer in May 1896, with promotion to vice admiral.

On 24 August 1897 Fisher became commander-in-chief on the North American and West Indies station, with his flag in HMS *Renown*, a fast but under-armed battleship he had inserted in the 1892 programme. He was quick to shake up this backwater post, exercising his ships and officers to see what they were capable of. He reportedly exuded 'something of the aura of an eastern potentate which was to mark his reign at the Admiralty', though he allowed his innate kindness to show through in personal matters.[27] Rather than fill his days with routine, Fisher used his time to think about the future of the service, enlisting the help of promising officers. His reveries were interrupted, however, by a sudden storm in Anglo-French relations over the headwaters of the Nile at Fashoda. He planned an immediate attack on the French West Indian possessions, while liberating the unfortunate Captain Dreyfus and landing him in France! If war came, he would leave the execution to his juniors: since the French had no battleships in the western hemisphere, he would reinforce the Mediterranean fleet. In the event, though, the navy that he had helped to build was so powerful that the French backed down. This, Fisher understood, was how deterrence worked.

In truth, the American command was an exercise in job creation, given because Fisher needed time at sea to stay on the active list. The Admiralty acknowledged as much by withdrawing him in March 1899, eighteen months before his term was up, to represent the navy in the British delegation at the forthcoming Hague peace conference. After this, he would take on the Mediterranean command – the pinnacle of a seagoing career. The Hague conference had been called by Tsar Nicholas II, who hoped to prevent further arms races which his vast, under-capitalised country could ill afford. A global naval arms race was rising to the boil, notably in Germany, an ambitious naval power. While Britain might benefit from a reduction in foreign construction, she would not accept any limit on her own effort – after all, Britain was a special case. In selecting Fisher Lord Goschen made a bold choice, ensuring Britain fielded the most senior officer at the conference. The decision also proved wise: between May and July 1899 Fisher's energy, seen to legendary effect on the dance floor, his open and direct conversation and his personal charm were tremendous assets. He also obtained much information, not least concerning German anxiety about the Baltic. He left the Germans to block Russian calls for a budget freeze, and adroitly avoided embarrassing the Tsar by voting against his personal opinion. When Captain Alfred T. Mahan USN opposed an otherwise universal ban on gas shells, Fisher had sidestepped the twin dangers of appearing frightful on the one hand and giving way on issues important to Britain on the other. Everyone praised his performance. Yet his unofficial conversations left no one in any doubt that he meant business and held no truck for agreement and arbitration. Might was right, and he would take no prisoners. His bellicose pose was carefully calculated. W. T. Stead recalled Fisher declaring, 'I am not for

war, I am for peace! That is why I am for a supreme Navy.'[28] This
was no more than the reiteration of a constant theme.

Mediterranean Plans

Although the Mediterranean remained the pinnacle of most sea officers' ambitions, Fisher really wanted to be First Naval Lord. When
Sir Frederick Richards stood down in 1899, the post went to Lord
Walter Kerr, only sixteen months Fisher's senior. It seemed that his
chance had gone, but he went to the Mediterranean determined to
make his mark. He was not interested in the old fetishes of paint,
brass-work and low-level drill; he took them for granted. This
frightened the fleet as much as Hornby's zeal for steam tactics, and
with good reason. Rumours soon spread of his 'Asiatic' origins – a
comment on his physiognomy and yellowing complexion, the latter
probably caused by dysentery. For officers who had made a career
out of neatness and drill, Fisher was indeed 'a tremendous
scoundrel':[29] he challenged their entire world view, and he was right
to do so.

Energy and determination overrode all obstacles: within a year
the fleet had stopped worrying about paint or the speed with which
torpedo nets could be got out and talked instead of 'tactics, strategy,
gunnery, torpedo warfare, blockade etc. It was a veritable renaissance and affected every officer in the Fleet.'[30] Although he had
rearmed the fleet with new long-range guns, Fisher had not considered how to use them effectively. This was curious, given his work
on *Warrior* and *Ocean*. Now younger men were overtaking him,
with Captain Percy Scott leading the way – extemporising telescopic
sights, communications equipment and fire control. Where a smaller
man would have condemned such unauthorised activity, Fisher
immediately grasped its significance. By June 1900 he was conducting long-range target practice.

Fisher's problem was time. There was much to do to prepare the
navy for war. The close-order fleet exercises of Hornby's day were
passé: guns were more powerful, accurate and rapid-firing, while
torpedoes threatened any fleet that held a steady course at medium
range. Fisher was an excellent communicator: his lectures were
fresh, stimulating and provocative, and he welcomed the input of
junior officers. By cultivating the best young officers Fisher speeded

up the process of change and upset the older generation. He broke the unwritten rule that admirals did not criticise their peers when talking with juniors. This would rebound on him later, when the old guard joined forces to have their revenge.

Once in supreme command he was not prepared to tolerate fools and displayed an arrogance that he himself recognised. Despite this self-knowledge, he caused a disastrous rift with Lord Charles Beresford, his second-in-command. Beresford was a fine seaman and a progressive officer with some good ideas, but he was also a pompous windbag whose inflated self-importance cried out to be punctured. When Beresford's flagship made a mess of anchoring at Malta, Fisher could not resist signalling in plain language, for everyone in the fleet to read, 'Your flagship is to proceed to sea and come in again in a seamanlike manner.'[31] Public humiliation has never been a particularly effective leadership technique, and in this case it had a painful legacy. If Fisher wanted to build a 'Band of Brothers', this was precisely the way to fail. Fisher's insult may have reflected his jealousy of Beresford's heroic reputation, fleet-handling skills and superior political connections; it also suggests that he would have failed the ultimate test of fleet command. On the day of battle his fleet would have been efficient and technically adept, but riven by petty, seething resentments. Fisher's open contempt for his less gifted contemporaries made it difficult for him to work effectively with colleagues. When Hornby court-martialled a sloppy officer, no one questioned his decision: his own seamanship was beyond reproach. From Hornby such actions were magisterial; from Fisher they were regarded as spiteful because no one rated Fisher as a seaman.

It was an indication of Fisher's success that Beresford rose above such spite, praising his achievement and acknowledging that the fleet was ready for war in every detail, from engineering reliability and coal stocks to intelligence gathering and gunnery. To secure the necessary ships and stores, Fisher had challenged the Admiralty. Alongside his work with the fleet, he was preparing to revolutionise the entire service. Fisher's constant public complaints cannot have endeared him to the Board, the very people he hoped would select him to be First Naval Lord. But his unconventional approach did not damage him as much as it might have because of his impressive ability to argue his case and because he was generally right. If Fisher could defeat the Admiralty from Malta, then he might be the man to fight the navy's battles in London. Having long since mastered the methods of newspaper warfare, Fisher extended his circle of contacts and fed them on a steady diet of facts, figures and hyperbole. He was not overly concerned about political affiliations, relying on the constant drip of press complaints to secure his object, and the agents served him well. He got the extra ships he needed to train his fleet at war strength. But this was purely a tactic: in 1906–9 he rejected exactly the same case when it was advanced by Beresford. Fisher was never consistent; geniuses rarely are.

Amid the politics and publicity, Fisher developed a good relationship with the new First Lord, the Earl of Selbourne. Selbourne had to argue the naval case to a Cabinet desperate to find savings amid the spiralling costs of the Second Boer War, fought between 1899 and 1902. With France, Russia, America, Japan and Germany all building battleships, Selbourne saw only two options: extra naval expenditure or a formal alliance with Germany. Fisher offered a third way: he advocated radical reform to reduce expenditure and increase Britain's warlike capability. To make his point properly, he needed to be back in Whitehall, so he began lobbying for the post of Second Sea Lord in January 1901. With his fleet up to strength and ready for war, he had had enough of sea service. The great armaments firm of Armstrong-Whitworth was ready to offer Fisher a staggering £10,000 a year to manage their business, but in February 1902 Fisher finally achieved the post for which he had been agitating for more than a year. Selbourne explicitly stated, however, that Fisher's appointment as Second Naval Lord did not imply he would succeed Lord Walter Kerr. It would be a test.

Initially Fisher planned to improve the intellectual capabilities of the service with a war staff, but as power came closer he preferred personal direction. He would cut obsolete, useless vessels, reduce the number of ships stationed abroad and concentrate the navy into five larger, more powerful fleets capable of moving with strategic effect to the principal areas of British interest. This would save manpower and money and reduce the demand for officers. At this stage the enemy was France, allied to Russia, with America a problem; Germany was only a minor concern. Fisher's plans focused on the Mediterranean, which he left on 4 June 1902, ending a remarkably short seagoing career.

The Second Naval Lord had oversight of personnel, and Fisher was quick to examine manpower and officer education with the same determination he had applied to mines, torpedoes, guns and ships. His solutions were radical, economical and provocative. He decided that all officers – executive, engineer or Royal Marine – should begin their careers under a common scheme, then specialise after the age of twenty. It was not his idea, but he adopted it with relish. The new Naval College building at Dartmouth was about to open, and Fisher could set the curriculum and thereby the tone of the service. He found an important ally in the brilliant naval historian Julian Corbett, a friend of Lieutenant Herbert Richmond, one of his bright young men. Corbett's well-informed *Monthly Review* articles on naval education helped gather support for Fisher's concept.

Fisher joined an Admiralty Board that resented his ceaseless criticism from the Mediterranean, but he forestalled any interference by arriving with his education scheme ready to print. He made time to work on reform by neglecting the routine paperwork that had bedevilled Hornby's term at the Admiralty and soured his view of naval administration; he expected his private secretary to tell him if anything important arrived! The common entry scheme was opposed by those who did not want lower-class officers on the quarterdeck, seemingly unaware that, as Fisher declared, this would exclude men like Nelson. He also opened up promotion from the ranks, following a Napoleonic vision of a service that rewarded talent. Improved conditions afloat were another way of improving recruitment, retention and job satisfaction. The results would be seen in war: the men of the Royal Navy stuck to the job to the end; those of the German navy mutinied.

Having made his mark, Fisher was quick to secure the prestigious appointment of Commander-in-Chief Portsmouth. He still hoped to return as First Sea Lord, and preferred to work on his reform project away from the stifling atmosphere of an organisation that he did not control. By July 1903, on holiday at Marienbad, his favourite German spa, Fisher was plotting his next move. He would offer the politicians a chance to economise: the navy would secure the home islands, the empire and commerce, reducing the army to a supporting role. His opportunity came when he joined Lord Esher's committee to reform the War Office, at the invitation of his friend King

Edward VII. Esher shared Fisher's delight in conspiracy, and his committee provided another platform for Fisher to display his reforming ideas. This was important because many senior officers were anxious to prevent him becoming First Naval Lord: he was considered too radical and lacking in respect for tradition. Sir Frederick Richards had been the model of a traditional First Naval Lord – strong, taciturn and almost incapable of formulating an argument – while the current incumbent, Lord Walter Kerr, was the son of a peer. Fisher was brash and far too clever. But even so, Selbourne invited Fisher to take the post on 14 May 1904.

During this year at Portsmouth Fisher refreshed his knowledge of shipbuilding and developed a serious interest in submarines. He was impressed by the potential of the crazy little boats, which could replace army engineers and their costly minefields to defend British ports or ferret enemy ships out of their harbours. This would be economical and increase the power of the dominant navy to annihilate an inferior fleet. The submarine gave him the germ of several ideas, not all of them compatible with each other. He invited key political allies to Admiralty House so they could see submarines in action, and briefed the prime minister, Balfour, on the economics of submarine defence. Fisher's position was reinforced when he became principal naval ADC to the King: once in office he focused his arguments on Balfour and the King, rather than Selbourne, whose support for Fisher's way of thinking had been gained on economic grounds. Once Fisher had secured the top job by undercutting his rivals, he realised that Selbourne was not content to maintain the existing level of expenditure: he wanted real cuts.

Having secured the succession, Fisher set to work with renewed zeal, and by late July 1904 he had prepared a reform programme that would dismay many in the navy. Never one to undersell his own work, he opened with a biblical quotation, heavily capitalised, and went on to promulgate a revolution.

ORGANISATION FOR WAR
'IF THE TRUMPET GIVE AN UNCERTAIN SOUND,
WHO SHALL PREPARE HIMSELF TO THE BATTLE?'
(St Paul, 1 Corinthians XIV, 8)[32]

The mottoes of his programme were FIGHTING EFFICIENCY and INSTANT READINESS FOR WAR. He promised 'a great reduction in the Navy Estimates!' but only if his entire programme was adopted. Having deprecated the role of the army in national defence, pointing out that the island would be starved if the navy were defeated, he planned new fleets, new ships and nucleus crews in the reserve fleet for rapid mobilisation, while scrapping old and useless ships. He must have wished he could apply the same criteria to his contemporaries on the flag list, but that was a step too far for Selbourne. Alongside the headline reforms, Fisher attacked every aspect of naval administration: regulations, stores, forms and routines.

Fisher took up his post on 20 October at the age of sixty-three, but there were few signs of physical decline and none whatsoever of mental atrophy. With his energy, enthusiasm and determination recharged by the position of authority, he became a dynamic dictator, delighting in power. Nor had his style mellowed: he still enjoyed a debate, becoming increasingly animated until he closed the discussion by banging a fist into the palm of his hand. Personally charming, vitality and enthusiasm compensating for a tendency to overbear, he was increasingly prone to give vent to his deeper feelings in writing. Furthermore, he kept everyone at arm's length: only he knew the full range of his policies and how they dovetailed. Fisher maintained not one but three separate 'brains trusts', dealing with ships, strategy and education, while employing the third estate to promote his big ideas and undermine his enemies. Achieving his ultimate ambition had not removed his tendency to make enemies: those who opposed him, and they were many, did not prosper. On too many occasions he allowed personal feelings to override the interests of the service.

It is easy to excuse Fisher his eccentricities at this remove: he was, in the main, right, his enemies wrong, and the navy needed him to get ready for the ultimate test of war. Fisher transformed the nature of naval power and the structure of the Royal Navy. In preparing for war he left nothing untouched: his navy was modern and effective, as ready for war as any armed force could be after a century of peace. He took no prisoners because he had no time to persuade the irreconcilable, and rushed because time was short. In little more than five years he would remodel the world's most successful fighting service and prepare it for the greatest challenge it had ever faced. That required genius and left no time for the old civilities.

It should never be forgotten that Fisher was preparing not for but against war. The whole purpose of his revolution was to enable the Royal Navy to keep Britain and the empire safe, stable and prosperous. In every word and deed, his regime as First Lord would be driven by the need to identify the most likely enemy, understand their weaknesses, both material and psychological, and apply maximum pressure to the key point. His opponents complacently assumed that Britain could afford to wait on events and respond when challenged. Fisher preferred pre-emption: he would kill off the competition before it got too serious.[33] The centrality of these concepts explains the apparent inconsistency of his words and deeds. Sound strategy must be flexible, and shortly after he took office it became clear that France was no longer the main enemy. When Japan destroyed the Russian fleet in 1904–5, that eliminated the other great bugbear of the last twenty-five years and finished off what little threat the Dual Alliance had ever posed. It also forced Paris and St Petersburg to concentrate on restraining Germany, which made them anxious for British support: as Germany was rapidly building a powerful battle fleet, mutual interest soon overrode old animosities. Never downcast by progress or change, Fisher soon hit his stride, and nowhere was this more obvious than in his policy on materiel.

Fisher never stopped thinking about ships: the concept of two new capital ships had been developed at Malta and refined at Portsmouth, along with improved destroyers and submarines. Everything was ready when he reached Whitehall. For all their technical novelty and increased power, the real purpose of the new designs was to facilitate major strategic changes. Historians and students of naval architecture have debated the merits and the necessity of the poster child of the Fisher revolution, the all-big-gun battleship HMS *Dreadnought*, but they miss the real object. Fisher replaced the mixed-armament design of the current ships – fifteen thousand tons with four twelve-inch and ten 9.2-inch guns, in a compact ship capable of no more than eighteen knots – with a 17,900-ton ship mounting twelve twelve-inch guns and easily capable of twenty-one knots, thanks to new turbine machinery and a radically different, modern profile. The *Dreadnought* became an instant design icon, linking a heroic name and battle honours stretching back to the Armada with the latest British technology. To ensure everyone sat up and took notice, she was built in record speed, a year and a day, and launched by the King in a blaze of publicity.

Dreadnought stunned the world, forcing every other navy to follow suit once they realised what she represented. Her size and cost posed a real problem, forcing the Germans to rebuild the vital Kiel Canal. Even if Fisher did not fully formulate all these arguments, his handling of the dreadnought question was entirely consistent with his purpose of deterrence and his love of theatre.

By contrast, Fisher's understanding of the new ship's superior fighting power was less certain. With a broadside of eight heavy guns, the new ship had the potential for long-range fire, if the guns could be centrally controlled and accurately directed. By 1912 Percy Scott's central-director system gave control of the entire armament to a single officer who had the best information on the range and bearing of the target.[34] Scott's work was essential to exploit the full potential of dreadnought battleships, as was the world's first practical mechanical analogue computer. To hit an enemy ship travelling at speed and on a diverging or converging course, gunnery officers needed to predict where the target would be by the time the shells arrived. Fisher expressed enormous enthusiasm for the target-prediction system of Arthur Pollen, but this waned once the system failed on trial.[35] He turned against Pollen in 1909, convinced he was an ally of Beresford and a Roman Catholic.[36] The rival system designed by Frederick Dreyer, a technically gifted naval officer, secured the market: it was cheaper and easier to maintain. The potential of the Pollen system was never proven, and Fisher's successors were content to let the matter drop when Pollen made outrageous financial demands for his imperfect apparatus.[37]

Fisher's initial enthusiasm for Pollen's system was linked to the development of big-gun armed cruisers, called battlecruisers from 1911. Initially conceived to deal with the threat to trade posed by France and Russia's armoured cruisers, they avoided the old policy of simply building more ships, which had been a major factor in the enormous increase in the naval estimates since 1890. The new ship would be bigger, while efficient, reliable turbine machinery made her faster and easier to maintain. These qualities would be exploited by an armament of eight twelve-inch guns, double that of any existing battleship. To keep the size and cost of the ship within acceptable limits, the protection was restricted to a cruiser standard of six-inch armour, against the nine or ten inches used on a battleship. Against French and Russian cruisers, the battlecruiser was a masterstroke. Fisher built three *Invincible*-class battlecruisers alongside the *Dreadnought*, and regarded them as the ships of the future, combining the twin attributes of speed and firepower.

The emergence of Germany as the potential enemy changed everything. The insignificant German cruiser threat did not require a fleet of *Invincible*s. When he discovered that Germany was building a battle fleet to fight in the North Sea, Fisher was forced to cut the procurement of battlecruisers in favour of cheaper but more powerful battleships. This development may explain his enthusiasm for Pollen's revolutionary fire-control system in 1906, when it had become clear that the battlecruisers might have to engage other capital units. However, this did not stop him developing a new strategy. From his pioneering work with destroyers in the 1890s, Fisher developed the concept of using flotilla craft to control the narrow seas. The emergence of practical submarines, a dramatic improvement in the range and accuracy of torpedoes and the shift of focus to the North Sea, which occurred around 1905, led him to a new system of naval warfare. His 'flotilla defence' concept used destroyers and submarines to prevent an invasion, while the main fleet remained outside the theatre of operations. While the equipment for this mission was still in development, notably radio, seaworthy destroyers and long-endurance submarines, the navy was forced to compromise between old and new concepts. But on the eve of war in 1914 it appeared that his vision would become reality: on his advice submarines replaced battleships in the last pre-war estimates.[38] If this strategy worked, it would release the main fleet for offensive action, allowing Fisher to exploit German fears about the Baltic.

He had occasion to exploit those concerns as soon as he took office. Germany responded to the Anglo-French Entente of 1904 and the Far Eastern distraction of France's long-term ally Russia by threatening war over the French occupation of Morocco and demanding heavy compensation. Britain backed France, and Fisher took the opportunity to employ his full repertoire of naval deterrence, calculated newspaper bluster and careful planning to gain maximum advantage from German insecurities. He allowed it to be known that he advocated 'Copenhagening' the German fleet – a scarcely subtle reference to the 1807 operation when the entire Danish navy had been seized by an overwhelming British expeditionary force. When Fisher put his finger on the Baltic, German resolve faltered. By late November the Kaiser was convinced the attack was imminent, and his chancellor was despondent. When the German army was ordered to plan for the occupation of Denmark, the general staff claimed it could not spare the troops. Germany agreed to a European conference to settle the Moroccan question at Algeciras – under the guns of the British Atlantic fleet, it should be noted. Meanwhile, Fisher sent the Channel fleet into the Baltic. This classic Fisher combination of acts, words and leaks prompted a 'Copenhagen complex' in Germany that was not exorcised for many years. It exposed the fact that the German navy was not ready for war, in mind or materiel, forcing Germany to redeploy money, guns and manpower to coastal defences.

The Kaiser responded by trying to bar the Baltic to British warships by treaty, without success. The British took care to ensure access to the Baltic was not compromised; Fisher had provided the ministers with a potent instrument to coerce Germany.[39] Fisher's ability to support foreign policy was priceless, and he also kept down costs – it was little wonder that the new Liberal government left him in office. His political views were closer to the Liberals than the Conservatives, placing him in a small minority among naval officers. While he did not make much of the fact, it would be critical to his later career: though the First Sea Lord was now technically apolitical, a degree of sympathy with the government helped to protect him from Conservative critics in the army and navy.

The astonishing haste of Fisher's opening year at the Admiralty in part reflected the fact that he was due to be retired on age in January 1906. He made that retirement unlikely by cutting £5 million from the estimates between 1904 and 1907, and was specially promoted to Admiral of the Fleet, securing another five years in office. It is not surprising that he could not sustain the effort through his last years in office, and one suspects that his initial object had been to get everything settled before 1906. No sooner had the Conservatives promoted Fisher than the Liberals came in and increased his pay. He was the most astute and adept First Naval Lord there had ever been, although he revived the older nomenclature of First Sea Lord. He

worked well with his political masters, especially the astute and incisive Reginald McKenna. They valued his political sense and his magnetic, mercurial personality. While lesser figures feared and
distrusted Fisher, men of experience and judgement valued him. Lord
Cawdor, able but ill, simply left him to run the Admiralty from
March to December 1905.[40]

Fisher's term at the Admiralty is associated with great changes,
and great feuds, as old animosities came back to haunt him. His
vision extended to a new national strategy in which homeland
defence, protection of commerce and imperial security were
entrusted to the fleet, the army becoming 'a projectile to be fired by
the Navy'. While the best British strategic minds, like Corbett and
Colonel G. F. R. Henderson, realised that Britain required a strategy
entirely distinct from the continental concept of mass conscript
armies meeting in decisive battle shortly after the declaration of war,
the British army had no desire to become a glorified marine expeditionary force for Fisher to throw ashore close by hostile naval
bases.[41] After the humiliation of the Boer War, the army rebuilt itself
along European lines, using the Anglo-French Entente to generate a
new mission, fighting alongside the French against Germany. Fisher,
who had no time for soldiers or allies, opposed this corruption of
the national effort, but the political value of the gesture – and with
only four divisions it was merely a gesture – outweighed his arguments. He helped to set up the Committee of Imperial Defence in
1904, expecting it to endorse his vision, only to see national strategy 'deflected' by short-term political needs. Little wonder he
became uncooperative.

By early 1906 the centre of naval effort was shifting from the
Mediterranean to the North Sea: Germany was not only the most
likely, but also the only realistic enemy. Russia was no longer a naval
power and the French navy had collapsed. Without the German
navy, British spending could have been cut. By scrapping old ships,
Fisher obviated the need to build new berths; he stopped work on a
new base at Rosyth, believing it unnecessary. He preferred to put his
money into new ships, about which he never ceased to brag,
attributing them with speed, protection and other qualities far in
excess of the facts. This all adds up to one thing: Fisher was determined to secure peace through deterrence, a mission in which
appearance counted for more than infrastructure. Many of the

weaknesses evident when the Royal Navy went to war in 1914 were the inevitable consequence of Fisher's overarching concept of deterrence. Had his policy continued to preserve peace after 1914, his reputation would stand higher than that of any other naval leader, perhaps even Nelson.

Fisher understood that Britain's vital interests, commerce, capital and sea control would not be improved by war. By 1900 Britain's empire was monumental, her trade and investments equally impressive, while a steady increase in profits and wealth were guaranteed so long as London remained the world's leading capital market.[42] Convinced the German challenge, like those of France and Russia, could be defeated by economic means, Fisher retrospectively used the *Dreadnought* to start a naval arms race and shifted the fleet to home waters to make the challenge clear. It was a high-stakes contest, spiced up by the threat to German security in the Baltic. Initially Fisher did not rush to get ahead – by 1908 Britain had ordered eleven dreadnoughts to Germany's nine – but even so he had complete confidence in the outcome. When the time came, he exploited his mastery of the press to whip up a nice little naval scare, much as he had back in 1884: he secured a massive eight-battleship building programme in 1909, which doubled the stakes and knocked the Germans out of the game. In 1912 Germany abandoned the naval arms race with Britain, unable to fund the necessary ships, and instead increased the army to meet a resurgent Russia. The naval arms race had been won by Fisher: the First World War was caused by Germany's fear of Russia.

Fisher was reluctant to set down his big programmes on paper because that would lock him into policies for long periods when he preferred to keep his position flexible. His critics called him inconsistent, and they were right. He changed his mind when he had to, and he did so without compunction, but he stuck with the big ideas of deterrence, coercion and arms races, confident that he could outmanoeuvre his enemies, whether they were German or British.

War Plans and Staff

To meet the economic agenda of the Liberal ministers, Fisher cut naval construction, confident Britain could always outbuild

Germany. His real concern was to shift funds from the army to the navy. However, entente with France gave the army an unusual prominence in British thinking. Suitably encouraged, the army raised the ancient bogey of invasion in order to justify conscription, and asserted its continental mission. The Liberal government disagreed but let the issue fester. Fisher responded by promoting the alternative priorities of economic blockade and Baltic operations. The war plans he developed in 1906–7, often derided as paper exercises meant to deflect criticism of his policy, contained important indicators of the way he saw naval warfare developing. While economic warfare would cripple Germany in the long term, it would be more useful to refine the deterrent threat that had served Britain so well in 1905. Fisher would concentrate his fleet to threaten the Baltic approaches, hoping to draw out the German fleet for battle. In 1907, before Germany possessed a single effective submarine, such strategies were entirely sound.

Fisher's ultimate plans for war were not put on paper: he kept them in his head, under constant development but ready to be promulgated at very short notice. The speed with which he operated in 1914–15 demonstrated that he could control the naval aspects of a major conflict with ease, and he did so despite the constant intervention of a troublesome First Lord. That such means were beyond lesser men was not a problem he cared to solve: instituting a dedicated staff would have atrophied the planning process, adding unnecessary complication to what was a relatively simple business. It might even have rendered the Royal Navy's thinking as dangerously simplistic as that of the German general staff. Maurice Hankey, a brilliant staff officer, concluded that with a good Director of Naval Intelligence and *ad hoc* committees of capable men, Fisher did not need a staff.[43] His successors did.

Fisher's relations with Lord Charles Beresford never recovered from the signal incident at Malta, and while Beresford was magnanimous enough to admit the value of Fisher's work, he and others of his class opposed the principle of interchangeable officers. They were equally incensed by the rather cavalier manner in which Fisher treated them. Although they fell out over matters of courtesy and style, Beresford was an obvious candidate to replace Fisher at the Admiralty, and it is highly significant that his animosity only became serious after Fisher's special promotion blocked that possibility. To Fisher's chagrin, Beresford was given the Channel command in 1907. This terrible decision poured fuel on the fire: Fisher responded by treating Beresford with contempt, reducing the size of his command and shifting the modern ships to a new Home Fleet. Fisher's vindictive, unpleasant schemes met with a bombastic response. Beresford formed a 'syndicate of discontent' among the wrong-headed admirals and captains who seemed, as if by magic, to coalesce around him. The quarrel split the service, and the country. Beresford had the support of the Conservative Party, the army (he was prepared to support their nonsensical talk of invasion) and the Prince of Wales; Fisher had on his side the Liberals, the King and the lower deck of the Royal Navy. He was right on the essentials but his methods were devious and divisive. He was definitely not a gentleman.

Fisher's opponents viewed war as a controlled, decent process in which civilians could be spared, private property respected and rules obeyed. They disliked Fisher's plans to open officer careers to common people and loathed him with that special contempt well-bred fools reserve for men of ability. Fisher might have been wise to pander to his opponents, but he did not have the time and would not risk the war-readiness of the fleet by waiting until they retired. And here Fisher held the ace. The Admiralty determined who served and who retired, and he ruthlessly passed over those he considered ineffective, ignorant or plain antagonistic. The extra five years allowed him to create a firebreak between generations, picking younger men for the top posts. Among them John Jellicoe, a quiet, unassuming man of relatively humble origins – his father was a Royal Mail steamer captain – possessed a remarkably acute technical mind and a personal charm that few could resist. Fisher cleared his path to the top. The dispute with Beresford and his aristocratic allies prompted Fisher to observe that the top 10 per cent of the country provided 90 per cent of all naval officers: 'This democratic country won't stand an aristocratic Navy!'[44]

These internal battles affected Fisher's health, and he became erratic, ill-tempered, resentful and bitter. He condemned officers who tried to resolve the dispute with Beresford or build a consensus, and demolished those who disagreed with him on matters of judgement. He held on to his post as long as he could, anxious to ensure his 'legacy' was not corrupted. When Beresford came ashore in March 1909, Fisher began to think about retirement, but only after he had pushed the government into building eight dreadnoughts in one year – the strike that settled the arms race with Germany. Beresford made a final attack, the spineless government set up a committee, and the mealy-mouthed report issued in August 1909 pleased no one. On 9 November 1909 Fisher was raised to the peerage as Baron Fisher of Kilverstone, the Suffolk property left to his son by Josiah Vavasseur. He left the Admiralty with great reluctance on 25 January 1910, his sixty-ninth birthday.

Awaiting Orders

Fisher took a well-earned rest but never took his eyes off the Admiralty. He possessed a sense of destiny, and reckoned the much anticipated war would begin in 1914, when the Kiel Canal was ready. He expected to be recalled in the event of war: no one would doubt that he was the man for the job, whatever their view of his character and conduct. Fisher's contact with the centres of power became more tenuous, however: his friend King Edward died in May 1910, and while Fisher kept up his correspondence with First Lord Reginald McKenna, his influence was limited.

He remained open to new ideas, notably that oil fuel and diesel engines should replace coal and steam turbines. Then Churchill replaced McKenna. While McKenna was far too level-headed to be swept along by Fisherite visions, Churchill, cut from the same cloth as the old admiral, quickly succumbed to his magnetic personality and wonderful flow of ideas. He came close to recalling him to office, but eventually restricted himself to employing him as a confidential adviser, reporting on the new fifteen-inch guns, improved conditions for the sailors, and much more. They fell out when Churchill appointed three of Beresford's acolytes to important posts over Fisher's bluntly delivered warnings. Churchill stuck to his guns but apologised profusely, and they went on much as before. Like any born conspirator, Fisher relished holding influence without responsibility. He chaired a Royal Commission in 1912 that recommended an oil-fuelled fleet.

In the last years of peace the navy's strategic concept shifted inexorably towards Fisher's concept of coastal defence by flotilla craft, leaving the main fleet to deal with any serious German movement or to threaten offensive operations. His protégé Jellicoe continued his rise to command, and the Fisherite trend of bigger, faster and more heavily armed warships seemed endless. By 1914 the new *Queen Elizabeth*-class battleships offered eight fifteen-inch guns on 27,500 tons, oil-fuelled to 24.5 knots. They were the best battleships in the world. Fisher's submarine paper of 1913 was visionary, predicting the methods used by German U-boats. While Churchill planned to recall Fisher if war broke out, he missed the chance to prevent war that might have been provided by drafting him earlier. No Cabinet advised by Fisher could have made such a blundering, incompetent, disastrous response to the July Crisis. The British trumpet gave a very uncertain sound in July, allowing the Germans to delude themselves that Britain might be neutral. With Fisher at the helm the fleet would have issued a much clearer note, and Germany would have paused. That was the ultimate purpose of Fisher's carefully crafted reputation for 'frightfulness' and the overwhelming impression of power that his fleet exuded. By holding out 'the possibility of ultimate action in the Baltic',[45] Fisher held the ace required to win the game.

War came in August 1914: the navy made mistakes, and men whom Fisher despised turned out to be failures. However, the contrast between the energy and enthusiasm of the young First Lord and the lackadaisical habits of First Sea Lord Prince Louis of Battenburg made Fisher's recall all but inevitable.

The strategic problem facing Britain in August 1914 was immense and fluid. Political and economic interests demanded a comprehensive, integrated global strategy, one that provided early and effective aid to France, if not to Russia, satisfied the Dominions and did not alienate major neutrals. The key would be sea control, the ability to use the world's oceans for military and economic activity, unhindered by hostile action. The strategic value of the sea for the Entente was incontestable; France needed military manpower and support from her overseas colonies and departments. Russia required industrial support, and Britain could only function at full capacity by sustaining her dominance of the global economy and bringing forward the resources of the Empire.[46] Although Britain dominated the war at sea she was no longer a free agent.

Initially Britain's strategy reflected her unique situation as a naval and economic power. In August 1914 Britain elected to wage a limited war. As one Cabinet minister observed:

We decided that we could win through by holding the sea, maintaining our credit, keeping our people employed & our own industries going – By economic pressure, destroying Germany's trade, cutting off her supplies we should gradually secure victory. This policy is steadily pursued – We have never thought we could successfully afford to compete with her by maintaining also a continental army on her scale – Our Navy, finance & trade was our life's blood & we must see to it that these are maintained.[47]

Entente strategy was based on Royal Navy sea control, secured by the 'Grand Fleet' which, together with other forces around the British coast, locked the German navy into the North Sea and Baltic. From this base all other operations flowed, but the Grand Fleet was not the offensive arm of the navy. Britain could not risk putting this at danger: as Churchill famously observed, Jellicoe was 'the only man who could lose the war in an afternoon'.

British strategy prioritised the long-term security of the Empire, recognising the threat posed by Russia, France, Japan and America. However, the failure of the French and Russian armies in 1914 accelerated the commitment of British ground forces, leading to battles like the Somme, and 'a significant diminution of [Britain's] economic power'.[48] British war policy was largely directed by the War Council, the key ministers and their professional advisers, who began meeting in late November 1914. Churchill was not prepared to wait on the defensive. He was anxious for battle and understood the political importance of defeating the enemy. His strategic model was essentially Fisher's:

> 1st Phase: The clearing of the outer seas.
> 2nd Phase: The clearing of the North Sea.
> 3rd Phase: The clearing of the Baltic.[49]

At each stage, the Royal Navy would use superior force to secure success. Access to the Baltic was central to Churchill's vision of naval strategy,[50] a point he had taken from Fisher.[51] While he had accepted Fisher's concept, he had not grasped the deeper purposes that informed the admiral's strategy. His anxiety to do something led him to propose schemes which relied on events and forces that were beyond his control. Yet the underlying theme remained consistent: 'It is to secure the eventual command of the Baltic that British naval operations must tend.'[52] While Churchill's thinking reflected Fisher's strategy, his plans were ill-digested and clumsy, operationally and diplomatically impossible. He envisaged steaming into the Baltic when the Foreign Office had written off any prospect of Denmark joining the Entente, and emphasised that British interests would be compromised if Germany occupied Denmark.[53] Fisher understood this, and his thinking evolved along far subtler lines.

Phase 1: The clearing of the outer seas

In August 1914 Germany had a number of warships and merchant auxiliaries deployed outside the North Sea, and these posed the only threat to British and Allied commercial shipping. Only a few visionaries, like Fisher, believed that submarines would be used to sink merchant ships without making provision for the safety of passengers and crew, as required by international law. Although the German cruiser threat loomed large in British planning and took some months to control, it was over by Christmas. German surface ships captured or destroyed a mere 2 per cent of British shipping, losses that were easily absorbed.[54] The combination of a global war plot[55] and the availability of overwhelming forces ensured that the cruiser war ended with the climactic battle of the Falkland Islands on 8 December. Britain could now concentrate on home waters.[56]

Phase 2: The clearing of the North Sea

From the first day of the war the German fleet conceded the initiative. Once the front line in France had stabilised, the ample superiority of the Royal Navy begged the question of how it could be used to defeat Germany. German forces suffered a serious defeat in the Heligoland Bight on 28 August at the hands of the Harwich Force and Grand Fleet battlecruisers.[57] Heligoland reminded the world that the 'magic of Trafalgar' had not dimmed, but it did nothing to halt the advance of the German army into France. The Royal Navy blocked German access to the outside world and secured Entente access to American industry and raw materials and the human resources of their overseas empires. The blockade was one half of the Entente strategy;[58] the other was to defeat the German army in France.

Churchill was quick to send submarines into the Baltic, probably on Fisher's advice.[59] The German response demonstrated that command of the western Baltic was a profoundly sensitive issue.[60] The Germans were unaware that the British had broken their radio codes. Decrypted signals, Churchill's 'priceless information', made it unnecessary to run any risks with the Grand Fleet.[61] Henceforth, while German motives remained unclear, information about fleet movements and even the departures of U-boats was served up on a plate.[62]

Phase 3: The clearing of the Baltic

For the first three months of the war Fisher was Churchill's unofficial adviser. Power without responsibility allowed him to indulge his hobby horses and pillory old enemies. On 20 October Prime Minister Asquith, desperately seeking some 'elan, dash, initiative, a new spirit',[63] approved Fisher's recall, and despite a stiff rearguard action by King George V, never an admirer, the seventy-three-year-old veteran returned, taking office on the 30th. While Churchill wanted him to energise the naval effort, Fisher ended up acting as a brake on the First Lord's wild schemes and unconstitutional assumption of executive authority. At least the two men agreed on the central place of the Baltic in British strategy: 'It was undoubtedly the prime goal of a naval offensive.'[64]

Churchill needed Fisher to develop and direct a war-winning strategy. Britain possessed a general command of the sea, but submarines, mines and the threat of coastal raids left the Royal Navy with some major problems, while the Germans had almost undisturbed possession of the Baltic. Fisher took office just as the battle-fleet balance of naval power turned decisively in Britain's favour. It was time to act.

Fisher began by detaching three battlecruisers from the Grand Fleet to avenge the defeat of a cruiser squadron on the Chilean coast. The Germans were annihilated at the battle of the Falkland Islands. He then ordered a massive new fleet for offensive operations, including shallow-draught monitors, light-draught battlecruisers, a host of minesweepers and motorised lighters.

Now that the outer seas had been cleared, the paramount need was to obtain a closer hold on the North Sea, with a view to the possibility of ultimately pressing our offensive into the enemy's waters. Such operations would involve coastal attack and inshore work, and required a special class of vessel.[65]

These operations had a very specific object. At the War Council of 1 December Fisher 'pointed out the importance of adopting the offensive'.[66] He had already instructed Corbett to examine Baltic operations. They agreed that any such plan would require careful development and could not be implemented in the short term. The intention was to be ready in case passive sea control and blockade failed to ruin the German economy as planned. The main item was the use of extensive minefields to keep the High Seas Fleet out of the North Sea while the British entered the Baltic.[67] Corbett concluded with a very clear statement of the rationale for a major offensive move:

The risks, of course, must be serious; but unless we are fairly sure that the passive pressure of our Fleet is really bringing Germany to a state of exhaustion, *risks must be taken to use our Command of the Sea with greater energy*.[68]

The paper was designed to persuade a hard-pressed War Council to back Fisher's concept, without revealing the details. Even Corbett was left guessing: he assumed the Grand Fleet would enter the Baltic.[69] Fisher knew this was impossible and unnecessary. Furthermore, Corbett was not clear how Fisher would stop German mines closing the Baltic.[70] Even so, Fisher was delighted.[71] He had plenty of minesweepers under construction,[72] which would be ready when the rest of his new 'Baltic' fleet entered service, and he had no intention of discussing the subject with politicians.

This measured approach did not please Churchill, who believed the war would be won in a year without new ships. He preferred opportunistic, improvised schemes.[73] Fisher used Corbett's strategic insight and the lessons of historical precedents to restrain Churchill.[74] But this was hard work and occupied much time that should have been devoted to waging war.

Fisher had no intention of sending the Grand Fleet into the Baltic. He required a new coastal warfare force. But Churchill, optimistic the war would be over in 1915, refused to sanction the new battle-cruisers Fisher demanded: 'Long before they can be finished we shall have smashed up the German Navy in harbour with our monitors, or they will have fought their battle in blue water, or peace will have been signed.'[75] At least he accepted that 'The Baltic is the only theatre in which naval action can appreciably shorten the war.'[76] This was enough for Fisher, who was perfectly happy to allow his energetic disciple to take the lead in public debates and Cabinet council.

Fisher persisted with his demands, using frequent threats of resignation to secure the new ships. When he was persuaded to withdraw his resignation in late January, he exacted authority from the War Council to order his *Courageous*-class light battlecruisers as part of the Baltic fleet – this was his price for supporting Churchill's Dardanelles plan.[77] Churchill reminded the War Council 'that the ultimate object of the Navy was to obtain access to the Baltic . . . this operation was of great importance as Germany was, AND ALWAYS HAD BEEN, very nervous of an attack from the Baltic. For this purpose special vessels were required, and the First Sea Lord had designed cruisers etc.' Chancellor of the Exchequer David Lloyd George immediately sanctioned the expenditure.[78] The new type of ship was 'imperatively demanded for the Baltic, where she can go through the international highway of the Sound owing to her shallow draught'. The Swedish side of the Sound was not mined, but it was shallow.[79]

Fisher's new fleet eventually included five battlecruisers, thirty-seven monitors,[80] minesweepers, motorised barges and armoured landing craft, while eight fast merchant ships were purchased to mine the North Sea. While waiting for the new ships, Fisher advocated a combined operation on the Belgian coast to close the submarine bases at Ostend and Zeebrugge.

The purpose of Fisher's new fleet was revealed in Corbett's paper:

even if the suggested operation is not feasible, a menace of carrying it out – concerted with Russia – might . . . disturb German equilibrium and force her to desperate expedients, even hazarding a fleet action or alienating entirely the Scandinavian Powers by drastic measures of precaution.[81]

While the last clause referred to a German invasion of Denmark, the underlying theme of deterrence reveals Fisher's input. This was the work of an arch-manipulator, trying to bend the minds of the German high command to act as he desired, something he had achieved on several occasions.[82] Fisher's pre-war form strongly suggests that the Russian army was no more part of his plan than using the Grand Fleet in the Baltic. The threat of Russian troops and British dreadnoughts would be enough. The real purpose of the Baltic plan was to bring the High Seas Fleet to battle in the North

Sea, probably in the Skagerrak, by threatening the Baltic Narrows. If the High Seas Fleet were sunk, Fisher could extend the blockade into the Baltic and ruin the German economy.[83]

From his position inside the planning process Corbett realised that, Fisher aside, the naval leadership, both civil and military, seriously overestimated the degree to which Germany was willing to use its fleet for offensive operations and thereby risk command of the Baltic. Without the Kiel Canal, which reopened for dreadnoughts in June 1914, Germany would never have gone to war.[84]

A Baltic operation, feint or stroke was the only way that the British could use sea power to influence the strategy of the war in the medium term and avoid total war mobilisation. Churchill accepted the Baltic concept, pressing it on Asquith on 29 December.[85] But his Cabinet memorandum outlined an amphibious campaign in which the risk of a naval disaster was only slightly less certain than the inevitability of alienating critical neutral powers. It was a far cry from Fisher's concept, in which Germany would be manoeuvred into violating Danish neutrality. However, Churchill's paper served Fisher's purposes, keeping the Baltic on the Cabinet agenda. As he expected, it leaked, alarming the Germans and the Danes.[86] Churchill's plan was damned by the simple fact that Asquith would not violate Danish neutrality, the Scandinavian states having signed a joint neutrality pact.[87] Yet the deadlock in France and Belgium left few options, and a Baltic strategy that played to Britain's strengths was the best option.[88] Fisher neatly sidestepped serious discussions of Churchill's ideas by stressing the need for troops.[89]

While critics argue that Fisher's 'Baltic' plans were based on wishful thinking and outmoded concepts, and would have been impossible to execute, the reality is more complex.[90] Fisher had known the Baltic was the key to a war against Germany since 1899. Only a serious threat to the Baltic communications would bring the German fleet to battle at a time and place of Britain's choice – as Corbett put it, 'the sublime moments of naval history have to be worked for'. Fisher was, as ever, rather more direct:

Make the German Fleet fight and you win the war! How can you make the German fleet fight? By undertaking on a huge scale, with an immense armada of rapidly-built craft, an operation that threatens the German Fleet's existence![91]

Fisher never produced a definitive version of his scheme, preferring to keep the details fluid. This much is clear, however: he did not plan to send the Grand Fleet into the Baltic or, in all probability, his new armada either until the High Seas Fleet had been greatly reduced or destroyed. The foolhardy plans of 1914 and 1915 were Churchill's. Fisher would talk up a good 'Copenhagen' scare, but this was the public rhetoric of deterrence, not the wisdom of a strategist. Notably reticent when the opportunity for a naval offensive arose at the turn of 1914–15, Fisher was not going to make his move until the opportunity was right.[92] It would have been good if others had been so restrained.

Searching for an Offensive

Fisher's faith in Jellicoe was amply rewarded. They were in constant communication from the day Fisher resumed office. Both Jellicoe and Beatty were greatly encouraged by Fisher's words and his willing response to their requests. After the German battlecruiser raid on Scarborough in November, the Grand Fleet was redistributed.[93] Several old battleships were withdrawn to attack Belgian ports being used by U-boats. Closing these bases and recovering complete control of the Channel would greatly ease the navy's defensive burden. On 23 November two battleships bombarded Zeebrugge, causing considerable damage.[94] Anything more serious would have required a combined operation, but both the French and Belgian armies proved unwilling to act.[95]

Nor was the prospect of drawing the High Seas Fleet out for battle ever very far from Fisher's mind.[96] The Belgian coast was the one place in Europe where the Entente could exploit command of the sea to assist a military operation. This operation was stifled by the carelessness of the commander of the Channel fleet, Vice Admiral Sir Lewis Bayly, just as Churchill's mercurial mind settled on the Dardanelles – an operation that offered enormous political and strategic benefits, and could be conducted without the new ships required for the Baltic.[97]

While Lord Kitchener persuaded the Cabinet to adopt an attritional strategy, assuming the Allies would win the war by outlasting Germany in human resources, Churchill, Lloyd George and War Council Secretary Colonel Hankey recognised that without some popular victories, and low casualties, enthusiasm for the war would begin to wane.[98] Such concerns dominated their response to an emerging alternative theatre in the eastern Mediterranean. Turkey had joined the war in November, putting pressure on Russia. When General Sir John French stated that the war could not be won on the Western Front, the government had to look elsewhere. Just when his matchless powers of advocacy and inspiration were required to persuade his colleagues to conduct a combined operation on the Belgian coast, Churchill launched his Dardanelles delusion.

By January 1915 Churchill was assuming executive authority, ignoring his professional advisers in an unconstitutional fashion. Furthermore, having pushed Vice Admiral Sir Sackville Carden to produce a plan for a naval attack on the Straits, Churchill, with typical effrontery, took it to the War Council claiming that Carden believed the operation was feasible. Fisher and Admiral Sir Henry Jackson, who had planned overseas operations since the outbreak of war, preferred a combined operation. Nothing daunted, Churchill carried on as if Fisher, Lloyd George and Kitchener were all in complete accord. He believed, and many of his colleagues were persuaded, that a naval expedition arriving off Istanbul would occasion the collapse of the 'Young Turk' regime and secure peace. This unwarranted assumption propelled his operational thinking. At the War Council on 7 January 1915 Kitchener finished off the Belgian offensive by refusing to release the necessary troops. Carden's plan for a steady naval advance through the Dardanelles, systematically destroying each fort and sweeping each mine, enabled Churchill to sidestep Kitchener's objection that he lacked the manpower to secure the Straits. The following day Fisher declared that a purely naval operation on the Belgian coast would be unacceptably risky, leaving the War Council to adopt the Dardanelles plan by default.[99] Carden would be reinforced with old battleships from the Channel and distant waters.

To an outside observer, the battlecruiser action on the Dogger Bank on 23 January reinforced the impression of effortless superiority established at Heligoland, encouraging Churchill's belief that he could commit considerable resources to the Dardanelles. Although Fisher was happy to deploy ships for a demonstration or diversion, he fundamentally disagreed with Churchill's strategy:

When the enterprise began to take on the aspect of a serious attempt to force the Straits, and reduce Constantinople, without military co-operation, he began to contemplate it each day with graver apprehension . . . So much, indeed, would have to be staked for success, that it would gravely prejudice, and even render impossible, the plans he was elaborating to secure a perfect control of Home Waters and the Baltic.

On 25 January Fisher sent a memorandum to Churchill, arguing that risking heavy ships on purely naval bombardments was playing into the hands of the Germans:

The pressure of sea power to-day is probably not less but greater and more rapid in action than in the past; but it is still a slow process and requires great patience. In time it will almost certainly compel the enemy to seek a decision at sea, particularly when he begins to realise that his offensive on land is broken . . .

. . . we ought to aim at a complete closure of the North Sea, and the declaration of a blockade . . . The sole justification for coastal bombardments and attacks by the fleet on fortified places, such as the contemplated prolonged bombardment of the Dardanelles forts by our Fleet, is to force the decision at sea, and so far and no further can they be justified . . .

It has been said that the first function of the British Army is to assist the fleet in obtaining command of the sea. This might be accomplished by military co-operation with the navy in such operations as the attack of Zeebrugge, or the forcing of the Dardanelles, which might bring out the German and Turkish fleets respectively. Apparently, however, this is not to be. The English Army is apparently to continue to provide a small sector of the allied front in France, where it is no more help to the navy than if it were at Timbuctoo . . .

Being already in possession of all that a powerful fleet can give a country, we should continue quietly to enjoy the advantages without dissipating our strength in operations that cannot improve the position.[100]

This reveals much of Fisher's strategic thought. The primacy of seeking a decision at sea and the vital role of the army in that object were critical to his 'Baltic' and North Sea plans. He had no interest in action for its own sake, and saw no reason to rush. This excellent critique of Churchill's relentless pressure for 'Action this Day'[101] appears to have been drafted by Corbett.

Churchill countered, arguing that the margin of superiority at home was perfectly adequate. With the Admiralty divided, the final decision rested with the War Council. Political concerns overrode

Fisher's professional advice.[102] He resigned rather than accept Churchill's plan, but Asquith persuaded him to remain. Rather than address the tough issues of authority and strategy, Asquith simply smoothed over the immediate problem and homogenised divergent views. Consequently, when the War Council met on 28 January Asquith backed Churchill's Dardanelles plan. Once again Fisher decided to resign; this time Kitchener dissuaded him, stressing the decisive political impact of a success at a time when his new armies were unready to take the field. This was correct advice. The political decision had been taken and, having made his protest to the minister responsible and privately informed the prime minister of his views, it was Fisher's duty to carry on. He consoled himself with the thought that if the attack failed, the ships could be withdrawn easily, as long as no troops were landed.[103]

Blockade

In home waters, the German fleet remained quiet, but the first unrestricted submarine campaign proved difficult to counter. Sinking merchant vessels without providing for the safety of passengers and crew was illegal, but the Germans had few options. British losses were embarrassing, especially as U-boats proved difficult to find or sink. Wordy exchanges about the legal issues of economic blockade and submarine warfare were little more than a smokescreen as the conflict escalated towards totality. Fisher emphasised that blockade was the one instrument that could make naval power effective on land. He agreed with Corbett that a commercial blockade of a vital trade route would ultimately force the enemy fleet to sea.[104] This would require the Royal Navy to threaten Germany's only vital maritime route: the iron-ore traffic across the Baltic.

Fisher developed an economic warfare policy for total war. On returning to office, he declared that the North Sea was so heavily mined that neutral ships must call at British ports for directions before proceeding. Suspicious vessels were then detained. By January 1915 the US government had accepted the British case for this policy.[105] When Germany warned that their response to British action might involve accidentally sinking neutral shipping, President Wilson sent a stiff protest. He ignored the illegal action by the British because an Allied victory served America's interest.[106] This paved the way for Allied victory in 1918 and 1945. In an age of total war no major power would willingly forego its major strategic asset unless forced to do so by neutral action or enemy reprisal. In 1914 the British developed new rules for war at sea. Only Sweden, secure inside the Baltic, could defy the British, largely because Russia depended on Swedish engineering products.[107]

The impact of the blockade was incremental. While German industry was not seriously affected before 1915, production never matched demand and gradually fell away.[108] However, economic warfare was too slow an instrument for Asquith's War Council.

By mid-February the Dardanelles had become, by default, Britain's only offensive option. Ministers anticipated massive diplomatic, strategic and economic gains from the collapse of Turkey, and Churchill persuaded them they could withdraw if the initial attack failed. Elsewhere, the real value of naval power was evident in Italy's decision to join the Entente. With her exposed coastline and dependence on imported coal and oil, Italy could not go to war against Britain.[109] Just as Churchill's naval plan was being put into effect, Hankey asked Corbett to produce a paper on the precedent of 1807 – the year in which the fleet successfully passed the Dardanelles without having any political effect on Istanbul.[110] This prompted Kitchener to release two divisions for the operation. Even so, Churchill insisted the Dardanelles was only a short-term commitment, telling the War Council on 3 March that the Baltic, 'our proper line of strategy', would be attempted 'later on when our new monitors were completed'.[111]

Vice Admiral Carden's careful plan of attack, steadily knocking out the main Turkish forts and sweeping the minefields, was conditioned by Churchill's admission that the supply of heavy ammunition was limited.[112] He hoped that a stately, imperial progress would undermine the morale of the defenders.[113] The opening stages of the Dardanelles attack went well, prompting a typically bombastic public outburst from Churchill which committed the government to carry the attack to a conclusion, ending any chance of an easy withdrawal. The purpose of his rhetoric was to enlist various Balkan powers in the war, but Greece, Bulgaria and Romania proved remarkably resistant to promises of a share when the skin of the Ottoman lion was divided. Fisher, anxious to secure military cooperation, directed Corbett to analyse analogous operations during the Russo-Japanese War.[114]

With the naval attack on the Dardanelles approaching completion, Churchill returned to the Baltic after two months' silence. He now proposed passing a squadron of fast capital ships into the Baltic to blockade the German coast.[115] This was visionary, and futile. Fisher neatly sidelined the plan by sending it for a second opinion and reminding Churchill that nothing could be done until the Turkish operation had been completed.[116]

As hopes for local support against Turkey withered, Churchill and Fisher, relying on radio intelligence that the forts were almost out of ammunition, raised the stakes. Churchill telegraphed Carden on 11 March to act 'vigorously': the potential results justified running risks.[117] They had some cause for optimism: so far there had been no fatal casualties afloat or any serious damage. However, Churchill ended up lecturing Carden on the effect of naval gunfire on forts, a subject of which he had neither practical experience nor theoretical comprehension. He was under enormous political pressure: the Grand Alliance and the British government demanded a positive result, and his head was on the block. One observer noted, 'Winston is very excited and "jumpy" about the Dardanelles; he says he will be ruined if the attack fails.'[118] Asquith realised Churchill was 'spurring' Carden on, but did nothing.[119] The following day, the 13th, Churchill demanded that 'operations should now be pressed forward methodically and resolutely by night and day, the unavoidable losses being accepted'.[120] Although browbeaten into acquiescence, Carden pointedly requested additional ammunition and fleet minesweepers.[121] While Churchill entertained dreams of glory, Fisher was anxious to get on or give up.[122] He understood that the Dardanelles dominated Churchill's thoughts, but his own energies were directed towards the Baltic.[123] Furthermore, the Dardanelles effort was draining away the very resources Fisher had prepared for the Baltic.

Faced with the prospect of forcing the Narrows, Carden broke down, handing the task to Rear Admiral de Robeck. On 18 March, his first day in command, de Robeck advanced into the Narrows. Three old battleships were lost, two on a small minefield; three more were damaged. British losses were no more than sixty killed. Despite initial enthusiasm, de Robeck did not try again. This was regrettable: it was a high-risk operation, but it might have worked, and the loss of a few twenty-year-old battleships did not threaten the Entente's

naval dominance. Churchill, Asquith and Kitchener favoured pushing on, but the Admiralty War Group backed de Robeck, and the
Cabinet of 23 March sanctioned an amphibious operation.[124] This
reinforced a naval rebuff with a military catastrophe. It might have
been possible to retire gracefully, if Churchill had not publicly committed the ministry. Fisher and the sea lords were concerned that the
new operation would drain away reserves of materiel and manpower
from the Grand Fleet. They did not care about old ships: they needed
skilled men for new warships. Fisher could see his Baltic strategy
being slowly whittled away, as Churchill inexorably fed every spare
ship and man into the Turkish adventure. The partial success of the
amphibious operation on 25 April was the worst possible outcome,
leaving the army perched uselessly on Turkish soil. Instead of assisting the naval attack, the troops now tied down a vast armada to support and sustain them.[125]

That said, the naval attack was doomed by details, not concept.
De Robeck's ships were astonishingly badly prepared for shore bombardment. Most were reserve fleet units, lacking specialist gunnery
training and high-explosive ammunition for their guns.[126] British
shells designed to sink armoured ships did little damage to earth-
work forts. Churchill's vision was not backed by attention to detail:
he actually boasted about using obsolescent ammunition!

Churchill's absolute and unashamed refusal to consider the advice
of the government's chosen professional expert, a man he had
appointed, demonstrated the complete breakdown of civil–military
relations at the Admiralty. It was high time he left the Admiralty –
although his political colleagues had yet to realise the fact. Nothing
could preserve the high-powered but unstable naval leadership.
Fisher had only agreed to the Dardanelles attack as a quick, decisive
blow. Even before the big naval attack he had reminded Churchill
that 'the decisive theatre remains and ever will be the North Sea'.[127]
When the amphibious landings of 25 April stalled on the beaches of
Gallipoli, turning Churchill's quick knockout into a long-term commitment, Fisher declared that the campaign would compromise 'his
own plans for the North Sea and Baltic'. His plans depended on the
early return of ships and men from Gallipoli, and if the War Council
backed another landing this would be impossible. On 14 May irrev-
ocable differences between Fisher and Churchill surfaced at the War
Council. Not only were the ministers committed to Gallipoli, but

Churchill was going behind his back and sending 'the new monitors which had been designed as an essential element in the North Sea plans' to join the campaign. 'Without them the offensive could not be pushed into German waters.'

'Lord Fisher's plan, which he believed was the only one that could give decisive results within a measurable period of time, was obviously to be postponed indefinitely. Feeling that he could no longer be responsible for the conduct of the war at sea, he resigned the next morning.'[128] His real object, however, was to remove Churchill and secure absolute control of the naval war. He planned to replace the other sea lords, abolish the War Staff and act as Lord High Admiral. These were the thoughts of an autocrat, not a leader. Arrogance and intolerance proved to be his fatal flaw. On 17 May Fisher sent his demands to Asquith and left the Admiralty. His naval colleagues did not back him, and their opposition was the final straw that persuaded Asquith to accept his resignation – but only on the 22nd.[129] Those at a distance were astonished, but Jellicoe understood the value of his action: 'We owe you a debt of gratitude for having saved the Navy from a continuance in office of Mr Churchill, and I hope that never again will any politician be allowed to usurp the functions that he took upon himself to exercise.'[130]

By resigning and bringing down Churchill Fisher saved the navy, and the nation. While his astonishing letter to the Prime Minster led many to question his sanity, Fisher was incensed, not insane. His carefully thought-out plans had been derailed by Churchill's impulsive, careless actions. A slightly more emollient letter might have served him better, as he realised when the passion had cooled. But it was too late. Those with a better grasp of the war, from the admirals afloat to Chancellor Lloyd George, regretted the loss of a man with the vision, energy and ideas to make a difference. Britain would fight the rest of the war with mediocre ideas and second-rate service leaders.

By no coincidence at all, the shortage of high-explosive ammunition in France caused a scandal, and Asquith took the opportunity to reconstruct his government as a coalition with the Conservatives, neatly avoiding the requirement for a general election.[131] The Conservatives' terms included removing Churchill from the Admiralty. Despite their faults, the dynamism, vision and energy of these two men, Churchill and Fisher, would be missed in the coming years.

Gallipoli was evacuated on 9 January 1916, just as beachheads became untenable.[132] This marked the end of a strategic era. In April 1916 the Cabinet committed the New Armies to France in an attempt to win the war by military operations in a single campaign. They did so in the knowledge that failure would risk bankruptcy.[133] This 'continental commitment' was a strategic leap in the dark.

Intrigue and Revenge

Fisher always expected to regain power, but had to content himself with the position of Chair of the Board of Invention and Research, soon nicknamed 'Intrigue and Revenge'. Pioneering work on submarine detection was the most obvious fruit of this effort, leading to improved hydrophones, depth charges and the basis of sonar. When Jellicoe became First Sea Lord, Fisher offered to return to the Admiralty as Third Sea Lord and Controller to deal with the growing U-boat crisis. Jellicoe knew better.

In July 1918 Lady Fisher died. She had been denied the peaceful retirement that might have compensated her for living alongside a volcano. Fisher placed her cremated remains at Kilverstone Church, along with the flag he had flown as admiral of the fleet. The funeral marked the death of earthly ambition, and the beginning of the end. In 1919 Fisher made his last appearance on the public stage, at the Paris peace conference. He remained full of energy on the dance floor and continued to tell wonderful stories. In 1920 he endured four operations for cancer, but he died within days of the last. It was a sad end to a titanic life. At his state funeral in Westminster Abbey, Jellicoe, the principal pall-bearer, wept. Afterwards his body was cremated and his ashes joined those of his wife.

John Fisher was the last titan to direct the Royal Navy. In an age of democratic politics and liberal values, there is no place for his unique genius. That may be for the best: we can no more rely on finding another Fisher than another Nelson. Yet we have lost a vital part of our humanity in the process. If we cannot aspire we will not achieve.

Fisher made a conscious effort to become a leader, learning to roar like a bull and keep the ship in first-class order, but he was bored by such trivia, preferring to master the latest technology. This was a field that exploited all his talents. He was quick to seize on the potential of new systems, often before they were actually service-able. His first period directing the Admiralty revolutionised the navy. It was necessary and, coming so late in the day, it was also shockingly brutal. The second redirected and reinvigorated a failing war effort and saved the nation from the worst of Churchill's follies.

Yet John Fisher was not a great leader: his energy and his genius made it hard for others to follow, and he always seemed short of time to explain his ideas. He lacked the natural authority and fleet-handling mastery of Hornby, the war record of Parker, and the human warmth of Nelson. Had he been more fortunate in any of these areas he could have achieved more. When thwarted, his nor-mally positive and enthusiastic nature quickly became suspicious, secretive and savage. He rarely forgave, and never forgot. His con-temporaries responded according to their own qualities: men of vision and energy loved him; small-minded pedants hated him and all his works.

As a strategist of deterrence he was unrivalled. His distaste for war, mastery of public relations and ability to harmonise different aspects of the task provided the nation with a navy that was entirely suited to its needs – economical and yet awe-inspiring. Had he been in office in July 1914 Britain would have been far better equipped to deter a war that cost millions of lives and ruined the empire he had lived to preserve.

9
RUTHLESS BOUNDER
David Beatty
1871–1936

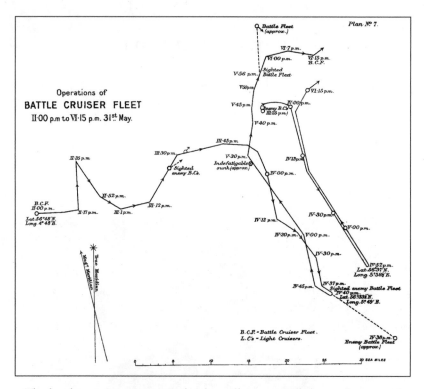

The battlecruiser action at Jutland cruelly expressed the weaknesses of David Beatty's command style. Haste, carelessness and a failure to see the big picture cost two ships and 2,200 lives

DAVID BEATTY WAS THE FIRST modern admiral.[1] His career was advanced by good fortune, publicity and money; his reputation reflected an image rather than reality; his victories only existed in the pages of wartime newspapers. In later life he waged a devious, if not downright dishonest, campaign to maintain the illusion of glory by traducing the reputation of another officer, splitting the navy down the middle in the process. Yet his eight-year term as First Sea Lord, after the glory days were over, transcended anything he had achieved at sea: his work ensured that the Royal Navy largely survived the inevitable post-war reductions and continued intact into the era of universal adult suffrage, strategic bombing and economic decline. Political skills honed in the vicious arena of service rivalries, bolstered by prodigious wealth and wartime glory, proved potent weapons. If he was not the Nelsonian leader the navy required in wartime, he proved to be a highly effective manager in the difficult days of peace.

Early Career

Born on 17 January 1871 at Howbeck Lodge near Nantwich in Cheshire, David Beatty, the second of four sons, grew up in a world dominated by social class, fox hunting and field sports. It was a world that he would never leave. His sister enjoyed the nickname 'Trot'; it may have been her first word – and his. His parents, Captain David Beatty, 4th Hussars, and Katherine Sadleir, were Irish, and Beatty considered himself 'essentially Irish'. By that he meant that he belonged to the Anglo-Irish Protestant elite, a largely forgotten branch of the British upper class. While his brothers followed their father into the army, David showed an interest in the sea and was prepared for the navy, with special schooling in the key subjects. At thirteen he passed into the Naval College at Dartmouth.

The 'college' comprised a pair of old wooden battleships tied up on the River Dart, providing a suitably spartan existence in which boys learnt to sail, navigate, command and, above all, be commanded. Beatty did not make his mark at Dartmouth: rigid discipline and endless routine clashed with his lively, sociable character. Having done well at entry he slipped down the term rankings. He was never selected to be a cadet captain and suffered several punishments before passing out halfway down the list in January 1886. After such an undistinguished performance, he was deservedly posted to the undesirable China station, but his mother, relying on shared Irish connections, appealed to Captain Lord Charles Beresford, the Fourth Sea Lord. Beresford moved his fellow Irishman from a backwater post to the navy's prize midshipman appointment: on the flagship of the Mediterranean fleet.

His Royal Highness the Duke of Edinburgh commanded from Hornby's old flagship, the *Alexandra*. Queen Victoria's unloved second son was a fine seaman and a good admiral. The flagship was painted white, both to keep her cool and to provide a showcase for the neatness, drill and display that did so much to sustain the Royal Navy's reputation. Inevitably the junior officers of the flagship included some of the brightest and the best connected; Stanley Colville and Colin Keppel would be role models and patrons. Fellow midshipmen Walter Cowan, Richard Phillimore and Reginald Tyrwhitt all served under Beatty in later years. Beatty's personal charm, polished manners and good looks made him popular with his contemporaries and the numerous guests who passed through the flagship. Exceptional horsemanship reinforced his social position. In these formative years he acquired an enduring taste for high society, while the contacts he made on the *Alexandra* did much to make his career.

After three years at sea, Sub-Lieutenant Beatty joined the wooden steam corvette *Ruby* in May 1889 for seamanship training. Eighteen months ashore at the Royal Naval College, Greenwich, and the gunnery training ship HMS *Excellent* at Portsmouth produced distinctly ordinary academic results. Although he could have secured six months' extra seniority by passing all three key subjects with first-class marks, he only did so in torpedoes. This suggests a lack of interest and application; he was perfectly capable of doing better. Beatty showed no enthusiasm for a career like Fisher's, driven by technical expertise. Instead, he would remain a non-specialist in a service dominated by gunners. Fortunately the small mid-Victorian navy was just beginning to expand, creating an insatiable demand for junior officers. It was a very good time to begin a naval career. Before being promoted to lieutenant on 25 August 1892, Beatty joined the royal yacht *Victoria and Albert* for the summer cruise, perhaps the ultimate testimony to his social acceptability. Another spell on *Ruby* in the West Indies and South Atlantic developed his seamanship and man-management skills. In October 1893 he rejoined the modern navy, in the form of the battleship *Camperdown* on the Mediterranean station. Transferring to the *Trafalgar* in 1895 he rejoined Commander Stanley Colville, the ship's executive officer. Colville had formed a high opinion of his potential back on the *Alexandra*.

Colville made Beatty's career. In 1896 an Anglo-Egyptian expedition under General Sir Herbert Kitchener began the re-conquest of the Sudan from the Islamic Dervish regime founded after the death of General Sir Charles Gordon at Khartoum in 1885. Kitchener's army depended on river gunboats for transport and fire support, and Colville was selected to command, taking Beatty as his second. While passing the cataract at Wady Halfa under heavy fire, Colville was seriously wounded, leaving Beatty in command. He did not hesitate, leading the flotilla upriver to outflank the Mahdist position at Dongola, forcing its evacuation. When the main army reached Dongola, Kitchener halted his offensive to build a railway line back to Egypt. Beatty went home for the winter, spending much of it hunting. He had made his mark, receiving the DSO, and Kitchener specifically requested his return for the 1897 campaign. This time the force was commanded by Colin Keppel, while Horace Hood and Walter Cowan were among the gunboat captains. The 1897 season did not begin well, but when Beatty's gunboat capsized and sank in a cataract, he simply moved to another and carried on. The new gunboats, armed with a quick-firing twelve-pounder gun, machine guns and a searchlight, moved ahead of the army, dispersing any Dervish forces that collected near the river. At the climactic battle of Omdurman on 2 September, the firepower and mobility of the gunboats provided vital support for the hard-pressed troops, who went about their work with a dash and daring that would characterise Beatty's leadership for the rest of his life. After Omdurman, with the Sudan firmly under Anglo-Egyptian control, Kitchener took his gunboats south to Fashoda, where a remarkable French expedition had crossed the continent and claimed the headwaters of the river. Kitchener arrived in style with a superior force. After an international showdown, France gave way.

Kitchener's final dispatch saw Beatty specially promoted to commander on 15 November 1898. As he was only twenty-seven, this moved him six years ahead of his contemporaries in the race for the rank of admiral. He had also become public property: his name joined those of the other young heroes of the Sudan, including Winston Churchill, chronicler of the campaign and of his own heroics in the last British cavalry charge.[2] While the story that Beatty tossed a bottle of champagne to the thirsty cavalry officer is apocryphal, their shared experience created an enduring bond.

Four months' home leave provided an early opportunity to savour the delights of his new-found fame. It was typical of Beatty that he fell in love with a woman who had the potential to ruin his career: she was beautiful, bold to the point of recklessness in the hunting field, married and fabulously wealthy. American heiress Ethel Tree was the only daughter of Chicago chain-store owner Marshall Field, and was separated from her husband. There was more than a hint of danger about her, perhaps the early signs of mental instability, but Beatty found her irresistible. He had little time to pursue Ethel before his career interrupted the horsy delights of an English leave.

Having outstripped his contemporaries with his heroics on the Nile, Beatty returned to the professional mainstream. Appointed captain of the battleship *Barfleur*, a flagship on the China station, Colville chose Beatty to be the ship's executive officer in April 1899. He had the opportunity to secure his next promotion in classic Victorian fashion, by ensuring the ship presented an unblemished appearance, was painfully clean internally and successful in competitive drills. He did not disappoint, but the exercise soon became irrelevant.

In May 1899 a large-scale anti-western insurrection gripped parts of imperial China, led by the Society of the Heavenly Fists, or 'Boxers'. Attempts by the Dowager Empress to deflect the movement from criticising the imperial regime backfired, and by summer 1900 the rebels had reached Beijing, where they murdered the German minister. Western residents took refuge in the Legation Quarter, under the protection of a tiny international garrison, reinforced by marines from the British fleet. Admiral Seymour led an international relief effort of two thousand soldiers, sailors and marines along the railway from Tientsin (Tianjin) towards Beijing. Beatty landed with a hundred and fifty men from the *Barfleur* the day after Seymour left Tientsin, joining an ill-equipped garrison of 2,400 men who faced at least fifteen thousand well-armed Boxers and imperial troops. Beatty took a prominent part in fierce fighting around Tientsin railway station. Severely wounded in the left arm and wrist on 19 June 1900, he discharged himself from hospital after minimal treatment.

When Seymour was forced to retreat by overwhelming opposition, his flag captain and chief of staff John Jellicoe among those badly wounded, Beatty led the relief column that met Seymour on the 26th. As more troops arrived, the sailors were left to control Tientsin, and Beatty missed the opportunity to join the successful Beijing relief expedition. Once again, he had displayed outstanding leadership, good command skills, an unusual ability to work with allies and the sort of personal bravery that came naturally to a fearless fox-hunting man. He received warm praise both from Admiral Seymour and from fellow Irishman Captain Edward Bayley RN, his commanding officer on shore.[3] Unable to disguise the seriousness of his injuries any longer, he was promptly ordered home. On 9 November 1900 Beatty was one of four commanders specially promoted to captain for his gallantry and leadership. While a second battlefield promotion was unusual, especially so soon after the first, Beatty had earned it. He was twenty-nine – the normal age for promotion to captain was forty-two. He would become an admiral before his contemporaries were captains.

David Beatty had not shown any star quality in his early service and did not specialise in any branch of the service. After the fortunate start secured by his mother, he was left trailing in the wake of determined contemporaries with greater mathematical aptitude and technical gifts. Indeed, without war service he would have been destined for an unremarkable career. When the chance came, however, he took command with the assurance of a veteran. Sheer good fortune saw him reach China in time to serve ashore and add to his laurels. Afloat or ashore, Beatty was a quick-thinking, decisive and confident leader who inspired commanders and followers alike. The double promotion was no more than he deserved – success in war marked him out as a future admiral.

Captain to Admiral

In September 1900 Beatty arrived in England, where a complicated operation restored the use of his left arm but left him with two paralysed fingers. He was soon back in the hunting field, and renewed his courtship of Ethel. Both were high-risk activities. She was fascinating and rich beyond the dreams of avarice – qualities that naturally attracted a young officer on the cusp of a great career. He was well aware of the social risks involved in a relationship with a married woman and in marrying a divorcee. The affair was conducted with great discretion, but mutual attraction overcame the opposition of both families and numerous other warnings. Ethel's husband divorced her in America on 12 May 1901, on the grounds of her abandonment. Ten days later she and David were married at Hanover Square Registry Office. Beatty was fortunate that the moral climate had eased with the accession of a new monarch: Edward VII was rather less censorious of other men's frailties than his mother had been. Beatty was a frequent guest of royalty, especially the Prince of Wales, but it would be several years before his wife was accepted at court. At least the marriage gave Beatty financial security. Ethel had money to burn, and this proved to be her favourite occupation – a distraction from the dull routine of waiting for her husband to come back from the sea.

Despite the lure of luxury and ease, Beatty did not allow the money or his demanding wife to distract him from his career. Instead, financial independence allowed him to be choosy about his postings. Despite affecting the demeanour of a fox-hunting squire, Beatty was a careful student of his profession and endowed with a powerful intellect. Once the medical board passed him fit for sea service, Beatty took command of the cruiser HMS *Juno*. While he had nothing to prove as a warrior, he had yet to demonstrate his ability to command in a major fleet, under the steely gaze of a senior admiral. Failure would have ended his career.

The Edwardian navy was facing a seemingly endless technological revolution, grappling with the tactical and strategic implications of new weapons, machinery and wireless radio. Fleet exercises provided opportunities to think about the future. While John Fisher's Mediterranean command had been the most spectacular, it was by no means unique. Beatty was set the hardest task: serving in the Channel fleet under the redoubtable Arthur Wilson. Known as 'Old 'Ard 'Art' for his refusal to consider the cares and comforts of officers and men, no one expected more of his captains than Wilson. Beatty handled his ship with skill and confidence, although he admitted to losing his temper with his rather pedestrian, rule-bound officers. Initially they did not share his zeal to excel in fleet drills, gunnery practice and exercises. His solution was pure Nelson. He entertained them and used dinner to make them think about their profession in a way that had clearly never been attempted before. Beatty was no autocrat. He believed in taking his officers into his confidence and making the best use of their talents, whatever they were. He expected them to share his concern for the higher aspects of the profession and to learn from the latest fleet exercises.

While Wilson was not a great communicator, he was significantly better than Beatty's next admiral. Lord Charles Beresford was now Commander-in-Chief Mediterranean, but he did not share Fisher's interest in the thoughts of his juniors. He micromanaged the fleet, depriving captains of any real authority, while bombarding them with endless orders and directions and setting outdated exercises. Beatty did not approve, but he took care not to get involved in the Fisher–Beresford squabble. On professional matters he agreed with Fisher, but he much preferred Beresford as a man – a judgement shared with many of his contemporaries.

After three months the *Juno* paid off, but Beatty took command of HMS *Arrogant* – clearly someone in the Admiralty had a sense of humour. He followed a second temporary posting by moving to the armoured cruiser HMS *Suffolk* in October 1904 to complete a three-year term. This allowed Ethel to join him in Malta, after months spent complaining about his attachment to his profession and absence from home. At Malta Ethel's money made for a hectic social life, while the arrival in 1905 of their first son, also named David, provided his father with much pleasure. A second son, Peter, was born in 1910. The family returned home in late 1905, and after a period of leave Beatty was appointed naval adviser to the Army

Council in December 1906. For the next two years he was closely involved in planning the movements the British Expeditionary Force to France would carry out in the event of a major war. His military background must have been a real asset, but Fisher's refusal to enter detailed planning arrangements with the army limited the value of the work. At least he was in London.

Lacking the sea time necessary to be promoted, Beatty took command of the battleship HMS *Queen* in December 1908, serving in the Atlantic fleet under Admiral Prince Louis of Battenberg. Once again the ship was a credit to her captain, while the admiral was more cerebral than the average, although somewhat lazy. The exercises had a greater sense of realism, reflecting the latest thinking on weapons and strategy. Though Battenberg's report helped to secure the special Order in Council required for Beatty's promotion to rear admiral on 1 January 1910, he still lacked sufficient sea time. The irrelevance of such regulations in this case could not have been more obvious. Beatty was a very good seaman, had commanded four ships and had nothing left to prove. At thirty-eight, he was the youngest admiral since Nelson.

The next two years were spent ashore, although attendance at the spring 1911 Naval War course in Portsmouth was highly significant, both for the opportunity to learn and for the intellectual stimulus it provided. In July 1911, fresh from the course, he turned down the post of second-in-command of the Atlantic fleet. Having told the First Lord's secretary that he wanted to join the Home Fleet or the Admiralty and not the Atlantic fleet, he refused the offer, missing an opportunity to serve under John Jellicoe in the process. While some saw this as arrogance, fuelled by wealth, others were simply jealous of anyone able to refuse an unwanted appointment. Although one-time naval captain King George V sympathised, Beatty was taking a risk. At least he had a safety net of dollars: his wife, newly admitted to court, would inherit her father's fortune. She was already heavily engaged in spending the money, buying and renting houses and finally a steam yacht, the *Sheelah*, which gave her wandering spirit some rest. But it was once again a sudden shift of personnel that would rescue Beatty from the prospect of early retirement.

Churchill

In October 1911 Winston Churchill became First Lord of the Admiralty, where he found the sea lords unwilling to offer Beatty further employment. With typical bravado, and no little wisdom, Churchill interviewed Beatty for the key post of the First Lord's naval secretary: he was greatly struck by 'the profound sagacity of his comments expressed in language free from technical jargon'.[4] A curious combination of the disapproval of his superiors and shared memories of Sudanese service ensured that Beatty was appointed on 8 January 1912. The naval secretary was the First Lord's confidential adviser on professional questions and a constant companion on his travels. It was a demanding job, and with Churchill at the helm it required tact, determination and the confidence to stand up to the boss on frequent occasions. The youth and arrogance of both parties made quarrels inevitable, but they soon understood one another and proved an effective team.

Many of those who had thwarted Beatty's ambition only six months earlier were now, to a large extent, in his power. Hitherto, Beatty's opinion of Churchill, a radical Liberal minister known for attacking naval budgets, had been anything but complimentary. But once he took the new post, Churchill became enamoured of his charge, and Beatty found the First Lord's enthusiasm a healthy alternative to the studied indifference commonly affected by the political elite. Churchill had the energy and the ability to make the navy's case to the Cabinet, and with Beatty's support he was rarely without a good argument. The position papers Beatty wrote at this time reveal a mature strategic concept and considerable attention to the latest thinking. He provided effective, intelligent responses to Churchill's questions and restrained the more extreme measures brought forward by the continuing influence of John Fisher. Beatty's advice on the disposition of the fleet in a German war, submitted in April 1912, was a very good basis for pre-war planning.[5]

Nor was Beatty backward in exploiting the opportunity to advance his career. As an experienced cruiser captain, he secured temporary command of an armoured cruiser squadron for the six-week period of the 1912 summer manoeuvres, quickly bringing his reserve fleet ships up to war readiness. This command was an ideal rehearsal for his next seagoing appointment and cannot have been an accident. His flag captain, Alfred Chatfield, had clearly made an impression on Beatty on the war course and would remain with him for the rest of his seagoing service.

Although Beatty was a bold huntsman with a zest for speed and initiative, he was anything but an unthinking fire-eater – a type with which the pre-war navy was amply provided. He was an educated, reflective officer, widely read and suitably instructed. He took a serious interest in naval history, while his comprehension of Clausewitz, the Prussian philosopher of war, reflected both the teaching at Portsmouth of the brilliant naval historian and strategist Julian Corbett and his own experience of combat.[6] His definition of the attributes of a good cruiser captain, too, was pure Corbett, drawn almost verbatim from that author's *The Campaign of Trafalgar* of 1910.[7] Beatty may not have been an intellectual, but he recognised their value, appointing the cerebral Reginald Plunkett to be his staff commander in 1913; it helped that Plunkett was also an aristocrat.[8]

Beatty had supported Churchill's proposal to introduce a naval staff, despite the reduction it would mean in the influence of his own office. However, he cannot have been satisfied by the half-baked scheme that resulted. Churchill's Admiralty War Staff lacked executive authority, which meant that it had little value; executive authority was the basis of the success of the Great German General Staff, the model of all such organisations. The common defence that the navy lacked the staff officers to run such an organisation is given the lie by Beatty, who was perfectly competent and significantly better equipped in intellect, experience and human understanding than either of Churchill's two pre-war choices, Ernest Troubridge and Doveton Sturdee. However, Beatty was not looking for another shore post. He had his eye on a prize for which any admiral would have given his right arm: commanding the battlecruiser squadron. Serving at the Admiralty, Beatty was intimately involved in the cycle of naval commands, using his position as a springboard to the coveted command. He had learnt a lot about politics, and even more about Churchill – lessons that would stand him in good stead in the years that followed.

Battlecruiser Admiral

Few naval officers have been so uniquely identified with a specific weapon system as Beatty. He took command of the British battle-cruiser squadron in early 1913, shortly after the ships had been reclassified, and led them for the next five years. By the time he left the command, the type had been largely discredited, and by the time his career was over the designation itself was rapidly fading into history.

The original battlecruisers, the *Invincible* class of 1906, combined battleship-calibre guns, high speed and cruiser levels of protection in a potent package. They were ideally configured for oceanic warfare, and ensured reliability by combining strong, high freeboard hulls, good crew space and powerful, relatively understressed machinery. The *Indefatigable* of 1908 offered a slight improvement, in speed at least, but in 1909 the *Lion* provided a quantum leap in firepower, with 13.5-inch guns, thicker armour and higher speed to counter German battlecruisers. When *Lion* entered service in 1912, she seemed to be the ideal modern warship, sailing at twenty-eight knots – or thirty if you believed Fisher – with eight heavy guns and three immense funnels. She was four thousand tons heavier than the battleships built that year, and far more impressive. This was the symbol of British naval deterrence.

Lion and her relatives were well-armed, seaworthy ships. They were adequately protected for their role, though protection was limited in order to save money and weight. Technology in this field was moving fast, however. Two ships funded by the Commonwealth countries, *Australia* and *New Zealand*, were built to the now outdated *Indefatigable* design, saddling the service with two more obsolescent vessels. In 1915 Beatty discovered Germany had adopted a very different design. They built fast battleships, accepting the disadvantages of low freeboard, cramped accommodation and highly stressed machinery in order to produce better fighting ships. For combat in the North Sea, they were superior to the British super-cruisers. The faster speed and heavier guns that the British ships offered were potentially valuable qualities largely negated by the poor performance of British heavy shell and the failure of human systems.[9]

Beatty developed the doctrine for the new force from existing cruiser practice. Long before the *Invincible*, armoured cruisers had combined fleet scouting with a fast flanking role in battle. Once equipped with battleship-calibre guns, the temptation to join the fight became irresistible. Beatty considered that his primary mission was reconnaissance superiority: his cruisers would use speed and firepower to demolish enemy scouting lines, pushing his forces within sight of the enemy fleet and providing his admiral with the best information. Once battle was joined he would deploy his force as fast wing, another Nelsonian concept developed in 1805 but not used at Trafalgar. The battlecruisers could fix the enemy, attack their flanks and conduct an effective pursuit of the defeated force.

Once in command Beatty began to exercise his ships at high speed. Early attempts at long-range gunnery revealed that their fire-control systems were ineffective at maximum range. The standard nine-foot base coincidence range-finders were inaccurate beyond fifteen thousand yards, and the sights of the early battlecruisers were limited to this range, although the guns were capable of firing to the horizon. Furthermore, firing at high speed added further complications: the ships vibrated and generated enormous quantities of coal smoke, which combined with spray and blast to obscure the view.

Unlike the battle fleet, where control and cohesion was the rule, Beatty placed a far higher premium on initiative and individual action. This was the essence of cruiser practice – and always had been. In combat he expected captains to follow his lead, which was easy while he led from the front. He believed that his subordinates should understand his ideas and methods, anticipate his actions or act in his absence. This was the model that Nelson had employed at the Nile and Trafalgar, one the Germans would recognise as *Auftragstaktik* or mission analysis. There were conscious echoes of the Trafalgar memorandum in his words and concepts, reinforcing the images of Nelson hanging on his cabin bulkhead. Beatty's concept was one that Fisher had understood but lacked the leadership to exploit. It was also what Hornby expected, once he had drilled his squadron to a suitably high standard, and formed the core of George Tryon's abortive tactical revolution in the early 1890s.[10]

Beatty led the largest, fastest and most imposing warships afloat, and tried to match his outsized persona to the task. He applied himself to motivating men engaged in the most arduous, endless, soul-destroying and filthy task on the ship, that of coaling – battlecruisers burnt enormous quantities of coal when steaming at high speed. Beatty visited the ships and spoke to the men, communicating his pride in the elite status of the force. The image he projected on the lower deck – the fearless horseman, bold, dashing and courageous – was ideally suited to the task in hand, though it somewhat misrepresented him. Journalists rushed to make him the navy's poster boy and his flagship, HMS *Lion*, the modern *Victory*. Much as he affected to hate being 'advertised',[11] public fame helped to insulate him from the penalties of failure, and he came to value matinee-idol status as something that helped advance his career.

In 1914 Beatty's force was dispatched to the Baltic for a courtesy visit to St Petersburg. As ever, court ceremonial found him on fine form: British hospitality was well calculated and hugely effective. But even as the toasts were being drunk, events in Sarajevo cast a dark cloud over Europe.

War

Like most of his naval colleagues, Sir David Beatty – newly awarded the KCB as a reward for a highly successful period of command – went to war with a sense of relief and brimful of confidence. Promotion to acting vice admiral on 2 August made him the senior cruiser admiral in the Grand Fleet, now assembled at Scapa Flow. The appointment of John Jellicoe to the chief command met with his approval. However, the widely anticipated naval Armageddon in the North Sea failed to materialise. The Germans, inferior in numbers and firepower, were unwilling to face the heirs of Nelson in open battle. Instead, the war developed into a series of skirmishes between light forces, with submarines taking an increasing toll of warships. Such invisible threats hampered the application of naval power, while diplomacy crippled the economic blockade and a lethargic Admiralty wasted the few opportunities that did occur.

After every fruitless sweep across the North Sea, the battlecruisers returned to Scapa Flow to resume the back-breaking misery of coaling ship. The failure to find and fight the enemy at a time when the army was heavily engaged in France and Belgium was especially frustrating for officers like Beatty, who had brothers at the front. Fortunately for his peace of mind, Beatty was soon in action. On 28

August his force was detached to support a sweep of the Heligoland Bight by cruisers, destroyers and submarines based at Harwich. Much confusion was caused by the failure of the Admiralty to inform the Harwich units that Beatty was in support, an oversight with potentially disastrous consequences. At 10.00 hours Beatty learnt that Commodore Reginald Tyrwhitt's force was heavily engaged with the German cruisers some forty miles to the south. This required him to make his first big decision of the war. After a pause to reflect on the risk from submarines and mines, he took the bold course, steaming to support Tyrwhitt. Two hours later, Beatty's five battlecruisers emerged from the mist, sinking three German light cruisers. Having secured a handsome victory, Beatty ordered a withdrawal before any German capital ships arrived. In the euphoria of victory some serious failures in command and reporting were overlooked.[12]

Quick to complain that his action had not elicited any praise from Whitehall, Beatty also blamed the Admiralty War Staff, and especially its chief, Admiral Sir Doveton Sturdee, for slow proceedings, pedestrian ideas and a complete lack of warlike spirit. Not surprisingly, he welcomed Fisher's return as First Sea Lord in October – 'he has energy, ideas and low cunning – which is what we need' – though he presciently predicted the relationship with Churchill would not last six months.[13] Fisher was devoted to the battlecruisers, and Beatty pressed for all ten British units to be collected under his flag: at the time two were in the South Atlantic, sinking Admiral von Spee's force, another was in the Pacific, escorting Australian troop ships, a fourth was guarding the Dardanelles, where an isolated German battlecruiser was hiding, and a fifth lay off the eastern end of the Panama Canal, just in case von Spee came that way. Six months would elapse before all ten were in home waters.

Beatty's assessment of Fisher reflected his own appreciation of what was required in war: he had little time for the routine, formulaic procedures that satisfied his contemporaries. His concept of leadership was permissive, dominated by character and conduct: the orders he produced for his fleet reflected that in their brevity and their insistence on the primacy of keeping contact with the enemy. These views ultimately led to clashes with Jellicoe, who believed that the Royal Navy's attempt to manage out the uncertainties of war would be harmed if senior officers were given much leeway to use their initiative. Beatty's own ability to deliver was undermined by a failure to attend to those details that admirals from James, Duke of York to 'Uncle Geoff' Hornby had rightly considered the foundation of success. Permissive tactics were only an option for thoroughly professional forces. Jellicoe may have lacked imagination, but he was a master of detail: his procedures did not fail.

On 15 December the German High Seas Fleet staged a major raid on the north-east coast of England. Rear Admiral Franz Hipper's battlecruiser force bombarded Scarborough, Hartlepool and Whitby before laying mines and retiring. The Admiralty had anticipated the operation by reading German radio signals, and placed Beatty and a battle squadron from Jellicoe's Grand Fleet to intercept. The strategic direction was excellent, although the British were unaware that the High Seas Fleet, which had sailed in support, came close to turning the tables. In the event thick, blustery weather complicated the work of the scouting cruisers on both sides, and Beatty lost contact with Hipper by sending a badly worded signal to his own cruisers, ordering them to resume their position when they were in action. Garbled reports of this skirmish led the German commander-in-chief to turn for home, leaving Hipper to his own devices. With Beatty's help, these proved adequate.

The inevitable post-mortem missed the key point. It was deeply worrying that Beatty either did not see or would not admit that errors committed by his staff had caused the loss of contact. Signal Lieutenant Ralph Seymour had been picked for his social graces: he was not a specialist and on at least four separate occasions he had issued misleading signals, with serious consequences. However, these errors were no more than a symptom of the 'amateur' culture of the battlecruisers. This culture developed in part because Beatty now sailed from Rosyth, on the Firth of Forth. This placed his ships closer to the central North Sea, and to the fleshpots of Edinburgh. While Jellicoe's Grand Fleet endured a monastic, spartan life at Scapa Flow, the battlecruisers had all the glory and far less hardship. The distance between the two bases denied Jellicoe and Beatty the opportunity for frequent personal meetings, the heart and soul of Nelsonian leadership. While their relationship was based on mutual regard, it needed more than polite correspondence to keep it alive through the hard days of war.

After 15 December, the Admiralty revised its procedures. When the Germans put to sea, the Admiralty would direct Beatty and the Harwich force until Jellicoe was at sea, when he would assume overall command. When Beatty's force went to sea in support of a seaplane raid on Christmas Day, and again in mid-January without heavy support, the Germans concluded that they could intercept him with their own battlecruisers. On 23 January Admiralty intelligence indicated that a battlecruiser sortie was imminent. Once again the strategic moves, largely directed by Admiral Sir Arthur Wilson, were excellent. Shortly after dawn on the following day Beatty completed a rendezvous with Tyrwhitt thirty miles off the Dogger Bank. The British were ideally placed to get between Hipper and his base, and they had all day to finish the job. Beatty had five battlecruisers; Hipper had three and a powerful armoured cruiser. As soon as he had identified the enemy, Hipper set course for home at his best speed, and Beatty followed on a parallel course to the south-south-east but several knots faster. This left *Indomitable* and *New Zealand* lagging behind *Lion*, *Tiger* and *Princess Royal*.

Once again the devil lay in the detail. Beatty's orders for the distribution of fire were misinterpreted by Captain Pelly of the *Tiger*, which left the *Moltke* to conduct undisturbed gunnery practice against the *Lion*. Hipper concentrated his fire on Beatty's flagship, but the British were the first to score an important hit, as *Lion* crippled the armoured cruiser *Blucher* early in the engagement and Hipper had no option but to abandon her to her fate. One down, three to go. One or two shells from *Lion* then smashed into Hipper's flagship, the *Seydlitz*: within minutes, both after-turrets had been burnt out, and the massive magazines came perilously close to exploding. *Lion* did not follow up this success, which allowed *Seydlitz* to maintain her speed.[14] The British scored no more significant hits. Despite being outnumbered, the Germans outshot their foes four to one, scoring twenty-two hits to six. Most of the hits were on *Lion*, which had outstripped the other British battlecruisers. Just when Beatty wanted to close for the kill, the flagship lost power from both engines and fell out of line. Moments earlier he had made an unnecessary turn to port, to avoid a mysterious 'periscope' that he, and he alone, had spotted. Without electrical power to send a radio message, Beatty had to rely on flag signals, and once again Ralph Seymour translated Beatty's thoughts into the worst possible mess. Rear Admiral Moore assumed command, reading the combination of flags flying from *Lion*'s halyards as an order to finish off the crippled *Blucher* rather than pursue Hipper. Beatty had condemned the appointment of Moore, well aware that they were not on the same wavelength. But Moore could only obey the signals that flew on *Lion*: an order is an order. By the time Beatty managed to board the *Princess Royal*, the enemy was out of reach. He turned for home, his crippled flagship under tow.

Whether the British could actually have completed the destruction of Hipper's ships had the signals not been misleading is a moot point. Modern research has shown that the British gunnery was anything but impressive, *Lion*'s being no better than the others'.[15] Hipper's ships shot better and proved very tough opponents: even the obsolete *Blucher* took a terrific pounding before she sank. Only *Tiger* had accurate range-finders, while the others lacked director control and some ships did not have a fire-control table. The under-practised British ships would have suffered heavily had they come to close quarters with the enemy. One useful side-effect of the action was that it provided breathing space, during which Jellicoe underwent a long overdue operation – piles had bedevilled his performance throughout the war!

While Jellicoe was under the knife, Beatty's force was renamed the Battlecruiser Fleet, with three squadrons each of three ships, in addition to the flagship. Removing the discredited Moore and changing a few senior officers ensured that Beatty was surrounded by old friends and kindred spirits. This allowed him to work his magic; his penetrating intellect impressed everyone. When Churchill visited *Lion* on 3 February, the usually phlegmatic Rear Admiral Pakenham took him aside and declared, with intense conviction, 'Nelson has come again.'[16] Pakenham, Osmond de Brock and Horace Hood commanded the three squadrons, while Beatty's old messmate Walter Cowan was Pakenham's flag captain. These men repaid their leader with unquestioning loyalty to the end of his life. They helped create the image of the Battlecruiser Fleet as a dashing, dynamic force, very much in their leader's image – the antithesis of the dull, regimented Grand Fleet.

Although he maintained his Nelsonian charisma in public, Beatty was depressed by the 'terrible failure' at the Dogger Bank and determined that it must not be repeated.[17] He criticised his subordinates for following orders, rather than the higher doctrine of ensuring the destruction of the enemy, though it was unfair to blame men who had served all their lives in a navy that prized control and obedience. They could not be expected to change their mental processes overnight. Beatty took an interest in his junior admirals and captains because he believed that they could effect the necessary cultural change, and he also adjusted his doctrine to profit from the first clash of dreadnought warships. He concluded that in any future action, ranges of twelve to fourteen thousand yards would be ideal, outside the range of enemy secondary guns or torpedoes. He believed his best ships were a knot or two faster than Hipper's average, and there had been nothing wrong with the engineering performance of the squadron, until *Lion*'s damage in action. The answer to the problem, he concluded, lay in increasing the rate of hitting, and to this end he ordered all the ships under his command to emphasise high rates of fire – in effect substituting numbers of rounds for precision. In this ill-conceived measure lay the seeds of catastrophe; no gunnery specialist would have advised such an approach. Within a year all the battlecruisers had removed the flash-tight interlocks from the ammunition hoists that carried cordite charges from the magazine, safe in the bowels of the ship, to the exposed gun mountings. Only one ship restored the safety measures before the next battle – HMS *Lion*. Newly appointed Warrant Officer Gunner Alexander Grant, a Grand Fleet man, refused to accept responsibility for the ship until they were replaced. By insisting on following correct procedure and rejecting Battlecruiser Fleet methods Grant saved himself, Beatty and the crew of the *Lion*.[18]

Beatty revised his standing orders in February to emphasise the primacy of initiative, and defined the role of the battlecruisers in a fleet action as being to achieve scouting dominance and deliver the enemy fleet up for destruction. It would only engage the enemy battle fleet when the Grand Fleet came into action. His real concern was to catch Hipper's force and to finish what he had begun on the Dogger Bank. His view of the war was dominated by the thought of this missed opportunity and the glory that had been within his grasp. This was his 'particular quarry', and no one was going to deny him the satisfaction of being 'in at the kill'.[19] The choice of language was revealing. But the Battlecruiser Fleet would have to wait another eighteen months for the next chase.

In the interval, reflections on the failure of 24 January did nothing to improve his mood or his relationship with Jellicoe. The two men agreed on all the essential points, but Beatty was always pressing to have more ships under his command, especially the five new twenty-four-knot *Queen Elizabeth*-class fast battleships. Jellicoe refused, well aware that with such reinforcements Beatty would engage the entire High Seas Fleet. Fisher's resignation in May was a profound shock: 'a worse calamity than a defeat at sea'.[20] Fisher had been an indulgent father to Beatty and the battlecruisers. Beatty had not restricted his concerns to the North Sea, troubled as he was by German Zeppelins, the Western Front and the submarine threat to merchant shipping. He had made frequent use of his access to Fisher and Churchill, fearing Jellicoe was not making the case for reinforcements with sufficient vigour. Now they had departed he lacked an outlet for his hopes and fears, and for the want of a better target he tended to blame Jellicoe for his problems, labelling him 'simple'.[21] Much of this friction could have been avoided if the two admirals had met regularly, but distance and the submarine threat made dinner and social calls impossible. When they met, on 3 February 1916, it was for the first time in five months.

Despite his dark moods and desperation to catch his elusive enemy, Beatty began 1916 with absolute faith in the ability of his officers, his men and his ships. This confidence was reflected in an increasingly rakish public image: he wore his cap at a jaunty angle and sported a non-regulation jacket with three rather than the obligatory four buttons. In doing so, he demonstrated a conscious disregard for trifling details, a character flaw that might seem innocent enough but would soon cost the lives of three thousand men.

Jutland: The Dawn of a Controversy

On 30 May 1916 the Admiralty, once again alerted by German radio traffic, concluded that a sortie was imminent and sent Beatty and Jellicoe to sea. They were to rendezvous in the Skagerrack the following afternoon. Beatty commanded six battlecruisers and four *Queen Elizabeth*-class battleships of the Fifth Battle Squadron, temporarily attached to his fleet while the Third Battlecruiser Squadron was at Scapa Flow for gunnery practice. Beatty had not troubled himself, or his staff, to brief Rear Admiral Evan-Thomas on

Battlecruiser Fleet doctrine and procedures: this mattered because Beatty's practice was quite distinct from Jellicoe's on such key issues as the importance of initiative and following the admiral's movements. The fleet was completed by twelve light cruisers, twenty-seven destroyers and a seaplane carrier.

If the German fleet was at sea, it would be Beatty's job to find it, crush its scouting forces and deliver it up to the guns of the Grand Fleet. This should have been easy: he had twice as many fast capital ships as Hipper. However, Admiral Reinhard Scheer's plan relied on Beatty rising to the lure of Hipper's scouting group, so it could be cut off and brought under the guns of the High Seas Fleet. The following day the Admiralty staff erroneously concluded that the High Seas Fleet was still in harbour, information that confirmed Jellicoe's decision to reduce speed, save coal and delay the rendezvous. More significantly, when Beatty encountered Hipper he had every reason to believe the German battlecruisers were alone.

The two battlecruiser forces made visual contact just before 15.30 on the 31st, when the First Scouting Group was steaming northwest. Although his squadrons were widely dispersed, Beatty immediately ordered a large turn to the east. However, the signal was made initially only by flags, which were not visible from the Fifth Battle Squadron. The same mistake had already resulted in the battleships trailing astern; now the gap opened further until the signal was repeated by searchlight. Even then, the order only required Evan-Thomas to maintain a parallel course. It seemed that Beatty, having realised that Hipper had only five ships, was determined to finish the job with his six battlecruisers. Hipper responded by turning about to the south-east, and subsequently to south-south-east, courses that would draw Beatty towards Scheer. Meanwhile, Beatty needed to bring his battlecruisers into line and dispose them to prevent mutual smoke interference, but they were still manoeuvring when the Germans opened fire. Beatty's ships had had no time to complete the necessary range-finding to predict the course, speed and range of their targets. In the event, only one ship, *Princess Royal*, took the necessary set of readings; the rest went into battle with hopelessly overestimated ranges. The position of the two slower ships of the Second Battlecruiser Squadron was made worse by the need to steam at full speed to regain their station. The resulting smoke and vibration made range-finding desperately difficult.[22]

When Beatty opened fire at 15.48, his initial salvoes went two thousand yards beyond the German ships. Having avoided both a radical alteration of course and excessive speed, the Germans used their superior stereoscopic range-finders to obtain more accurate opening ranges. Heavy ship gunnery required the firing ship to achieve a straddle – that is, shells landing on either side of the target – before going to rapid salvo fire, literally sending a deluge of heavy projectiles onto the enemy vessel, until the observers could see that they had lost the target. Then the process started all over again with deliberate ranging fire, based on fire-control predictions.[23] Beatty seriously compromised this process with his impulsive turn to contact, and slack procedure exacerbated the problem. The Germans found the target long before the British – aided by the conditions that silhouetted Beatty's ships against the hazy light of the setting sun.

To make matters worse, the fire-distribution plan failed, as it had at the Dogger Bank, leaving *Derfflinger* unengaged for a precious ten minutes. One of the first ships to suffer was *Lion*, and at 16.00 her midships turret was hit and burnt out. Only Warrant Officer Grant's insistence on refitting the safety interlocks saved the ship when a massive cordite fire flared up some minutes later. Then, at 16.03, the rear ship, *Indefatigable*, was hit by two salvoes from *Von der Tann*: she rolled over onto her side and blew up with the loss of 1,026 men. Beatty pressed on, but twenty-three minutes later *Queen Mary* followed her elder sister under the choppy waters of the North Sea, taking 1,266 men with her and leaving behind a truly apocalyptic pall of smoke that rained debris onto the following ships. At this point Beatty turned to his flag captain, Alfred Chatfield, and observed, 'There seems to be something wrong with our bloody ships today.' As he would admit two days later, there was rather more wrong with the system than the ships. Beatty and his fleet had thrown away the advantages of speed, range and weight of fire, allowing the smaller and less heavily armed Germans to turn a five to six inferiority into a five to four advantage in under thirty minutes. The Germans were hitting four times faster than the British, totalling twenty-two to six.[24] Already 'decisively beaten',[25] Beatty was on the verge of annihilation because he had blundered into battle against a cool professional. At this rate Hipper would finish him off before Scheer arrived. Beatty was forced to open the range.

Beatty was saved by the timely arrival of Evan-Thomas's squadron shortly after *Indefatigable* went down. When Beatty's staff finally repeated the signal by searchlight, a simple procedure that should have been carried out at the time it was originally sent, Evan-Thomas cut the corners to bring his ships into long-range action with the rear of Hipper's force. Fifteen-foot-base range-finders and superior gunnery procedures enabled the Fifth Battle Squadron to turn the tables in minutes. Reeling from the impact of massive fifteen-inch shells, *Von der Tann* was forced to turn away. The other German ships followed to avoid a destroyer attack that Beatty had ordered. Hipper's battle report stressed the accuracy and power of Evan-Thomas's gunnery and contrasted it with the ineffective performance of the British battlecruisers.

Just when it seemed he had snatched victory from the jaws of defeat, Beatty was stunned by reports from his light cruisers that the High Seas Fleet was steaming into view. That changed everything. Instead of fighting a second Dogger Bank, he faced the prospect of a second Trafalgar, and his role in the Grand Fleet battle plan took precedence over his lunge for glory. At 16.40 he reversed course to lead Scheer towards Jellicoe, whose presence was unknown to the Germans. It was Beatty's job to keep the Germans blind until Jellicoe opened fire. Once again he failed to make his intentions clear. Evan-Thomas continued south, exchanging fire with the leading elements of the High Seas Fleet until 16.48; *Barham* had been heavily damaged before Beatty belatedly ordered him to turn.

The rival battlecruisers resumed action on the opposite course at 17.40, but the light conditions now favoured the British, who made significantly more hits. While his ships were making a better job of battle, Beatty failed to carry out the fundamental task of a scouting commander: he did not provide Jellicoe with accurate information on the course and speed of the enemy. The frustrated and annoyed Jellicoe nonetheless ultimately deployed the fleet at the perfect moment, 'crossing the T' of Scheer's advancing line and pouring in a series of crushingly accurate broadsides at ten to twelve thousand yards that forced the German admiral to make the first of two emergency 180-degree turns. Much of the credit for keeping Hipper from spotting Jellicoe belonged to Rear Admiral Hood, whose Third Battlecruiser Squadron demolished the German light cruisers and drove Hipper back, although his flagship, the *Invincible*, followed her sisters to the bottom of the sea at 18.33, broken in half by another catastrophic explosion that took Hood and 1,016 others to their deaths.

By this time Beatty was leading the Grand Fleet south. At 19.47 he signalled Jellicoe requesting that the leading battleship division follow him to cut off the Germans. Jellicoe concurred, but Admiral Jerram never closed up. Beatty was furious, and took out his frustration on Hipper's ships, but he lost contact with them as night fell – when another blunder compromised the Grand Fleet night-recognition signal.

Beatty displayed commendable resolution, clear judgement and the right spirit at Jutland, but his leadership was vitiated by major errors in procedure and detail that demonstrated an ignorance of the basic weapons system of his force and the connection between it and the handling of the ships. By contrast, Jellicoe proved unimaginative, cautious and conventional, but the professionalism of his Grand Fleet left the Battlecruiser Fleet looking shambolic. Yet for all his failings, Beatty was a great commander, able to see the larger picture and to grasp complex issues. He expected his subordinates to use their skill and judgement, to show initiative. But he failed to explain himself with the clarity that had been the basis of Nelson's success, and left everyone guessing. Jellicoe had little faith in his followers and preferred to do everything himself. Hand-picked by Fisher to execute the tactical command of a fleet under the operational direction of an all-seeing Admiralty, Jellicoe performed at his best when the Admiralty failed him, but his default setting was to avoid losing command of the North Sea.

That night, as Beatty led the fleet south, Scheer fought his way through the light forces stationed to the rear of the Grand Fleet, without Jellicoe knowing what was going on. By the next morning he was safely out of range. The Admiralty had intercepted a critical message revealing Scheer's route home but failed to pass it on.

On 2 June Beatty arrived back at Rosyth, depressed by the heavy losses his force had suffered and the growing realisation that a second, far greater victory had slipped through his fingers – and he had been the last flag officer in contact with the High Seas Fleet. While Beatty comforted himself by unfairly blaming Jellicoe for failing to press his advantage, his objection to the Admiralty's pessimistic press release, which accepted German reports of their losses at face value, was shared by the entire service. The British lost three battle-cruisers, three old armoured cruisers and some destroyers; the Germans lost a battlecruiser, an old battleship, several light cruisers and destroyers. In addition, Hipper's ships were out of action for months: their stout protection had kept them afloat and steaming, but their turrets and control systems had been destroyed. British casualties were slightly more than double those of the Germans, almost all of them from five big ships that blew up. After the battle, Beatty tacitly admitted his responsibility for the three battlecruiser losses, on 2 June symbolically ordering that the flash-tight interlocks be restored. After repeating his fateful words to Chatfield about something being wrong with 'our bloody ships', he added, 'and our bloody system too!'[26] But even when tormented by a sense of fail-ure, Beatty never let drop the public image of a confident, dynamic commander.

The Germans had also learnt a harsh lesson: they could not face the Grand Fleet in battle, and had been lucky to get home without much heavier losses. After a nervous sortie in August, they would not come out again. Running away is not the same as victory.

Commanding the Grand Fleet, 1916–19

In November 1916 Jellicoe was appointed First Sea Lord, largely to deal with the U-boat threat to merchant shipping. As the only other admiral with a high public profile, Beatty was specially promoted on the 27th and took over the Grand Fleet the following day, on board Jellicoe's flagship, the *Iron Duke*. It was a big step up from the Battlecruiser Fleet to command the entire Grand Fleet, but Beatty took the translation in his stride, as he had every other promotion in his remarkable career. Now he had to motivate and invigorate thirty-five thousand men, to convince them that next time they would get their Trafalgar. His public performances exuded Nelson-ian confidence and commitment, securing the admiration of officers and men and helping to maintain the navy's public image at a time when the army was heavily engaged. He was also careful to ensure that his reputation was maintained: in concert with Jellicoe he sup-pressed a report by the Corps of Naval Constructors that identified the real cause of the loss of the three battlecruisers, publicly main-taining that it was due to inadequate armour protection. The lie was necessary if morale was to be maintained. That the morale of the Grand Fleet held up ranks amongst Beatty's greatest achievements.

Delegating the technical lessons of Jutland to trusted subordinates, Beatty concentrated on the strategic ramifications. Although still anxious for a decision, he was far too astute to take unnecessary risks. He preferred not to risk battle until the armour-piercing shells had been improved, and saw no good reason to enter the southern North Sea. He believed that the economic blockade, steadily tightened as the war progressed, would bring Germany to her knees, pressing for more resources and stricter implementation. He received little support from Jellicoe, who greatly underestimated the impact of British economic warfare. Beatty rejected calls to shift some of his heavy forces south against a wholly imaginary invasion threat, and began work on new methods of attack. Significantly, he supported the development of aircraft carriers for strike missions against German bases.

As might have been expected, Beatty quickly replaced Jellicoe's mandatory Grand Fleet Battle Orders with two pages of optional 'Instructions', emphasising the need for subordinates to use their initiative. He stressed the need for continuous pursuit and the maximum use of all means of attack, moving his flag to the twenty-four-knot *Queen Elizabeth* to ensure he was not confined to the line of battle. When the United States joined the war in April 1917, an American battle squadron joined the fleet. Beatty rose to the challenge, bringing the Americans into line with British procedures without offending them or risking their inexperienced ships coming into contact with the Germans. Although the chance of a fleet action receded as the Germans focused on the U-boat campaign, their battleship crews already showing signs of the unrest that would ultimately destroy the fleet, Beatty kept his own fleet ready, despite shifting destroyers to the anti-submarine campaign. Although profoundly unimpressed by Jellicoe's efforts as First Sea Lord, and by his lightweight subordinates, Beatty had no desire to replace him. Instead, he provided Prime Minister Lloyd George with an alternative source of advice and helped to hasten the introduction of defensive convoys. His position gave him the authority to contribute to Allied command decisions, and he made sure his views were heard. In contrast to the pessimistic Jellicoe, Beatty exuded confidence. At a time when there was much to be gloomy about, this was a valuable quality. In his dealings with the King, politicians, allies and soldiers Beatty was the complete naval statesman. His elevation to the First Sea Lord's office was only a matter of time – but it would be a time of his own choosing.

If his career was proceeding apace, then his private life had become increasingly turbulent. His highly strung wife vociferously objected to sharing Beatty with the navy and the nation, and both were unfaithful. Beatty had begun a long-term affair in late 1916 with Eugénie Godfrey-Fausset, the wife of a naval officer and royal equerry. Although Beatty remained close to Ethel, the relationship caused him much pain, and the chance to release his cares in correspondence with Eugénie was a priceless asset at what would otherwise have been a grim and depressing period. That correspondence reveals Beatty as more intellectually rounded than is sometimes believed: he requests that she send him a copy of Plutarch, as his is packed away at home, and the pair engage in mutual study of Arabic and Persian verse, exchanging amorous confidences in those scripts.[27] Beatty was an educated man, possessing a remarkable ability to master details and process information. He gloried in men of talent, from the unreflective zeal of Roger Keyes to the incisive intellectual arrogance of Herbert Richmond. He did not try to micromanage: he believed in using the right man for the job, trusting his staff and, on most occasions at least, making allowance for human failings.

By 1918 it was clear that the High Seas Fleet was wasting away, stripped of the best officers and men for the submarine war. Beatty took the entire Grand Fleet to sea for the last time on 23 April 1918, St George's Day, when Scheer tried to catch one of the Scandinavian convoys. Thereafter he was content to exercise command of the seas with detachments. Jellicoe had been dismissed in late 1917, replaced by Beatty's old friend Rosslyn Wemyss, another cultivated and urbane seaman. They worked well together – until the end of the war.

When Germany accepted an armistice in November, Beatty insisted that the entire High Seas Fleet must surrender unconditionally and that all submarines should be handed over to Britain. His ultimate triumph had been delayed but could not be denied. On 21 November the German fleet arrived in the Firth of Forth between two lines of British warships. The shabby, unkempt appearance of the German ships betrayed only too clearly that mutiny and revolutionary turmoil had wrecked the imperial navy. Beatty did not share this moment with Fisher or Jellicoe, who had done so much to make it possible, and the oversight was deliberate: the internment was stage-managed as a victory parade. When the German ships came to anchor, Beatty sent an entirely unauthorised but deeply pondered signal to their admiral: 'The German flag will be hauled down at sunset today, Thursday, and will not be hoisted again without permission.'[28] Three days later the First Battlecruiser Squadron, led by his old flagship HMS *Lion*, escorted the Germans to Scapa Flow to await the outcome of the peace negotiations. Beatty made sure that his battlecruisers were seen to have won the war.

Command and Control

Throughout the war Beatty was unhappy with the amount of information being passed to him from the Admiralty. The debacle at Jutland reinforced his concern that the shore-based strategic and operational control was error prone and left the men on the spot with too little information to form their own opinions, while the instructions issued were so definite that there was no occasion for the exercise of independent critical judgement. While Jellicoe seems to have been groomed for the role of technocratic executor of other men's policies, Beatty's strengths were entirely different. His active, wide-ranging mind refused to get bogged down in the minutiae of modern war: he left that to his staff. He wanted to grasp the big picture and see his role in the larger context. Consequently Beatty protested when the Admiralty took decisions that affected him, from foisting unwelcome officers on his force to withholding intelligence.

Beatty's real goal was to exercise command in Nelsonian fashion. Nelson had been the model for naval education when he began his career, and rightly so, but the development of wireless radio in the early twentieth century allowed the Admiralty to take operational control. The technical ability to transmit signals was no sooner perfected than senior officers ashore – and politicians as well, whenever Churchill was at the Admiralty – were using it to interfere in the business of the commander afloat. By a potent combination of intellect, resolve, charisma and political skill, Beatty managed to stem the tide of change: he exercised naval command in the heroic mould, as much in appearance as reality, right to the end of the war. When the German fleet was interned, he flouted his orders, treating them as defeated and surrendered foes whose violation of the rules of war did not entitle them to the usual civilities. In this he reflected the mood of the nation and the fleet, rather than the aims of British diplomacy. As Captain Stephen Roskill observed, he was 'the last naval hero'.[29]

The art of the admiral was changing, and the space in which Beatty operated was being eroded. By the end of Hornby's career, the submarine telegraph limited the admiral's ability to direct theatre strategy. Operational issues were still under his command, but the ability to communicate globally, which the British state pioneered, was steadily eroding that role. The emergence of radio – and its revealing by-product, radio-based cryptanalysis – privileged the centre, which collected, processed and analysed intelligence, while depriving the man on the spot of access to the raw material.

Fisher wanted to be a shore admiral long before technology had provided the tools for operational control. Beatty's move to Whitehall was more reluctant: he was a seaman through and through, but recognised that once the guns fell silent he needed to be in the place where the decisive actions would be fought. After 1919, his work would be carried out at a desk and around the Cabinet table.

Peace

When the peace negotiations began, Beatty wanted Britain to recover the strategic island Heligoland and retain the modern German ships. He would be disappointed on both counts. Foolish politicians were content to disarm Heligoland, and on 21 June 1919 the Germans scuttled their ships. At least they were denied to potential rivals: France, Italy, Japan and the United States. By then the ships were no longer Beatty's responsibility. Specially promoted to Admiral of the Fleet on 3 April 1919, at forty-eight the youngest ever, he hauled down his flag on the 7th. After cruising around the Mediterranean with his wife, he led the naval contingent at the London victory parade. On 6 August he became an earl – Baron Beatty of the North Sea and of Brooksby – with the courtesy title of Viscount Borodale for his eldest son, recalling his Irish ancestry. He also received a parliamentary grant of £100,000.

Beatty had seen more combat than anyone else in the fleet, taking a leading role in three significant engagements. He had built a matinee-idol image: cap at a rakish angle, firm jaw jutting into the breeze, every inch the admiral. Sadly he had been nowhere near as good at the business of command as appearances suggested. In two engagements, errors of judgement had allowed the enemy to escape or caused unnecessary losses, while his astonishing and largely unwarranted self-confidence infected his officers and men, leading to slack procedure in key areas. His men lacked the hard-nosed Jervis-like professionalism of their colleagues in Jellicoe's Grand Fleet. At Jutland three battlecruisers exploded and sank with catastrophic loss of life because of sloppy ammunition-handling procedures. His own performance was patchy: poor signalling procedure left his support squadron in the dark, but he did find the enemy and brought it under the guns of the Grand Fleet. The events of 31 May 1916 would be a problem for the rest of Beatty's life, and he devoted much of it to an overt campaign to shift responsibility for the failure onto Jellicoe. While this was unfair, revealing the darker side of Beatty's character, rewriting history was also necessary to sustain his reputation as a successful wartime commander.

Clearly Beatty was not content with his war record. No sooner had his vast command been dispersed than Beatty expected to become First Sea Lord. He was still under fifty, and unlike other wartime leaders, his response to five years of unbroken strain was to carry on. However, Wemyss's plans to make way, accepting the Mediterranean command and the governorship of Malta as a suitable recompense, were blocked by the army, while the government considered Sir Rosslyn an excellent member of the negotiating team in Paris. Furthermore, Churchill, once again in high ministerial office, spoke for many when he suggested that it would be useful to impose stringent reductions on the navy before Beatty took office: he advised Prime Minister Lloyd George that 'once Beatty is enthroned he will be in a position to champion the particularist interest of the Admiralty to an extent which would be quite impossible for Wemyss'.[30] This was a high compliment, if a backhanded one. But Beatty, supported by a powerful press campaign, behaved like a spoilt child; and his wife even managed to upstage him by publicly turning her back on Walter Long, the inoffensive First Lord.

Nonetheless, the post was finally offered: Beatty accepted without hesitation, entering the Admiralty on 1 November 1919 and becoming a model colleague.

First Sea Lord

When the war ended, Beatty was still a young man: his meteoric career left him ample time for shore service. He would hold the post of First Sea Lord for eight years, longer than anyone else in the twentieth century, and it would be here, rather than at sea, that he demonstrated true greatness as an admiral. His apprenticeship under Churchill paid dividends: the future wartime leader proved to be his most dangerous opponent in the political battles to maintain the naval budget against pacifists, economists and the newly created Royal Air Force. As he explained to Ethel, who wanted him to herself: 'You would not have me go down in history as the 1st Sea Lord of the day who made so bad a struggle that our rulers gave up the heritage of Command of the Sea which we have held for over 300 years.'[31] A potent cocktail of concern for his place in history and anxiety to spend as little time as necessary with his wife ensured that Beatty would serve long and hard.

Beatty moved easily in government circles and had no difficulty working with the first Labour ministers. This was vital because his success was largely dependent on the ability of the First Lord and the Junior Civil Lord to win political battles with the Treasury. He served five First Lords, only one of whom did not reciprocate his absolute commitment to the navy: Arthur Lee thought Beatty was 'suffering from a swollen head, that he is of the dashing "cavalry leader" type, without deep or great intelligence, and that Brock is really the *brain*'.[32] This last point was not so much untrue as ill directed. Beatty's ability to present the naval case proved a major asset at civilian meetings, notably the Committee of Imperial Defence, and he did rely on battlecruiser veterans like Brock, the Deputy Chief of Naval Staff, for the intellectual aspects of the argument. He knew how to use a staff: the old traditions of the 'silent service', displayed to good effect by Frederick Richards only thirty years before, were as obsolete as HMS *Victory*. A quick brain and a ready flow of argument were essential in the altogether more complex world that Beatty faced. At every meeting other than Cabinet,

Beatty led the Admiralty team, wartime authority adding weight to his words. Social contacts, too, helped him cultivate political support for the navy: this was an essential part of the job.[33] Well aware that Churchill and Curzon were unusual in appreciating the role of sea power in national strategy, Beatty sent Lloyd George a biography of Sir Francis Drake.[34]

While the navy enjoyed the spectacle of the First Sea Lord giving the law to slippery politicians, Beatty was storing up future problems for the service. Modern scholarship provides a rather different picture of Beatty as 'a formidable, if arrogant and politically naïve, spokesman for the Admiralty'.[35] It appears he was never entirely persuaded that democratic politics had a place in making defence policy, being rather impatient with the inevitable compromises of high office. When he presented the cash-strapped post-war governments with very large demands for new warship construction, he did not anticipate having to haggle and horse-trade: he expected them to behave like gentlemen and pay up. When the Cabinet jibbed at Beatty's demands, the naval members of the Board threatened to resign on several occasions. In the short term Beatty's tactics worked because he possessed a degree of public prestige that they dared not cross, but in the long term treating the Cabinet like errant lieutenants was not a good idea. The politicians simply bided their time and had their revenge in the years that followed.[36]

In the meantime, though, Beatty provided the politicians with an education in the realities of running a global empire. He brought the best of the fleet to serve under him, grooming future naval leaders like Alfred Chatfield and Osmond de Brock while relieving himself of the detailed work that had never been his forte. Fleet Paymaster Frank Spickernell, his secretary for over a decade, continued organising his working routine and ensured he arrived at meetings well briefed.[37] Beatty would have been a great advocate, a barrister of real weight, but, one suspects, an erratic judge. He exploited talent wherever he found it, using spiky intellectual Herbert Richmond to write powerful public speeches,[38] educate naval officers and inaugurate the new Imperial Defence College, where the tri-service relationships that proved vital to the next war were built.

Beatty took office convinced that the strategic needs of the British Empire could only be met by naval superiority. This would provide security and allow Britain to rebuild the essential economic portfolio of trade, investments and shipping. To sustain naval might without risking economic recovery required a delicate balance. The big issues facing Beatty were the resumption of naval construction in the largest classes after a wartime hiatus, the pay and conditions of officers and men, new bases to face the threat of war with Japan, and control of naval aviation. In the first three tasks he proved successful: the Royal Navy won most of the budget battles with the Treasury and had more money to spend than the other two services. Beatty prevented the bureaucrats imposing cuts in naval pay when the cost of living fell, and in 1922, in the absence of his sickly First Lord, he was left to make the case for a major new naval base at Singapore, and he won.[39] The new base would have been ideally placed to sustain the fleet required to meet Japan in 1941 – if the navy had possessed enough ships.

The lack of ships in 1941 was a direct result of the Washington Treaty of 1921 and the naval building limitations that persisted until 1936. In 1921 the United States, already sliding into isolationism and alarmed by the prospect of a naval arms race with Japan and Britain, called an international conference. Under the treaty Britain, for the first time, accepted binding limits on the number, size and characteristics of her warships. The Royal Navy no longer enjoyed worldwide supremacy: it was now only equal in status to the United States Navy. Beatty accepted the diplomatic requirement to avoid a clash with America, but he stressed the critical point, one that his political masters took too lightly: that Britain, unlike the United States, was utterly dependent on her ability to use the seas. Despite the evident truth of this point, political considerations made a settlement with the United States imperative. Lloyd George acknowledged that Beatty's argument against a total ban on new battleships were 'powerful' but continued:

Nevertheless, we feel that the advantages of a ten year absolute naval holiday in capital ships are so great for the causes of peace and disarmament throughout the world, that we are prepared to face the technical objections and inconveniences inseparable from it.[40]

But Washington was the only significant disarmament measure, leaving armies and air forces with unlimited manpower and weapons.

Wemyss had derailed American plans for naval dominance at the Paris peace conference in 1919, and the Washington Treaty removed the risk of a costly arms race, allowing Britain a decade of cheap security. But the real prize – American engagement in world affairs – never materialised. The United States turned its back on Europe and the League of Nations, and furthermore did not build up to the treaty limits for more than a decade. The real object of American naval policy was cheap security. In 1927, just as Beatty was leaving office, the follow-up Geneva conference tried to lower the limits to those the Americans currently possessed, giving them naval superiority without shedding blood or dollars. Beatty was scathing: 'The damned Yanks thought they could get it for nothing!'[41]

The Washington process gravely weakened Britain, artificially limiting the navy on which her great-power status depended, while armies and air forces were wholly unrestricted. In 1939 Britain was of less account in world affairs than it had been in 1914 because the Royal Navy was far smaller – and in key areas its ships were obsolescent. Beatty did his best, but ultimately the politicians decided.

Before the Washington process began, Beatty had won a difficult battle over new capital ship construction. He emphasised the continuing invulnerability of modern battleships to all weapons and the need to sustain British industry by resuming construction. Prophetically, he warned that 'specially skilled labour, accustomed to special warship work, is being dispersed, and the longer warship construction is put off, the more difficult it will be to find suitable skilled labour'.[42] The government was persuaded, and four forty-five-thousand-ton battlecruisers were ordered. Once the Washington Treaty had been signed they were cancelled, replaced by two slow thirty-five-thousand-ton battleships. In effect, vastly improved versions of Beatty's ideal warship, all speed and glamour, had been replaced by dour dreadnoughts, more to Jellicoe's taste. These two new ships aside, the battle fleet was made up by ships like the *Queen Elizabeth*, designed before the war. A fifteen-year battleship-building holiday followed Washington, years in which the key industries that produced armour and gun mountings atrophied, causing serious problems when rearmament began with a rush of orders. Beatty's call for these industries to be subsidised in late 1920 had been ignored.[43]

Before the Washington Treaty was signed, Beatty returned to London to oppose savage cuts that the Geddes Committee wanted to apply to all three armed forces. In this 'terrible battle to preserve what can be saved of the Navy for the Empire',[44] he was largely successful. The 1922–3 estimates, the first to be considered after the Washington Treaty, were a major test of Beatty's authority. He refused to accept the proffered figures unless the government publicly reduced the one-power standard, set only the previous year. This forceful, resolute response won the day but did not win any friends at the Treasury: 'Despite intense pressure, Beatty had prevented any further cuts than were inevitable given the naval treaty. The navy was in a far better position to define and defend a new policy than was the army.'[45] Unable to breach Beatty's defences, the Treasury took its pound of flesh from the army, which bore the brunt of defence cuts. This was the correct outcome.

Throughout Beatty's time in office the naval estimates were under enormous pressure, and Treasury inquiries into every aspect of the profession constantly called his attention away from the positive aspects of the job. He met Treasury demands for savings by ensuring the navy's house was in order and then refusing to compromise. Little wonder First Lord William Bridgeman considered his Admiralty 'a remarkably capable set of men, they produced economies much in excess of what I had ventured to hope for'.[46] Such troubles and time-wasting for experienced officers, and the impressive Treasury mandarins who were deployed in opposition, reflected a fundamental failure by government. Time after time Beatty had to hammer home the same points: that the Empire depended on sea communications, while Britain depended on imports of food, fuel and raw materials for her survival. Yet such principles were ignored in the constant pressure for cuts. Restringing the financial sinews of war was essential, but rich, under-defended countries have a habit of becoming victims of aggression by poor, well-armed rivals. Navies and the industries that sustain them are slow-growing organisms.

For Beatty the main threat to Britain in the 1920s and beyond came from imperial Japan, an increasingly militaristic power with extensive ambitions in China. Like most Europeans of his age, Beatty was not immune to racist fears of a 'yellow peril', and realised that the success of an Asian nation in a traditionally European role would call into question the validity of the imperial project. Only a major fleet, equal to that of the Japanese and based in the region, would be an effective deterrent: the new Singapore base was essential for operations in the eastern arc of Empire. Beatty envisaged waging war by blockade, slowly crushing the vitals of the Japanese Empire, much as he believed Britain had crushed those of imperial Germany. The same strategy would work, at a push, against the United States. If such options were to be considered, the Royal Navy had to be at least equal to the United States Navy or, in more realistic measures, equal to those of Japan and at least one major European power, so that it could act as a deterrent in two regions.[47] Pacific operations would place a premium on effective coordination with the Australian and New Zealand navies, but Beatty's hopes for a Dominion naval compact foundered on local political sensitivities. The setback was not severe, however, as close naval cooperation was ensured by officer exchanges and the use of standard procedures and equipment.

With battleship building at a standstill for a decade, Beatty secured a large cruiser programme and kept up a modest level of replacement in other classes. The new ten-thousand-ton cruiser armed with eight-inch guns had been defined by the Washington Treaty. Beatty ensured that Britain built more of them than any other power during his term of office. The 'County' class, like the battlecruisers of the Edwardian era, were big, seaworthy ships with a long steaming radius but only light protection. They were ideal for oceanic commerce protection but were deficient in combat strength. They were part of an ambitious project to replace the entire surface fleet, other than the battleships, before the Washington process ended and new battleships could be built. Nor was Beatty slow to exploit an opening. When Prime Minister Stanley Baldwin suddenly decided that cruiser construction could mop up unemployment ahead of a general election in 1923, the naval staff quickly produced a suitable programme.[48] Attempts to restrain naval budgets with a 'ten-year rule', demanding that the armed forces plan on the assumption that there would be no major conflict for a decade, were defeated by reference to the Washington Treaty standard, which Beatty insisted had to be met to maintain parity with the United States.[49]

Naval Aviation

Nineteen twenty-three would turn out to be the high-water mark of Beatty's success as First Sea Lord. He was once again succumbing to the fault of believing his own public relations, becoming increasingly unreasonable in the process: 'The Admiralty's uncompromising attitude as, for example, over naval aviation in July 1923, led statesmen to see sailors as petulant and unreasonable. These perceptions ultimately cost the navy dear.'[50] Beatty's only major defeat as First Sea Lord came in the uncharted area of shipboard aviation. In 1914 the Royal Navy had its own fledgling Royal Naval Air Service (RNAS), which developed from small beginnings into a major service in its own right, with armoured cars, strategic bombers, maritime patrol aircraft and shipboard aviation. In 1917 Beatty had pushed for a torpedo-bomber attack on Wilhelmshaven, yet he supported the creation of an independent Royal Air Force on All Fools' Day 1918, a decision he would live to regret. Many in the navy saw the RNAS as an ill-disciplined, irregular adjunct, and were not sorry to see it go, but Beatty may have bought the original argument for the RAF: that a single force would ensure effective control of aircraft and engine manufacture.

In practice, the RAF had no intention of being merely an aviation supplier to the other two services. It was quick to carve out a unique mission statement, with strategic bombing as its *raison d'être*. Furthermore, it was dominated by officers with an army background, uninterested in shipboard aviation or maritime patrol. By the time he took office at the Admiralty, Beatty knew that the arrangements for the RAF to supply squadrons for naval service were not working, and he began moves to recover control of shipboard aviation. In 1920 Air Marshal Sir Hugh Trenchard, head of the Royal Air Force, promised that the naval units of the RAF would gradually become part of the navy, with the RAF merely supplying pilots and planes. By accepting this offer of jam tomorrow, Beatty displayed his political naivety: Trenchard was playing for time, desperate to sustain his fledgling service at a time when economy was the order of the day. After Trenchard's bad faith, Beatty rejected his 1923 offer to locate naval aviation command at the Admiralty. He wanted naval aviation to be wholly naval, but overplayed his hand.[51]

A Cabinet committee considered the subject in 1923 and concluded that Beatty's object was to weaken the Air Ministry. The sea lords came very close to resigning, only to be read a lesson in democratic politics by First Lord Leo Amery.[52] In 1924 Deputy Chief of Naval Staff Roger Keyes secured a compromise agreement which at least ensured a small supply of naval officer pilots and observers. Only in 1939 was the Fleet Air Arm restored to full naval control. The legacy of inter-war chaos was painful: the Royal Navy went to war with too few aircraft and pilots to equip its carriers, and the aircraft in production were obsolescent.

The naval aviation question was part of the larger tri-service battle for funds. The RAF did not want to give up any air assets, as it would lose budget share, and counter-attacked with the claim that aircraft could carry out many, if not all of the roles currently filled by naval and land forces. This 'substitution' was politically attractive, if wholly fraudulent. Beatty resisted these claims, strongly supported by successive army chiefs of staff. Despite these battles Beatty was an early convert to the idea of a single defence ministry with a single secretary of state – the system that exists today. His work on the Chiefs of Staff Committee and at the Imperial Defence College were important elements in building the sophisticated, effective strategic-command systems used in the Second World War.

Sadly, his domestic life continued to afford him no relief from the pressures of work: the pleasures of chase and grouse moor were only temporary respites from the torment caused by his unstable wife. Lacking any sense of purpose or belonging, Ethel gave way to depression, making the lives of everyone around her unbearable. It seems that she broke the marriage vows at least as often as he did, perhaps more. While Beatty found some solace outside marriage, he never considered leaving Ethel. They were only too well matched: fast, dangerous people who burnt everything they touched, including one another. He loved her to the end.

Jutland Refought

Altogether less edifying was his attempt to rewrite Jutland. His purpose was clear: 'There are so many interests involved. The outstanding one & the only one which should be considered is what is best for the Navy. That is my guiding consideration.'[53] Though Beatty had proved invaluable to the navy by protecting the defence budget from the threat of cuts, he was also guilty of exploiting his office to sustain his reputation. Fortunately, Jellicoe and the official historian managed to block the worst excesses of his ego-driven obsession.

Despite all the evidence to the contrary, Beatty remained convinced that Jellicoe had not done enough to pursue and destroy the enemy after the Battlecruiser Fleet had delivered Scheer to him on a plate. He was equally certain that the gunnery of his ships was at least as good as that of the Grand Fleet. With his customary arrogance, he could not see that others might take different views without intending to be hostile, or that the evidence did not support his position. He could do little about the fact that the majority of publications in the 1920s were on the whole more favourable to Jellicoe than to the Battlecruiser Fleet. But when the relevant volume of Sir Julian Corbett's official history was sent to the Admiralty for vetting, he objected to this magisterial work, which supported Jellicoe's decisions. Unable to alter the text, the Admiralty inserted a damning disclaimer ahead of the title page:

The Lords Commissioners of the Admiralty . . . are in no way responsible . . . for the accuracy of its statements.

Their Lordships find that some of the principles advocated in this book, especially the tendency to minimise the importance of seeking battle and of forcing it to a conclusion, are directly in conflict with their views.[54]

The master historian and strategist who had produced the book – a man whose work had influenced both Fisher and Beatty before 1914 – died eleven months before the book appeared. Corbett's demise was surely hastened by the impossible task of creating an 'official' history that would also satisfy the outsized egos of error-prone men like Churchill and Beatty.[55]

Beatty also suppressed the very 'matter of fact' Harper Report, compiled by a leading navigation officer, commissioning his own 'Staff Appreciation' in its place. These actions did far more to raise controversy than the events of 31 May 1916. Jellicoe's supporters – but not Jellicoe himself, it should be noted – published their own versions, increasingly critical of the Battlecruiser Fleet's actions and methods. In 1925 Admiral Bacon's vitriolic *The Jutland Scandal* was reprinted, much to Beatty's exasperation. For him, 1916 mattered because it was part of his political armoury: 'That bloody Bacon book annoys me, and has added to my despondency, and the difficulties I am having with the government are not so easily overcome, & I think they don't pay so much attention to my advice as in the past.'[56]

Even if Beatty were inclined to moderation, Alfred Chatfield – captain of the *Lion*, Battlecruiser Fleet gunnery officer and a key member of the Admiralty team – was deeply committed to defending the gunnery record of the force. He had far more to lose than Beatty – indeed, he kept the question alive after the other protagonists had died. While the matter might now appear rather arcane, it was a matter of public notoriety throughout Beatty's term in office. Questions were asked in Parliament about Harper's report, while Jellicoe refused to take up his post as governor general of New Zealand unless the staff account was either radically altered or suppressed. The Harper Report eventually appeared after Beatty left office, and all one hundred copies of the 'Staff Appreciation' were ordered to be pulped, although Beatty kept his!

However, Beatty was far too astute to let this issue rankle in public once he no longer needed the public éclat of heroism. Magnanimously, he advised the government to appoint Admiral Sir Charles Madden, Jellicoe's brother-in-law and his chief of staff at Jutland, as his successor. With that, the issue was left to the tender mercies of retired officers and historians. In private, Beatty still relished the fight and delighted in new accounts that backed his opinions – but he also preserved the key documents from both sides of the argument among his private papers. If he abused his position to protect his reputation, he did so with good reason: he did not take the issue as seriously as his critics have suggested.

Failure

In 1925 the naval staff prepared a highly ambitious long-term construction programme to replace every ship in the navy, except battleships, between 1925 and 1931. This time Beatty had overplayed his hand, and proceeded to mismanage the game. He offered no room for compromise and no ground for negotiation. At a time of straitened public finances and political turmoil, this only reinforced the navy's arrogant image. Despite Ethel's predictable public disparagement, Churchill, now Chancellor of the Exchequer, came up with a very generous long-term programme that came close to meeting Beatty's terms: he asked only for a year's delay in commencing the work. This was the best chance the navy had to secure long-term construction in the fifteen years after 1918, but Beatty persuaded the political head of the Admiralty to reject it. The navy secured a better settlement for 1925, but it would pay a heavy price for this minor tactical success in the years to come; indeed, it was still paying that price when war broke out in 1939. The Cabinet responded to Beatty's bullying by setting up the Colwyn Committee to cut the 1926–7 service estimates, a major development in the steady implementation of Treasury control over defence spending. Beatty also exposed a flank to the RAF, which Trenchard was quick to exploit. He offered to defend Singapore with aircraft, and to do so for far less outlay than the fixed defences the navy required.[57]

When Beatty retired, Maurice Hankey, long-time secretary of the Committee of Imperial Defence and a keen student of the civil/military interface, told him:

You are the only First Sea Lord I have known in my 26 years who could really talk on even terms to the highest Cabinet ministers and stand up to them in argument. Fisher is an exception, but Fisher was a crank, and even he didn't really state a case clearly.

This has meant everything in starting the Chiefs of Staff Committee. Without a really first class chairman we might have failed, and that would have been disastrous.[58]

Despite its whiff of sycophancy, Hankey's assessment was not too far from the truth. Beatty had stood up to the politicians; indeed, he often stood over them, dictating lessons in sea power. Yet such success had not brought wisdom, and in the arrogance of his power Beatty left a bitter legacy for less charismatic men who could not sustain his success.

In retirement Beatty remained active and involved – in part, one suspects, out of a desire to escape from the dark, melancholy world in which Ethel existed. 'I have paid a terrible price for my millions,' he admitted. He attended the Committee of Imperial Defence, spoke effectively in the House of Lords and supported naval charities, but there was not enough to satisfy a man of his enormous energy. He still rode with the reckless daring of a subaltern, and suffered accordingly. In 1922 he had fractured his breastbone in a car accident; after retirement his bulldog jaw was shattered by a horse's hoof, which also broke an arm and several ribs. By 1935 he was suffering from breathing problems and coronary damage but ignored medical advice to rest. After Ethel's death in 1932, he continued to hunt with the vigour of youth, rather than the wisdom required by advancing years and failing health.

After 1927, the feud over Jutland subsided: Beatty was still all too certain that he was right, but it no longer mattered. Jellicoe died suddenly in November 1935, and despite his own ill health, Beatty insisted on attending the funeral as a pall-bearer to show that the divisions had healed. When George V died in January 1936, Beatty once again left his sickbed; this time he caught pneumonia and died of heart failure at his London home on 12 March 1936. Four days later Beatty followed Jellicoe to the grave. He was only sixty-five, his body worn out and weakened by the endless pursuit of glory and vermin.

He was buried in the crypt of St Paul's, close by the tomb of his immortal exemplar. It was an honour that no one merited more than Beatty. He was not perfect, but he rose to every challenge that was set, and matched his style and his methods to the task at hand with remarkable consistency. His defence of the navy and its budget in difficult times between 1919 and 1927 remains unequalled in the annals of modern civil–military relations, but as with everything he ever attempted, the results were by no means clear-cut, and in the end the details did for him.

David Beatty was not a 'nice' man: along with his talent and his charisma came an overbearing arrogance and 'some elements of a bounder'. Beatty and Ethel were the spoilt children of fortune – his personal and opportunistic, hers monetary. Both suffered for their treasures. Beatty shared the values and sentiments of his class and his age: his attitude towards the men on the lower deck was authoritarian, tempered by paternalistic concern, while an all-consuming love of hunting, shooting and horses revealed the inner man. He exploited his chances, in life, love and service, with a ruthless selfishness that in a lesser man would have been truly appalling. Nor did success and wealth bring him happiness or long life. He lived for his career and his country; he died young, worn out by hard work, mental anguish and the same carelessness about his health that he applied to such minor matters as magazine safety.

The sublime moments of Beatty's career were the explosive destructions of his own ships, not those of the enemy. This was an instructive contrast with Nelson: where Nelson mastered the details before building his system, Beatty did not. Those details were the difference between winning and losing, between true genius and a close-run thing.

In a navy filled with officers who did as they were told, David Beatty was different. He brought an original and powerful mind to bear on the matter of command, and he looked for something more than order and regulation. He emphasised the object, not the method, and stressed the need for initiative. In this he went against the grain, but he was right. Two combat promotions in two years brought him to high command very early. Unfortunately this heir of Nelson found himself leading dutiful, obedient, unimaginative officers who responded to his mission-analysis methods with varying degrees of incomprehension. The navy relearnt much about war, leadership and command in the First World War, and the benefits of that experience would be seen two decades later.

In 1936 battleship building resumed, and the navy decided to name ships for the recently departed Jutland admirals. By the time the thirty-five-thousand-ton monsters were ready to launch in February 1940, Churchill felt that the proposed names would only revive old squabbles, and the ships were renamed *Anson* and *Howe*. Jellicoe and Beatty had to make do with busts in Trafalgar Square: it was an honour they would share with the last admiral.

TRANSCENDENT TALENT
Andrew Cunningham
1883–1963

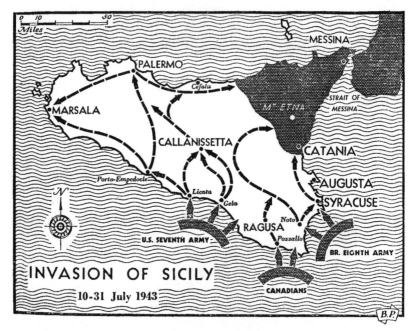

The fruits of naval victory are always found on land. Having evacuated
the British army from Greece and Crete, Andrew Cunningham directed
the invasion of Sicily and Italy

ANDREW CUNNINGHAM WAS the last admiral – the last to command an entire theatre from the bridge of his flagship. He won two major battles, staged two major evacuations, directed the Allied landings in North Africa, Sicily and Italy and finished the Second World War as First Sea Lord. The finest fighting seaman of the war, and a master of command, he earned his place in Trafalgar Square with a truly Nelsonian performance.[1]

Andrew Browne Cunningham was born at 42 Grosvenor Square, Dublin, on 7 January 1883, the third of five children. His father was Professor of Anatomy at Trinity College, but both parents were Scottish – a matter of great pride.[2] After early schooling in Dublin, the boy was dispatched to Edinburgh Academy, living with his aunts. In 1893 Professor Cunningham sent a telegram asking his ten-year-old son if he would like to join the navy. Cunningham would recall his response years later: 'Yes, I should like to be an admiral.' At the time of the telegram, Geoffrey Hornby was the admiral; Cunningham would be the last of his heirs.

Professor Cunningham's timing was significant: Gladstone had recently lost his battle against naval expansion. With the navy set to grow, it was an opportune moment to begin a sea career. This was also a relatively cheap option, which may have been part of the attraction. Cunningham spent the next three years at Foster's School in Fareham, just across the harbour from Portsmouth naval base, preparing for Dartmouth. Although clever, Cunningham never did any more than was absolutely necessary. After a good exam performance, he joined the old wooden wall HMS *Britannia* in January 1897. Like Beatty, Cunningham was bored by Dartmouth, preferring to spend his time sailing or fishing – the latter a lifelong passion. He was never a cadet captain, and passed out tenth of sixty-five cadets in May 1898. First-class marks in mathematics and seamanship earned him seven months' seniority, however, and after a month at sea he became a midshipman.

Having requested service on the African station, Cunningham arrived in Cape Town that summer, joining a small cruiser based at Zanzibar. In October 1899 he joined the flagship, just as the Second Boer War broke out, and in February 1900 mustered with the inevitable Naval Brigade. Although the senior officer took a marked dislike to him, General Lord Roberts, a family friend, ordered him to the front. He had a baptism of fire at the battle of Diamond Hill on 10 June 1900, under Roberts' command. After meeting his father, who was in Pretoria inspecting medical facilities, he went home after six months' shore service. Following time in a battleship and a sail-training brig, he passed for sub-lieutenant on his nineteenth birthday but found the gunnery school, HMS *Excellent*, not to his taste. Although the torpedo school HMS *Vernon* proved more interesting, he never became a specialist: Cunningham, like Beatty, remained a 'salt-horse', perennially sceptical about the claims of gunnery officers. There was something different about the young Cunningham; he didn't like being ordered about by officers who lacked the skill or the authority to command respect. These included gunnery instructors and his first half dozen captains. He learnt well from these early experiences: when his own turn came to take command, he was firm, but never mindless; sharp, but always recognised the talent of others.

Commissioned in March 1903, Cunningham found life on a Mediterranean fleet battleship boring. Within six months he had secured a transfer to a destroyer. Once given a responsible position, the indolent Cunningham was transformed, securing excellent reports from his commanding officer. He made it his business to impress the senior officers of the flotilla, who served him well in later years. Cunningham was unusually forward-thinking, and he loved to be in command. Further service in a sail-training brig and the cruiser of cultured Scots aristocrat Captain Rosslyn Wemyss, later First Sea Lord, interrupted his love affair with destroyers. Wemyss was impressed, recommending him for a coveted destroyer command in 1908, when he was barely old enough.

Cunningham would remain a destroyer commander for an unprecedented eleven solid years, at a time when the Admiralty invariably moved officers between large and small ships. Taking his first command at twenty-five, Cunningham would command every ship he served on until he became an admiral. This was very unusual, but very deliberate.

Cunningham honed his natural leadership skills while his contemporaries spent their time ashore learning to be specialists and serving at sea in subordinate capacities, a career pattern that narrowed and atrophied their individuality and delayed the test of command until they had become set in their ways. This early, sustained period of responsibility was very unconventional. It put him outside the norm, just like Beatty. The normal career pattern for Edwardian officers filled the navy with good seconds, capable seamen and technical experts – qualities required by the vast majority of officers in any navy. But such regimentation does not generate wartime leaders. Cunningham was a brilliant seaman and a leader of men, although an abiding hatred of paperwork led him to prefer incineration to response.

Leadership ultimately requires innate abilities that cannot be taught. These are not intellectual attributes; indeed, intellectuals often fail the test of war. It is no coincidence that the professional admirals in this study obtained command early: real leaders seek out opportunities to lead. Confidence and self-awareness are vital. Jellicoe queried his promotion to command the Grand Fleet in August 1914 three times; he should have been sacked on the spot. By contrast, Cunningham rose to every challenge that the navy threw at him; he was a natural. While he avoided technical subjects, Cunningham was no fool. He possessed a remarkably capable intellect and was clever enough to avoid posts ashore and subordinate positions. The officers he admired were men of character, like Reginald Tyrwhitt, Roger Keyes and Beatty's old friend Walter Cowan, whose diminutive chest was already weighed down with medals before 1914.

Destroyer service was active, physically demanding and required the highest standards of seamanship. This suited Cunningham, who possessed nerves of steel, a cast-iron constitution and a passion for the sea. In 1911 he took over HMS *Scorpion*, retaining the command for seven years. He made mistakes, getting an official reprimand for cursing a signalman, and narrowly avoided more serious trouble when the *Scorpion* ran down and sank a small sailing ship. Realistic training involved real risks.

War

When war broke out in 1914, Cunningham was already a veteran. His flotilla was in the Mediterranean, and nearly came into action with two German ships on 7 August, only for Admiral Troubridge to back off, having decided that the German ships constituted a 'superior force'. In his memoirs Cunningham made his feelings clear, but concluded, 'I will not comment on this decision.'[3] After a brief sortie into the Adriatic, *Scorpion* settled down to watch the Dardanelles, whence the German warships had fled.

After a cold, dull winter, the opening of Churchill's offensive in March 1915 provided some relief. After four years in command, Cunningham's ship-handling had been honed to a fine edge: he enjoyed rushing into harbour, bringing the *Scorpion* up smartly alongside her collier and having his crew at coaling stations in seconds. That kind of skill impressed everyone and made the crew feel special. Despite being fitted for minesweeping, *Scorpion* sat at anchor off Tenedos throughout the great Dardanelles attack of 18 March 1915. On 25 April the destroyers swept for mines ahead of the battleships, providing fire support for the amphibious landings. Then, their work complete, they lay off the beach with strict orders not to fire on the Turkish defences. This foolishness did not last long: the battleships were forced to retreat by a U-boat, leaving the destroyers to provide fire support. Cunningham was in his element. Supporting the advance at Cape Helles on 28 June, his forward gun fired so quickly that the contact breaker failed and had to be remade with heavy-duty wire. That night *Scorpion*'s searchlights covered the approaches to the British trenches and Cunningham went to sleep. When the Turks tried to shoot out the lights, it was obvious that a counter-attack was imminent. He closed in and laid down a point-blank barrage that destroyed the Turkish assault force. Relentless determination to attack, the audacity with which he operated and absolute professionalism made Cunningham the best destroyer skipper at Gallipoli. He swept mines under fire with calm precision, re-fuelled with celerity and kept his little ship neat and seamanlike under the strain of constant work. *Scorpion*'s taut discipline and exemplary seamanship impressed his seniors. He stood out from a crowd of bold and brave fellows and was promoted to commander in 1915, overtaking some 250 officers on the Navy List.

Like all good officers of his generation, Cunningham took a paternal interest in the welfare of his men, arranging football matches, runs ashore, opportunities to swim and supplies of fresh food. He even enlisted his mother as an unofficial aid committee for those with families near Edinburgh. Those who let him down were invariably punished, and he never found a first lieutenant who met his standards; they passed through the ship with alarming frequency. At least he never bore a grudge, and understood that junior officers needed to be encouraged, as well as instructed.

After a month's leave at Malta, *Scorpion* returned to play a prominent part in the evacuation of the Gallipoli bridgehead: it would not be the last time Cunningham would rescue the army from a beach. He was awarded the DSO in recognition of his efforts. Further Mediterranean service ranged from semi-independent coastal operations against Turkish shipping to convoy duty, both of which were quickly mastered. No ship in his convoys was sunk, which he attributed to accurate station-keeping and good fortune. By mid-1917 he had seen enough of the Mediterranean, turning down command of the Malta destroyer flotilla. In December he took his tired ship home, having been offered destroyers at Harwich under Reginald Tyrwhitt or at Dover under Roger Keyes. These were leaders he could follow: bold seamen, and relentlessly aggressive. He was not overly concerned with intellectual skills, preferring to keep war simple and direct.

A brief spell with the Grand Fleet destroyers did not impress, and he accepted Keyes' offer of HMS *Termagent* in April. Based at Dunkirk, he was kept busy escorting troop convoys and patrolling the straits. Then Keyes gave him command of the old battleship *Swiftsure*, prepared for another attempt to block the harbour at Ostend. The Germans evacuated the base just before the operation, and Cunningham saw out the war in the *Termagent*, earning a bar for his DSO. During the armistice he acted as chauffeur to the great and good as they shuttled across the Channel: Beatty, Rosy Wemyss, now First Sea Lord, royal princes, foreign rulers and even Prime Minister Lloyd George enjoyed Cunningham's dynamic ship-driving in the Channel storms.

Cunningham had learnt about war the hard way: amphibious operations, command failure, tactical success, convoy work and coastal attacks. The experience came at a critical period in his career: unlike Beatty, Fisher and Hornby, he would reach the high command with a wealth of relevant experience. Zeal, energy and, above all, a ready assumption of responsibility made him an obvious candidate for higher command. He was brave, professional and thorough; but beyond that he had displayed genuine initiative while acting independently in command of his own ship and of small formations.

Peace

In 1919 Cunningham led a flotilla to the Baltic, placing his pennant in the new destroyer HMS *Seafire*. With Walter Cowan in command, this was always going to be active service. It was also brief, but Cunningham made his mark, clearing German troops out of the Latvian port of Libau to earn a second bar to his DSO. Cowan considered him 'as good an officer as I can remember', stressing his 'unfailing promptitude and decision . . . an officer of exceptional valour and unerring resolution'.[4]

Cunningham came ashore in late 1919, being promoted to captain at the turn of 1920. At the age of thirty-seven he was once again ahead of his contemporaries and well on the way to becoming an admiral. It was a good time to be conspicuously talented: when the Geddes Axe of 1922 decimated the service, Beatty's Admiralty took care to retain future leaders. After a year overseeing the destruction of German forts on the North Sea island of Heligoland, an odd task for a destroyer leader, Cunningham secured a flotilla command. His flotilla exercised at high speed in all aspects of destroyer work, quickly achieving the standards of neatness and discipline that he expected. One officer recalled Cunningham's three favourite expressions as 'Duty is the first business of a sea officer', 'NDBGZ – No Difficulty Baffles Great Zeal', and finally 'Let intelligent anticipation be your watchword.'[5] The first paraphrased Nelson, who had written thus to his betrothed shortly before their wedding; the motto reeked of Cunningham's single-minded dedication to his profession, a Calvinist zeal for hard work and long hours at sea.[6]

In 1926 Walter Cowan became commander-in-chief on the North

America and West Indies station. Cunningham was offered the post of flag captain and chief staff officer, which he accepted with alacrity. As captain of the light cruiser *Calcutta*, he quickly imposed his own ideas on the ship, and enjoyed working with Cowan. His memoirs reveal a delight in seamanship and problem-solving, while he 'particularly enjoyed visiting the old dockyard at English Harbour (Antigua), which had been used by Nelson'.[7] Although the endless cycle of port visits and social occasions soon became wearing, he met his future wife Nona Byatt at Government House, Trinidad, where her brother was the governor. Cowan taught him the rudiments of squadron command and high-level leadership, essential after a career spent in small ships. Cowan was quick, decisive and determined, but like his friend Beatty, he made mistakes. Cunningham did not: he was too professional. Nonetheless, the two men remained good friends for the rest of Cowan's long, eventful life.

Returning home in 1928, Cunningham was dispatched to the army senior officer's course at Sheerness, where he learnt about battlefield logistics and the selection of ground before joining the Imperial Defence College, now the Royal College of Defence Studies. The IDC had been one of Beatty's better ideas, and in Admiral Sir Herbert Richmond it had an ideal founding director. The IDC brought together the future leaders of all three armed forces, their imperial and Dominion contemporaries and civil servants in an environment where they could exchange ideas, form useful contacts and grasp a national concept of strategy. After a career spent carefully avoiding anything intellectual, from gunnery to the minutiae of staff work, Cunningham was apprehensive about his mental faculties. They were merely dormant; he had not tested them unduly in the past two decades, but he soon mastered the work. The IDC was critical to the development of effective inter-service co-operation in the Second World War.

On 21 December 1929 Cunningham and Nona were married. He was forty-seven, and she forty; he was a dedicated professional seaman, she shy and retiring. They were happy, and although they had no children they took great delight in their numerous nieces and nephews. Soon afterwards, Cunningham took command of the navy's newest and largest battleship, the awe-inspiring *Rodney*, built to meet the Washington Treaty limits, with all nine massive sixteen-inch guns mounted in triple turrets ahead of the bridge. This represented a dramatic change of emphasis for a man accustomed to small ships: she would be a challenge to handle in confined waters, but success would be the obvious prelude to flag rank. The ship was soon humming to Cunningham's tune: well-drilled, neat, highly proficient at competitive sports, a successful ship in the Atlantic fleet led by Sir Alfred Chatfield, who as First Sea Lord for most of the 1930s held the final decision about Cunningham's career. This may have been why his immediate superior Rear Admiral Drax declared: 'Cunningham, on no account allow yourself to become entangled in the technicalities of this great ship.'[8] Drax need not have worried: nothing could have been further from Cunningham's mind.

The commission only lasted one year, to allow as many potential admirals as possible to have the opportunity to prove themselves. Cunningham went to command the barracks at Chatham, which provided crews for ships as they commissioned. This post was dominated by the Invergordon Mutiny of September 1931, which saw sailors of the Atlantic fleet refuse to obey orders after the Admiralty Board reduced their pay. However, there was only one incident of disaffection at Chatham. Cunningham combined a fearsome reputation with an old-fashioned paternalistic attitude to the lower deck. He may have treated the men like enthusiastic children, but he was genuinely concerned for their well-being and took the trouble to listen to some five hundred complaints. After a career in destroyers, Cunningham understood and appreciated the ratings and the petty officers who were the backbone of the service. Invergordon cast a dark shadow over the navy's public image and its self-confidence that was not dispelled until 1939.

Admiral

Promoted to rear admiral in September 1932, Cunningham remained at Chatham until the following February, largely for want of a suitable post. Attending the senior officers' technical and tactical courses filled the interval before his next period at sea: tactics proved far more to his taste than technology, laying the foundations for combat command.

On 1 January 1934 Cunningham was appointed Rear Admiral Destroyers Mediterranean Fleet. This was the post that he craved, crowning the career of a great destroyer man. From his light-cruiser flagship he directed three nine-ship flotillas in Vice Admiral Sir William Fisher's fleet. Fisher, known as 'the great Agrippa' thanks to his impressive stature and silent demeanour, was a highly intelligent officer and absolute master of his fleet. He preferred bold and direct methods and close-quarters action, relying on the superiority of the Royal Navy's people, methods and training. Consequently his fleet operated at a very high standard, prepared for night action, with initiative devolved to junior admirals and captains. Fisher used his staff to great effect and encouraged Cunningham's preference for this method of command. Destroyer exercises emphasised speed of thought, precision of manoeuvre and accurate torpedo work. The destroyers also drilled extensively with the new Asdic sonar system for anti-submarine defence. Inspired by his example, many of the officers under his command would become outstanding leaders in their turn. Visits to the Dalmatian coast reminded him of Nelson's brilliant protégé William Hoste, who had served ashore and afloat in that region.[9]

In the middle of 1935 the Abyssinian crisis led to the rapid reinforcement of the fleet – to the fury of Fisher and Cunningham, the chiefs of staff considered it unready to wage war on Italy. Justifiably confident that their men and their ships were ready, the two admirals were planning a major offensive for the outbreak of war. The morale of the fleet was high, facilities were improved, and the welfare of the men was constantly under review. The government backed away, but the lessons of 1935 would be revived in 1940. No one in the Royal Navy considered the Italian fleet a serious opponent. Among the reinforcements Cunningham obtained a flotilla of old destroyers led by newly promoted Captain Philip Vian, 'for whom I had especially asked'.[10] In March 1936 the crisis passed, to the relief of Fisher and Cunningham.

Facing the prospect of two years on half pay, Cunningham and his wife leased Palace House at Bishop's Waltham – close to Portsmouth, and within easy reach of London. Promoted to vice admiral on 22 July 1936, he chaired a committee on the internal arrangements and ventilation of warships. But any chance of rest ashore disappeared as the navy's high command was decimated by death and disease. William Fisher died in July 1937, and Geoffrey Blake, second-in-command in the Mediterranean, had two heart attacks. Cunningham went out as a temporary replacement, but Blake had to retire and the job became permanent. With his flag in the mighty battlecruiser *Hood*, the largest warship in the world, Cunningham completed the transformation from destroyer captain to fleet commander. He spent much of his time on the Spanish coast, ensuring the safety of British merchant vessels and restricting the savagery of the Spanish Civil War to the shore. Commander-in-Chief Sir Dudley Pound was an arch centraliser, given to issuing extensive, detailed and rather rigid orders. While Pound and Cunningham were friends and colleagues, their early careers had been very different, and this was reflected in their command styles. Pound, the distilled essence of the Grand Fleet, was impressed by the effortless manner with which Cunningham took up his post.

In August 1938 Cunningham was ordered home to become Deputy Chief of Naval Staff; in effect, he would be the Admiralty's dedicated strategic planner. He warned the new First Sea Lord, Sir Roger Backhouse, that he lacked the necessary experience or aptitude, but as events would soon show, this was little more than laziness. He needed a period of service in the political environment of the Admiralty to prepare him for command of the Home or Mediterranean fleets. Although the Munich crisis of October 1938 greatly increased Backhouse's workload, he was another micro-managing centraliser and reluctant to delegate. Cunningham was able to take responsibility for the Spanish situation, but only because he had local knowledge. His mission to Berlin to dissuade Germany from accelerating naval construction failed. In March 1939 Backhouse was diagnosed with a brain tumour, and by July he was dead. This left the newly knighted Sir Andrew Cunningham acting First Sea Lord in the months before war broke out, dealing with the demands of mobilisation, rearmament and alliance-building.

He used the opportunity to drive through a major change in strategy. Plans made in the inter-war years had presumed that Japan was the main threat and the primary naval task was the dispatch of a fleet to Singapore. Cunningham shifted the focus to the Mediterranean, confident that Italy could be knocked out relatively quickly by naval pressure, aerial bombardment and overseas land offensives. This policy harmonised with the aims of France, once again Britain's strategic partner in attempting to restrain the aggressive intentions of Germany. Backhouse's death forced another shuffle among the top posts. Pound was recalled to the Admiralty, and Cunningham took over the Mediterranean fleet. He had been at the Admiralty a mere eight months, and was promoted to acting admiral as he took command.

Master of the Mediterranean

Skill, fortune and opportunity saw Andrew Cunningham reach the post ideally suited to his talents just in time for the start of the war. He was fifty-seven, a decade older than Nelson at Trafalgar, but his energy and aggression had not been tempered by the years. Long marked out for an active command in war, Cunningham had the ability to size up situations immediately and to make lightning-fast decisions without doubts or second thoughts. His orders were simple, direct and coherent: no one misunderstood his meaning, and he picked a professional staff to ensure his wishes were met. He was not an easy man to serve. He did not suffer fools or failures; he was quick to judge and rarely changed his mind. He hated charlatans, mountebanks and lightweights – a category that included many of the better-known senior officers of all three services. He abhorred publicity and never cared about his popular reputation. But although his staff generally arrived with a mixture of awe and trepidation, inspired by his fearsome reputation and none-too-gentle tongue, they quickly came to admire him.

A man of medium height and spare build, his weather-beaten complexion spoke of a life spent on a destroyer's open bridge. Those pale blue, watery eyes seemed to be on everyone and conveyed more than a hint of menace. His standards were little short of perfection, and he did not appreciate delay. But he was as hard on himself as he was on others, and his bark was frequently followed by a vulgar joke and a comforting remark. How far he generated his fearsome persona as a command tool and how far it reflected the inner man is hard to judge. Like Jervis he had an inherently kindly nature, but he did not take it to work.

Like all great admirals Cunningham cared about his people: success depended on them, not the machines they controlled. The same approach to man management that he had employed in the First World War was revived for the Second, on a grander scale. He would ask the impossible of his people, and they would oblige because they admired him and trusted him to be careful with their lives. To the fleet, 'ABC' was a talisman, an icon who guaranteed success.

Above all Cunningham was a hands-on commander. He had learnt his business at sea, exercising, testing and developing. His instincts were to seek out the enemy, secure command of the sea in battle, and use it to attack the enemy's vitals. In this way he would impose his will on the enemy. It did not require a profound intellect to be an admiral: being quick, certain and positive were the key assets. Although he possessed a fine mind, Cunningham never micromanaged. He expected his juniors to use their own judgement within the overall brief, and he already knew most of them. He used his staff more effectively than any previous admiral, and did so with confidence because they were tested men. He would drive them hard, using them up at a frightening rate, to meet the myriad demands of modern war. That was the secret of his durability: by making appropriate use of those beneath him, he avoided working himself into an early grave or a nervous breakdown.

These qualities fitted him for squadron command but, like Nelson, he also possessed a clear concept of operations. His ability to act as a strategic commander had been developed over the past decade, from the IDC to his lengthy period as a junior admiral under Fisher and Pound. He knew the theatre of war better than any officer in the Royal Navy, having visited many of its harbours and key locations. He had operated in every season and every storm that the Mediterranean had to offer, and spent at least five years preparing for war with Italy.

Cunningham arrived at Alexandria on 5 June 1939, relieving Pound the following day. No one doubted that war was imminent, but in the Mediterranean it remained to be seen whether Italy would join Germany or wait in the wings. Japan was still the dominant concern for some decision-makers and the intended destination of Cunningham's fleet in the event of war. Throughout the 'phoney war' Britain attempted to draw Italy away from Germany, but Churchill's return to the post of First Lord on the outbreak of war in September 1939 indicated a major shift of focus: Churchill was committed to a Mediterranean strategy, confident Italy could be defeated.

Within weeks of taking command Cunningham found his fleet

reduced from three battleships, an aircraft carrier, half a dozen cruisers and three destroyer flotillas to a half-flotilla of old Australian destroyers. The Mediterranean was untouched by war, and the ships were needed elsewhere. To make matters worse, the main base at Malta lacked any serious defences against air attack, despite the Sicilian airfields being only sixty miles distant. Shortly before Italy declared war, the fleet moved to the commercial harbour at Alexandria, which was utterly unprepared, lacking a large dock, ammunition stores, workshops or defences of any sort. Pressure from Cunningham, and the endorsement of First Sea Lord Dudley Pound, secured anti-aircraft guns and a floating dry dock, and much was achieved locally. Even so, Cunningham never had the luxury of a secure base.

A degree of cooperation was established with France, largely through Cunningham's personal relationship with Vice Admiral Godfroy. He was equally successful working with General Wavell and Air Marshal Longmore, who shared his strategic views and his sense of the woeful lack of resources. All three services saw the Italian colony of Libya as a threat to Egypt and an opportunity for an early strike. British intelligence had penetrated many Italian radio codes and ciphers before the war, enabling Cunningham to anticipate Mussolini's intervention and secure reinforcements.[11] By early June 1940 he commanded a sizeable fleet, but the return of his flagship, the modernised Jutland veteran HMS *Warspite*, disguised the fact that his pre-war elite formations had been widely dispersed, taking heavy losses off Norway and Dunkirk. ABC went to war with a fleet of odd units, but he had picked many of his staff and junior admirals. He made his own luck – these were his choices. He went to war with only three battleships, two essentially unmodernised and one of them painfully slow. His aircraft carrier was also a veteran, with too few aircraft to defend the fleet or to mount an effective torpedo strike.

Relying on the French fleet to hold the western basin of the Mediterranean and stage an offensive along the Riviera, Cunningham planned to open the war by challenging the Italians with a major sweep through the central Mediterranean. His relationship with Pound provided a sounding board, stout support and absolute confidence. Pound knew there was no better man for the job, despite their distinctly different approaches to the art of the admiral. His confidence was vital as Churchill, now prime minister, frequently tried to interfere, sending bold, breezy and banal signals which did not improve Cunningham's opinion of the new leader. The steely-eyed professional warrior had little but contempt for the ill-advised interjections of an amateur strategist: without the emollient Pound, one of them would have been forced out.

ABC's determination to take the war to the enemy, briefly thwarted by Italy remaining neutral, soon paid dividends. On 10 June 1940 Mussolini sneaked into the war, hoping to pillage some trifles from the stricken corpse of France. Never one to stand on ceremony, Cunningham's destroyers were in action against Italian submarines two hours before war was declared![12]

When France surrendered, Cunningham was left with a powerful French squadron in Alexandria harbour. Churchill decided that the French navy had to be kept out of enemy hands, even if that required sinking the ships. Cunningham did no such thing: by exploiting decrypted French radio traffic and his relationship with Godfroy he avoided bloodshed.[13] After fraught negotiations and a hastily improvised broadcast to the French crews, Godfroy agreed to disarm and land his fuel. By ignoring Churchillian imperatives ABC found time to resolve the impasse. That said, he was now well placed to sink the French if they proved recalcitrant, but he went out of his way to avoid wounding the *amour propre* of his erstwhile allies. He managed this despite the terrible events at Mers-el-Kebir, when over thirteen hundred French sailors were killed. Having disarmed the French, ABC was quick to set about the enemy. He kept his fleet at sea, well aware that the Italian army in Libya depended on substantial convoys for food, fuel and reinforcements.

British submarines went into action immediately, but they were cumbersome old boats and suffered heavy losses in Italian minefields. The huge Italian submarine force did little better: they sank a small cruiser on an early sortie, but their patrol lines, betrayed by signal decrypts, were frequently rolled up by Cunningham's destroyers. Their numbers were never translated into results.

Back in London, Pound seriously considered abandoning the Mediterranean, if only temporarily, but Cunningham and Churchill were adamant that the addition of a few ships to the Atlantic fleet would achieve little. Confident the Germans could not invade Britain,[14] Cunningham stressed that Malta was the ideal base from which to strike Italian convoys to Libya, if it had adequate air defences. However, he had major convoys of his own to escort, and precious few escort vessels. Lacking sloops or corvettes, his limited force of destroyers had to do double duty, escorting the fleet and the convoys. This left little time for rest and refit. With over twenty-five thousand men under his command, Cunningham carried a heavy responsibility for welfare, recreation and morale. It was one that he addressed with the same concern he had shown as a destroyer skipper, earning the admiration of the fleet by his devotion to their interests.

On 9 July the two fleets met off the Calabrian coast, both escorting valuable convoys. Using superior intelligence and effective air reconnaissance, Cunningham tried to slow the two Italian battleships with Swordfish torpedo bombers from the carrier HMS *Eagle*. Against an enemy manoeuvring at high speed a handful of slow planes were unlikely to be successful. Instead, *Warspite*, miles ahead of the other heavy ships, opened fire on the Italians at the unprecedented range of twenty-five thousand yards – over thirteen miles. The latest gunnery-control computer ensured the opening salvo was accurate, and within a few minutes a fifteen-inch shell smashed into the Italian flagship *Giulio Cesare*. Stunned and alarmed, the Italians fled through a heavy smokescreen, leaving their air force to attack the British. Now only twenty-five miles from the enemy coast, Cunningham broke off the action, having no desire to be drawn into the submarine and air ambush that his intelligence had revealed.[15] As one of his staff observed, 'ABC enjoyed himself like a schoolboy.'[16]

The 'battle' off Calabria gave the British a moral ascendancy that would last the rest of the war. Sadly, Cunningham would not see another Italian battleship for three years. Working in tandem with his Dartmouth term-mate and friend James Somerville, who was commanding Force H, a battle group based at Gibraltar, Cunningham ensured that the British dominated the Mediterranean. The Royal Navy was better trained, better equipped and far better led. Many of the Italian ships were outdated and their gunnery equipment was markedly inferior. Moreover, they were hampered by an excessively centralised system of naval command: when HMAS *Sydney* sank an Italian cruiser of the same type and badly damaged a second, Captain John Collins was acting on brief, permissive orders that stood in marked contrast to the strict control exerted from Rome and allowed him to display the Nelsonian spirit that carried the day.

Taranto

At the beginning of the war Pound reminded Cunningham of the 1935 plans for a torpedo-bomber attack on Taranto. The new armoured aircraft carrier *Illustrious* arrived at the end of August 1940 to reinforce *Eagle*. Furthermore, her modern Fulmar fighters made short work of Italian scout planes and broke up the target-practice conditions in which *Regia Aeronautica* had hitherto operated. She was accompanied by several ships equipped with radar, which provided early warning of air attacks. Rear Admiral Lumley-Lyster took command of Fleet Air Arm operations.

The Italian invasion of Greece on 28 October allowed the British to occupy Suda Bay on the north coast of Crete as an advanced base, but this meant further convoys had to be escorted by the over-stretched destroyers. Cunningham and Lumley-Lyster planned to attack Taranto once the RAF acquired the necessary reconnaissance aircraft. The date initially set – 21 October, exploiting echoes of Trafalgar – was abandoned after a small fire on *Illustrious*. The next moonlit night, 11 November, found *Eagle* suffering from contaminated aviation fuel, a legacy of many near misses by Italian bombs. Five of her Swordfish and eight other air crews moved to *Illustrious*. Operation 'Judgement' was part of a large, complex combination of shipping and naval movements. The fleet covered the arrival of reinforcements from Gibraltar, convoys to Suda Bay and the Piraeus, the movement of the monitor *Terror* from Malta to Suda Bay, a cruiser raid on shipping in the Adriatic and the carrier strike. Timetabling these interlocking events made considerable demands on ABC's staff, but it all ran like clockwork. Cunningham directed the reinforcements, a battleship and two cruisers, to call at Malta. They entered Grand Harbour with the sides manned and bands playing – a massive boost for local morale.

The main fleet left Alexandria on 6 November, the Fleet Air Arm dispatching several Italian scouting aircraft during the passage. The reinforcements linked up on the 10th; the following evening *Illustrious*, escorted by cruisers and destroyers, broke away without

being observed. Air reconnaissance confirmed that all six Italian battleships were anchored in the main harbour at Taranto. Twelve
Swordfish flew off at 20.35 from a position about forty miles west
of Cephalonia, a second wave of nine following at 21.28. They carried flares, torpedoes or bombs. Although one aircraft had to return
and others became dispersed, the attack was a complete success. The
six torpedo planes of the first wave avoided anti-aircraft fire and
barrage balloons to drop their weapons at sea level. They scored
three hits, while flares and bombs dropped on the oil-storage depot
added to the confusion. The *Littorio* and the *Cavour* sank to the
bottom of the shallow harbour, leaving their superstructures above
water. One plane was shot down, but the rest returned at around
02.00. The second wave also lost a plane to mechanical failure but
scored two hits with three torpedoes, adding to *Littorio*'s woes and
sinking *Duilio*. The bombers wrecked the seaplane base and hit the
destroyer moorings, while badly directed anti-aircraft fire did considerable damage to the town. A repeat attack the following night
had to be abandoned when the weather turned foul.

While all three Italian ships were eventually refloated, and two
returned to service, Taranto shattered Italian morale and boosted
that of the British at a time when they had nothing else to celebrate.
The Italian fleet retreated to Naples, greatly simplifying the task of
reconnaissance, while the three sunken ships allowed Cunningham
to send home two slow battleships. His battle line – *Warspite*,
Barham and *Valiant* – were all veterans of the Fifth Battle Squadron
at Jutland. Only *Barham* was unmodernised. A late convert to air
power, Cunningham was profuse in his praise of the air crew and
their remarkable achievement. Soon he was expecting rather more
of the air arm than it could deliver. He recognised that Taranto had
'greatly increased our freedom of movement in the Mediterranean
and has thus strengthened our control over the central area of the
sea'.[17] Improved air defences at Malta meant he could translate control into offensive action against the Libyan convoys. In December
he took *Warspite* into Grand Harbour as if to signify his success.
The army smashed into Libya in early December, with extensive
naval fire support and logistics. The Italians were soon in full
retreat, enabling the RAF to operate shore-based fighters over the
Malta convoys.

The first six months of war had gone very well. Italy had been beaten on land, sea and in the air, and Cunningham was the master of the Mediterranean. Clear-sighted strategic assessment, good inter-service cooperation and a refusal to be dictated to by Churchill had secured success. His bold, decisive leadership empowered those under his command and allowed them to excel. He radiated success, and with modern cruisers, destroyers and submarines joining the fleet he could have been forgiven a little self-satisfaction. But that was not his way: he anticipated German intervention. The year ended with his promotion to full admiral, and a KCB followed in March.

By February 1941 the army was on the verge of clearing the Italians out of North Africa – a massive strategic success, turning the tables in dramatic style. But a new enemy was on the horizon.[18] On 10 January the fleet was at sea for another interlocking ship-ping-escort mission when two Italian torpedo bombers pulled *Illustrious*'s fighters down to sea level. Right on cue, forty-three German Ju 87 'Stuka' dive-bombers of the elite anti-shipping detachment *Fliegerkorps X* arrived overhead. Despite a massive anti-aircraft barrage, the attacks were pressed home with skill and determination worthy of a better cause. As Cunningham noted, 'We were watching complete experts.'[19] Six bombs hit the carrier and over a hundred men were killed, including many of the air crew from Taranto. Armoured decks, stout construction and outstanding fire-fighting kept the carrier afloat, and three hours later she was heading for Malta at seventeen knots; another hit later in the day made little difference. The next day the cruiser *Southampton* was sunk by the same aircraft.

Cunningham had lost his carrier. Despite being well aware that she was the prime target, he had ignored the urgent request of Lumley-Lyster and Captain Boyd that the ship be detached from the fleet. With only six serviceable fighters her defences were weak, and there was no radar warning of the attack. While mistakes were made at the tactical level, Cunningham had been stressing the need for additional fighters for months, a concern that the arrival of the Luftwaffe only emphasised. His protests were unavailing. The Mediterranean did not have top priority for air assets. The ongoing air campaign in northern Europe and the battle of the Atlantic had first call on resources.

Fortunately the small, quiet U-class submarines were taking their toll on the Axis convoys to Libya. Further intelligence insights, courtesy of the Luftwaffe, persuaded ABC to move a destroyer flotilla to Malta on 8 April. It demonstrated the value of surface command only eight days later by annihilating an entire convoy.[20] Within twelve months, a third of Italy's merchant shipping had been sunk. With precious few replacements being built, such losses made the outcome of the North African campaign inevitable. Unable to send the ships and fighters needed to stop the Axis convoys, Pound came up with a ludicrous scheme to block the harbours at Tripoli and Benghazi with the battleship HMS *Barham* and a small cruiser. Cunningham was disgusted, well aware that such operations rarely achieve anything and unwilling to risk useful ships and their priceless crews on such foolishness. Behind Pound's nonsense lay Churchill, the arch-exponent of the futile gesture. Since the outbreak of war with Italy he had been obsessed with the idea that Cunningham – of all people – was insufficiently aggressive. On 12 April he told Pound that the navy was 'sitting passive' despite an overriding need to stop Axis convoys. Fortunately Pound had the sense to keep this insult from Cunningham.[21] On 21 April the fleet bombarded Tripoli, doing significant damage.

The main reason that Cunningham could not concentrate on attacking the Axis convoys was his need to supply the isolated fortress at Tobruk, a constant, costly commitment, and to escort fifty-eight thousand troops to Greece in pursuit of another Churchillian initiative. Just as the Italians were on the verge of being expelled from Africa, much of Wavell's successful army was moved to a new theatre. The Greeks had beaten off an initial Italian attack in 1940, but German air and ground forces soon turned the tables. They attacked on 6 April, forcing the British to evacuate almost as soon as they arrived. Having protested in vain at the decision to push the fleet into waters where they had no air cover, Cunningham, an amphibious veteran, ordered his staff to prepare for another Dunkirk.[22] The loss of priceless ships, men and, above all, opportunities for other operations made the entire Greek episode utterly futile. The fleet paid a high price for Churchill's political gesture.

Matapan

With convoys carrying an army to Greece, Cunningham expected an Italian attack. The target was simply too tempting, and a powerful force led by the new battleship *Vittorio Veneto* set out on the night of 26 March to sweep the area around Crete. Slapdash procedures for air–sea cooperation left Admiral Iachino without air cover or reconnaissance, while Luftwaffe radio traffic gave British codebreakers vital information. This 'Ultra' intelligence was carefully disguised by dispatching a flying boat to make visual contact.[23] Cunningham quickly marshalled his forces and diverted the troop convoys, leaving Alexandria himself late on the 27th. He spent the day, as he always did when at sea, pacing up and down on the flag bridge; his staff called this the 'caged tiger' routine, but it gave him time and space to think. At 08.00 the following morning British and Italian cruisers exchanged fire, although without scoring any hits. Outnumbered and outgunned, Rear Admiral Pridham-Wippell retired towards Cunningham. Iachino's trap was sprung, with the British cruisers caught between his battleship and his cruisers. Cunningham responded quickly: he committed the torpedo bombers of the newly arrived carrier *Formidable*, which he had been holding back for a short-range strike to cripple the enemy. The attack forced Iachino to turn away, although he avoided any damage. Iachino had at least a five-knot speed advantage, and Cunningham depended on his aircraft to slow him down. Contact was lost until mid-afternoon, when a second strike was flown off. One plane pressed home to point-blank range and torpedoed the Italian battleship, although it was shot down in the process. The torpedo caused severe flooding and temporarily brought the forty-five-thousand-ton ship to a standstill. However, the *Vittorio Veneto* was soon under way, managing a speed of almost twenty knots. Thoroughly chastened, Iachino gathered his fleet around the flagship for added security and headed home.

Despite the advice of his staff, ABC decided to press on and seek a night action. He knew the Italians were unprepared, did not have radar and were already rather shaky. Furthermore, he might never get another opportunity. Another air strike crippled the ten-thousand-ton cruiser *Pola*, which was left wallowing in the wake of the fleet. Cunningham sent his cruisers ahead to find the enemy, so the destroyers could conduct a torpedo attack. Sensing a first-rate battle was within his grasp, his decisions were quick, clear and precise. The three battleships, *Warspite*, *Valiant* and *Barham*, with the *Formidable* in company, pressed on. Just after 22.00 *Valiant* reported radar contact with a large ship, but as the fleet changed course two cruisers were sighted about two and a half miles ahead on the starboard bow. Not realising that Cunningham was so close, Iachino had detached *Zara* and *Fiume* with three destroyers to find their sister ship. Caught completely unawares, their main armament trained fore and aft, the gun crews not at action stations, the cruisers were sitting ducks. Ordering *Formidable* out of the battle line, Cunningham swiftly brought the broadsides of his battleships to bear and opened fire at 3,800 yards, point-blank for fifteen-inch guns. It took only seven minutes to reduce the Italian ships to blazing wrecks. Two destroyers were sunk by British forces before the crippled *Pola* was located. The crew was taken off and the ship was sunk. British losses were two aircraft and their brave crew.

Despite the British success, the big prize had escaped. Shortly after sinking the two cruisers, an excited, determined Cunningham sent a badly worded signal to his cruisers and destroyers, despite advice from his staff, and they never made contact with the main Italian force. However, it is unlikely they lost an opportunity: neither was heading in the right direction! Had they found Iachino, an action early the next morning might have been possible, but the fleet would have been very close to the Italian coast and exposed to heavy air attack.

Cape Matapan was a major success, finishing off the morale of the Italian fleet and ensuring it remained shackled to shore-based air support for the rest of the war. Cunningham had demonstrated a mastery of fleet action and the high quality of his fleet. He responded to each twist and turn of the action instinctively, with only one minor error.

Disaster

As the Germans advanced into Greece, the navy began evacuating the troops. Cunningham detailed Rear Admirals Pridham-Wippell and Baillie-Grohman to conduct the evacuation; they rescued over fifty thousand troops. Cunningham expected everyone to share his absolute commitment: when the captain of HMAS *Perth* abandoned an evacuation without sighting the enemy, he was immediately relieved of his command. The Greek tragedy left the fleet exhausted, and any fresh ships that arrived quickly took their turn in the Mediterranean meat grinder. ABC's inspirational leadership and example was never seen to greater advantage than in this tense situation. He expected everything from his fleet, and gave his all to the officers and men under his command.

Many of the troops removed from Greece were deployed to Crete, ill organised and short of heavy equipment. Suda Bay had become a major forward base for the fleet, although the defences were flimsy, the cruiser *York* being sunk by an explosive motor boat in late March. An Axis attack was anticipated, and 'Ultra' intelligence laid bare the entire operational plan: the Germans would combine a parachute landing with seaborne invasion. Only the precise date was unknown. Cunningham deployed cruisers and destroyers to intercept troop convoys but held the heavy ships back.

In between the two evacuations Cunningham restructured his command system so he could stay ashore to cooperate with his army and air-force colleagues. Superior shore-based communication links enabled him to receive sensitive information through the 'Ultra' sources. The fleet was deployed in four dispersed formations:

After deep consideration I had decided against going to sea personally. It was imperative that I should be in Alexandria in good communication with all the four dispersed forces at sea, and to direct the naval side of the operation as a whole. It was necessary, too, that I should be in the closest touch with my colleagues, the other Commanders-in-Chief.[24]

This was a difficult decision for Cunningham: his instincts and his experience told him that admirals commanded at sea, but intelligence, communications and joint-service command made his presence ashore essential.

On 20 May the Luftwaffe launched a heavy attack on the defences of Maleme airfield, and then dropped a large force of paratroopers, who captured the landing strip. Reinforcements were quickly flown in, and the Germans gained the upper hand. The seaborne invasion was a complete failure: no German troops reached Crete by sea, as Cunningham's excellent dispositions ensured his ships drove off or sank the makeshift assembly of coasters and caiques that passed for military transport. But the cost of these operations was high. On the 21st massed Stuka attacks left *Warspite* damaged, with two cruisers and a destroyer sunk; two more, including Lord Louis Mountbatten's *Kelly*, were lost the next morning. Cunningham found it difficult to coordinate his forces from his shore headquarters. As the battle hung in the balance, he was still sending in military reinforcements, and on 24 May he issued a characteristic signal to the fleet: 'The Army is just holding its own . . . we must NOT let them down.'[25] When Churchill interfered, forcing the Admiralty to countermand his orders, Cunningham simply repeated them.

Desperate to relieve the pressure on the fleet, Cunningham made a second serious mistake with a carrier. He sent *Formidable*, with only four serviceable fighters, to bomb the airfield at Scarpanto. Not only was the bombing ineffectual, but twenty Stukas crippled the carrier and a destroyer. *Formidable* followed *Illustrious* out of the theatre, leaving Cunningham without air cover. This time there were no replacements. Having risked his greatest asset on a trifling operation, he lost air cover and torpedo strike.

There was no time for reflection: the battle for Crete had been lost, and the following night the evacuation began. Most of the troops were taken off a shallow beach on the south coast by worn-out destroyers with fragile crews. The ships and their khaki-clad passengers suffered heavy losses on the passage to Alexandria, and even Cunningham briefly questioned the wisdom of carrying on. But despite the cost, and utterly bereft of air cover, the fleet carried on. Everyone was stretched beyond endurance, and it required all Cunningham's experience and skill to keep the officers and men at their posts. Captain Lees of the anti-aircraft cruiser HMS *Calcutta*, Cunningham's old ship, had protested when ordered back to Crete, but Cunningham 'talked to me quietly, like a father, explaining everything, including his own misery at being ashore whilst the ships of his Fleet were being decimated'. The next morning Cunningham was on the jetty at Alexandria when HMS *Carlisle* brought in *Calcutta*'s survivors. She had been sunk on the way to Crete with the loss of a hundred and fifty officers and men. Cunningham boarded the cruiser: 'as we walked up and down on the quarterdeck, he was in tears'.[26] It was a rare insight into the mind of a man who appeared to the world the very model of resolution and confidence. He was deeply troubled by the belief that had he been at sea, some ships might have been saved by better tactical choices. This was the central dilemma of modern command: he had to delegate such decisions to the men on the spot and restrict himself to providing intelligence and support. If they failed, they were relieved.[27]

The air–sea battle off Crete had been lost – the Germans had pre-vailed at the cost of thirty to forty aircraft – but once again the bulk of the army, some 16,500 troops, had been withdrawn. Without air cover the fleet found their anti-aircraft fire inadequate in the face of mass attacks. Only concentrated forces could survive, using well-organised barrage fire to cover threatened ships and employing vio-lent evasive manoeuvres. Big ships were sitting ducks, though that said half a dozen well-placed Fulmars could break up any dive-bomber attack. Slow Stukas were easy meat for modern fighters: 'In my opinion three squadrons of long-range fighters and a few heavy bombing squadrons would have saved Crete,' he declared.[28]

Despite serious losses of ships and men, Cunningham refused to give up: even when Wavell said he had done enough he insisted on going back another night because 'the Navy had never yet failed the Army in such a situation, and was not going to do so now; he was going in again that night with everything he had which would float'.[29] As he told his staff when they advised him to call off the operation, 'You can build a new ship in three years but you can't rebuild a reputation in under three hundred years.'[30] Crete had cost the navy 1,828 dead and 183 wounded; plus the loss of three cruis-ers and six destroyers, and serious damage to two battleships, a car-rier, two cruisers and two destroyers. Furious that London had failed to provide the essential air assets, Cunningham contemplated resignation.[31]

However, true greatness triumphs over adversity. Cunningham evacuated the army from Greece and Crete, under relentless attacks from the Luftwaffe. When his officers began to crumble under the intense pressure, Cunningham used every trick in the book, from fatherly chats to the threat of a court martial, to keep the evacua-tion going long enough to snatch an army from the jaws of a German prison camp.[32] His example inspired tired men to carry on, brave men to surpass themselves, and bold men to be more auda-cious. He was the driving intellect of the naval war.

Not that there was much hope that the navy could improve the situation while the enemy held the upper hand in the air. London seemed unable to provide fighters, leaving Cunningham restricted to night operations and occasional forays relying on feeble RAF shore-based cover. Yet he bounced back from the despondency of the Cretan disaster and found some peace ashore on the golf course or at home with his wife and the inevitable collection of lively young people. But as soon as he returned to work he assumed the mask of command, bullying his staff and demanding the impossible. Those who met his standards received the praise they deserved, however. When Rear Admiral Bernard Rawlings, who commanded the fleet during the Crete operation, went home exhausted, ABC singled out his 'capability of rapid and courageous decision in tight corners . . . he seemed instinctively to do the right thing'.[33] Rawlings ended the war in operational command of the British Pacific Fleet.

Admiral Ashore

With few serviceable destroyers and no naval air cover, the battle fleet spent the rest of the year in harbour. Forced onto the defensive, Cunningham found his situation deeply galling, as Philip Vian later recognised:

As I see it one of the most difficult of the Commander-in-Chief's jobs is keeping up the morale of the sailors, the sea-going ones, in present circumstances. It is not easy to sit in an armchair and send ships out, well knowing the time they are going to have until they return to harbour.[34]

With the supply run to Tobruk taking a heavy toll on his smaller ships, and Malta effectively isolated, he warned Pound that 'We are on the edge of a disaster here.'[35] To make matters worse, Air Marshal Longmore was replaced by Arthur Tedder, whom Cunningham considered 'capable but crooked', interested only in the 'glorification of the RAF',[36] while the army suffered further defeat at the hands of Erwin Rommel's Afrika Korps. Concern that the French regime in Syria was preparing to link up with the Germans prompted a diversion of naval assets to support an invasion in early June. It took six weeks to force the French to settle, costing the fleet aircraft and ships it could not afford. When Sir Claude Auchinlek replaced Wavell, Cunningham found himself isolated: Auchinlek was utterly ignorant of the valuable naval support he received, and agreed with Tedder that Cunningham should be replaced by someone more pliable. At least all three men agreed on the need to secure Egypt as the base for all future British operations – and dismissed Churchill's absurd call that they plan to invade Sicily. Wavell and Longmore had been sacked for failing in missions that they lacked the political courage to refuse. ABC survived because he was tougher and refused to act against his judgement.

Cunningham's new colleagues complained when he went to sea with the fleet, seemingly unaware that admirals had always been in the thick of the fighting, not taking decisions in air-conditioned offices. He refused to move his headquarters to Cairo, preferring to fly in once a week. Disgusted by Tedder's inadequate provision of air support, in contrast to Longmore's more collegiate approach, Cunningham launched a successful campaign to secure operational control of significant air assets for the naval war. Tedder called for Cunningham to be relieved, but Churchill and the chiefs of staff backed him. It must have been a relief to defeat this bloody-minded airman. Tedder bent before the decision and got on with his job. Cunningham soon realised that Tedder possessed valuable organisational and management skills. While air assets were vital, they were no substitute for surface ships in exploiting command of the sea.

In October Cunningham detached another intelligence-led surface striking force to Malta to support Operation Crusader.[37] Force K paid dividends, destroying seven out of eight merchant ships and three out of four escorts in a night action. Further successes followed, including the destruction of two cruisers carrying Rommel's petrol. Clearly the Germans were desperate. Later the same month a handful of U-boats entered the Mediterranean with immediate impact. They sank the carrier *Ark Royal* off Gibraltar and then the battleship *Barham* on 25 November, during Cunningham's last operation with the fleet. Finally, early on 19 December, an Italian human torpedo attack crippled his last two battleships. The *Queen Elizabeth* and *Valiant* were left resting on the bottom of Alexandria harbour, just like the Italian battle fleet thirteen months before. Cunningham maintained the appearance of power by keeping his office on the former, which was upright, if a little low in the water. On the same day, the Malta striking force was destroyed by a minefield, two more cruisers were lost and other ships were simply incapable of operating. The loss of the *Prince of Wales* and *Repulse* off Malaya, in addition to all the other calamities, made late 1941 a terrible time for the Royal Navy. The only positive note was that the Italians, lacking fuel and confidence, were not minded to use their fleet, despite the lack of British capital ships in the eastern Mediterranean. Cunningham was left to worry about the Suez

Canal, the army's lifeline, which was frequently bombed and mined, and Malta, the linchpin of the entire theatre. The Malta supply run was essential, and for this mission he had secured the navy's best combat commander, Rear Admiral Philip Vian. Vian had served under ABC in the 1930s, and his war record was unequalled. Like ABC he was single-minded, hard-driving and overbearing, but tactically astute – an inspiring leader full of invention.

On 15 December 1941 Vian sailed with three light cruisers and seven destroyers to escort a tanker and search for a convoy that 'Ultra' information had revealed would sail that night. Just before he met the Malta striking force, he was surprised by an Italian force of three battleships, two heavy cruisers and several destroyers. Already under heavy air attack, Vian immediately established a thick smokescreen, and by threatening torpedo attacks kept the enemy at a distance until nightfall, while handing the tanker to ships from Malta. He could not locate the Italian convoy that had crossed his path, but he managed to get home unscathed. The first battle of Cape Sirte ended in a draw: Malta was refuelled, but the Axis convoy delivered vital ammunition just in time to repulse Operation Crusader.

A repeat operation on 12 February was less successful: two out of three merchant ships heading for Malta were sunk, the third forced to turn back. Malta had been reinforced with fighters, enabling naval and air forces to use it as a base to attack Axis convoys to North Africa, but food and fuel were short. Another convoy would have to be sent, with supporting operations by the air force and army to distract the Luftwaffe. Vian left Alexandria on 20 March with three cruisers and sixteen destroyers, later joined by a cruiser and a destroyer from Malta to escort four fast merchant ships. When Vian asked what he should do if a superior Italian surface force appeared, Cunningham told him to use his initiative, but that 'if he made enough smoke the Italian Fleet would not come through it'.[38] Vian took no chances, exercising his force in small-unit surface-warfare tactics and smoke-laying. Like Cunningham he made sure all his captains knew exactly what he expected, to minimise the need for communication during the battle. For two days he avoided air attack, but on the 22nd a hundred and fifty Axis planes were driven off by effective barrage fire and long-range Beaufighter aircraft. Then, with the wind and sea rising to a storm, an Italian force of cruisers and destroyers was sighted to the north-east. Vian detached the convoy with an anti-aircraft escort comprising one cruiser and four destroyers; the remaining ships steered towards the enemy. After an inconclusive forty-five-minute engagement the Italians broke off, only to reappear a little over an hour later, this time with a second formation, led by the battleship *Littorio* in concert. They were looking for the convoy. Vian laid a massive smokescreen, and for the next three hours, every time the Italians tried to work round it, he extended the cover and threatened a torpedo attack. Although the range briefly came down to six thousand yards, before a torpedo attack forced the enemy to sheer off, the sea conditions and heavy smokescreens did not favour accurate gunnery, and Vian's ships only scored a single hit. Unwilling to fight at night, the Italian admiral broke off the action at dusk, leaving two British destroyers badly damaged but the convoy unscathed, despite repeated air attacks. In action, Vian was remarkably similar to Cunningham.[39]

While all this was going on, Cunningham, who had spent the greater part of his career preparing for just such an action, was forced to wait and listen with his staff at Alexandria. This was a strange situation for him:

Never have I felt so keenly the mortifying bitterness of sitting behind the scenes with a heavy load of responsibility while others were in action with a vastly superior force of the enemy. We could visualise so well what was happening . . . We could imagine it all, yet there was nothing we could do to help.[40]

In reality Cunningham handled the situation perfectly: he helped Vian by leaving him to fight the battle. He had real-time radio communication with the squadron, a very good picture of the unfolding drama and the penetration to know what needed to be done, but he left the decisions to the man on the spot. No sooner had he thought of the right response than Vian had executed it, prompting shouts of 'Good boy!' and 'There you are, he is right again.'[41] Cunningham displayed his true greatness by not interfering. When Vian reached Alexandria, Cunningham went aboard his flagship to congratulate him on 'one of the most brilliant naval actions of the war, if not the most brilliant'.[42]

Unfortunately the tactical success came at a price. Four destroyers were sunk during the operation, and only two remained serviceable, while the three ships that reached Malta were destroyed by air attack before much of their cargo could be unloaded. Cunningham advised the Admiralty that any future convoys would require much greater air cover. Axis air attacks were wearing down Malta, and only a massive reinforcement of modern fighters, not the obsolescent Hurricanes that were being sent, would enable the island to operate as a striking base. Forty-seven Spitfire Vs arrived at the same time as Vian's convoy, flown in from the west by carriers, and they began to turn the tide, but not before all naval units had been withdrawn from the island. Fortunately the First and Tenth Submarine flotillas, under Cunningham's direction, became increasingly effective against Axis shipping, while major air reinforcements soon arrived with a dedicated command for anti-shipping missions.

Washington

On 3 April 1942 Cunningham flew home to London, handing over command of the Mediterranean fleet. Without a fleet there was little prospect of taking the offensive and little purpose in remaining. By driving his officers, men and ships to the absolute limit, Cunningham kept Britain in the Mediterranean, Malta in British hands, and the Eighth Army in action. His departure was not announced, in case the enemy took heart.

He had been detailed to add weight and experience to the British Admiralty delegation in Washington, but before that he took the opportunity for a long-overdue rest, visiting his relations and fishing. Despite his constant criticisms, Churchill now asked Cunningham to replace his friend Vice Admiral Tovey as Commander-in-Chief Home Fleet. Cunningham refused point blank, unless Tovey dropped dead! After strong-arming the Treasury into providing a chauffeur-driven Rolls, Cunningham and Nona flew to Washington in late June. Acutely aware of the need to make the right impression, representing his country as well as his service, ABC didn't miss a trick when he moved from theatre command to defence diplomacy. The American Chief of Naval Operations, Admiral 'Ernie' King, would be the most formidable foe he ever faced.[43] King combined a powerful intellect and superb organisational skills with a thoroughly unpleasant character and vitriolic hatred of the Royal

Navy. He was little better disposed towards the United States army, and reckoned the war in the Pacific should take priority. While King had ridden roughshod over his predecessor, Cunningham called his bluff, using his meetings with the American joint chiefs of staff and some pretty blunt language to clear the air. He also insisted on receiving the latest 'Ultra' briefs, to ensure he was fully up to date when he met the Americans.[44] Success in Washington laid the foundations for the next stage of his career: American decision-makers were impressed by his clear and cogent strategic analysis, integrity, unrivalled command experience and willingness to cooperate.

Despite Ernie King and his generals, President Roosevelt decided in July 1942 to conduct an Allied invasion of French North Africa, Operation 'Torch'. Cunningham agreed: the Mediterranean was the only place where the Allies could use sea power and the rapidly expanding American army to achieve a strategic success in the next eighteen months. Anticipating opening the Mediterranean sea lanes and knocking Italy out of the war, he pressed Pound for the naval command. The American army acknowledged his expertise and liked anyone who stood up to Ernie King. Although King opposed the operation, he cheered the appointment: 'They got *a man*,' he declared. 'He would fight like Hell.'[45] ABC was an equally astute judge of men, making it his business to work closely with the inexperienced American commanding general, Dwight D. Eisenhower, his junior in age and rank. Without ever overstepping the lines of authority, the veteran warrior made it his business to educate Ike about sea power and the Mediterranean, laying the foundations for a harmonious partnership.

Cunningham's role would be overall naval command, leaving the detailed planning of the landings and supporting operations to his force commanders, both British and American. The central task, getting the troops ashore at three widely dispersed points, was handled by Admiral Sir Bertram Ramsay, architect of the Dunkirk evacuation and a master of detailed operational planning. Torch was his first big operation; his masterpiece would be D-Day. Although he recognised Ramsay's talent, Cunningham treated him badly, partly because he was jealous of another brilliant flag officer, and partly because Ramsay worked well with his *bête noire*, General Sir Bernard Montgomery. It required all the tact his staff could muster to keep ABC's signals to Ramsay from causing a rupture.[46] With such capable subordinates, and a hand-picked staff, ABC could concentrate on the real problem: ensuring harmony among the Allies. His good humour, common sense and realism held the whole project together. Landings at Casablanca, Oran and Algiers went ahead on 8 November 1942, quickly overcoming Vichy French resistance. When the Vichy leader Admiral Darlan changed sides, the balance of the war in Europe swung heavily in the Allies' favour. ABC played a key role in bringing Darlan to the Allied side; Harold Macmillan, the government's Minister Resident, considered him 'a splendid man and absolutely first class and a most amusing and agreeable companion'.[47]

The Vichy collapse forced Germany to spread its forces more widely, threatened Italy and ended any possibility that Spain might join the Axis. Only Admiral Godfroy, still tied up inert at Alexandria, refused to change sides. He waited until May 1943, when all North Africa had been cleared. By late November Ike and ABC were living ashore in adjacent villas at Algiers. Success and frequent social occasions developed the curious partnership between the American back-room general and the salt-horse fighting seaman. Ike was particularly struck by ABC's aggression, his toughness and the inspirational effect he had on British servicemen.[48]

Cunningham believed that Tunisia would be the key to the campaign's success. If the Allies could seize it before the Germans, North Africa would be cleared quickly, but he predicted that the failure to push the Torch landings far enough east would be costly. The British First Army was left to advance overland from Algiers, supplied through the small port of Bône. It was like Tobruk in reverse, with costly air–sea battles to push the supplies through. Despite growing Allied success against Axis convoys, Rommel got to Tunis first, but Cunningham used 'Ultra' intelligence decrypts to make him pay heavily.

Despite his wide-ranging command, Cunningham was never too busy to find time for the men. He visited the small ports and isolated commands, spoke to the sailors and conveyed something of his energy and determination to those who were on the front line. His insistence that seamen be properly dressed, even those recently liberated from Vichy prison camps, might have seemed slightly odd, but he wanted his men to take pride in their work. He remained an old-fashioned, autocratic leader, a man who made up his own mind and did not allow his staff, even the impeccable Ramsay, to influence his judgement. His directions remained clear, decisive and resolute, but he unveiled hitherto unexpected qualities of cooperation, tact, diplomacy and patience in pressing forward the strategic agenda. While he worked his chosen officers hard, he also took a fatherly concern for their health and career prospects. Typically, he had the apparently irreplaceable Vian relieved from his cruiser command in September 1942; in this way Cunningham ensured that Vian would be rested for the second half of the war, when Cunningham would find ever more demanding tasks to tax his talent.[49]

By May 1943 the Axis convoy system to North Africa had been irredeemably broken. Once the Allies had command of the air, surface ships barred the route. That month Cunningham took his revenge for Greece and Crete, launching Operation 'Retribution' with the direction: 'Sink, burn and destroy: Let nothing pass.' Nor was he overly squeamish about the enemy: when a young destroyer commander reported running down a boat-load of German soldiers, ABC 'shook him warmly by the hand and left him without enquiring further'.[50] Two hundred and fifty thousand Axis prisoners were taken, as many as at Stalingrad – a major triumph.

The headquarters at Algiers were visited by Churchill, whose late hours and interference proved as much of a trial for his host as they had been for Fisher. ABC's solution was to live on board a headquarters ship! By contrast, King George VI, who had fought at Jutland, delighted Cunningham by asking to visit Malta. The arrival of the King on board HMS *Aurora* on 20 June 1943 did wonders for the morale of population and servicemen alike. Alongside his numerous awards Cunningham became Commander-in-Chief Mediterranean for a historic second term as the momentum grew for an Allied invasion of Italy. Having secured complete command of all naval assets in theatre, he persuaded Eisenhower to make Tedder overall air commander; much as he disliked the man and his doctrine, he recognised his ability. Sadly Tedder lacked the character to rise above partisan backbiting and resented having to set aside aircraft for naval cooperation.

When the Allies decided on an invasion of Sicily, planning was hampered by the need to finish the North African campaign and the distance between the various headquarters. The self-absorbed, bombastic contributions of General Montgomery did not help. Monty, by now revelling in his celebrity, was apt to think himself the supreme arbiter of all military issues, expecting everyone else, American and British, to fall in with his demands. ABC remained deeply unimpressed.

Massive naval forces, including six battleships and two aircraft carriers, supported the Sicily landings, Operation Husky, on 10 July. Eisenhower joined ABC at Malta to exploit the excellent communications links. Even so, he visited the beachheads on D-Day and went ashore at Augusta on D+8, by which time half a million troops had been landed. He pressed the generals to use the landing craft to leapfrog Axis defences, but only George Patton took advantage of the option, hastening the conquest of the island. Montgomery resolutely refused. By early August the enemy was in full retreat across the Straits of Messina, but the Allies were unable to make much impression on this effort. Even with good intelligence Cunningham and his American task commander Admiral Hewitt were reluctant to risk heavy ships in the enclosed waters.[51] Crete remained a painful memory, to which he frequently referred.

On 25 July Mussolini was dismissed by the King of Italy, paving the way for surrender. Cunningham sensed the time was ripe to strike again, anxious to secure the Italian fleet and release his ships for service elsewhere. The invasion of the mainland began on 8 September, but Cunningham's involvement was largely indirect. His only direct contribution was to organise the rapid movement of the British First Airborne Division to Taranto, settling the fate of the Italian fleet. When the American landings at Salerno came under intense German counter-attacks, he sent reinforcements, including *Warspite*. An eleven-thousand-ton naval bombardment did the trick. Predictably, the Germans had an answer: new radio-controlled glider bombs sank HMS *Spartan*, before crippling *Warspite* and an American cruiser.

ABC received the surrender of the Italian fleet at Malta on 12 September 1943, signalling to the Secretary to the Admiralty: 'Be pleased to inform Their Lordships that the Italian Battle fleet now lies anchored under the guns of the fortress of Malta.'[52] This was his triumph. He was also present when Eisenhower accepted the surrender of Italy at Malta on 29 September, a ceremony very deliberately staged on board HMS *Nelson*. And with that, the Mediterranean ceased to be a significant naval theatre. It was a long time since Cunningham had been an admiral in the Nelsonian sense:

he did not command from the bridge of his flagship; he operated ashore alongside the essential communications and intelligence links, supported by a vast staff. Ironically Cunningham's finest moment as an admiral came during the second battle off Cape Sirte, when he left Vian to fight his own battle.

First Sea Lord

No sooner was the Mediterranean naval war won than Cunningham was needed elsewhere. His old friend Pound suffered a stroke at the Quebec conference, and despite Churchill's anxiety to keep ABC from the post, fearing another clash of wills with a formidable, outspoken admiral, he was the inevitable choice as the new First Sea Lord. ABC refused the poisoned chalice of the South East Asia Command, which went to Mountbatten.[53] He took office on 5 October 1943, and completed the handover of the Mediterranean command on the 16th.[54] This time he was able to thank his officers and men, with tears in his eyes – shed both for the end of his seagoing career and because he was departing before the job was done. The new post, so much coveted by Fisher and Beatty in earlier decades, had never been his ambition. Nor was it the critical role that it had been in 1940–2. The naval war was largely won: the focus had shifted to army and air-force operations, with naval support. Furthermore, the Americans were now dominant at sea. In truth, Cunningham took the job because it was his duty.

He arrived at the Admiralty with a matchless war record and the support of the entire service. In high command over the past year he had revealed a mastery of strategic and political issues that surprised many, reflecting both innate ability and a rare talent for making the best use of a staff. He delegated the routine, and focused on the critical. He and First Lord Harold Alexander, a long-serving Labour politician, had little in common, which may have helped build an effective team. Cunningham worked closely with his fellow chiefs of staff, General Brooke and Air Marshal Portal, all three of them passionate fishermen who were careful to settle their differences in committee without involving the politicians. Having offended the old man of the sea once too often, Churchill expected to be repaid in kind, ascribing to ABC a degree of influence over his two colleagues that was flattering but largely unwarranted.[55]

ABC ran the Admiralty the same way he had run the fleet: he focused on finding the right men for the senior commands, and trusted them to do the job. When Admiral Bruce Fraser engaged the German battleship *Scharnhorst* on Boxing Day 1943, Cunningham remained at home in Bishop's Waltham, using a tele-printer to make sure all the relevant intelligence was sent. He did not interfere, which was all the more remarkable as he did not have a particularly high opinion of Fraser. However, his masterly eye was cast over operational orders before they were sent, and occasionally he would improve them.

Although permanently short of manpower and resources, the most difficult task was forestalling Churchill's endless parade of bizarre strategies. He took office just as one such scheme was launched: the seizure of the Dodecanese Islands. Predictably it did not end well: six destroyers were sunk and the Mediterranean fleet took a battering. In case anyone had missed the utter folly of Churchill's second Greek tragedy, the Germans evacuated the islands a few months later! While Pound had managed Churchill by keeping things smooth, Cunningham preferred to engage the war lord. He soon discovered that once brought to close action, the prime minister's lack of detailed knowledge ensured his schemes quickly disappeared in a cloud of late-night cigar smoke. 'What a drag on the wheel of war this man is. Everything is centralised in him with consequent indecision and waste of time before anything can be done,' Cunningham complained in the privacy of his diary.[56] When Churchill was absent, the war was prosecuted more effectively under the chairmanship of Deputy Prime Minister Clement Attlee, who did not keep such curious hours or try to advise the experts on their business.

The major concerns of Cunningham's time at the Admiralty were the invasion of north-west Europe, the shift of British naval power to the Pacific, and the inevitable post-war demobilisation. He was wise enough to leave alone the areas where he had neither knowledge nor experience, such as the Battle of the Atlantic. Here the relentless Max Horton had ground the U-boats into defeat by the time Cunningham reached Whitehall. By contrast, he took a large role in the planning for D-Day, building good teams, appointing tried men and keeping Churchill from interfering. Ramsay masterminded the five-division landing, and with overwhelming air and

sea support the Allies had established a solid bridgehead by nightfall. Cunningham must have reflected on the bitter defeat at
Gallipoli thirty years earlier, when teamwork, firepower and experience were sadly lacking. Over the next few days naval gunnery
defeated every German counter-attack. When the Allied break-out
drove into the Low Countries, Cunningham was disgusted by
Montgomery's failure to clear the estuary of the River Scheldt in
time to use the undamaged port of Antwerp. It required a major
assault landing at Walcheren to rectify the blunder, one that ensured
the war in Europe would go on into 1945. This risked a revival of
the U-boat effort.

This was worrying because Germany was now mass-producing
advanced Type XXI U-boats and developing radio codes that would
be impenetrable to British decryption. 'Ultra' was going to be
switched off just as the fast deep-diving boats came on stream. In
January 1945 ABC warned the War Cabinet that a renewed U-boat
offensive was imminent. In response, bombing-target priorities were
shifted and half the escort vessels slated to join the Eastern Fleet
were kept at home.[57] Lacking in-depth knowledge of the situation,
Cunningham met the danger by over-insuring.

While Churchill wanted to use the navy to recover the eastern arc
of Empire in Burma and Malaya, Cunningham and the other chiefs
of staff were determined to join the main American attack on Japan,
a task for which the navy was ideally suited. Despite prime ministerial interference, and the hostility of Ernie King, Cunningham
ensured that a modern British fleet operated in the Pacific in spring
1945. Defeating Ernie King was almost as satisfying as winning the
war.[58] While Fraser commanded the British Pacific Fleet from
Sydney, Cunningham protégés Bernard Rawlings and Philip Vian led
the fleet and the carrier force at sea. After learning American procedures, new techniques for afloat replenishment and sustained air
operations, a force led by four battleships and six fleet carriers performed very well in the latter stage of war, dealing with kamikaze
aircraft, typhoons and Ernie King's resentment with equal success.
Units of the fleet, including two battleships, represented Great
Britain at the Japanese surrender in Tokyo Bay in August 1945.
Elsewhere, British warships took the Japanese surrender at
Singapore, Hong Kong and Saigon. It was important for Britain to
be there, and important for the Royal Navy that it rather than the

Royal Air Force represented Britain. When the RAF publicly claimed to have won the Battle of the Atlantic, ABC's fury knew few limits.[59]

War's End

By August 1945 Cunningham was exhausted and depressed. After six years of constant warfare he needed a break, but his sense of duty would not let him give up his post until he had set the navy on the right course for the future. A new Labour government, a shattered economy and a seemingly limitless demand for manpower dashed any hopes of a substantial post-war fleet. By late 1947 only ninety-eight thousand men remained, and the fleet was massively over-committed to post-war occupation, reconstruction, relief and diplomatic support. One possible response to this situation was the retention of female personnel, the WRNS or 'Wrens'. ABC, for his part, showed his unreconstructed Edwardian attitude by arguing that there was no reason to sacrifice either thirteen-year-old entry at Dartmouth or the clear distinction between officers and ratings, but the new government was determined, and he lost both battles. At least he kept the key commands in the hands of his followers, helping to set the tone of the post-war service.

New ships were hard to come by, while many old warriors were pensioned off into the reserve. The navy needed time to digest the lessons of war: new threats from atomic bombs, fast submarines and jet aircraft renewed old doubts about surface ships. It was fortunate that ABC did not have the chance to do much in this area: his mania for small, cheap warships, allied to a visceral dislike of new 'gadgets', left him mired in the past. This mattered because the events of 1940–1 were no longer much use as a guide to the next war. There was no longer an enemy for a classic fleet to fight: the Americans were not an option, and no one else had a navy worth a damn – indeed, Canada ended the war in third place, behind the two larger anglophone navies. It was time to demobilise, save money, plan for the future and see what shape the post-war world would take. Having met Stalin at Yalta, ABC recognised his skill, ruthlessness and determination. Anxious to keep the latest technology from the Soviets, he rushed to strip captured German dockyards of useful equipment and destroy German naval resources. Britain secured the latest German submarine technology, including the advanced air-independent power plant designed by Dr Walther. They also hired the doctor.[60]

Having fought long and hard to keep Britain in the Mediterranean, against Italian, German and American pressure, Cunningham was forced to watch as his legacy slipped away. A hundred and fifty years of British pre-eminence in the Mediterranean ended on his watch. It was sickening – but inevitable. By the time he left office the US Navy was top dog in those classic waters; Britain could not afford the honour. On the positive side, ABC gave the Royal Marines a new identity, as amphibious experts, and prepared the ground for another battle with the Royal Air Force over naval aviation, especially the shore stations. In March 1946 he suffered a heart attack, and although he made a full recovery it sealed his decision to lay down the burden. On 8 June he handed it on to his chosen successor, his namesake (but not relation) John Cunningham. He was sixty-three and had given his country fifty years of service – his profession had been his life. He never retired as an admiral of the fleet, remaining on full pay for the rest of his life, but there were no more jobs for him. He turned down a royal invitation to be governor general of Australia, ostensibly on health grounds, although his real concern was the expense he would incur.

Retired

In retirement ABC took pride in renewing his Scots identity: he became a knight of the Order of the Thistle in January 1945, and when a viscountcy was forced on him a year later, he chose the title Viscount Cunningham of Hyndhope, an obscure Scots village from which his ancestors hailed. At least the title enabled him to speak on naval matters in the House of Lords. He collaborated closely with the official historian of the navy's war, Captain Stephen Roskill, ensuring the past was moulded into a form that would serve the navy's current agendas. His autobiography, a task he undertook with considerable reluctance, proved to be a best-seller, once it had been suitably polished by Captain Taprell Dorling, an old destroyer colleague and experienced naval author. He chose the tenth anniversary of Matapan to launch the book. This was a professional life, revealing very little of the man, and it carefully toned down his real feelings about those who thwarted him – especially the real 'enemy' of his war, Winston Churchill.[61]

Cunningham reinforced his Scots identity by taking the office of Lord High Commissioner of the Church of Scotland in 1950 and 1952, when he lived at Holyrood House. Otherwise he lived at Palace House, which he had been able to purchase, enjoying trophies of his career, a bust of Nelson and a large garden, his real pleasure. Annual pilgrimages to fish in Scotland provided some variation, as did visits from officers who served under him in the war – Tovey, Rawlings, Vian, Royer Dick, Manley Power – and young relatives, including his great-nephew Jock Slater, who followed in his footsteps as First Sea Lord and admiral of the fleet.

After fifty years of hard service, Andrew Browne Cunningham enjoyed fifteen years of peaceful, slightly self-indulgent retirement. Having outlived the biblical term by a full decade, he died suddenly and quietly in a taxi halfway between his club and Waterloo Station on 12 June 1963. The decisive quality of his heart attack was typical of a man who didn't have much time for sentiment – there was no need for any fuss. Six days later the mortal remains of Admiral Lord Cunningham of Hyndhope were buried at sea, dropped into the Solent from the deck of a destroyer, in the presence of the Board of Admiralty and his family. With that the age of the admiral passed. On 2 April 1967 a bust of the last admiral joined those of Jellicoe and Beatty at the north end of Trafalgar Square, in the mighty shadow of Nelson.

Cunningham was a throwback to the heroic age of naval command. While his contemporaries balanced their careers between ship and shore, he avoided the latter with a single-minded passion that reflected an innate dislike of office, routine and politics. His was a career of unsurpassed commitment and professionalism, topped off by an uncanny ability to rise to any challenge that the service threw at him, from rescuing defeated armies and disarming truculent Frenchmen to managing raw Americans. Making his name as a destroyer commander in the Dardanelles, he missed Jutland and the Beatty–Jellicoe feud. Between the wars, he reached the top of his profession via a succession of sea postings, a few educational opportunities and the failing health of colleagues who spent too much time in unhealthy offices. The final shuffle of the admirals' pack in mid-

1939 took him from the Admiralty to the Mediterranean, just when his resource and determination were most required.

As Commander-in-Chief Mediterranean, Cunningham became a household name in Britain, the Empire and the world. He was magnificent in victory, unbreakable in defeat, possessing the spirit and determination to carry on, the intellect to know what was right and the political courage to defy his superiors. He refused to fill his head with unnecessary information: specialist knowledge never compromised his single-minded concern to reach the highest standards and win. He kept the business of war at sea simple, and he made it work. Nelson would have been proud. He had the right instincts and the professionalism to ensure they were translated into effective action.

Philip Vian understood perhaps better than anyone what it took to be a great fighting commander in the Mediterranean, and his praise for Cunningham knew no bounds: he had 'lightning reactions at sea . . . unrivalled powers of observation . . . he was a seaman through and through . . . His known character did the rest.' There was a certain 'relentlessness in the pursuit of excellence . . . and utter fearlessness and composure in adversity'. Above all, Vian realised that 'Behind the bluff façade . . . there lay a very acute and a very astute brain', 'a kind heart and great humanity'. However, the last line contained the sentiment that would have pleased Cunningham the most, not least because it came from another great destroyer commander: 'He was a leader whose orders could never be questioned and whom it would be unthinkable to let down.'[62]

EPILOGUE

Reflections on a Lost Age

By the second decade of the twentieth century, global cable and wireless networks enabled political authorities to take the higher strategic direction of war into their own hands. By 1942 admirals afloat were restricted to operational command: the key players operated ashore, surrounded by large staffs, tied to secure communications, and alongside their political masters. It was the end of a unique art. The men who feature in this book were fortunate to live in a world where the 'rules of engagement' were clear. The added strain produced by modern limited wars came through all too clearly in the Falklands campaign.[1]

Early on 2 May 1982 Rear Admiral John 'Sandy' Woodward ordered the nuclear submarine HMS *Conqueror* to sink a large Argentinian warship that threatened his task force and the British mission to recapture the Falkland Islands. Simple enough, one might think. *Conqueror* took in the signal, and did nothing. Woodward had no authority to order the submarine to engage: his message had been issued to ginger up the command team back in Britain, where the necessary authority lay. The political sensitivities of war and of nuclear-powered warships had persuaded the government that final authority must remain at home. We know exactly what Nelson would have made of such attempts to finesse war: he demonstrated his views at Copenhagen. But Woodward had no 'blind eye': the electronic systems of 1982 gave Fleet Headquarters at Northwood in west London an ability to direct his movements that Sir Hyde Parker did not possess in 1801, even though he could see Nelson's ships.

Woodward's 'order' had the desired effect, but it was a crude,

ADMIRALS

cumbersome method of waging war, one that placed his ships in
unnecessary danger. It also marked the end of the line for the art
of the seagoing admiral. Naval command had evolved and developed over the previous four hundred years to meet the demands
posed by changes in ships, weapons, theatres and political align-
ments. But in the twentieth century the big decisions slowly leeched
away from the seagoing commander to his superiors ashore, who
had more access to information, better communications and closer
proximity to the political leadership. In the First World War the
Admiralty tried to run the Grand Fleet by radio, with decidedly
mixed results, but systems improved and by 1943 Andrew
Cunningham was obliged, much against his wishes, to command
the Mediterranean from a bunker. He had been the last admiral to
command a major theatre from a flagship while exercising tactical
control of the fleet.

Politics and communications meant that Rear Admiral Wood-
ward had significantly less freedom of action off Port Stanley than
Lord Howard off Gravelines in 1588. The Falklands campaign was
controlled by the Commander-in-Chief Fleet, Admiral Sir John
Fieldhouse, from the headquarters at Northwood. He supervised
Woodward's campaign, while the Chief of Defence Staff, Admiral
Sir Terence Lewin, worked hard to insulate the operational com-
mander from the more damaging aspects of political control.
However, it is worth quoting Woodward's account of how he receiv-
ed the key order of the war:

I received my orders personally from the Commander in Chief, Fleet,
Admiral Sir John Fieldhouse. As expected they were succinct. He gave me
permission to proceed with the landing, using my own local judgement as
to the day chosen . . . The C-in-C had left the decision on timing to me
alone.[2]

This demonstrates that the traditional skills of the admiral still
count for something: Woodward's account contains more than an
echo of the relationship between Cunningham and Vian, between
Nelson and his captains, between all great commanders and their
trusted subordinates. While it is highly unlikely that any future
admiral will exercise command in the same way as the men in this
book, it is equally clear that naval command will remain a vital task,
increasingly positioned in the political dimension.

The admirals in this book developed and defined their art: they shaped the systems and methods of command, directing the grim business of war and often equally fraught days of peace with a rich mix of skills, as seamen, diplomats, warriors, administrators, politicians and innovators. The variety of assets required for success at the highest level was ceaselessly recombined to address the complex problems posed by wind and weather, war and peace, economic hardship and novel technology. These men, among the best ever to hold that rank, demonstrate that there is no single template against which admirals can be measured. While no two admirals faced the same problems, larger patterns emerge. Successful admirals possessed the confidence to lead, the ability to see beyond the fog of battle, to deal with political masters as demanding as Elizabeth I and Winston Churchill, and the ability to make the right decisions. None could succeed without education – both professional and humane. Only an educated mind has the ability to master the business in hand and see its wider importance. Such insight provides the proper context for decision – the ability to get inside the enemy's decision-making cycle, seize the initiative and apply force with skill. Tough decisions require courage – physical and, above all, moral. The ability to issue orders that will lead to the deaths of many in the interests of a higher aim and to question the judgement of those in superior authority is essential. These were the qualities Nelson valued above all others, ones he found lacking in many of his otherwise brave and brilliant contemporaries. To translate insight and decision into action and success, admirals rely on leadership: the ability to engage with the moral and mental resources of the people who alone can make a fighting force great, inspiring them with the conviction that their cause is just, their equipment effective and their commander successful. While this task has a critical moral dimension, there is no requirement for admirals to be admirable people. Many great leaders have been truly appalling human beings – including James II. The fact that Nelson was universally loved merely emphasises his unique genius.

Counter-intuitive though it may seem, seamanship has never been a primary requirement for a great admiral. In retirement John Fisher observed: 'To be a good admiral, a man does not need to be a good sailor. That's a common mistake. He needs good sailors under him.'[3] Some of the admirals in this study were skilled sailors: Anson,

Hood, Jervis, Parker, Hornby and Cunningham. Lord Howard, Blake and James, Duke of York were not professionals, though, while Fisher was at best an ordinary seaman, and Beatty's panache was frequently compromised by carelessness. Nor is it necessary to be an expert in contemporary weapon systems. Seamanship and technical expertise may be useful for admirals who also possess the other command and leadership attributes, but they are no substitute for them. Similarly the finest intellects rarely succeed in command, although they may play a critical role in war.

Although the distinction can be exaggerated, wartime command is very different from peacetime management. Nelson was not successful in his only peacetime command: he was a warrior, impatient with the compromises and constraints of peace. However, he was unusual. Many more admirals have failed in war, rendered cautious and steady by careers spent dealing with the bureaucratic demands of peace.

Ultimately commanders cannot be made by training or education: only a combination of innate qualities, refined by self-education and experience, can generate and sustain the highest levels of understanding and confidence. This is as it should be. Navies do not need all their officers to be commanders in the Nelsonian mould. In truth they need far fewer commanders than managers, junior officers who follow orders, support staff and impart specialised technical knowledge. Training and education must be geared towards the development of an officer corps that is coherent, professional and capable: it must prepare officers for promotion and help to find future leaders, but it is no substitute for practical experience.

Although they face peculiar demands and operate in a particularly dangerous environment, admirals share many concerns with other professional leaders. The evolution of their art is a reminder of what is possible, and how the impossible can be attempted. Each and every one of these admirals had a glimpse of genius: they found a sublime, defining moment amid the everyday cares of command and leadership. Lord Howard's triumph came when the Spanish made a bonfire of their ships at Cadiz in 1596, but the fruits of his labours were frittered away by a vainglorious earl. Robert Blake knew that God was an Englishman when the Spanish ships blew up at Santa Cruz. Better known as a bad king, James II found his defining moment as Lord High Admiral, in the fiery destruction of van

Obdam's flagship. While George Anson earned his name circumnavigating the globe, it was the fall of Havana, a triumph that occurred after his death, that marked his genius. If Samuel Hood and John Jervis could not match his standards, their defining moment was provided by their protégé on 21 October 1805. For William Parker the bloodless resolution of the Portuguese Civil War demonstrated the qualities that made him the example of the age. Similarly Geoffrey Hornby's handling of the Turkish crisis of 1877–8 secured a triumph that the feeble ministry scarcely deserved. John Fisher defeated the German naval threat and saved the navy from Winston Churchill. David Beatty's defining moment will always be the catastrophic destruction of three battlecruisers on 31 May 1916; sadly they were British, a fact that exposes a culture of carelessness that vitiated his leadership. By 1942 admirals commanded their fleets from ashore: Andrew Cunningham demonstrated true greatness by letting a talented subordinate fight his own battle. We may never see their like again, but their example is enduring – as Napoleon observed, those who wish to lead must study the lives and careers of leaders.

While each man in this study brought something unique to the business and reached the highest levels in at least one aspect of the profession, none equalled Horatio Nelson, the admiral who rounded off the careers of the first six men discussed, and inspired the last five. His sublime genius, the ultimate expression of naval command, looms over them. While his fellow admirals might have matched him in some aspects of the business, none came close to rivalling his all-round excellence.

Notes

Introduction

1. Articles of War, Clause 2, 1749: Rodger, N. A. M. ed., *The Articles of War*, Havant, 1982.
2. HMS *Victory* log book 21.10.1805: TNA PRO ADM 51/4514, part 3.
3. On 17.10.1794 Nelson quoted from Addison's journal *The Spectator* of March 1711. The passage on the Sublime is in the June–July edition of 1712.
4. Wilton, A. and Barringer, T., *American Sublime: Landscape Painting in the United States 1820–1880*, Princeton UP, 2002, pp. 11–13.
5. Baugh, C., 'Loutherbourg, Philippe Jacques de (1740–1812)', *Oxford Dictionary of National Biography*, http://www.oxforddnb.com/view/printable/17037.
6. Translation taken from Heuser, B., *Reading Clausewitz*, London, 2002, p. 72.
7. Clausewitz, C., *On War*, Howard, M. and Paret, P. eds and trans., Princeton, 1984, p. 100.
8. I am indebted to my friend Beatrice Heuser's discussion of this subject in *Reading Clausewitz*, London, 2002, pp. 72–4.
9. Collingwood–Dr Carlyle 24.8.1801: Hughes, E. ed., *The Private Correspondence of Admiral Lord Collingwood*, London, Navy Records Society, 1957, p. 130.
10. *On War*, p. 112.
11. *On War*, p. 119.
12. Collingwood–Pasley 16.12.1805: Nicolas, Sir N. H. ed., *Letters and Dispatches of Admiral Lord Nelson*, London, 1847, Vol. VII, p. 241.
13. *The Oxford English Dictionary.*

Chapter 1: Charles, Lord Howard

1. Rodger, N. A. M., *The Safeguard of the Seas: A Naval History of Britain, Volume One 660–1649*, London, 1997, p. 171.
2. Clowes, W. L., *The Royal Navy: A History from the Earliest Times to the Present, Vol. I*, London, 1897, pp. 456–7.
3. Kenny, R. W., *Elizabeth's Admiral: The Political Career of Charles Howard, Earl of Nottingham, 1536–1624*, Baltimore, 1970, p. 146.
4. Kenny, pp. 6–7.
5. Both pictures are in the Collection of the National Maritime Museum.
6. Sugden, J., *Sir Francis Drake*, London, 1990.
7. Sugden, p. 178.
8. Howard–Walsingham 24.1.1588: Laughton, J. K. ed., *State Papers Relating to the Defeat of the Spanish Armada*, London, 1893, 2 vols. Vol. I, pp. 46–8.
9. Howard–Walsingham 27.1.1588 and 9.3.1588: Laughton I, pp. 48–9, 103–4.
10. Wernham, R., *Before the Armada: The Growth of English Foreign Policy 1485–1588*, London, 1966, p. 394.
11. Howard–Walsingham 15.6.1588: Laughton I, p. 205.
12. SP 12/211. fol. 50 cited in McDermott, Howard, Charles, *ODNB*, 2004–5, www.oxforddnb.com/view, accessed 30.06.2005.
13. Parker, G., 'The *Dreadnought* Revolution of the Sixteenth Century', *Mariner's Mirror*, Vol. 82, August 1996, pp. 269–300.
14. Howard–Burghley 29.2.1588: Laughton I, p. 84.
15. Pierson, P., *Commander of the Armada: The Seventh Duke of Medina Sidonia*, New Haven, 1989.
16. Rodger, p. 259.
17. Howard–Burghley 29.2.1588: Laughton I, pp. 85–6. It should be noted that Howard's praise occurs in a letter to the Lord Treasurer, who was no student of ships but an Argus-eyed guardian of the Queen's limited funds.
18. Burghley–Walsingham 10.4.1588: Laughton I, pp. 141–2.
19. Wernham, pp. 402–5.
20. Howard–Walsingham 7.4.1588: Laughton I, p. 133.
21. Howard–Burghley 28.5.1588: Laughton I, p. 190.
22. Sugden, p. 221.
23. Howard–Walsingham 13.6.1588: Laughton I, pp. 195–7.
24. Walsingham–Howard 9.6.1588: Laughton I, pp. 192–3.
25. Howard–Walsingham 14.6.1588: Laughton I, pp. 199–201.
26. Howard–Walsingham 6.7.1588: Laughton I, p. 245.
27. Howard–Walsingham 13.7.1588: Laughton I, pp. 256–7.

28. Kenny, p. 146. As hare coursing is now illegal in Britain, modern admirals will have to find another sporting metaphor.
29. Pierson, p. 126.
30. Howard–Walsingham 21.7.1588: Laughton I, p. 289.
31. At this point Rodger's chronology breaks down: he has the fighting begin on the 20th, then the day of inaction caused by Drake, only to resume combat off Portland on the 21st, pp. 266–7. Kenny is quite opaque on the first days of the campaign, pp. 145–7. Laughton remains the best guide, p. liii.
32. Pierson, pp. 147–54.
33. Winter–Walsingham 27.7.1588: Laughton I, p. 332.
34. Rodger, p. 269.
35. Howard–Walsingham 29.7.1588 and Drake–Walsingham 29.7.1588: Laughton I, pp. 340–2.
36. Winter–Walsingham 1.8.1588: Laughton II, p. 11.
37. Howard–Walsingham 7.8.1588: Laughton II, p. 54.
38. Council of War 1.8.1588: Laughton II, p. 6.
39. Winter–Walsingham 1.8.1588: Laughton II, p. 13.
40. Howard–Walsingham 7.8.1588: Laughton II, pp. 53–5.
41. Walsingham–Burghley 8.8.1588: Laughton II, p. 69.
42. Walsingham–Burghley 9.8.1588: Laughton II, p. 82.
43. Burghley–Walsingham 9.8.1588: Laughton II, p. 84.
44. Return: Laughton II, pp. 90–1.
45. Howard–Walsingham 9.8.1588: Laughton II, pp. 91–3.
46. Howard–Burghley 10.8.1588: Laughton II, pp. 96–7.
47. Laughton II, pp. 101–4.
48. Howard–Privy Council 22.8.1588: Laughton II, p. 141.
49. Drake–Walsingham 23.8.1588: Laughton II, pp. 146–8.
50. Edward Winter–Walsingham 24.8.1588: Laughton II, pp. 149–52.
51. Hawkins–Burghley 26.8.1588: Laughton II, p. 163.
52. Howard–Walsingham 27.8.1588: Laughton II, p. 167.
53. Hawkins–Burghley 28.8.1588: Laughton II, pp. 175–9. The lists and notes that Hawkins provided were remarkably clear and thorough.
54. Howard–Walsingham 29.8.1588: Laughton II, pp. 183–4.
55. Wernham, R. B., *After the Armada: Elizabethan England and the Struggle for Western Europe, 1588–1595*, Oxford, 1984, p. 11.
56. Hawkins–Burghley 4.9.1588: Laughton II, pp. 211–2.
57. Allowance for ships burned October 1588: Laughton II, pp. 287–8. Howard–Burghley December 1588: Laughton II, p. 303.
58. Martin, C. and Parker, G., *The Spanish Armada*, London, 1988, p. 254.
59. Knerr, D., 'Through the "Golden Mist": A Brief Overview of

Armada Historiography, *The American Neptune*, 1989, Vol. 49, pp. 5–6.

60. Adams had been drawing charts for the defence of the Thames before the battle; see Armesto, F., *The Spanish Armada: The Experience of War in 1588*, Oxford, 1988, pp. 112–13.

61. Russell, M., *Visions of the Sea: Hendrick C. Vroom and the Origin of Dutch Marine Painting*, Brill, Leiden, 1983, pp. 111–13.

62. Russell, pp. 149–51. This picture, painted in 1600, is now in Innsbruck.

63. Wernham 1984, pp. 151, 271, 533.

64. For an extended contemporary account, see 'Relation of the Voyage to Cadiz 1596 by Sir William Slyngsbie', ed. Corbett, J. S., in Laughton, J. K., ed., *The Naval Miscellany Vol. 1*, London, Navy Records Society, 1901, pp. 23–92.

65. Wernham, R. B., *The Return of the Armadas: The Last Years of the English War against Spain 1595–1603*. Oxford, 1994, pp. 84–113.

66. 'Of the true Greatness of Kingdoms and Estates', Bacon, F., *Essays*, 1597. In Mattheson, P. and E., eds, *Francis Bacon*, Oxford, 1929, pp. 85–6.

67. Wernham 1994, pp. 114–29.

68. Kenney, pp. 205–6.

Chapter 2: Robert Blake

1. The most recent life of Blake is Baumber, M., *General at Sea: Robert Blake and the Seventeenth Century Revolution in Naval Warfare*, London, 1989. See also Baumber's *ODNB* entry, 'Blake, Robert', accessed 19.01.2006.

2. Dixon, W. H., *Robert Blake. Admiral and General at Sea*, London, 1852, p. 14. Despite such reservations this is a work of considerable merit. See also Hannay, D., *Admiral Blake*, London, 1886, a reduced version of Dixon.

3. Capp, B., *Cromwell's Navy: The Fleet and the English Revolution 1648–1660*, Oxford, 1989, p. 117.

4. Hill, C., *God's Englishman: Oliver Cromwell and the English Revolution*, London, 1970, p. 58.

5. A miniature by Samuel Cooper, now at the National Maritime Museum, Greenwich.

6. Cromwell's decision to live at Hampton Court and to retain the astonishing series of paintings by Andrea Mantegna, *The Triumph of Caesar*, purchased by Charles I reveals a man with an eye for images of power. Lloyd, C., *Andrea Mantegna: The Triumph of Caesar*, London, 1991.

7. Capp, p. 118.
8. Powell, J. R., *Letters of Robert Blake*, London, Navy Records Society, 1937, p. 46.
9. Blake–King of Portugal 10.3.1650: *Letters*, pp. 54–5.
10. Blake–Council of State 14.10.1650: *Letters*, pp. 64–6. Baumber, p. 89
11. Blake–Council of State 21.12.1650: *Letters*, pp. 69–70. Baumber, p. 92.
12. Proceedings at Scilly: *Letters*, p. 134.
13. *A True Accompt of the late Reduction of the Isles of Scilly*, London, 1651: *Letters*, pp. 118–28.
14. Fox, F., *Great Ships: The Battlefleet of King Charles II*, London, 1980, for the ships of the period.
15. Blake–Speaker of the House of Commons (then the English Head of State) 20.5.1652: Gardiner, S. R., ed., *Letters and Papers relating to the First Dutch War Vol. I (FDW 1)*, London NRS, 1898, pp. 194–5.
16. Baumber, p. 127.
17. Blake–Tromp 30.5.1652: *FDW 1*, p. 257. Fortunately 'Royal Navy' soon came into use.
18. Baumber, p. 128.
19. The *Resolution* was built as the *Prince Royal*. At this time the *Sovereign* was often referred to as the *Commonwealth*: Capp, p. 52.
20. Blake–Council of State 2.10.1652: *FDW 2* 1900, pp. 272–5.
21. Blake–Admiralty Commissioners 1.12.1652: *FDW 3*, Gardiner and Atkinson, C. T., 1905, pp. 91–3.
22. Capp, p. 130.
23. Blake–Council of State 4.12.1652: *FDW 4*, Atkinson C. T., ed., 1909, pp. 114–15.
24. Abbott, W. C., ed., *Writings and Speeches of Oliver Cromwell*, Cambridge, Mass., 1945, Vol. II, 1939, p. 606.
25. Capp, p. 120.
26. Capp, p. 121.
27. Capp, p. 120.
28. Capp, pp. 79–82.
29. The Generals at Sea–Speaker 27.2.1653: *FDW 4*, pp. 163–9.
30. Ibid. The belated report reflected the difficulty of getting Monck over to the *Triumph*.
31. Abbott II, 1939, pp. 620–1.
32. Rodger, N. A. M., *The Command of the Ocean: A Naval History of Britain Volume Two, 1650–1815*, London, 2004, pp. 16–17.
33. Blake–Council of State 2.6.1653: *FDW 5*.
34. Rodger 2004, p. 17.

35. Blake and Monck–Council of State 4.6.1653: *FDW* 5, p. 82.
36. Blake and Monck–Council of State 4.7.1653: *FDW* 5, pp. 248–51.
37. Powell, *Letters*, p. 238.
38. Instructions for the Better Ordering of the Fleet in Fighting 29.3.1653: *Letters*, pp. 467–71. Baumber, pp. 182–8. Palmer, M., *Command at Sea: Naval Command and Control since the Sixteenth Century*, Harvard, 2004, pp. 41–50. Tunstall, B., *Naval Warfare in the Age of Sail: The Evolution of Fighting Tactics, 1650–1815*, London, 1990, p. 21.
39. Instructions for the Better Ordering of the Fleet in Sailing 29.3.1653: *Letters*, pp. 471–6.
40. Ibid., pp. 472–3.
41. 'Instructions for Fighting', ibid., p. 470.
42. Capp, p. 127.
43. Jones, J. R., *The Anglo–Dutch Wars of the Seventeenth Century*, London, 1996, pp. 136–42.
44. Baumber, p. 189. Capp, p. 138, argues that Blake supported Cromwell.
45. Hill, p. 158.
46. Hill, p. 168.
47. Abbott III, p. 297.
48. Baumber, p. 191. Rodger, p. 25, attributes the quote to Mountagu, but admits there is no certain reference. It conveys the meaning of loyalty, and Blake had accepted the point long before Mountagu went to sea.
49. Blake–Secretary of State Thurloe 18.4.1655: *Letters*, p. 294.
50. Corbett, J. S., *England in the Mediterranean: A Study of the Rise and Influence of British Power within the Straits 1603–1713*, London, 1904, Vol. I, p. 268. A brilliant, if dated, strategic analysis.
51. This fulfilled Cromwell's orders of 22.7.1654: Abbot III, p. 379.
52. Blake–Thurloe 18.4.1655: *Letters*, p. 295.
53. Cromwell–Blake 13.6.1655: Abbott III, pp. 745–6.
54. Blake–Cromwell 30.8.1655: *Letters*, pp. 306–10.
55. Cromwell–Blake 13.9.1655: Abbott III, pp. 823–4.
56. Abbott III, pp. 547–8.
57. Abbott III, p. 804.
58. Christopher Hill contended this move would have displeased Blake: Hill, p. 149: *Letters*, p. 333.
59. Capp, p. 142.
60. Blake–Lord Protector 12.6.1655: *Letters*, p. 298, appears to be the first such address.
61. Nelson survived his fatal wounds far longer than modern physicians

would expect, something that can only be attributed to will power – a potent element in leadership.

62. Blake's will of 13.3.1656: *Letters*, p. 342–5.

63. Fox, p. 69. At the Restoration this mighty vessel became the *Royal Charles*, only to be captured by the Dutch in 1667.

64. Cromwell–Blake and Mountagu 28.4.1656: Abbott IV, p. 148.

65. Blake and Mountagu–Committee of Admiralty 9.5.1656: Blake and Mountagu–Cromwell 19.6.1656: *Letters*, pp. 347–9, 358–61.

66. Cromwell–Blake and Mountagu 6.5.1656: Abbott IV 1947, p. 154–5.

67. *Letters*, p. 327.

68. Council of State–Blake and Mountagu 9.6.1656: Abbott IV, pp. 183–4: letter received 30.6.1656: *Letters*, p. 328. Blake and Mountagu–Lord Protector 1.7.1656: *Letters*, pp. 366–7.

69. Lord Protector–Blake and Mountagu 28.8.1656: Abbott IV, pp. 239–40. Firth, C. H., *The Last Years of the Protectorate, 1656–1658*, London, 1909, Vol. I, pp. 237–8.

70. Blake–Mountagu 10.10.1656: Firth Vol. I, p. 239, and also *Letters*, p. 376. Blake–Cromwell 29.9.1656: *Letters*, pp. 374–5.

71. Blake–Mountagu 9.2.1657: *Letters*, pp. 381–2.

72. Ibid.

73. Blake–Committee of Admiralty 11.3.1657: *Letters*, pp. 383–5.

74. Firth, Vol. I, p. 240.

75. Abbott III, pp. 864–9.

76. Capp, p. 297.

77. Firth, Vol. I, p. 249.

78. Stayner's account, the most detailed, was written some years later for Charles II, who knighted him afresh, in lieu of Cromwell's dubbing. Stayner downplayed Blake's role. The general was by then both dead and thoroughly discredited with the new regime. Firth, C. H., ed., 'A Narrative of the Battle of Santa Cruz, written by Sir Richard Stayner, Rear Admiral of the Fleet', in Laughton, J. K., ed., *The Naval Miscellany Vol. II*, London, Navy Records Society, 1910, pp. 123–36.

79. Baumber, p. 234.

80. Campbell, J., *Lives of the British Admirals and other Eminent British Seamen*, London, 1785, Vol. II, pp. 224–6.

81. Abbott IV, p. 540.

82. Elliot, J. H., *Imperial Spain 1469–1716*, London, 1963, p. 175.

83. Firth I, pp. 261–2.

84. Stradling, R. A., *Philip IV and the Government of Spain 1621–1665*, Cambridge, 1988, pp. 292–5. Lynch, J., *Spain under the Habsburgs II*, Oxford, 1969, pp. 122–3.

85. Firth I, p. 259.
86. Firth I, p. 260. Cromwell–Blake 10.6.1656: Abbott IV, pp. 548–9.
87. Abbott IV, pp. 601 and 615.
88. Campbell II, p. 220.
89. Clarendon, Earl, *The History of the Rebellion and Civil Wars in England*, Macray, W. D., ed., Oxford, 1888, Vol. VI, p. 38.
90. Capp, p. 324.
91. This concern for his people dominates the Navy Records Society edition of his *Letters*.
92. Nelson–Earl St Vincent 12.4.1797: Nicolas, Sir H., *Letters and Dispatches of Admiral Lord Nelson*, Vol. II, London, 1845, pp. 378–90.
93. Firth, Vol. I, p. 258.
94. Books about Blake began to appear in the mid-nineteenth century, and a scholarly examination of the First Dutch War was undertaken as part of the intellectual revival of the Royal Navy, but it took the navalist revival of the late nineteenth century to restore Blake to public prominence, even in his home town. In 1900 a lively, if highly improbable, statue was erected in Bridgewater, a memorial garden was opened soon afterwards alongside the River Parrett, and in 1926 the Blake Museum opened in the house where he was born, in a street renamed in his honour.

Chapter 3: King James II

1. Capp, p. 349.
2. Imlah, A. I., *Lord Ellenborough*, Cambridge, Mass., 1939, p. 239. Ellenborough shared the duke's political ineptitude, twice having to resign from high office after embarrassing faux pas.
3. Macaulay, T. B., *History of England*, London, 1848–61, 5 vols. The basic text for this 'Whig' interpretation.
4. Jones, E., *John Lingard and the Pursuit of Historical Truth*, Brighton, 2001, pp. 93–5.
5. Callow, J., *The Making of King James II: The Formative Years of a Fallen King*, Stroud, 2000, pp. 14–20. Callow's judgement of his subject allows little room for his naval career to be a success, and he accepts the critical judgements of partial sources without reflection. The treatment of naval issues is not convincing.
6. James II and VII: Speck, W., www.oxforddnb.com/view, accessed 30.06.2005.
7. Callow, pp. 55–7.
8. Callow, pp. 111–12.
9. Callow, p. 128.

10. Callow, p. 127.
11. Callow, pp. 117–18.
12. Coventry was an important contributor to the creation of Restoration naval policy, although generally overlooked in favour of the more accessible Pepys.
13. Fox, pp. 11, 80–3.
14. Fox, p. 104.
15. Rodger 2004, p. 96.
16. Tanner, J. R., ed., *Samuel Pepys Naval Minutes*, London NRS, 1926, p. 338.
17. Rodger 2004, pp. 114–17.
18. Davies, J. D., *Gentlemen and Tarpaulins: The Officers and Men of the Restoration Navy*, Oxford, 1991, p. 160.
19. This is the conclusion of Davies, pp. 231–3.
20. Rodger 2004, p. 121.
21. Rodger 2004, pp. 102–3.
22. Hutton, R., *Charles II: King of England, Scotland and Ireland*, Oxford, 1989, p. 432.
23. Callow, pp. 192–9.
24. Callow, pp. 199–204. Tanner, p. 418.
25. Tanner, p. 416.
26. Callow, pp. 206–7.
27. Davies, pp. 139–40.
28. Rodger 2004, p. 131.
29. Tunstall, W. C. B., *Naval Warfare in the Age of Sail: The Evolution of Fighting Tactics 1650–1815*, Tracy, N., ed., London, 1990, pp. 22–3.
30. Dyer, F., *Sir John Narborough*, London, 1931, p. 24.
31. These were originally dated to 1672–3, but the latest research places them squarely in the period between the Four Days and the St James's Day battles. Palmer, p. 57.
32. Callow, p. 208.
33. Hutton, p. 432.
34. Anderson, R. C., ed., *The Journal of Edward Mountagu, First Earl of Sandwich 1659–1665*, London, Navy Records Society, 1929, pp. lii–liii.
35. Dyer, p. 21.
36. Tunstall, p. 25.
37. Anderson, R. C., *The Journal of Edward Mountagu, First Earl of Sandwich*, London NRS, 1929, p. 228.
38. Davies, p. 150.
39. Tanner, p. 320. Callow, pp. 117–8, 215–222, is highly critical of James's conduct but underestimates the difficulties of exercising

command in the seventeenth century and blames James for failing to order the pursuit to be carried on when he turned in, missing the point that he left the fleet pursuing the enemy, and no one had the authority to change that order.

40. Hutton, pp. 222–3.
41. Anderson 1929, p. lvii.
42. Duke of York–Albemarle 28.5.1666: in Pearsall, A. W. H., ed., *The Second Dutch War, 1665–1667*, National Maritime Museum, 1967, p. 16.
43. See Powell, J. T. R. and Timings, M. A., eds, *The Rupert and Monck Letter Book 1666*, London Navy Records Society, 1969, for this campaign.
44. Rodger 2004, p. 79.
45. Tanner, *Pepys*, pp. 36–8.
46. Davies, p. 160. Rodger 2004, p. 81.
47. Narborough's journal in Anderson, R. C., ed., *The Third Dutch War*, London, 1946, pp. 96–7.
48. Fox, p. 138.
49. Narborough, p. 104.
50. Rodger 2004, p. 85.
51. Tunstall, p. 34.
52. Callow, pp. 225–8.
53. Rodger 2004, p. 85.
54. Hutton, pp. 299–300.
55. Davies, p. 165.
56. Penrose was an astute and experienced student of fleet tactics. Penrose, J., *Lives of Vice Admiral Sir Charles Vinicombe Penrose and Captain James Trevenen*, London, 1850, p. 173.
57. Callow, pp. 214 and 237.
58. Callow, p. 93.
59. Hutton, p. 308.
60. Fox, p. 171.
61. Dyer, p. 203.
62. Davies, p. 198.
63. Rodger 2004, pp. 110–11. Tomalin, C., *Pepys: The Unequalled Self*, London, 2003, p. 343.
64. Rodger 2004, p. 135.
65. Bold, J., *Greenwich: An Architectural History of the Royal Hospital for Seamen and the Queen's House*, Yale, 2000, p. 95.
66. Bold, pp. 98–100.
67. Davies, pp. 128, 137, 148.
68. Rodger, pp. 137–9.

69. Davies, pp. 199–211.

70. James took an inordinate interest in his written legacy, preserving his papers with remarkable zeal in a shipwreck of 1682 when everything else was in chaos; and in the shipwreck of his monarchy he took more interest in his records than his life or those of his followers. Callow 2000, pp. 2–3.

71. Callow, J., *The King in Exile. James II: Warrior, King and Saint*, Stroud, 2004, p. 75.

72. Palmer, pp. 70, 335.

73. Callow 2004, p. 198.

74. Callow, p. 200.

75. Aubrey, P., *The Defeat of James Stuart's Armada 1692*, Leicester, 1979, p. 121.

76. Symcox, G., *The Crisis of French Sea Power, 1688–1697*, The Hague, 1974.

77. Callow 2004, p. 202.

78. Callow 2004, p. 210.

79. Callow 2004, ch. 8.

80. When George III had his son William, Duke of Clarence, promoted before he had served his proper time, it ended his hopes of a serious naval career. William's naval pretensions could be indulged in peacetime, but he spent the French Revolutionary and Napoleonic wars, 1793–1815, on the beach. Queen Victoria's naval son Alfred, Duke of Edinburgh, had a successful career because he was not especially privileged.

Chapter 4: George Anson

1. Earle, P., *The Pirate Wars*, London, 2003, examines one aspect of this station.

2. Barrow, Sir J., *Life of George, Lord Anson*, London, 1839, pp. 14–15. Barrow compensated for the paucity of surviving evidence about Anson's career by compiling a broad-based naval history of the era, lightly seasoned with flattery of King William IV.

3. For a detailed study of a contemporary naval officer, a friend of Anson who prospered in colonial society, see Gwynn, J., *The Enterprising Admiral: The Personal Fortune of Admiral Sir Peter Warren*, Montreal, 1974.

4. Thompson, E. K., 'George Anson and the Province of South Carolina', *Mariner's Mirror*, 1967, Vol. 53, pp. 279–80.

5. Tunstall, B., *Admiral Byng and the Loss of Minorca*, London, 1928.

6. Williams, G., *The Prize of All the Oceans: The Triumph and Tragedy of Anson's Voyage Round the World*, London, 1999, p. 10.

7. These older men died early in the voyage – only one officer returned to England. Williams, pp. 18–22.

8. Williams, p. 58.

9. Williams, pp. 111, 118.

10. Williams, pp. 147–8.

11. Heaps, L., ed., *The Log of the Centurion*, London, 1973, pp. 222–7. Based on the journals of Captain Philip Saumarez.

12. Williams, pp. 160–75.

13. Rodger, *Command*, 2004, p. 245.

14. Anson–Hardwicke 14.6.1744: Yorke, P. C., *The Life and Correspondence of Philip Yorke, Earl of Hardwicke*, Cambridge, 1913, 3 vols, Vol. I, p. 346.

15. Namier, L., *The Structure of Politics at the Accession of George III*, 2nd edn, London, 1957, p. 144.

16. Williams, p. 218.

17. Sedgewick, R., ed., *The History of Parliament: The House of Commons, 1715–1754*, London, 1970, Vol. I, pp. 319, 358–9 and 415–16.

18. Williams, pp. 222–30.

19. Anson–Hardwicke 14.6.1744: Williams, G., ed., *Anson's Voyage*, London, Navy Records Society, 1967, pp. 222–4.

20. Barrow, p. 100.

21. Barrow, pp. 404–16, retails many examples of this loyalty.

22. Russell, J., ed., *The Correspondence of John, 4th Duke of Bedford*, 3 vols, London, 1842–46, Vol. II.

23. Baugh, D., *British Naval Administration in the Age of Walpole*, Princeton, 1965, pp. 78–9.

24. Ibid., p. 79.

25. Admiral Vernon–Admiralty 13.12.1745: Ranft, B. Mcl., ed., *The Vernon Papers*, London Navy Records Society, 1958, p. 554.

26. For a summary, see Rodger, 2000, p. 183.

27. Lavery, B., *The Royal Navy's First Invincible*, Portsmouth, 1988, p. 21.

28. Palmer, p. 99.

29. Admiral Sir Peter Warren: Rodger, 2000, p. 183.

30. Tunstall, pp. 92–7.

31. Lavery, p. 24, from Anson's official report.

32. Baugh, p. 112.

33. Warren–Bedford 18.5.1747: Gwynn, J., *An Admiral for America: Sir Peter Warren, Vice Admiral of the Red, 1703–1752*, Gainesville, Florida, 2004, p. 131.

34. Palmer, pp. 102–4.

35. Anson–Bedford 11.5.1747: Russell, *Duke of Bedford* II, pp. 213–15.

36. Baugh, p. 281.

37. Anson–Bedford 3.4.1747: Baugh, p. 308.

38. Anson–Sandwich 14 and 15.2.1748: Barrow, pp. 199–202. Sandwich was one of the treaty negotiators at Aix-la-Chapelle, forcing Anson to commit his thoughts to paper.

39. Anson–Bedford 17.4.1747: quoted in Rodger, 2000, p. 189.

40. Williams, p. 229.

41. Baugh, p. 504.

42. Hardwicke–Newcastle 4.10.1748: *Hardwicke* I, p. 678.

43. Middleton, R., *The Bells of Victory: The Pitt–Newcastle Ministry and the Conduct of the Seven Years' War, 1757–1762*, Cambridge, 1985, pp. 33, 76, 78 etc.

44. The quote from Walpole's published *Memoir of the last Years of George II* is in Barrow at p. 109. The passage in quotes is from the unpublished MS of Walpole's *Memoir*, published in Sedgwick at p. 416.

45. Most of Nelson's ships at the Nile were seventy-fours of Slade's design.

46. Gardiner, R., *The First Frigates*, London, 1992, pp. 10, 13, 90, establishes Anson's critical role in developing new cruising ships from captured French models.

47. Lavery, B., *The Ship of the Line: Vol 1. The Development of the Battlefleet 1650–1850*, London, 1983, pp. 96–115.

48. Anson–Hardwicke 6.12.1756: Add MSS 35,359, f.384, in Mackay, R., *Admiral Hawke*, Oxford, 1965, p. 136.

49. Middleton, p. 6.

50. Hardwicke–Anson 18.6.1757: Barrow, pp. 290–3.

51. Middleton, p. 33: Sainty, J. C., *Admiralty Officials 1660–1870*, London, 1975, p. 24.

52. Middleton, p. 21.

53. Middleton, p. 28.

54. Rodger, N. A. M., *The Wooden World: An Anatomy of the Georgian Navy*, London, 1986, p. 147.

55. Anson–Hardwicke 6.10.1757: Yorke III, p. 186.

56. Anson–Newcastle 15.6.1759: Namier, pp. 33–4. While Namier portrayed Anson as an opponent of Newcastle's methods, the evidence demonstrates that he was an active, if sophisticated, player of mid-eighteenth-century politics.

57. Anson–Newcastle 15.2.1755: Namier, pp. 249–50.

58. Namier, p. 32.

59. Namier, p. 307.

60. Middleton, p. 56.

61. Middleton, p. 116.
62. Rodger 2000, p. 197.
63. Namier, p. 41.
64. Anson–Holdernesse 25.7.1755: Rodger 2000, p. 195.
65. Mackay, pp. 195–6.
66. Mackay, p. 197.
67. Palmer, pp. 111–12.
68. Middleton, p. 87. Anson–Hardwicke 29.6, 22.7.1758: Yorke III, pp. 215–18. These letters are largely concerned with military affairs and the King of Prussia's campaign.
69. Middleton, p. 120.
70. Middleton, p. 112.
71. Middleton, pp. 67–76.
72. Middleton, pp. 121–5, 136.
73. Baugh, D., *British Naval Administration in the Age of Walpole*, Princeton, 1966, p. 379.
74. Newcastle–Bedford 18.11.1759: Middleton, p. 143.
75. Middleton, p. 145.
76. Hardwicke–Newcastle: Yorke III, p. 580.
77. Middleton, pp. 169–71.
78. Middleton, p. 195.
79. Barrow, pp. 380–1.
80. Anson–Saunders October 1761: Staffordshire Record Office D615/P(S)/1/10/34.
81. Middleton, pp. 204–5.
82. Tracy, N., *Manila Ransomed: The British Assault on Manila in the Seven Years War*, Exeter, 1995, pp. 12–13.
83. Syrett, D., ed., *The Siege and Capture of Havana, 1762*, London, Navy Records Society, 1970, p. xiii.
84. Pocock–Admiralty Secretary Cleveland 14.7.1762: Syrett, p. 237.
85. Newcastle–Thomas Anson (brother) 9.6.1762: Barrow, pp. 389–91.
86. Barrow's biography was written at the behest of William IV, George III's naval son. Corbett, J. S., *England in the Seven Years War: A Study in Combined Strategy*, London, 1907, 2 vols, Middleton.
87. Corbett's book was based on a lecture series given to the Naval War Course.
88. Rodger 2000, p. 181. What standing Horace Walpole and Sir Charles Williams had in making sneering asides about Anson is hard to fathom.
89. Williams 1999, p. 207.
90. Rodger 2000, p. 199.

91. Baugh, pp. 494–5.
92. Middleton, p. 214.
93. Middleton, p. 104.

Chapter 5: Samuel Hood and John Jervis

1. Maitland, F., *Narrative of the Surrender of Bonaparte*, London, 1826, p. 99.
2. Hood, D., *The Admirals Hood* (London n.d.) is the only full-length treatment, although Hood shares the book with his younger brother Alexander, Lord Bridport, and his cousins Alexander and Samuel, one of Nelson's captains at the Nile. Hannay, D., ed., *Letters Written by Sir Samuel Hood (Viscount Hood) in 1781–2–3*, London Navy Records Society, 1895, offers a valuable record of Hood's thinking. Duffy, M., 'Samuel Hood, First Viscount Hood 1724–1816', in Le Fevre, P. and Harding, R., *Precursors of Nelson: British Admirals of the Eighteenth Century*, London, 2000, pp. 249–78, is the best modern analysis.
3. Hannay, intro. *Hood*, pp. xv–xvi.
4. Duffy, p. 250.
5. Duffy, p. 251.
6. Rodger, N. A. M., *The Wooden World: An Anatomy of the Georgian Navy*, London, 1986, pp. 216–17.
7. Knight, R. J. B., ed., *Portsmouth Dockyard Papers 1774–1783: The American War*, Portsmouth, 1987.
8. Duffy, p. 256.
9. Knight, pp. li–lii, 164.
10. Hannay considered them brilliant, inconsistent and often unfair. *Hood*, pp. vi–xlvii.
11. Palmer, pp. 140–4.
12. Hood Enclosure 6.9.1781: Hannay, p. 31.
13. Graves–Hood and Hood–Graves 13.9.1781: Hannay, pp. 34–5.
14. Hood–Stephens 20.1.1782: Hannay, p. 62.
15. Captain Lord Robert Manners–Duke of Rutland 8.2.1782: Hannay, p. 79. Manners was the captain of HMS *Resolution*.
16. Manners–Rutland 22.2.1782: Hannay, p. 81.
17. Ibid., p. 83.
18. Hood–Stephens 22.2.1782: Hannay, pp. 89–92.
19. Hood–Stephens 23.2.1782: Hannay, p. 95.
20. Hood–Jackson 16.4.1782: Hannay, p. 102.
21. Hood–Jackson 16.4.1782: Hannay, p. 101.
22. Hood–Stephen 16.4.1782: Hannay, pp. 101–7.
23. In the event she never made it, sinking in a hurricane. Instead, the

British built a new *Ville de Paris* to remind the French who ruled the ocean.

24. Lambert, A. D., 'Sir William Cornwallis, 1744–1819', in Lefevre, P. and Harding, R., *Precursors of Nelson: British Admirals of the Eighteenth Century*, London, 2000, p. 358.
25. Palmer, pp. 151–7.
26. Nelson–Cornwallis 30.12.1804: Leyland, J., ed., *Dispatches and Letters Relating to the Blockade of Brest, 1803–1805*, London, Navy Records Society, 1899–1902, Vol. I, p. xvi.
27. Lambert, 'Cornwallis', pp. 352–75.
28. Mahan–Laughton 14.8.1895: Lambert, A., ed., *Letters and Papers of Sir John Knox Laughton; 1830–1915*, London Navy Records Society, 2002, pp. 111–12.
29. Mahan, *Nelson I*, pp. 37–8.
30. Hood–Stephen 24.8.1782: Hannay, pp. 143–4.
31. Hood–Stephen 29.1.1783: Hannay, pp. 155–6.
32. Duffy, p. 267.
33. Hood–Stephens (Secretary of the Admiralty) 25.8.1793: Rose, J. H., *Lord Hood and the Defence of Toulon*, Cambridge, 1922, p. 20.
34. Rose, p. 59.
35. Rose, pp. 40–3.
36. Rose, p. 51.
37. Rose, p. 61.
38. Elliot II, p. 199, cited in Rose at p. 70.
39. Crook, M., *Toulon in War and Revolution*, Manchester, 1991, pp. 144–60.
40. Rose, pp. 88–9.
41. Duffy, p. 268.
42. Gregory, D., *The Ungovernable Rock: A History of the Anglo–Corsican Kingdom and its Role in Britain's Mediterranean Strategy during the Revolutionary War (1793–1797)*, Cranbury, NJ, 1985, pp. 64–9.
43. Nelson–Cornwallis 23.5.1794. *HMC Various MS Vol. VII*, London, 1909, p. 388.
44. Hood–Pitt 9, 18 and 28.4.1795: TNA PRO 30/8/146 f. 7, 9, 11 and 13. Hood–Spencer 18.3.1795: BL Add 75780. Hood–Admiralty 28.4.1795: ADM 1/393 111.
45. Admiralty–Hood 1.5.1795 (Secret) ADM 2/1349 57–9. Spencer–King 3.5.1795: BL Add 75780.
46. Nelson–Father 29.7.1795: Nicolas II.
47. Nelson–Wm Nelson 8.6.1795 and Nelson–Rev. Dixon Hoste 22.6.1795: Nicolas II, p. 146.

48. Admiralty–Admiral Hotham 15.4.1795: ADM 2/128 105.

49. Lambert, A. D., 'William, Lord Hotham', in Lefevre, P. and Harding, R., eds, *British Admirals of the Napoleonic Wars: The Contemporaries of Nelson*, London, 2005, pp. 23–45, for Hotham's command.

50. Stirling, A. M. W., *Pages and Portraits from the Past; Journals of Sir William Hotham* (Admiral Hotham's nephew). London, 1919, Vol. II, p. 44.

51. Duffy, p. 251.

52. Duffy, p. 270.

53. Rose, p. 10.

54. Duffy, p. 259.

55. Hood, p. 125.

56. Hood, p. 132.

57. Hannay, pp. vii and xxxi.

58. For a well-balanced treatment, see Crimmin, P. K., 'John Jervis, Earl of St Vincent 1735–1823', in Lefevre, P. and Harding, R., *Precursors*, pp. 324–50. Crimmin, P. K., 'Jervis, John, Earl of St Vincent (1735–1823)', www.oxforddnb.com/view/printable/14794, accessed 08.03.2006. Arthur, C. B., *The Remaking of the English Navy by Admiral St. Vincent – Key to the Victory over Napoleon: The Great Unclaimed Naval Revolution (1795–1805)*, Lanham, MD, 1986, while a very one-sided eulogy of the great man, has the merit of prompting further thought and research, unlike older biographies.

59. Jervis–his father 21.1.1770: cited in Crimmin, *ODNB*.

60. Duffy, M., *Soldiers, Sugar and Sea Power: the British Expeditions to the West Indies and the War against Revolutionary France*, Oxford, 1987, pp. 41–135, esp. pp. 106–14 on plunder.

61. Palmer, pp. 170–7, provides a fine analysis of the battle.

62. Ehrman, J., *The Younger Pitt. Vol. III*, London, 1996, pp. 3–16.

63. Nelson–Jervis 19.4.1797: *Nelson Dispatches*, Vol. II, pp. 378–81.

64. Lambert, A. D., *Nelson: Britannia's God of War*, London, 2004, p. 239.

65. Lambert, A., 'Sir William Cornwallis 1744–1819', Lefevre, P. and Harding, R., 2000, pp. 353–76.

66. St Vincent–Earl Spencer 23.1.1801: Phillimore, Sir A., *The Life of an Admiral of the Fleet: Sir William Parker, Bt. GCB*, Vol. I, London, 1876, p. 180.

67. Morriss, R., *The Royal Dockyards during the Revolutionary and Napoleonic Wars*, Leicester, 1983, pp. 193–8, quote, p. 194.

68. Phillimore, Vol. I, p. 244.

69. St Vincent–Benjamin Tucker 11.9.1822: Tucker, J. S., *Memoirs of Earl St Vincent*, London, 1844, Vol. II, pp. 425–6.
70. Naval Chronicle VI, p. 418, cited in Nicholas IV, p. 520.

Chapter 6: William Parker

1. Phillimore, Sir A., *The Life of Admiral of the Fleet Sir William Parker, Bt. GCB*, 3 vols, London 1876–1880. A monstrous work of close on two thousand pages, crammed with undigested correspondence, offers any serious student of Parker's career a rich resource, although it contains little critical analysis and no criticism. Phillimore worshipped the old admiral as a living link with Nelson, the fount of all naval wisdom.
2. It has taken the navy 160 years to relearn this lesson!
3. Parker–Captain Robert Tryon 30.10.1847: Phillimore III, pp. 263–4.
4. John Jervis–George Parker 14.7.1792: Phillimore, pp. 5–6.
5. Phillimore, p. 8. Anson had excellent patronage, but there was no need to tell the boy that sort of truth.
6. Pope, D., *The Black Ship*, London, 1963, examines this catastrophic failure of leadership.
7. Parker–his mother 7.3.1801: Phillimore I, pp. 151–2.
8. Parker–his father 15.11.1801: Phillimore I, p. 166.
9. Cornwallis–George Parker 7.12.1801: Phillimore I, p. 170.
10. Phillimore I, pp. 139, 188.
11. Built at Woolwich Dockyard 1796–9, the thirty-eight-gun *Amazon* fought at Copenhagen, her captain, Edward Riou, commanding Nelson's frigate squadron, losing his life in answering Admiral Hyde Parker's infamous recall signal. Gardiner, R., *The Heavy Frigate: Eighteen Pounder Frigates. Volume I, 1778–1800*, London, 1994, pp. 54–5, 88.
12. Phillimore I, p. 208.
13. Phillimore I, p. 193. Phillimore was Parker's flag lieutenant at the end of his career and knew him well.
14. Phillimore I, pp. 195–203.
15. Wareham, T., *The Star Captains*, London, 2001, pp. 207–8.
16. Privateers were privately owned, state-licensed commerce destroyers who relied on captures to pay their way. They did far more damage to British merchant shipping than regular warships in the sailing-ship era, posing a serious threat to the economy. Little wonder successful frigate captains were well rewarded by the shipping and insurance industry.
17. Parker–George Parker 25.12.1803, Parker–his mother 25.12.1803: Phillimore I, pp. 225–6.

18. Nelson–St Vincent 14.2.1804 and 17.3.1804: Phillimore I, pp. 228 and 234.

19. Sir William Hoste (1780–1828) had no peer as a frigate captain. His brilliant squadron victory at Lissa in 1811 and dynamic amphibious operations were unparalleled. His early death means that his story belongs to a study of captains.

20. Phillimore I, p. 289.

21. Corbett, J. S., *The Campaign of Trafalgar*, London, 1910, pp. 265–6.

22. Gardiner, R., *Frigates of the Napoleonic Wars*, London, 2000, pp. 148–67.

23. St Vincent–Warren n.d.: Phillimore I, p. 328.

24. Broke captured the USS *Chesapeake* in 1813 in the outstanding single-ship action fought under sail.

25. *Amazon* was broken up in the immediate post-war years, being beyond economic repair.

26. Wareham, pp. 128 and 133, deprives Parker of his last two years in command.

27. Clarence–Parker 14.10.1828: Phillimore I, p. 490.

28. Parker–wife 18.7.1829: Phillimore I, p. 494; see also p. 183.

29. Phillimore II, p. 86.

30. Graham–Parker 9.9.1831: Phillimore II (1880), p. 32.

31. Graham–Parker 19.12.1831: Phillimore II, p. 58.

32. Graham–Parker 30.6.1832: Phillimore II, p. 94.

33. Grey–Graham 18.9.1832: Howick MSS University of Durham (2).

34. Parker–Graham 9.9.1832: Phillimore, p. 103.

35. Parker–Captain Markland HMS *Briton* 4.9.1832: Phillimore II, p. 132.

36. Diary 10.7.1832: Blakiston, G., *Lord William Russell and his Wife, 1815–1856*, London, 1972, p. 253.

37. Parker–Russell 23 and 24.10.1832: Phillimore II, pp. 142–3.

38. Lord John Russell–Lord William Russell 16.11.1832: Blakiston, p. 264.

39. Lord William Russell–Lord John Russell 9.11.1833: Blakiston, p. 264.

40. Lord W. Russell–Palmerston 16.8.1833: Blakiston, p. 278.

41. Parker–Captain Hyde Parker (no relation) 13.11.1833: Phillimore II, p. 148.

42. Napier–Lima undated, replying to the offer of 1.2.1833: Napier, Papers. National Maritime Museum (NMM), NAP/11 f7.

43. Phillimore, Sir A., *The Life of Admiral Sir William Parker*, London, 1880, Vol. II, pp. 209–10.

44. Parker–Napier 17.6.1833: Phillimore, p. 223.

45. Parker–Graham 3.7.1833; Phillimore, p. 237. For the Portuguese telegraph system, see Wilson, G., *The Old Telegraphs*, London, 1976, pp. 183–4.

46. Lord W. Russell–Palmerston 25.6.1833, no. 55: Foreign Office Papers (FO), The National Archives (TNA), 63/399.

47. Parker–Graham 3.7.1833: Phillimore, pp. 237–9.

48. Russell–Palmerston 3.7.1833, no. 56: FO 63/399.

49. Hoppner–Shee 25.6.1833, no. 117: FO 63/405.

50. Napier–Parker 7.7.1833: Phillimore II, p. 243.

51. Parker–Napier 20.7.1833: Phillimore II, p. 251.

52. Russell–Palmerston 15.7.1833, no. 58: FO 63/399.

53. Napier–Dundas 10.7.1833: British Library Additional Manuscripts (Add.), Add. 40.019 f.84.

54. Graham–Palmerston 14.7.1833 endorsed 'Sunday night': Broadlands MSS GC/GR 39.

55. Russell–Palmerston 25.7.1833, no. 61: FO 63/399. Parker–Admiralty 25.7.1833 rec. 3.8.1833, no. 252: Admiralty Papers (ADM) at TNA, ADM 1/360.

56. Grey–Graham 4.10.1833: Howick MSS (5).

57. Graham–Parker 26.3.1834: Phillimore II, p. 343.

58. Hardy was now Governor of Greenwich Hospital. Graham–Parker 8.4.1834: Phillimore II, pp. 349–51.

59. Parker–Graham 14.4.1834: Phillimore II, p. 353.

60. Parker–Admiralty Secretary Captain George Elliot 21.6.1834: Phillimore II, p. 388.

61. Graham–Parker 3.6.1834: Phillimore II, pp. 378–9.

62. Phillimore II, pp. 388–9.

63. Codrington–Parker 16.8.1840: Codrington Papers (COD), NMM, COD/20/2 ff. 14–15.

64. Parker–Codrington 7.10.1839: COD 20/4. Codrington–Parker 8 and 10.10.1839: COD 17/3 ff. 146–9.

65. Parker–Codrington 9.10.1839: COD 20/4.

66. This period is covered by Phillimore II at pp. 394–425, largely devoted to a résumé of domestic politics.

67. Navies of Great Britain, France etc.: Barrow, J., *Life of George, Lord Anson*, London, 1839, pp. 421–84.

68. Napier–Parker 1840–41: Parker Papers (PAR), NMM, PAR 163/11.

69. Palmerston–Elliot 12.6.1837: FO 228/6/30, cited in Melancon, G., *Britain's China Policy and the Opium Crisis: Balancing Drugs, Violence and National Honour, 1833–1840*, Aldershot, 2003, pp. 58–9.

70. Melancon, pp. 78–9.

71. Melancon, pp. 101–7.

72. Minto–Palmerston 20.10.1839: Broadlands Archive, GC/MI 410.

73. Phillimore II, pp. 428–42.

74. Rait, R. S., *The Life and Campaigns of Hugh, First Viscount Gough, Field-Marshal*, London, 1903, 2 vols, Vol. I, pp. 200–94, for the military campaign and *ODNB* at www.oxforddnb.com/view/print-able/11135.

75. McLean, D., 'Surgeons of the Opium War: The Navy on the China Coast, 1840–41', in *English Historical Review*, April 2006, pp. 487–504, for the latest research on medical issues.

76. The British 18th, 26th, 49th and 55th Regiments, the 36th Madras Infantry, with artillery and engineers.

77. Collinson, T. B., ed., *Journal of HMS* Enterprise *on the Search for Sir John Franklin's Ships 1850–1855 by Sir Richard Collinson; with a memoir of his other services*, London, 1889, pp. 479–89.

78. Fay, P. W., *The Opium War, 1840–1842*, New York, 1976, p. 315.

79. Rawlinson, J. L., *China's Struggle for Naval Development 1839–1895*, Cambridge, Mass., 1967, pp. 19–28.

80. Secret Dispatch of 31.12.1841: quoted in Graham, G. S., *The China Station: War and Diplomacy 1830–1860*, Oxford, 1978, p. 200.

81. Secretary of State for War–Admiralty 4.2.1842: Graham, p. 205.

82. Ellenborough–General Gough 25.3.1842: Graham, p. 207.

83. Pottinger–Gough 1.7.1842: Phillimore II, p. 473.

84. Parker–Auckland 9.4.1843: Phillimore II, pp. 546–7.

85. The two surveying officers would have distinguished careers, and a decade later led expeditions searching for Sir John Franklin in the Arctic.

86. Parker–Admiralty 26.7.1842: Phillimore II, pp. 482–9.

87. Fay, pp. 354–9.

88. Graham, pp. 224–5.

89. Wong, J. Y., *Deadly Dreams: Opium and the Arrow War (1856–1860) in China*, Cambridge, 1998.

90. Collinson, pp. 488–9, repeats the praise heaped on these officers by Parker, Gough and Pottinger.

91. Graham, p. 229. For the subsequent history of this station, see Graham, p. 230 *et seq.*

92. Graham–Parker 1.1.1843: Haddington–Parker 5.12.1842: Phillimore II, pp. 505–9.

93. Phillimore II, p. 515.

94. Parker–Admiralty 26.7.1843: Phillimore II, pp. 548–50.

95. Parker–Pottinger 15.7.1843: Phillimore II, p. 552.

96. Parker–Belcher n.d; also Parker–Belcher 18.9.????: Phillimore II, pp.

616–19. Sadly Belcher did not take the hint, ending his career under a similar cloud after abandoning his squadron in the Arctic in 1854.

97. Parker–unknown: Phillimore II, pp. 616–17.

98. Parker–Lord Auckland 18.8.1847: Phillimore III, p. 256.

99. Parker–Captain H. Chads 19.3.1846: Phillimore III, p. 44.

100. Many of the British Museum's major classical pieces were brought home by the Royal Navy.

101. Phillimore III, pp. 48–50.

102. Auckland–Parker 3.7.1846 and Parker–Auckland 13.7.1846: Phillimore III, pp. 64–5.

103. Parker–Captain George Willes 3.5.1847: Phillimore III, pp. 162–3. The letter had all the more force because Willes was a friend of fifty years' standing; Parker wept when he died a few months later.

104. Phillimore III, pp. 185–207.

105. Auckland–Parker 7.7.1847: Phillimore III, p. 223.

106. Phillimore III, pp. 234–42.

107. Lord Palmerston–Prime Minister Lord John Russell 9.8.1837: Bourne, K., ed., *The Foreign Policy of Victorian England, 1830–1902*, Oxford, 1970, p. 275.

108. Parker–Sir Edmund Lyons 18.10.1847: Phillimore III, p. 261.

109. See fn. 3.

110. Phillimore III, p. 299.

111. Lord Palmerston–Lord Auckland 7.8.1848: Phillimore III, pp. 368–9.

112. Phillimore, pp. 376–7.

113. Parker–Commander A. C. Key 17.1.1849: Phillimore III, p. 456.

114. Temperley, H., *England and the Near East: The Crimea*, London, 1936, pp. 264–6, 499–506.

115. Canning–Parker 2.11.1849: Phillimore III, p. 577.

116. Parker–Canning 7.11.1849: Phillimore III, p. 581.

117. Palmerston–Mr Wyse 15.2.1850: Phillimore III, p. 620.

118. It is curious how often the self-interested actions of France are mistaken for wisdom in Britain.

119. Lord John Russell in the House of Commons: Phillimore III, p. 647.

120. Parker–Graham: Phillimore I, pp. xiii–xiv, and III, p. 718.

121. Admiral Sir George Seymour–Miss Parker: Phillimore III, pp. 752–3.

Chapter 7: Geoffrey Hornby

1. Egerton, F., *Admiral of the Fleet Sir Geoffrey Phipps Hornby*, London, 1896. Mrs Egerton was Hornby's daughter, and her book has a more human feel than many of the dutiful memoirs compiled in this period.

2. Peel was admired by the entire service, and greatly lamented.
3. Hornby–Stopford 4.9.1842: Simon's Bay. Egerton, pp. 14–17.
4. His new captain, Christopher Wyvill (1792–1863), had seen active service in the Napoleonic Wars, including two years with Charles Napier. He was reckoned a very smart officer. O'Byrne, W., *A Naval Biographical Dictionary*, London, 1849, p. 1,332.
5. Egerton, p. 23.
6. Egerton, p. 36.
7. Egerton, p. 44.
8. Completed in 1853, the thirty-one-gun *Tribune* displaced 2,200 tons, with a crew of 330.
9. Hornby–Admiral Hornby 21.12.1858: Egerton, pp. 52–4. These 'professional' letters reflect a shared ethos. The admiral had seen extensive war service, notably at Lissa in 1811 under Hoste's command.
10. Hornby–wife 5.8.1859: Egerton, p. 66.
11. Colonel Moody–Sir John Burgoyne 8.8.1859: Egerton, pp. 66–7.
12. Gough, B. M., *The Royal Navy on the Northwest Coast of North America 1810–1914*, Vancouver, 1971, pp. 140, 159–60. In 1871 the island was awarded to the Americans.
13. Fremantle, E. R., *The Navy as I Have Known It*, London, 1904, pp. 132–3. Fremantle served on the *Neptune*.
14. Hornby–Admiral Hornby 20.10.1860: Egerton, pp. 81–2.
15. Gordon, G. A. H., *The Rules of the Game: Jutland and British Naval Command*, London, 1996, p. 184, claims Hornby accepted the position. That he did not is of the first importance. Hornby did not share Martin's concern for drill as an end in itself.
16. Hornby–Dacres 1.4.1863: Egerton, pp. 99–100.
17. Gordon, p. 185.
18. Lambert, A. D., 'Politics, Technology and Policy-making: Palmerston, Gladstone and the Management of the Ironclad Naval Race, 1859–1865', *The Northern Mariner*, Vol. VIII, July 1998.
19. Hornby–wife 17.8.1865: Egerton, p. 115.
20. Hornby–wife 26.7.1865: Egerton, pp. 117–18.
21. Hornby's notes on the Bight of Benin 1866–1867: Egerton, pp. 123–5. Thomas, H., *The Slave Trade: The History of the Atlantic Slave Trade 1440–1870*, London, 1997, pp. 769–85.
22. The new Admiralty Board took office on 18.12.1868 in Gladstone's first ministry.
23. Instructions: Egerton, pp. 139–42.
24. Mackay, R. F., *Fisher of Kilverstone*, Oxford, 1973, shows how one talented officer got on, p. 93 *et seq.*
25. *Report of a Committee to examine the Designs upon which Ships of*

War have recently been constructed, London, 1872, HMSO. Committee appointed on 12.1.1871, reported on 26.7.1871. I am indebted to my friend John Roberts for this report.

26. Hornby Diary 15.9.1873: Egerton, p. 181.

27. Egerton, p. 186.

28. Fremantle, pp. 133, 143.

29. Clowes, W. L., *The Royal Navy: A History from the Earliest Times to 1900*, Vol. VII, London, 1903, p. 291.

30. Mahan–Nelson 14.8.1895: Lambert, A. D., ed., *Letters and Papers of Professor Sir John Knox Laughton, 1830–1915*, Aldershot, Navy Records Society, 2002, p. 212.

31. Egerton, pp. 195–8. Beeler, pp. 173–4.

32. Hornby Diary 13.1.1875: Egerton, pp. 192–3.

33. Diary 10.7.1876: Egerton, pp. 197–8.

34. Derby Diary 19.1.1877: Vincent, J., ed., *A Selection from the Diaries of Edward Henry Stanley, 15th Earl of Derby (1826–1893)*, Camden Fifth Series, Vol. 4, London, 1994, p. 368.

35. Fisher–Hornby 6.3.1877: Mackay, *Fisher*, p. 132.

36. Waterfield, G., *Layard of Nineveh*, London, 1963, pp. 357–420.

37. Hornby–Smith 12.1.1878: Egerton, pp. 225–6.

38. Entries for 23 and 24.1.1878: *Derby Diary*, pp. 489–91.

39. Hornby–W. H. Smith 19.2.1878: Egerton, pp. 252–4. Waterfield, p. 404.

40. Hornby–W. H. Smith 14.2.1878: Chilston, Viscount, *W. H. Smith*, London, 1965, pp. 105–6.

41. Smith–Hornby 15.2.1878: Chilston, p. 106.

42. 22.2.1878: *Derby Diary*, p. 514.

43. Disraeli–Queen 8.3.1878: Chilston, p. 110.

44. Roberts, A., *Salisbury: Victorian Titan*, London, 1999, pp. 194–202.

45. Hornby–Admiral Wellesley (First Naval Lord) 2.4.1878: Egerton, pp. 256–8.

46. Smith–Hornby 20.4.1878: Chilston, p. 116.

47. See Roberts, p. 194, for Salisbury's dismissive response to Hornby's complaints. Salisbury had a marked contempt for the opinions of naval and military experts, but he misjudged Hornby.

48. Hornby–Derby 12.11.1878: Egerton, pp. 297–300.

49. Chilston, pp. 126–7.

50. Hornby–W. H. Smith 4.1.1879: Egerton, pp. 340–5.

51. Fisher, Lord, *Memories*, London, 1919, pp. 142–3. Cited in Mackay at p. 140.

52. Ballard, G. A., *The Black Battlefleet*, Lymington, 1980, pp. 180–1. Willis, G. H. A., *The Navy as I Saw It*, London, 1924, pp. 19–27.

53. Fremantle, pp. 293–4.

54. Egerton, pp. 329–30.

55. Colomb, P. H., *Memoirs of Admiral Sir Astley Cooper Key*, London, 1896, pp. 412–14. Beeler, pp. 173–4. Egerton, pp. 195–6.

56. Lambert, A. D., *The Foundations of Naval History: John Knox Laughton, the Royal Navy and the Historical Profession*, London, 1998, pp. 76–8.

57. Colomb, *Key*, pp. 474–5.

58. Brassey, Lord, ed., *The Naval Annual 1886*, Portsmouth, 1886, pp. 110–40. Marder, A. J., *The Anatomy of British Sea Power: British Naval Policy 1880–1905*, London, 1940, p. 111.

59. Marder, pp. 134–5.

60. Report in *The United Service Gazette*, quoted in Egerton, pp. 358–9.

61. Smith, S. R. B., 'Public Opinion, the Navy and the City of London: The Drive for British Naval Expansion in the Late Nineteenth Century', *War and Society*, Vol. 9, no. 1 (1991), pp. 29–50.

62. Marder, pp. 131–2.

63. Smith, pp. 34–9. Kynaston, D., *The City of London: Volume One 1815–1890*, London, 1994, pp. 377–8.

64. Sumida, J. T., *In Defence of Naval Supremacy: Finance, Technology and British Naval Policy 1889–1914*, London, 1989, pp. 20–1.

65. Egerton, p. 399.

66. Beresford, Admiral Lord Charles, *Memoirs*, London, 1916, 4th edn, p. 355.

67. Wilkinson, H. S., *The Command of the Sea*, London, 1894, p. 68. Wilkinson, the founder of the Navy League, was a leading civilian commentator.

68. Luvaas, J., *The Education of an Army: British Military Thought 1815–1940*, London, 1964, p. 195.

69. Hornby–Laughton 16.6.1894: Lambert, ed., *Papers of Professor Sir John Knox Laughton*, p. 102.

70. Gordon, pp. 280–3.

71. Hornby–Culme-Seymour 30.6.1893: quoted in Gordon at p. 302.

72. Hornby–Laughton 16.6.1894: Lambert, ed., *Laughton*, p. 102.

73. Marder, p. 49.

74. Luvaas, pp. 265–6.

75. John Fisher–Austen Chamberlain 22.12.1893: Marder, A. J., ed., *Fear God and Dread Nought: The Correspondence of Admiral of the Fleet Lord Fisher of Kilverstone. Volume 1: The Making of an Admiral 1854–1904*, London, 1952, p. 119.

Chapter 8: John Fisher

1. I exclude from this category Ruddock Mackay's exemplary study *Fisher of Kilverstone*, Oxford, 1970, the basis of all serious scholarship on the subject. Fisher's Service Record is in ADM 196/15, pp. 3 and 9.

2. Nelson also tried to create a suitable past for himself. See Lambert, A. D., *Nelson: Britannia's God of War*, London, 2004, pp. 92–3.

3. Fisher–Mrs Warden 25.6.1860: Marder, A. J., ed., *Fear God and Dread Nought: The Correspondence of Admiral of the Fleet Lord Fisher of Kilverstone. Volume 1: The Making of an Admiral 1854–1904*, London, 1952, pp. 57–8.

4. Fisher–wife 2.5.1879: Marder, p. 94.

5. Phillimore, Sir A., *The Life of Admiral Sir William Parker*, London, 3 vols, 1880–3.

6. Lambert, A. D., *The Foundations of Naval History: John Knox Laughton, the Royal Navy and the Historical Profession*, London, 1998, pp. 21–6.

7. Lambert, A. D., 'Under the Heel of Britannia: The Bombardment of Sweaborg 9–11 August 1855', in Hore, P., ed., *Seapower Ashore*, London, 2000.

8. Lambert, A. D., '"Part of a long line of Circumvallation to confine the future expansion of Russia": Great Britain and the Baltic, 1809–1890', in Rystad, G., Bohme, K.-R. and Carlgren, W. M., *In Quest of Trade and Security: The Baltic in Power Politics, 1650–1990*, Vol. I, Lund, 1994, pp. 297–334, provides an overview of British Baltic policy in the nineteenth century. For Fisher's mature views on this pivotal theatre, see: Lambert, A. D., '"This Is All We Want." Great Britain and the Baltic Approaches 1815–1914.' In Sevaldsen, J., ed., *Britain and Denmark: Political, Economic and Cultural Relations in the 19th and 20th Centuries*, Copenhagen, 2003, pp. 147–70.

9. Colomb, P. H., *Memoirs of Sir Astley Cooper Key*, London, 1896.

10. Lord Charles Beresford, after speaking in the House of Commons, was famously described as not knowing what he was about to say before he spoke, nor what he was saying while he was talking, and not recalling what he had said when he sat down. And he was among the best of them!

11. Lambert, A. D., *The Foundations of Naval History: John Knox Laughton, the Royal Navy and the Historical Profession*, London, 1998, pp. 21–6.

12. Mackay, pp. 36 and 40–1.

13. Fisher–wife 9.12.1869: Marder, p. 70.

14. Fisher–Tryon 31.5.1871: PHI/132 Hornby MS.
15. Gray, E., *19th-Century Torpedoes and their Inventors*, Annapolis, 2004.
16. Fisher–wife 9.6.1872: Marder, p. 85.
17. Marder, *Fear God*, p. 65.
18. Fisher–wife 30.6.1882: Marder, p. 106.
19. Hogg, O. F. G., *The Royal Arsenal Vol. II*, Oxford, 1963, pp. 1,435–6.
20. Fisher–Seymour 12.9.1882 and Fisher–Nathaniel Barnaby 25.1.1883: Marder, pp. 110–11 and 114.
21. Fisher–wife 9.10.1882: Marder, p. 112.
22. Lambert, 'Part of a long line'.
23. Lambert, A. D., 'Palmerston, Gladstone and the Management of Ironclad Naval Race', *The Northern Mariner*.
24. Le Masson, H., *Histoire du Torpilleur en France*, Paris, 1963, pp. 58–62.
25. Paper of 1 February 1891.
26. Lyon, D., *The First Destroyers*, London, 1996, pp. 14–22.
27. Mackay, p. 213.
28. Mackay, p. 223.
29. Remark retailed by Lord Hankey, then a Royal Marine captain in the fleet. Mackay, p. 225.
30. Hankey: Mackay, p. 226.
31. Mackay, p. 233.
32. Mackay, p. 310.
33. Only four years earlier, when Commander-in-Chief Mediterranean, he had recommended 'We ought to begin [ships] much later and complete them sooner.' Marder, *Fisher I*, p. 177.
34. Brooks, J., 'Percy Scott and the Director', *Warship 1996*, London, 1996, pp. 150–70.
35. Sumida, J. T., *In Defence of Naval Supremacy*, London, 1989. A major study linking the long-term financial problems that pre-dated Fisher's revolution with the potential solution offered by Pollen's equipment.
36. Brooks, J., *Dreadnought Gunnery and the Battle of Jutland*, London, 2005, provides an alternative view of the Pollen–Dreyer argument to Professor Sumida. See pp. 107, 110–13 and 200–4.
37. Brooks, 2005, pp. 118–26 and 211–14.
38. Lambert, N. A., *Sir John Fisher's Naval Revolution*, Columbia, South Carolina, 1999.
39. Lambert, 'This Is All We Want', 2003, pp. 162–6.
40. Mackay, p. 341.

41. This was exactly what Fisher wanted: Mackay, pp. 331–2.
42. The standard account is Cain, P. J. and Hopkins, A. G., *British Imperialism: Innovation and Expansion 1688–1914*, London, 1993. See pp. 125–77.
43. Mackay, pp. 421–2.
44. Mackay, pp. 426–7.
45. Winston Churchill–Sir Edward Grey 21.8.1914: Gilbert, M., *Winston S. Churchill. Vol. III Companion Part I*, London, 1972, p. 48.
46. French, D., *British Strategy and War Aims: 1914–1916*, London, 1986, pp. x–xi. A very important book that would have been improved by consulting Corbett's *Naval Operations* and Admiralty material.
47. J. A. Pease–brother 28.8.1914: French, p. 27.
48. French, p. xi.
49. Churchill statement to the War Council of 28.1.1915: Gilbert, M., *Winston S. Churchill. Vol. III Companion Part I*, London, 1972, p. 463, henceforth *Companion*.
50. Gilbert, M., *Winston S. Churchill. Volume III 1914–1916*, London, 1971, pp. 44, 52–3, 84, 202, 225–6, 228, 231, 237, 246, 259, 265, 272, 348 and 400. Henceforth Gilbert. Churchill–Grey 3.8.1914: Gilbert, *Companion*, p. 15.
51. Lambert, A. D., 'Great Britain and the Baltic, 1890–1914', in Salmon, P. and Barrow, T., eds, *Britain and the Baltic: Studies in Commercial, Political and Cultural Relations, 1500–2000*, Sunderland, 2003, pp. 215–36.
52. Churchill–Jellicoe 8.10.1914: *Companion*, pp. 180–2 at p. 182.
53. Kaarsted, T., *Great Britain and Denmark 1914–1920*, Odense, 1979, pp. 8, 31–46.
54. Marder, A. J., *From the Dreadnought to Scapa Flow: II*, p. 127.
55. Lambert, N., 'Strategic Command and Control for Maneuver Warfare; Creation of the Royal Navy's "War Room" System, 1905–1915', in *The Journal of Military History*, 69, April 2005, pp. 361–410..
56. Strachan, p. 475.
57. Strachan, p. 416.
58. Grainger, J., ed. *The Maritime Blockade of Germany in the Great War: The Northern Patrols 1914–1918*, Aldershot, 2003.
59. Gilbert, p. 53.
60. Corbett I, p. 237.
61. Churchill–Fisher 21.12.1914: *Companion*, p. 326.
62. Beesly, P., *Room 40*, is the standard account.
63. Asquith–Venetia Stanley 2.11.1914: *Companion*, p. 247.

64. Churchill, *World Crisis II*, p. 39. Cited in Mackay at p. 462.

65. Corbett II, p. 3.

66. War Council Minutes 1.12.1914: *Companion*, p. 290.

67. Fisher, Lord, *Records*, London, 1919, pp. 217–22, and missing paragraphs in Marder, ed., *Fear God III*, p. 45.

68. Fisher, *Records*, p. 222. The careful use of language and potent historical analogy leave no doubt this was Corbett's work. His staff college lecture series, published as *England in the Seven Years War: A Study in Combined Strategy*, London, 1907, invests his paper with considerable weight. While Marder argues for Fisher's authorship in *Fear God III*, p. 45, his case is unconvincing. Marder's oversight explains why Gilbert, ed., *Churchill Companion*, pp. 284–7, does not mention Corbett.

69. *Records*, p. 220.

70. Schurman, pp. 159–60.

71. Fisher–Corbett 3.12.1914: Marder, *Fear God III*, p. 45.

72. The British had secured a wealth of information on Japanese minesweeping in 1904–5: Cabinet Papers, TNA, CAB45/1.

73. In fairness Churchill had been thinking about this subject since 19.8.1914: *Companion*, pp. 44, 75, 83, 95.

74. Corbett, p. 161.

75. Churchill–Fisher 21.12.1914: Marder III, p. 105 and *Companion*, pp. 323–4.

76. Churchill–Fisher 22.12.1914: *Companion*, pp. 325–6.

77. Gilbert, pp. 272–3.

78. Fisher's notes of the meeting in Fisher–Churchill 13.3.1918: Marder *Fear God III*, pp. 521–2.

79. Fisher–Churchill 25.1.1915: *Fear God III*, p. 145, Lambert, 'This Is All We Want'. Kaarsted, p. 46. These ships, the *Courageous* class, are the most misunderstood of all Fisher's creations, but they were designed to meet a real need.

80. Buxton, I., *Big Gun Monitors*, Tynemouth, 1979, an exemplary study of these craft.

81. *Records*, pp. 221–2.

82. See Lambert, A., 'Fisher's Formative Years: the Education of a Strategist', unpub. conference paper given at the British Joint Services Staff and Command College, Shrivenham, October 2004.

83. Offer, A., *The First World War: An Agrarian Interpretation*, Oxford, 1989, on the development of blockade ideas and Fisher's thinking.

84. Hankey–Fisher 28.5.1917: Fisher, Lord, *Records*, London, 1919, pp. 214–15. Fisher–Hankey 28.5.1917: Marder, A. J., *Fear God III*, p. 429.

85. In 1930 Churchill condemned Fisher for not wanting to enter the Baltic! Mackay, p. 464. Seligman, M., *Spies in Uniform: British Military and Naval Intelligence on the Eve of the First World War*, Oxford, 2006, p. 194.

86. Gilbert, pp. 225–6. Churchill–Fisher 22.12.1914; Marder, p. 107. Churchill Cabinet Memorandum 31.12.1914: *Companion*, pp. 347–9. Kaarsted, p. 53.

87. Kaarsted, pp. 51–3.

88. Gilbert, pp. 228, 231.

89. Fisher–Churchill 4.1.1915: *Companion*, pp. 371–2.

90. It is worth noting that most criticism is based on partisan contemporary sources, usually those without any understanding of what he intended. Fisher took his plans with him to the grave.

91. Fisher–Lloyd George 11.7.1917: Marder, *Fear God III*, p. 465.

92. Lambert, A. D., 'The Royal Navy 1856–1914: The Strategy of Seapower', in Errington, J. and Nielsen, K., eds, *Navies and Global Strategy*, Kingston, 1996.

93. Corbett II, pp. 4–5.

94. Corbett II, pp. 9–12.

95. Corbett II, p. 19.

96. Fisher–Jellicoe 11.12.1914; Marder III, p. 93.

97. Gilbert, pp. 237, 246–7.

98. French, p. 66.

99. War Council 8.1.1915: *Companion*, p. 396.

100. Fisher Cabinet Memorandum 25.1.1915: Gilbert, pp. 263–4.

101. The legend on a stamp Churchill used as Prime Minster, 1940–5.

102. Corbett II, p. 105.

103. Fisher Memorandum 25.1.1915: Marder, *Fear God III*, p. 49. *Companion*, pp. 452–5.

104. Corbett 1988, p. 185.

105. Coogan, J. W., *The End of Neutrality: The United States, Britain and Maritime Rights, 1899–1915*, Cornell UP, Ithaca, 1981, pp. 170–215, for the long-running argument of the Americans.

106. Coogan, pp. 222–33.

107. McKercher, B. J. C. and Nielsen, K., 'The Triumph of Unarmed Forces: Sweden and the Allied Blockade of Germany', *Journal of Strategic Studies*, 1984, p. 199.

108. Halpern, P., 'The Blockade of World War One', in Ellerman, B. A. and Paine, S. C. M., *Naval Blockades and Sea Power: Strategies and Counterstrategies 1805–2005*, Abingdon, 2006, pp. 91–103. Osborne, E. W., *Britain's Economic Blockade of Germany 1914–1919*, London, 2004, provides a less positive interpretation.

109. French, pp. 74–8.
110. Schurman, p. 161; see also TNA CAB 24/1 of 5.2.1915. With typical disregard for history that did not support his own opinions, Churchill would condemn this paper in his *World Crisis II* at p. 303n.
111. Gilbert, p. 324.
112. Churchill–Carden 5.2.1915: *Companion*, p. 487.
113. Gilbert, p. 276.
114. Corbett–Fisher 1.3.1915: *Companion*, pp. 604–5.
115. Churchill–Jellicoe 9.3.1915: *Companion*, pp. 656–8.
116. Fisher–Churchill 3.3.1915: *Companion*, p. 622.
117. Churchill–Carden 11.3.1915: Gilbert, p. 337.
118. Lord Esher Diary 20.3.1915: *Companion*, p. 719.
119. Asquith–Venetia Stanley 12.3.1915: *Companion*, p. 683.
120. Gilbert, pp. 342–3.
121. Carden–Churchill 14 and 15.3.1915: *Companion*, pp. 693, 696–7.
122. Fisher–Churchill 15.3.1915: *Companion*, p. 698.
123. Fisher–Churchill 16.3.1915: *Companion*, pp. 701–2.
124. French, p. 85.
125. For the latest scholarship on the land campaign, see Travers, T., *Gallipoli 1915*, Stroud, 2001.
126. McCallum, I., 'The Riddle of the Shells, 1914–1918: The Test of Battle, Heligoland to the Dardanelles', in Preston, A., ed., *Warship 2004*, London, 2004, pp. 13–20.
127. Gilbert, p. 347; French, p. 86.
128. Corbett II, pp. 409–10.
129. Mackay, pp. 501–4.
130. Jellicoe–Fisher 29.5.1915: Mackay, p. 505.
131. French, pp. 94–5.
132. French, pp. 140–51.
133. French, pp. 159–63.

Chapter 9: David Beatty

1. Beatty has been fortunate in his biographers. Admiral Chalmers served on his staff. Captain Roskill knew his navy and many of his junior offices, while Professor Ranft was a model of historical scholarship. More recently Professor Gordon has used his experience of naval service to open up aspects of Beatty's command style that have restored him to the curriculum of modern naval education in several countries. Chalmers, W. S., *Life and Letters of David Earl Beatty*, London, 1951. Roskill, S. W., *Admiral of the Fleet Earl Beatty: The Last Naval Hero: An Intimate Biography*, London, 1980. Ranft, B.

McL., ed., *The Beatty Papers*, 2 vols, London, Navy Records Society, 1989 and 1993. Gordon, A., *The Rules of the Game: Jutland and British Naval Command*, London, 1996. Ranft, B., 'David, Earl Beatty', *ODNB*, accessed 08.03.2006.

2. Ziegler, P., *Omdurman*, London, 1973.
3. Bayley's 'Journal of the Siege of Tientsin', in Sharf, F. A. and Harrington, P., eds, *China 1900: The Eyewitnesses Speak*, London, 2000, at pp. 101–23. Beatty is mentioned favourably on several occasions.
4. Churchill, R., *Winston S. Churchill*, p. 550.
5. Ranft, *Beatty*, pp. 36–45.
6. Ranft, *Beatty*, pp. 33 and 60. Corbett, J. S., *Some Principles of Maritime Strategy*, London, 1911, contains an expanded version of Corbett's Naval War Course notes on Strategy.
7. Beatty I, p. 59.
8. Roskill argues Beatty was a terrible snob: pp. 59–60.
9. Campbell, N. J. M., *Battlecruisers: The Design and Development of British and German Battlecruisers in the First World War Era*, London, 1978. Roberts, J., *Battlecruisers*, London, 1997, is the best guide to these controversial ships.
10. Gordon, A., 1996, contains a masterly dissection of the subject.
11. Beatty I, p. 66.
12. Roskill, pp. 83–5. Brooks, J., *Dreadnought Gunnery and the Battle of Jutland*, London, 2005, p. 217.
13. Roskill, p. 98.
14. Brooks, p. 219.
15. Campbell, p. 40, and Roskill, pp. 118–19.
16. Roskill, p. 116. The quote is from Churchill's *World Crisis*, Vol. II, p. 89.
17. Roskill, p. 114.
18. Lambert, N., '"Our Bloody Ships" or "Our Bloody System"? Jutland and the Loss of the Battle Cruisers, 1916', *Journal of Military History*, 62, January 1998, pp. 29–56.
19. Roskill, p. 155.
20. Roskill, p. 127.
21. Ibid.
22. I am indebted to my friend Dr John Brooks for his masterly exposition of this phase of the battle in *Dreadnought Gunnery*, pp. 232–67.
23. Brooks, pp. 248–9.
24. Brooks, p. 243.
25. Brooks, pp. 4 and 242.

26. Roskill, p. 183.
27. At his death his son burnt a large collection of correspondence concerning his love life.
28. Roskill, p. 279.
29. Roskill, *Admiral of the Fleet Earl Beatty: The Last Naval Hero.*
30. Churchill–Lloyd George 1.5.1919: *Beatty II*, p. 37.
31. Beatty–Lady Beatty 23.1.1931: *Beatty II*, pp. 148–9.
32. Lady Lee's diary of 2.3.1921: *Beatty II*, p. 165.
33. Roskill's treatment in *Naval Policy Between the Wars Vol. 1*, London, 1968, is coloured by his experience of less forceful naval leadership in Whitehall and the degree of bias to be expected from a career officer.
34. Ferris, J. R., *Men, Money and Diplomacy: The Evolution of British Strategic Foreign Policy, 1919–1926*, Ithaca, 1989, p. 61. The obvious book was Corbett's brief life from the 'Men of Action' series. We do not know what use the recipient made of the text.
35. Ferris, p. 5.
36. Ferris, p. 6, demonstrates this conclusively, while Roskill asserts that the threat was never made.
37. Ferris, p. 5.
38. His installation speech as Lord Rector of Edinburgh University on 28.10.1920 is typical. See Chalmers, *Beatty*, pp. 454–66, and Hunt, B. D., *Sailor–Scholar: Admiral Sir Herbert Richmond*, Waterloo, Ontario, 1982.
39. *Beatty II*, p. 78.
40. Lloyd George–Arthur Balfour (leader of the British Delegation) 1.12.1921: *Beatty II*, pp. 196–7.
41. Beatty–Bridgeman 6.8.1927: *Beatty II*, p. 355.
42. Gordon, G. A. H., *British Seapower and Procurement between the Wars: A Reapprisal of Rearmament*, London, 1988, p. 76.
43. Gordon, *British Seapower*, p. 82.
44. Beatty–Lady Beatty 20.1.1922: *Beatty II*, p. 198.
45. Ferris, pp. 113–15.
46. Bridgeman Diary, January 1926: *Beatty II*, p. 311.
47. Ferris, pp. 79–80.
48. Ferris, pp. 135–6.
49. Ferris, p. 28.
50. Ferris, p. 138.
51. Ferris, p. 123.
52. *Beatty II*, pp. 250–8.
53. Beatty–Lady Beatty 6.3.1923: *Beatty II*, p. 242.
54. Corbett, J. S., *History of the Great War Based on Official*

Documents: Naval Operations Vol. III, London, 1923.
55. Schurman, J. S., *Julian S. Corbett, 1854–1922: Historian of British Maritime Policy from Drake to Jellicoe*, London, 1981, pp. 152–98.
56. Beatty–Eugénie Godfrey-Faussett April 1925: *Beatty II*, p. 290.
57. Ferris, pp. 165–9.
58. Hankey–Beatty 30.4.1927: *Beatty II*, p. 349.

Chapter 10: Andrew Cunningham

1. Cunningham, Lord, *A Sailor's Odyssey*, London, 1951. Winton, J., *Cunningham: The Greatest Admiral since Nelson*, London, 1998. Simpson, M., ed., *The Cunningham Papers. 2 vols*, Aldershot, Navy Records Society, 1999 and 2006. Simpson, M., *Cunningham of Hyndhope: Admiral of the Fleet*, London, 2004.
2. His younger brother Alan (1887–1983) became a general.
3. *A Sailor's Odyssey*, p. 56. He may have done so out of consideration for Troubridge's son, who served under him in 1943, p. 477.
4. Simpson, p. 18.
5. Simpson, p. 22.
6. Lambert, *Nelson*, p. 15. Nelson actually wrote 'Duty is the great business . . .' but the sentiment is unchanged.
7. *Odyssey*, p. 128.
8. *Odyssey*, p. 142.
9. *Odyssey*, p. 168.
10. *Odyssey*, p. 175. Vian, P., *Action this Day*, London, 1960, p. 17.
11. Hinsley, F. H. *et al.*, *British Intelligence in the Second World War*, London, 1979–88, Vol. I, pp. 199–201.
12. Hinsley I, p. 205.
13. Reynolds, D., *In Command of History: Churchill Fighting and Writing the Second World War*, London, 2004, p. 196.
14. Hinsley I, p. 276.
15. Hinsley I, p. 209.
16. Simpson, p. 68, quoting Geoffrey Barnard.
17. Simpson, p. 74.
18. Signals Intelligence revealed the Germans were coming, but the information did not reach ABC in time. Hinsley I, p. 385.
19. Simpson, p. 80.
20. Hinsley I, p. 400.
21. Simpson, *Life*, p. 83.
22. Reynolds, p. 267.
23. Hinsley I, p. 405.
24. Cunningham, p. 367.
25. Simpson, p. 99.

26. Lees in *The Naval Review*, 1963, p. 262, quoted in Simpson at p. 101.

27. Winton, p. 243, for his views on Admiral King, who commanded the 15th Cruiser Squadron off Crete.

28. Winton, p. 221.

29. Winton, p. 219.

30. Simpson, p. 100.

31. Reynolds, p. 267.

32. Winton, pp. 215–16, for the court-martialling of four men who jumped ship rather than sail to Crete again.

33. Winton, p. 257.

34. The words are Cunningham's: quoted in Vian, p. 93.

35. Cunningham–Pound 28.5.1941: Simpson, *Life*, p. 106.

36. These observations are Manley Power's. Winton, p. 226.

37. Hinsley II, p. 320.

38. Simpson, p. 118, quoting from Cunningham's notes.

39. Roskill, S. W., *The Art of Leadership*, London, 1964, p. 166.

40. Cunningham, p. 452.

41. Winton, pp. 261–2.

42. Cunningham, p. 454.

43. Winton, p. 266.

44. Hinsley II, p. 47.

45. Winton, p. 275.

46. Winton, citing Manley Power, p. 312.

47. Simpson, p. 146.

48. Winton, p. 278.

49. Vian, p. 99.

50. Simpson, p. 150.

51. Hinsley III, p. 99.

52. Simpson, p. 171. Winton, p. 328.

53. Reynolds, p. 401.

54. Pound died on Trafalgar Day 1943. Winton, p. 336.

55. Reynolds, pp. 404–6.

56. Simpson, pp. 179–80. Quote from Cunningham's diary entry of 8.8.1944.

57. Hinsley IV, pp. 499, 622, 852.

58. Winton, p. 359.

59. Winton, p. 375.

60. Madsen, C., *The Royal Navy and the Disarmament of Germany 1942–1947*, London, 1998. Winton, p. 376.

61. Reynolds, p. 512.

62. Vian's Obituary Notice of ABC in *The Naval Review*, 1963, p. 263.

Epilogue
  1. Woodward, Admiral Sir John, *One Hundred Days*, London, 1992.
  2. Woodward, p. 238. Freedman, Sir L., *The Official History of the Falklands Campaign. Vol. II: War and Diplomacy*, Abingdon, 2005, pp. 450–5.
  3. Fisher, Lord, *Memories*, London, 1911, p. 45. See also Gordon, A., *The Rules of the Game*, p. 354.

Index